HENRIETTA MARIA

HENRIETTA MARIA

By Honthorst

"The Happiest Woman in the World"

Reproduced by kind permission of the
National Portrait Gallery, London

HENRIETTA MARIA
"The Happiest Woman in the World"

Henrietta Maria

Carola Oman

WHITE LION PUBLISHERS LIMITED
London, Sydney and Toronto

First published in Great Britain
by Hodder & Stoughton Ltd., 1936
Reprinted 1951

Copyright © Carola Oman

White Lion edition 1976

ISBN 7274 0154 8

Made and printed in Great Britain
for White Lion Publishers Limited,
138 Park Lane, London W1Y 3DD
by Hendington Limited,
Lion House, North Town, Aldershot, Hampshire

CONTENTS

PAGE

BIBLIOGRAPHY ix

CHAPTER I

THE LITTLE MADAM 1

CHAPTER II

OBERON AND TITANIA 37

CHAPTER III

THE HAPPIEST WOMAN IN THE WORLD . . . 72

CHAPTER IV

GENERALISSIMA 106

CHAPTER V

LA REINE MALHEUREUSE 158

CHAPTER VI

THE WIDOW OF THE MARTYR 197

CHAPTER VII

THE QUEEN MOTHER 226

CHAPTER VIII

THE MOTHER OF MADAME 267

CHAPTER IX

THE INDIAN SUMMER 306

INDEX 347

LIST OF ILLUSTRATIONS
Between 176-177

HENRIETTA MARIA, by Honthorst. "The Happiest Woman in
   the World" . . . . . . *Frontispiece*
> Reproduced by kind permission of the National Portrait
> Gallery, London.

HENRIETTA MARIA. The Bride . . . . .
> Reproduced by kind permission of Sir Guy Nugent, Bt.

CHARLES I, AS PRINCE OF WALES, by Daniel Mytens. The
   Bridegroom . . . .
> Reproduced by kind permission of the National Gallery of
> Canada, Ottawa.

CHARLES II, AS PRINCE OF WALES, by Vandyck. "Mi deare
   sone, the Prince" . . . . . .
> Reproduced by gracious permission of His Majesty the King.

FIVE OF THE CHILDREN OF CHARLES I, by Vandyck . .
> Reproduced by gracious permission of His Majesty the King.

HENRIETTA MARIA, after Vandyck . . . .
> Reproduced by kind permission of the Nationalmuseum,
> Stockholm, from the portrait at Gripsholm Castle, Sweden.

HENRIETTA MARIA, by Vandyck . . . .
> Reproduced by gracious permission of His Majesty the King.

HENRIETTA ANNE, from a drawing by Claude Mellan.
   "Minette" . . . .
> Reproduced by kind permission of the Nationalmuseum,
> Stockholm.

HENRIETTA MARIA, by Claude le Fevre. "The Widow of the
   Martyr" . . . .
> Reproduced by kind permission of J. G. Morrison, Esq.

ix

BIBLIOGRAPHY

AIRY, O., *Lauderdale Papers*. Camden Society, London, 1884–5.

Ashmole, E., *Diary from original manuscripts of*, ed. R. Gunther. Oxford, 1927.

AVENEL, VTE. G. D', *Lettres, instructions diplomat: et papiers d'état de Richelieu*. Docs. inéd., Paris, 1853–77.

Baillie, Rev. R., *Letters and Journals*, ed. D. Laing. Bannatyne Club, London, 1842.

BAILLON, COMTE C. DE, *Henriette-Marie de France*. Paris, 1884.
Lettres inédites de Henriette-Marie.

BALLARD, G., *Memoirs of Learned Ladies in the 17th and 18th Centuries*. London, 1825.

Bassompierre, *Mémoires du Maréchal de*. Amsterdam, 1723.

BEAUREGARD, MARQUIS C. DE, *Mémoires historiques sur la Maison Royale de Savoie*. Turin, 1816.

Bibliotheca Regia. London, 1659.

Biographie Universelle. Paris, 1852–66.

Bodleian Library, Oxford. Clarendon, Douce, Rawlinson and Tanner Manuscripts.

Bossuet, J. B., *Oraisons Funèbres du Cardinal*. Paris, 1816.

BREVAL, J., *History of the most illustrious House of Nassau*. Dublin, 1758.

Brienne, *Mémoires du Comte de*, ed. M. Petitot. Paris, 1824.

British Museum. Additional, Sloane, Egerton and Harleian Manuscripts.

BROMLEY, SIR G., *Collection of Original Royal Letters*. London, 1837.

BRUCE, J., *Charles I in 1648*. Camden Society, London, 1856.

BRYANT, A., *Letters, Speeches and Declarations of King Charles II*. London, 1935.
King Charles II. London, 1931.

BUCHAN, J., *Marquis of Montrose*. London, 1913.
Oliver Cromwell. London, 1934.

BULSTRODE, SIR R., *Memoirs and Reflections upon the Reign and Government of King Charles I and King Charles II*. London, 1721.

BURNET, G., *History of My Own Time*, ed. O. Airy. London, 1900.
Supplement to, ed. H. Foxcroft. Oxford, 1902.

Cabala. London, 1691.

Calendar of State Papers Domestic, 1625–73.

CAPEFIGUE, J., *Anne d'Autriche et la minorité de Louis XIV*. Paris, 1861.

CARPENTER, W., *Memoir of Sir A. Van Dyck*. London, 1844.

CARTE, T., *Life of James, Duke of Ormonde*. Oxford, 1851.

CARTWRIGHT, J., *Madame*. London, 1894.

Clarendon, Life of Edward Hyde, Earl of, by himself. Oxford, 1827.
State Papers. Oxford, 1767–86.
History of the Rebellion and Civil Wars in England, by Edward, Earl of Oxford, 1888.

COLES, J., *History and Antiquities of Wellingborough*. Wellingborough, 1837.

COTOLENDÌ, CARLO, *Vie de Henriette-Marie de France*. Paris, 1690.

Court and Times of Charles I, illustrated by Authentic and Confidential letters, ed. J. Brewer. London, 1848.

DE GAMACHE, FATHER C., *Memoirs of the Mission in England of the Capuchin Friars of the Province of Paris, from 1630–69*, ed. J. Brewer. London, 1848.

DE LA FAYETTE, MADAME, *Memoirs of the Court of France, 1688–9*.
Secret History of Henrietta, Princess of England, ed. J. Shelmerdine. London, 1929.

De Montpensier, Mémoires de Mademoiselle, ed. M. Petitot. Paris, 1825.

De Motteville, Mémoires de Madame, ed. M. Petitot. Paris, 1824.
Memoir on the Life of Henrietta Maria, ed. M. Hanoteaux. Camden Society, London, 1883.

De Retz, Mémoires du Cardinal. Paris, 1824.

DÈ THOU, J., *Mémoires*. Amsterdam, 1704.

DE WITT, MADAME G., *Lady of Lathom, Original letters of Charlotte de la Trémoille*. London, 1869.

D'ISRAELI, B., *Commentaries on the Life and Reign of Charles I*. London, 1828.
Curiosities of Literature. London, 1849.

DODD, REV. C., *Church History*, ed. Rev. M. Tierney. London, 1840.

DREUX DU RADIER, J., *Historiques, critiques et Anecdotes des Reines et Régentes de France*. Amsterdam, 1776.

DUGDALE, SIR W., *The Life, Diary and Correspondence of*, ed. W. Hamper. London, 1827.

DUPLEIX, S., *Histoire de France*. Paris, 1632.

ELLIS, H., *Original Letters illustrative of English History*. London, 1827.

Evelyn, J., Diary and Correspondence of, ed. W. Bray. London, 1895.

Exact Account of the Attempts made upon the Duke of Gloucester, 1655, ed. W. Scott. London, 1811.

FALKNER, J., *History of Oxfordshire*. London, 1899.

Fanshawe, Memoirs of Lady, wife to Sir R., Ambassador from Charles II to the Courts of Portugal and Madrid, written by herself, ed. B. Marshall. London, 1905.

FEILING, K., *England under the Tudors and Stuarts*. London, 1927.
     British Foreign Policy, 1660–72. London, 1930.

FERRERO, H., *Lettres de Henriette-Marie à sa sœur Christine, Duchesse de Savoie*. Turin, 1881.

FULLER, T., *History of the Worthies of England, 1662*. London, 1811.

GARDINER, S., *History of England, 1600–42*. London, 1883.
     History of the Great Civil War. London, 1893.

GREEN, M. EVERETT, *Letters of Queen Henrietta Maria*. London, 1856.
     Lives of the Princesses of England, vol. vi. London, 1855.

Hardwick Papers, vol. ii. London, 1878.

HARTMANN, C., *Charles II and Madame*. London, 1934.

HAYNES, H., *Henrietta Maria*. London, 1912.

Henrietta Maria de Bourbon, Life and Death of. London, 1685.[1]

Herbert of Cherbury, Life of Edward, Lord, by himself, ed. H. Walpole. London, 1792.

HERBERT, SIR T., *Memoirs of the last two years of that Unparallel'd Prince of very Blessed Memory, Charles I*. London, 1702.

HÉROARD, J., *Journal de 1601–28*, ed. E. Soulié et E. de Barthélemy. Paris, 1868.

HOWELL, J., *Historiographer to Charles II, Familiar Letters of, 1645–55*, ed. J. Jacobs. London, 1890.

---

[1] Referred to in notes throughout this biography by the abbreviation 'H. M. de B.'

Hutchinson, *Memoirs of the life of Col.*, by his widow, ed. H. Child. London, 1904.

JESSE, J., *Memoirs of the Court of England during the Reign of the Stuarts.* London, 1855.

JUSSERAND, J. J., *A French Ambassador at the Court of Charles II.* London, 1892.

Lambeth Manuscripts, King's Cabinet Opened. London, 1675.

Laud, W., *The Works of the most Reverend Father in God, sometime Lord Archbishop of Canterbury*, vol. iii. Oxford, 1853.

L'Estoile, P. de, *Mémoires-Journaux, 1574–1611.* Paris, 1888.

LE VASSOR, M., *Histoire du règne de Louis XIII.* Amsterdam, 1700.

Leveneur de Tillières, *Mémoires inédits du Comte*, ed. M. Hippeau. Paris, 1863.

LINGARD, J., *History of England to 1688.* London, 1849.

MACRAY, W., *Privy Council Notes of Charles II and Lord Clarendon.* Roxburghe Club, London, 1896.

MATTHIEU, P., *Histoire des dern: troubles 1560–1613.* Paris, 1613.

MÉZERAY, F. DE, *Marie de Medicis. Histoire de la Mère et du Fils.* Paris, 1730.

NAPIER, M., *Memoirs of the Marquis of Montrose.* Edinburgh, 1856.

NEEDHAM, R., and WEBSTER, A., *Somerset House: Past and Present.* London, 1905.

Nicholas, Sir E., *Correspondence of*, ed. G. Warner. Camden Society, London, 1886–97.

Panzani, G., *Memoir of*, ed. Rev. J. Berington. London, 1793.

Pepys, S., *Diary of*, ed. H. Wheatley. London, 1893.

PÉRÉFIXE, H. DE, *Histoire du Roy Henry le Grand.* Paris, 1749.

PETRIE, SIR C., *Letters, Speeches and Proclamations of King Charles I.* London, 1935.

Public Record Office, *State Papers, Foreign;* French and Roman Transcripts.

RANKE, L., *History of England.* London, 1874.

Regicides. *The Indictment, Arraignment, Trial & Judgment at large of 29 of the Murtherers of his most sacred Majesty.* Anon. London, 1714.

Reliquiae Sacrae Carolinae. Hague, 1651.

Reresby, Sir J., *Memoirs of.* London, 1734.

SPALDING, J., *History of the Troubles, etc., in Scotland in the Reign of Charles I.* Aberdeen, 1792.

State Trials, ed. T. Howell, vol. iv. London, 1816.

STRAFFORDE, Letters and Despatches of Thomas, Earl of. London, 1739.

STRICKLAND, A., *Lives of the Queens of England,* vol. viii. London, 1857.

Sully, Mémoires du Maréchal de Béthune, Duc de, 1634–62, ed. Petitot. Paris, 1821.

TAYLOR, I., *Life of Queen Henrietta Maria.* London, 1905.

Thurloe, J., A Collection of the State Papers of, ed. T. Birch. London, 1742.

TOWNSHEND, D., *Life and Letters of Mr Endymion Porter, sometime Gentleman of the Bedchamber to King Charles I.* London, 1897.

WARWICK, SIR P., *Memoirs of the Reign of King Charles I.* London, 1701.

WISHART, G., *Memoirs of James Graham, Marquis of Montrose,* translated from the Latin of, with original letters. Edinburgh, 1819.

WOTTON, SIR H., *Reliquae.* London, 1685.

---

* In the footnotes to this book, where original manuscripts, some of which have never been published, are quoted, the exact reference is given, but where the authority is one which has been frequently reprinted, only the author's name is stated: the edition from which the quotation is made is to be found in the bibliography.

CHAPTER I

THE LITTLE MADAM

I

SHORTLY after four o'clock on the afternoon of Friday, May 14th, 1610, Henri IV, King of France, left his palace of the Louvre to pay a private visit. He was due to set out upon a new campaign, into Germany, on the following Wednesday, and had kept this one day in a harassing week free of engagements so that he could attend to his own affairs. But he had found himself unable to settle to any business, or even to rest. When an officer of the Guard had suggested that his majesty might like to take the air the king had agreed instantly and called for his coach. This vehicle was large and heavy; its body was slung upon leathern braces and possessed extra seats, known as the "boots", projecting between the front and back wheels. Six or seven gentlemen prepared to embark in it with the king, who ordered the curtains shrouding its windows to be looped up. While this was being done, M. de Vitry, Captain of the Guard, approached to offer his services but was dismissed. As he stepped into the coach, the king asked what day of the month it was, and appeared amused when two of his companions supplied different answers; then, with one of his characteristic sudden changes from gaiety to melancholy, he repeated "Between the thirteenth and the fourteenth" in a disturbed voice, and told the coachman to drive in the direction of the Hôtel de Longueville. As the vehicle lumbered out of the courtyard a tall and bulky man, who had been sitting for a long time upon the stones at the gate of the palace where footmen waited for their masters, rose

I

silently and followed it. He had hoped to find his victim seated next to the window, but the king happened to have taken the Duc d'Epernon on his right hand.

Henry of Navarre was now in his fifty-seventh year. He was of medium height, small-boned and wiry, his long nose had a hook in it, the vigorously curling hair of his head and short beard was quite grey; he had the glittering eye of the inveterate gambler and lady-killer. His forehead was noble, his air martial rather than majestic, his manner restless, his dress of black satin elaborate but not foppish. He was going, this fine spring afternoon, to call upon his Superintendent of Finances and Grand Master of Artillery. The Duc de Sully had been wounded at his his side, twenty years before, on the field of Ivry. "I have no great inclination to go to the Arsenal," said Henry, "because I shall put myself into a passion." This one of his oldest friends, who had remained a Protestant, was frugal, taciturn and often disapproving. But the duke had been ill, and the king wanted to see the decorations in the streets. At last, in spite of persistent prophecies that it would prove fatal to him, he had consented to his second wife's coronation. The ceremony had been performed with great splendour at St Denis yesterday, and as his massive Florentine queen had passed beneath a window from which he was watching, Henry had playfully dripped some scented water on her head.[1] His divorced first wife had taken part in the procession too, though in tears of chagrin at the inferior position allotted to her.[2] It was nearly twenty-eight years since his wedding with Marguerite of Valois, and the Massacre of St Bartholomew. He had resigned himself to both his marriages from utterly mundane motives. Two days after meeting his second bride he had left her to follow him to Paris. Nevertheless, Marie de Medicis had brought him a fine family. Their sixth child, and third daughter, had been born[3] at the Louvre on November 25th of the previous year. Cardinal

---

[1] Dupleix.   [2] L'Estoile.   [3] At 10 P.M. Héroard.

Barberini, papal nuncio, paying a visit of congratulation, had expressed the hope that this princess might become a great queen. "That will come to pass when you are a great pope", replied the proud mother to the future Urban VIII.[1] Henry had declared that he would have given a hundred thousand crowns for another boy, and no cannon had been fired or rejoicings ordered in honour of Henriette-Marie, the first of their children to be named after both parents.[2] Still, it was after the birth of this infant that he had given way to her mother on the subject of the long-deferred coronation, and this morning he had sent for her and her two-year-old brother Gaston "to divert his thoughts".[3] His happiest moments, as he had once told Sully, were those spent playing with his children, who were the prettiest creatures in the world.

His contemporary, Charles Emmanuel, Duke of Savoy, would not undertake a journey without a reassuring report from an astrologer, and Henri IV's amazing career had been suitably attended by prophecy. Recently the supernatural injunctions delivered to him had been impressive in volume and somewhat exacting. Cardinal Barberini had begged him not to stay in any large city this year, especially between March and July, as he was threatened with assassination by an unfrocked monk of saturnine temperament born in his own realm. From Constantinople his ambassador transmitted a message striking a note of Oriental lavishness. The Sultan Achmet urged his brother potentate, immediately on receipt of this letter, to strike off the heads of the six principal nobles of France, and immure for life the chief woman of the court and her three advisers.

Henry had begun to allude to his imminent death. He told Sully that he was doomed "to be murdered at a public ceremony and in a coach". But it had always been his pleasure to dis-

---

[1] Panzani.   [2] L'Estoile.
[3] H. M. de B., 1685.

concert courtiers by touching upon delicate topics.[1] Actually he
was seriously out of spirits this spring. He who confessed that
he "dreaded domestic dissension more than foreign warfare"[2]
was sick of the ten years' feud between a wife who had never
amused nor attracted him and a mistress[3] of whose unfaith-
fulness he was convinced; also he had been crossed in a new
enterprise. The fifteen-year-old Charlotte de Montmorency,
wife of his cousin, had been removed from his kingdom by a
suspicious bridegroom. The king's detractors announced that
he was about to take the field rather to regain possession of
the Princesse de Condé than to preserve his territories. The
forthcoming campaign might be ill-advised—he had always
been a better soldier than strategist—but Henry had never yet
allowed private inclination to interfere with political expediency. Expediency had dictated his choice of religion and friends;
he had gone to the wars at sixteen, and, after his accession at
the age of six-and-thirty, had struggled for another ten years
against the League and Spain before he had won his kingdom.
At fifty-seven he was cynical and fretful, but his country was
flourishing, and with the bulk of his people, who knew that
he often disregarded the counsels of his nobility, he had successfully cultivated a gay personal touch. His *bons mots*, his tennis,
his gambling, his generosity towards a series of ladies whose
beauty was only surpassed by their cupidity, were all appreciated in Paris, where he had built the great gallery of the
Louvre, the Hôtel de Ville and the Place Royale, and completed
the Tuileries. Five years previously, on his Pont Neuf, as he rode

[1] "There are three things that the world will not believe, and yet they
are certainly true; that the Queen of England [Elizabeth] died a maid; that
the Archduke [Albert of Austria, sixth son of Maximilian II] is a great
captain; and that the King of France is a very good Catholic." L'Estoile.
[2] Sully.
[3] Catherine Henriette de Balzac d'Entragues, d. of Marie Touchet, mistress of Charles IX, and François de Balzac. Created Marquise de Verneuil,
1595. She boasted that she possessed a written promise of marriage by the
king, and called her son by him "the Dauphin".

home in a winter's dusk after a day's hunting, a man had tried to stab him, but this attempt, like that of an Orleans wheelwright in 1593, had been the act of a maniac.

He had beautified his capital, but an English traveller,[1] ten year after this date, described the mud of Paris as indelible, and its streets "generally foul all the four seasons of the year" as so narrow that traffic-blocks were half a mile in length and of two hours' duration. The Cross of Tiroir, to which Henry presently directed his coachman this afternoon, having dismissed further attendants, was literally a plague-spot, and passing from it to the Cemetery of the Innocents his vehicle was brought to a standstill. At the corner of the Rue de la Feronnerie, where shops were built against the cemetery wall, a vintner's cart had met a hay wain. All but a couple of the royal footmen slipped ahead so as to rejoin the coach at the top of the street; of the two remaining, one attempted to clear a passage, while the other took advantage of the halt to readjust a garter. François Ravaillac, the tall and somewhat bulky man who had followed the king all the way from the Louvre, holding his cloak around him with his left arm so as to conceal the knife which he grasped in his right hand, and sliding between the shops and the coach as if he were trying to pass by like others, raised himself by leaping with one foot on a stone and the other upon a wheel-spoke of the stationary vehicle. The king in that instant turned towards him, either to catch the light upon a letter which he was reading, or to make some remark to the Marshal de Lavardin, seated near the opposite "boot", and François Ravaillac struck Henri IV a little above the heart, between the third and fourth ribs. Henry exclaimed "*Je suis blessé!*" and flung up an arm, and Ravaillac repeated his blow, this time with fatal effect. Blood was gushing from the king's heart and mouth before anyone in the coach realized what had happened. "It is

[1] Howell. Letter of J. Howell to Capt. F. Bacon, Paris, March 30, 1620.

nothing," said Henri IV faintly, and died before Ravaillac struck for the third time "as into a bottle of hay".[1]

II

One of the six noblemen in the coach warded off Ravaillac's third blow, but had not the murderer stood transfixed, still grasping his weapon, he might have escaped, for the courtiers now all dismounted "with such precipitation that they hindered each other from seizing the parricide", and upon one of them exclaiming "The King is dead!" a panic ensued. The Duc d'Epernon then "suddenly bethought himself of saying that the king was only wounded, and had fallen into a swoon", and wine was called for. Before it could be fetched the coach doors were shut, its curtains drawn, and the equipage bearing the dead body of Henri IV set off at top speed for the Louvre. An hour later, only the inhabitants of the palace knew for certain that the king was dead. The invalid Duc de Sully, pressing through the streets in a high fever at the head of a hundred and fifty alarmed gentlemen on horseback, received three warnings that if once he entered the Louvre he would never escape alive. Paris was in an uproar, and wild contradictory reports of a second St Bartholomew's Massacre, and plots organized by Spain, Madame de Verneuil and the Queen Mother, were widely credited. Sully, after having sent word to his son-in-law to move six thousand Swiss troops towards the capital, and ordered all available bread in the shops and markets to be seized and brought into the Bastille, retired to await

---

[1] The description given here of the happenings of May 14, 1610, is drawn from the accounts of de Péréfixe, Matthieu, Sully, L'Estoile, the continuator of De Thou, and the *Mercure Français*, 1610, but these contemporaries differ as to the number of persons in the coach at the time of the tragedy, the number of wounds received by the king, his last words, and other details. The murder took place outside the house of a notary named Poutrain, on a site occupied by the present No. 11 Rue de la Feronnerie.

hostile developments. But François Ravaillac,[1] although subjected to unspeakable tortures, eventually died asserting that he had been alone in his enterprise.

Gradually the citizens of Paris realized their loss, and "some became motionless and insensible, thro' grief; others ran about the streets quite frantic; others threw themselves on the ground . . . one might see women with their hair dishevelled, crying and lamenting; fathers said to their children, 'What will become of you? You have lost your father.' "[2] All shops were shut; the triumphal decorations in honour of the queen's entry were hastily torn down, and the route to St Denis was hung with black.

The six children of the murdered king spent the night closely guarded in the Louvre. At supper the new king's tutor knelt to serve him. The boy, who was not yet nine, first burst out laughing, then began to cry, and said that he wished his younger brother could become king instead of him: "Because I am afraid they will kill me as they have done my father". Next midday, mounted on a white pony, and enveloped in a mourning-cloak of violet velvet, he went to meet his Parliament. The Queen Regent, swathed in crêpe, sat on his right hand at the ceremony, and was at first unable to utter for tears.[3] Sully, in answer to repeated messages, ventured to the Louvre, and a promising scene took place, at which the widow said to the boy king, "My son, this is M. de Sully; you must love him well, for he was one of the best and most faithful servants of

---

[1] He was the son of a poor lawyer of Angoulême, thirty-two years of age, a bachelor, and had been a novice in the monastery of the Feuillants. That community had rejected him "because he had visions", amongst which was finding that, when he sang the Psalms of David, he had in his mouth a trumpet "which made a sound as loud as that which is made in war". While serving a term of imprisonment four years previously, he had conceived the idea of killing the king "because he had heard it reported that the king intended to make war upon the Pope" (*The Tryal of F. Ravaillac for the Murder of Henry the Great*, 1610).

[2] Péréfixe.   [3] L'Estoile.

the king your father, and I entreat him to continue to serve you in the same manner".

But one of her first acts on hearing of her son's accession had been to order the removal of his bed into her room. Her hour had come, and she intended to allow no rival influence with her first-born. The boy's tutors were continually changed, and the late king's advisers soon found themselves supplanted by the Regent's foreign favourites.

III

Henrietta Maria's entrance into the world had been a hasty one, and she appears to have been vivacious from the day of her birth. Her eldest brother, admitted after some remonstrance to his mother's bedchamber, declared that his new sister was laughing at him and squeezing his hand.[1] Henrietta's first public appearance had been at her mother's coronation. Twelve days later she was again borne in her nurse's arms to St Denis, this time to cast holy water on the corpse of her father. With autumn the whole royal nursery took the road into Champagne, and at her brother's coronation in the Abbey of Rheims, the black-eyed infant of eleven months was carried by the dazzlingly fair Princesse de Condé, herself only sixteen.[2]

His youngest daughter had been considered by Henri IV to resemble him. Two early family groups represent her as a very dark, round-faced, healthy-looking child, grotesquely over-dressed in the miniature replica of an adult court costume. She began to grow up, quick of speech, gesture and temper. From her father she may have inherited her curly hair, het courage and a large handwriting.[3] By her unstable, elaborate-minded mother she was instructed in absolute devotion to the

---

[1] Héroard.   [2] H. M. de B.
[3] The first four letters of Henri IV's signature "Henry" and his daughter's "Henriette-Marie" are almost identical.

Catholic faith and exaggerated notions of royal despotism. Marie de Medicis was an unattractive woman. Her appearance suggested the similes of the cabbage-rose or the over-blown peony. Rubens did his best for a liberal patroness, and depicted again and again, with meticulous care, the pear-shaped pearls and voluminous sable draperies which formed a telling background for the Queen Mother's peach-like complexion and metallic gold coiffure; but with her sorrows and years her girth increased. Floors, as well as courtiers, trembled at the approach of this emphatic and portentous royal widow. By a curious chance, all her children were dark; both surviving sons even swarthy. They inherited some of her solidity, but her three daughters were all small, slight and quick-witted. Marie de Medicis was possessively devoted to her children, with the exception of her eldest son, whose majority would mean her retirement. Louis XIII developed into an ignoble example of the result of female despotism. A clumsy, black-a-vized, sullen boy, he stammered, he was secretive. He displayed fondness for nothing but his dogs (with whom he conversed in a language invented by himself[1]), his falcons, his horses and the study of gunnery.

Marie de Medicis knew that she was not a stupid woman; she refused to recognize that it would have taken a much cleverer woman to manage the discordant nobility of France at this period. She had been lucky in managing to rear every one of her six royal infants. When her second son, Henry, Duke of Orleans, died suddenly in his fifth year, her unpopularity was already so great that she was obliged to invite all the princes and princesses of the blood to pay a solemn visit of inspection to her nursery. She proceeded to conclude the treaty of a double marriage between her eldest son and daughter and the eldest son and daughter of Philip III of Spain, an alliance from which Henry IV had always been averse. Henrietta was again dis-

[1] Bernard, *Histoire de Louis XIII.*

played at the festivals attendant on these contracts, and three years later, on Sunday, June 15th, 1614,[1] she was publicly christened together with her brother, the Duke of Anjou. Gaston-Jean-Baptiste had as sponsors his father's first wife and the Cardinal de Joyeuse, and Henriette-Marie her own elder sister and the Cardinal de la Rochefoucauld. The two dark children were dressed alike in white satin. They shared a learned tutor, M. de Brévis, who was certainly more merciful than the little king's governors, and Henrietta received extra religious education from a distinguished Carmelite, Mère Magdeleine of St Joseph.[2] Over the royal nursery presided a distant cousin of the Queen Mother, a Madame de Montglat, affectionately known as "Mammanga", and Henrietta's first letter is one of apology to Mammanga for a little burst of temper. "I cannot be good all of a sudden, but I will do all I can to content you; meanwhile I beg you will no longer be angry with me."[3] Mammanga's beautiful daughter, "Mamie St George", Jeanne, wife to Hardouin de Clermont, Seigneur de St George, occupied a post of sub-governess.

The boy king's first physician, M. Jean Héroard, kept an explicit journal of his royal patient's doings, in which mentions of "Monsieur", the little Duke of Anjou, and "Mesdames", the princesses, are frequent. Louis XIII rose at six-thirty, performed his devotions, breakfasted about eight, studied for an hour, dined at eleven-thirty, and studied again till half-past one. He played billiards, "paille-mail" and tennis, went hunting and hawking, made bridges over the ornamental waters in his mother's garden, and had battles with lead or silver toy soldiers. On wet or cold days he diverted himself in the galleries of the palace. With Madame Elizabeth, his eldest sister, he performed amateur cookery; he harnessed two pet bulldogs to his little coach, usually drawn by six dun ponies, played cards and "Colin Maillard" (a species of blind-man's-buff), and gave audience

---

[1] Héroard.   [2] Bossuet.   [3] Strickland.

to such thrilling personalities as the Muscovite Ambassador and a merchant bringing rarities from China. The fare described at his frequent meals is rich—hippocras, canary and sometimes claret to drink, kidney soup, larded fowls, various *pâtés* and preserved fruits to eat. Whenever he arrived at St Germain he went to sup with his brother and sisters at six-thirty. Bedtime for the eldest of the children of Henri IV was supposed to be about nine o'clock, but all too often there are entries of supper with the queen at eight, before the Italian comedy, or the marionette show, or the fireworks on the terrace. The princesses, as well as their brothers, learnt to ride, and there are continual mentions of dancing-lessons and theatricals.

The background of Henrietta's infancy was a beautiful one—the galleries of the Louvre, the Orangery of the Tuileries, the forest of Fontainebleau, the terraces of St Germain and St Cloud—yet throughout her childhood the principal nobility of France were in arms against the Crown, and she was from the first accustomed to talk of civil war, a situation which never actually affected her personal comfort. Her mother was dominated by the Concini, a curious couple. Madame was small, sallow and self-effacing. She had been Leonora Galigai, daughter of the Regent's nurse and a carpenter. Monsieur, born Concino Concini, and son of a Florentine notary, but now raised to the rank of a Marshal of France, was dashing, handsome, and repaid with interest the insolence of the exasperated aristocracy of his adopted country. But even he advised the queen not to leave Paris open to the advance of the Prince de Condé while she proceeded into Guienne with all her family, to accomplish the Spanish marriages on which her fancy was fixed. Henrietta was in her sixth year when she set out on this journey, her longest hitherto, and the weather in which she first saw Touraine and Poitou was some of the hottest in the memory of man.[1] The summer of 1612, "*l'année des magnificences*", was one of

---

[1] Héroard.

splendid sunshine. By Amboise and Orleans the procession reached Poitiers, where the Queen Mother fell ill and the bride developed smallpox. They had quitted Paris in August; they entered Bordeaux by barge, early in October. The two proxy weddings took place, as had been arranged, at Burgos and Bordeaux simultaneously, on October 18th; Marie de Medicis said farewell to her eldest daughter, "quickly, for fear of tears",[1] two days later, and in midstream of the Bidassoa, on November 9th, the exchange of Madame Elizabeth for the Infanta Anne was effected with much pompous ceremony. Rubens subsequently depicted this scene in a vast allegorical painting, one of the twenty-one representing the career of the Regent, ordered by her to decorate her new palace of the Luxembourg. Judging by his portrait of the future Queen of Spain, a strong resemblance existed in youth between Henrietta and the eldest sister whom she was never to see again. Madame Elizabeth left France a merry, sparkling brunette of thirteen. The bridegroom who awaited her in decadent Spain was a frightening-looking boy of ten, with a long, pallid face, sandy hair, thick red lips, an enormous under-jaw and roving luminous eyes. Both physically and mentally he was a poorer specimen than his sister, who arrived at Bordeaux on November 21st. The Infanta Anne of Austria was well-grown, fair and plump, eager to see the husband from whom she had received accomplished love-letters.[2] She was five days his senior by the calendar, and charming, as she reclined, Moorish fashion, on a pile of cushions, dressed in green satin trimmed with silver and gold and diamond buttons, with a close ruff, and a jaunty cap of green velvet with a black heron's feather. Disillusionment set in for her at once. When he had been asked whether he would rather ally himself with England or Spain, the child Louis XIII had answered Spain, because it was much grander, a point of view which coincided with that of his short-sighted mother. But at fifteen he did not

[1] Héroard.   [2] de Motteville.

want a wife, and in any case was prepared to dislike a companion of the Regent's providing. He preferred to go hunting with a M. de Luynes, whose father had been an archer of the bodyguard, and grandmother the excellent housekeeper of a certain Canon Ségur of Marseilles. As far as birth was concerned Louis was not much more fastidious than his mother in his choice of intimates.

Concini, who appears to have been quite unsuspecting that his successor in royal favour had arrived upon the scene, had been right in attempting to dissuade the Regent from leaving Paris. She was not able to return there until May of the following year, when, after a solemn reconciliation with the rebellious princes of the blood, she made a state entry. Henrietta is mentioned as taking part in the procession. Eleven months later, on the morning of April 24th, 1617, Concini was arrested in the king's name, and, before he could defend himself, shot dead in the courtyard of the Louvre. In answer to cries of "Vive le Roi!" Louis XIII appeared at a window overlooking the shocking scene, and, hoisted onto a billiard table, he received the homage of the many who flocked to the palace mistakenly believing that the fall of the Regent's faction would be the salvation of France. At a council of war held in the hall of the Augustine Monastery seven months previously, she had declared that she was no weak woman to be intimidated, quoted the career of Elizabeth of England to her consternated audience, and announced that, unless the hand of friendship which she offered was accepted, she intended in future to resemble a lioness. She was now banished to Blois, and the seven-year-old Henrietta, who was amongst the group that witnessed her departure,[1] cannot have failed to realize that her mother was a prisoner and two most familiar figures had met violent ends. Concini's wife, who valiantly replied to her judges that the only sorcery she had employed over the queen was that of a

[1] Brienne.

strong character over a weak one, was publicly executed, her body burned, and her ashes scattered to the winds. In place of the Italian favourites the Queen Mother's circle learnt to become accustomed to the noiseless tread and dry cough of Armand du Plessis, Bishop of Luçon, afterwards famous as Cardinal de Richelieu. He had been introduced to her by Concini, and when she fell from power he begged leave to go with her into exile, a request which was granted, as he kept de Luynes privately informed of all her doings. It suited the sickly prelate to retire for a while from Paris and watch their due fates overtaking his rivals. De Luynes was soon as unpopular as ever Concini had been. But the bishop had been removed from the Queen Mother's retinue when, on the night of February 21st, 1619, she made her escape from the château of Blois. A ladder had been placed against the casement of her closet. The window was small, the Regent large. She emerged at length after such painful struggles that, when she reached a second ladder giving access to the ditch of the fortress, her nerve broke and she declared herself unable either to go back or go on. Ultimately the Comte de Brienne, two faithful male attendants, and one maid, lowered her sately to the ground enclosed in a strong cloak. A carriage awaited her at the bridge-head, and, joined by the Duc d'Epernon at Loches, she made on to Angoulême, where a great gathering of the disaffected welcomed her. De Luynes and Louis XIII were humiliatingly reduced to recalling Richelieu to make terms for them.

Henrietta was an occupant of òne of the fifty coaches that arrived at the château of Consières in the following September, to take part in a festival of reconciliation, but the Queen Mother refused to return to Paris. She proceeded to ensconce herself at Angers, to the discomfiture of her son, and Henrietta "durst not follow her mother to the displeasure of her brother".[1] She was now "Madame", the only unmarried princess of

[1] H. M. de B.

France, and the king had already received one request for her hand.

IV

Marie de Medicis had designed that all her daughters should become queens. She had married Elizabeth, her eldest, to the heir of Spain. Henry, Prince of Wales, had been her choice for her second. Three days after the untimely death of this promising youth, while the Louvre was still plunged in sympathetic gloom, James I of England had startled French notions of etiquette by a prompt substitution of his surviving son, Charles, as bridegroom for the princess Christine. But during the Queen Mother's captivity Christine had been given to the Prince of Piedmont. Victor Amadeus, afterwards Duke of Savoy, was a judicious young man of twenty-four, personally brave, hard-working, and devoted to horse-racing. He made a good husband, and, upon the whole, the only one of Henri IV's daughters who did not attain queenly rank had the happiest life. Her relations by marriage bullied her, her brother went to war against her husband (as he did against all his brothers-in-law), and she was widowed at the age of one-and-thirty, but she reigned successfully for eleven years as regent for her sons,[1] and to the day of her death, at the age of fifty-seven, her influence was paramount in Turin.[2]

Marie de Medicis was obliged to acquiesce formally to her second daughter's marriage, and when a match for her third with the sixteen-year-old Comte de Soissons was discussed, she could not object. Actually de Luynes, in an effort to detach England from Spain, was already sending secret envoys offering the hand of Henrietta to Charles, Prince of Wales. His first agent, a Sieur du Buisson, a person of no great rank or conse-

---

[1] During her regency, however, took place the massacre in Piedmont celebrated by Milton in "Avenge, O Lord, Thy slaughter'd Saints . . .".

[2] Beauregard.

quence, was despatched to England on the pretence of buying horses for the Prince de Condé. The Comte de Tillières, French Ambassador in London, tactlessly kept in ignorance of the arrangement, was horrified, when out hunting with the king, to be told that James I regretted he could not entertain proposals from France, as he was already pledged to Spain. De Tillières hastily and haughtily repudiated du Buisson, saying that it was not the custom to seek husbands for the princesses of France, but the egregious de Luynes subsequently sent a second agent, who met with no better success than his predecessor. In Paris, the little princess, being told that her religion had militated against the English match, remarked that "a wife ought to have no other will but that of her husband".[1]

Marie de Medicis became her son's prisoner again, and not until the sudden death of de Luynes in December 1621 while upon a punitive campaign against the Protestants, did she return to a semblance of her old authority. Unaware that the day of Richelieu was now come, and that he was not to prove her friend, she spent her time jealously sowing dissension between her son and his "little queen", and she encouraged Henrietta to follow her example.

V

On February 21st, 1623, two handsome young Englishmen, calling themselves John and Tom Smith, arrived in Paris from Boulogne, took lodgings in an inn in the Rue St Jacques, and went out to see the sights of the capital. They bought a couple of large bushy perukes and went to the Louvre, where they observed the Queen Mother dining and the king walking in a gallery of the palace. Their appearance must have inspired confidence, for when they introduced themselves to the Duc de Montbazon as travelling noblemen they were admitted to a large and dim hall, whence string music sounded, and they

[1] Herbert of Cherbury.

found themselves spectators at the rehearsal of a masque performed by the ladies of the court. Anne of Austria was taking the chief part, that of Juno, and the little princess Henrietta, aged thirteen, was dancing "rarely well, as she could" in the character of Iris. That night the shorter and less flamboyant of the Smiths wrote to his father in England that the sight of the queen, whom he had considered the belle of the "fair dancing ladies", had quickened his desire to see her sister. At about the same hour, Lord Herbert of Cherbury, English Ambassador in Paris, was being asked by "one Andrews, a Scotchman, whether he had seen the prince". The ambassador enquired "What prince?" and was told the Prince of Wales. A maid who had formerly sold linen in London had recognized him. The secret was out, and next morning when Lord Herbert roused the Secretary of State betimes, that dignitary anticipated his news with—"I know your Business as well as you". The future Charles I, on his romantic incognito journey into Spain to woo the Infanta Maria, had set eyes for the first time upon the princess who was destined to be the queen of his country and his heart, but it had not been a case of love at first sight. He had left Paris again at 3 A.M., to the great disappointment of the royal ladies, whose ballet he had beheld unobserved. Anne of Austria, although he was *en route* to woo her own sister, regretted that he had seen her sister-in-law under such disadvantages, by a poor light and at a distance, for "her face and person have most loveliness considered nearer", and Henrietta herself said that it was a pity he had gone so far to seek for a wife. "He might have had one neerer hand." [1]

VI

Charles, Prince of Wales, rode south for a fortnight, at the rate of sixty miles a day, down France, and over the rough

[1] Brienne; Le Vassor; de Motteville; Bassompierre; H. M. de B.

mule-tracks of northern Spain. He was twenty-two, slight, shy, and believed himself to be passionately in love with the far-away princess whom he had never seen. By his side rode George Villiers, Duke of Buckingham, one-and-thirty, and in the full pride of the dark beauty which, unattended by·any striking mental attainments, had won him the post of king's favourite. James I had wept openly at the thought of his "Steenie" (as he called the duke, from a fancied resemblance to a picture of St Stephen) and his "Baby Charles" undertaking this dangerous expedition, but the duke had been determined and the prince ardent. Besides, the bluff Count Gondomar, Spanish Ambassador in London, had held out flattering hopes of the effect of a personal visit to Madrid by the pair, and James hoped, as a result of the Spanish marriage, for the reinstatement in the Palatinate of his needy son-in-law, Frederick of Bohemia.

The knights-errant arrived at length at "the house of the seven chimneys" in a retired street off the Calle de Alcala, and Buckingham, taking the lead as usual, went into the residence of Lord Bristol, English Ambassador in Madrid, while Charles held the horses outside. That night, Gondomar, who was in the capital, visited the most important man in Spain, Gaspar de Guzman, Count of Olivarez, Duke of St Lucar. The Count-Duke remarked that the Ambassador to London looked as jolly as if he had the King of England in Madrid, and Gondomar replied that he had the next best thing—the Prince of Wales. He believed that they could now squeeze James I to agree to almost any proposition. But Olivarez, who foresaw that a feeble monarch was unlikely to compel his Parliament to agree to the reversal of half a century's religious policy, agitatedly pushed back his *toupet* of false hair, grasped his crutch and hurried off to see his nominal master. Before dawn, Philip IV, in one of his bursts of religious ecstasy, had bound himself by an inviol-able oath never to give his sister to a heretic. The only course open to the Spaniards was to overwhelm the unwelcome guests with magnificent entertainment. They did this for over five months, at the end of which time, Charles, who had gained universal admiration by his politeness, and Buckingham, whom the Spaniards made the scapegoat of the unsuccessful negotiations, departed empty-handed. The Queen of Spain, born the beautiful Elizabeth of France, but doomed to grow stony-eyed and shapeless after repeated efforts to supply her unfaithful husband with a healthy male heir, seized an early opportunity to warn the prince that he would never win her sister-in-law, and had better apply himself to her sister. Years afterwards, Charles told Henrietta Maria that he had experienced great difficulty in getting speech with Elizabeth, who had whispered to him when he began to talk to her in French, that etiquette forbade her to converse in her native tongue. When she had obtained her husband's permission to do so, she warned the prince, in the royal box at the Opera, "never to speak to her again, for it was the custom in Spain to poison all gentlemen suspected of gallantry towards the queen–consort".[1] Charles never saw the Infanta in private, although at one point in the game of deluding him, she was actually saluted as Princess of Wales, and their betrothal was celebrated by a bullfight at which three-and-twenty bulls were slain. She was a fair, silent, pious, uninformed girl of nineteen, with protruding lips and a high nose. Two years later she made the match which had always been intended for her, with Ferdinand, King of Hungary, by whom she became the mother of the Emperor Leopold I.

VII

The humiliating Spanish expedition had at any rate accustomed England to the unpopular prospect of a Catholic queen, and the way now seemed open for the willing Henrietta.

On a Sunday afternoon in February 1624, a secret envoy from

[1] de Motteville; Cabala; Howell.

England arrived at the Louvre. Henry Rich, Lord Kensington, was excellently suited for the post which he himself described as that of "wooing Ambassador". He was a favourite both with James I and Buckingham, "a very well-bred man, and a fine gentleman", thirty-five, remarkably handsome, and not sufficiently intellectual to cause any companion embarrassment. The Duchesse de Chevreuse was the most important court beauty and greatest friend of Anne of Austria. De Luynes had been the first husband of the heiress of Rohan-Montbazon; shortly after his death she had made a marriage more suited to her birth. Kensington went, on the very evening of his arrival, to the apartments of the Duc and Duchesse de Chevreuse, whom he found much engaged, attiring themselves for the queen's masque. Nothing deterred—indeed his embassy was to entail the task of making love to the Duchesse—he stayed with them for an hour, and was rewarded by an informal meeting with the Queen Mother and the princess. That night he sent home the first of a series of stirring descriptions of "The little Madam", as he invariably called Henrietta. She had that night, he was flatteringly assured by his hosts, looked unusually happy. They left him to guess the reason. Marie de Medicis, remembering the ignominious manner in which her daughter had been hawked to England by de Luynes, had replied guardedly to his first solicitation "the maiden must be sought, she may be no suitor",[1] but the distinguished Englishman assured her that his private mission was directly from the King and the Prince of Wales, whereupon she admitted that her daughter was still disengaged.[2]

Charles's own engagement to the Infanta had not yet been formally broken off, and the Spanish Ambassador tried to hinder Kensington, whose errand he guessed. Henrietta presently had three suitors. The Comte de Soissons, prodded on by a determined mother, was still in the field, and Philip IV

[1] Cabala.   [2] Le Vassor.

now sent an offer of his younger brother, Don Carlos. His
suggestion was that the young couple should reside with the
Archduchess Isabella at Brussels, until her demise, upon which
he would obtain for them the sovereignty of the Catholic Low
Countries. But Richelieu, always the enemy of Spain, advised
the Queen Mother and Louis XIII to a definite refusal of so con-
ditional an offer. Kensington meanwhile toiled on amiably (he
was to get an earldom for his success), charming the French court
and reconciling the dejected Charles to the idea of a child-bride.

The truth was that Henrietta was small, even for fourteen,
and her accomplishments were few, but the wooing ambassador was adroit with scanty material.[1] The little Madam was,
according to him, "the loveliest creature in France and the
sweetest thing in nature". "Her growth is very little short of
her age; and her Wisdom infinitely beyond it." He had heard
her "discourse with her Mother and the Ladies about her, with
extraordinary discretion and quickness" and "they all swear
that her Sister, the Princess of Piedmont (who is now grown
a tall and goodly Lady), was not taller than she is, at her age"
Her dancing and singing were beyond praise, and she had herself told Kensington that she was devoted to riding on horseback, a taste unusual amongst French ladies. (Charles was an
expert horseman.) Presently there was an inflammatory hint of
another suitor. The Comte de Soissons had been behaving with
such "childish incivility" that when the Englishman had received
a message from him, he had quite expected it to be a challenge.
The Comte, however, proved to be unromantically set upon
buying an English horse.

Kensington's pen raced—to the prince, to his "most dear and
noble lord" the Duke of Buckingham, to the Lord Conway,
Secretary of State. He went about wearing a locket containing
a miniature of his young master hanging round his neck.
Anne of Austria had asked to see it and had shown it to her

[1] Harl. MS. 1581, f. 35.

ladies "with infinite Commendation of your Person". Everyone, in fact, except "the poor young Lady" most concerned,
had been at liberty to inspect it at close quarters. Then came a
delicious little scene of mystification. "The gentlewoman of the
House where I am lodged", who had once been an attendant
upon Henrietta, came to the Ambassador with a mysterious
request for a loan of his master's portrait. The princess was the
secret borrower. "As soon as she saw the party that brought it,
she retired into her Cabinet, calling only her in; where she
opened the picture in such haste as shewed a true picture of her
passion, blushing in the instant at her own guiltiness. She kept
it an hour in her hands and when she returned it she gave it
many praises of your Person. Sir, this is a business fit for
secrecy. . . . I would rather dye a thousand times than it should
be published, since I am by this young Lady trusted, that is for
Beauty and Goodness an Angel."[1]

In May, James Hay, Earl of Carlisle, arrived in Paris, openly
accredited with Kensington, joint Ambassador-Extraordinary
to treat for the French marriage. Hay had been one of James
I's poor Scottish gentlemen. Having twice married heiresses,
he was now renowned for his wealth and refinement. His
suppers were famous. His countenance, perhaps, was not handsome, but his figure was perfect.[2] "Camel-face", as his master's
high-spirited daughter, the Queen of Bohemia, called him,
had brought letters from the king and prince and Charles's
portrait. Henrietta received her mother's permission to accept
them and, with tears in her eyes, read Charles's letter twice
over before slipping it into the bosom of her dress. James's
epistle she put into her cabinet. Her portrait was duly given in
exchange to the ambassadors for transmission to their young
master, and Kensington next begged for a private interview
with the princess. Marie de Medicis demurred and wished to
know what he would say to her daughter. The courtier

answered loftily, "Nothing unfitting for the ears of so virtuous a princess", but the stout widow, thoroughly enjoying herself, insisted upon hearing a sample of "the more free and amorous kind of Language" which the handsome proxy considered suitable for employment in a wooing so far advanced. Evidently Kensington acquitted himself to admiration, for "*Allez! allez!*" smiled she, when he had finished. "There is no danger in any of that. I put my trust in you! I put my trust in you!" "Neither", reports the triumphant deputy, "did I abuse her trust, for I varied not much from it in delivering it to Madam . . . who drank it down with Joy, and, with a low Courtesie, acknowledged it to the Prince, adding that she was extremely obliged to his Highness." The ambassador then turned his speech to "the old Ladies that attended", and detailed to them how Charles kept his future bride's picture in his cabinet "and fed his Eyes many times with the sight and contemplation of it". Henrietta, standing by, did not, he noticed, miss a word of what he was saying.[1]

All thus seemed on the surface to be going well, but the negotiation was yet to come close to a breakdown. Kensington's letters to England described nothing but success in his dealings with the Queen Mother, whom he considered the most important person to be placated, but Carlisle, the senior envoy, sent warnings to his employers directly he had got into close touch with Richelieu, the true ruler of France. The Cardinal desired the English alliance as a curb to the power of Spain and Austria, but he demanded the insertion in the marriage treaty of a clause engaging that the penal laws in force against the Catholics of England should be abolished. Carlisle strongly advised his master against concessions which James had publicly assured his Parliament that he would not make. From Rome, the Pope refused to grant a dispensation for the marriage, although this projected treaty gave Henrietta as much liberty

[1] Harl. MS. 1581, f. 31.

in the exercise of her religion as that drawn up on behalf of the
Infanta a year before. Urban VIII foresaw that unless the King
of England continued severities against his Catholic subjects
the Protestants of his country would not long brook his rule.
Whether the concessions demanded by France were made or
not, therefore, he prophesied unhappiness for Henrietta. Months
passed, and in August Charles, growing exasperated, wrote to
Carlisle bidding him either make or break the match. But for
the respect he had for the princess he would not give a
farthing for the friendship of "the Mounseers". On a late
September evening the ambassadors announced that an agreement had been reached, and Henrietta told her younger brother
that this was the happiest day of her life; but on October
23rd (O.S.) a London writer's report was merely that "the
French match goes on by fits; the Lady . . . grows melancholy
when any obstacle occurs".[1] In December bonfires blazed in
England "for the forwardness of the French match", but on
March 27th (O.S.) James I died, and all was uncertainty again.
Marie de Medicis, determined to see her youngest daughter
a queen, now redoubled her efforts and began to consider
offering to celebrate the marriage without waiting for a dispensation, but Charles I at once renewed the negotiations on his
own authority, and in the end Richelieu obtained almost everything for which he had asked. Even the freedom of the English
Catholics was assured by the definitive treaty, though in
secret clauses. A refusal from Charles to agree to their publication closed the tedious haggling. He had already promised more
than he could fulfil. On the evening of May 8th, 1625, Henrietta was solemnly betrothed in the king's great chamber in
the Louvre, and three days later, on the old English "May-
Day", her marriage took place.

[1] *Cal. S.P.D.*, 1624.

VIII

Henrietta spent the day before her wedding in the convent
in the Faubourg St Jacques, to which she had been accustomed
to go throughout her childhood for quiet days, taking her
problems and anxieties to Mère Magdeleine for solution. Now
the saintly Carmelite's work was done. For the last time she
solemnly advised her wayward and innocent pupil as to her
future conduct in life.[1] Henrietta knew that her destiny was a
glorious one. She was to be the guardian angel of the Catholics
in her new country. Already she had brought happiness into
hundreds of English homes. Three months before his death
James I had ordered the release of all persons imprisoned on
account of their religion. She would not be alone in her battle,
for the marriage treaty generously ensured her chapels, ora-
tories and chaplains in every English royal palace; a bishop and
twenty-eight priests were to accompany her and all her domestic attendants were to be French Catholics. Furthermore, the
children whom she must now hope to bear were to be left
in her keeping until they were thirteen years old, so there was
every hope that the next king of England would bring his
country back to the old faith. She had received a wonderful
letter from the Pope telling her that the eyes of the whole
world and of the spiritual world were upon her. She was to
be the Esther of an oppressed people, the Clothilda who had
brought a pagan husband into the fold, the Aldiberga whose
wedding had introduced Christianity into Britain. She had
readily given the Pope and her brother, the king, her written
promise that if it pleased God to make her fruitful she would
have her children reared by no heretics.

The wedding-day dawned wet, and there were other causes
for irritation. The Archbishop of Paris, who considered that
he—not the bride's godfather—should have been called upon

[1] Bossuet.

to officiate in his own cathedral, had left the capital in a pet. The nuptial mass could be said by the Bishop of Chartres, his senior suffragan, but unfortunately the archbishop's example had infected his clergy. Strange singers from the chapels royal had to be hastily substituted for the defiant choristers of Notre Dame.

In spite of her host's defection Henrietta went, as had been arranged, to the archbishop's palace to dress for her wedding. The royal procession was not timed to appear until five o'clock in the evening but people had been waiting overnight in the cathedral square, where stands had been erected. The neighbouring streets had been barricaded and patrols of the Swiss Guard were in charge of the complicated traffic arrangements. The wedding itself was to take place under a canopy of cloth of gold on a temporary platform outside the west door of Notre Dame. Henrietta's wedding-gown was of cloth of silver and gold patterned with gold fleurs-de-lis. She wore many coloured jewels as well as a crown of diamonds with a famous pearl in front. Her pale-blue velvet and cloth of gold train proved to be so heavy that the three ladies deputed to carry it had to engage a gentleman to walk underneath it, supporting some of its weight on his head and hands. One of these ladies was the widowed Comtesse de Soissons, whose son, ardent to the last, had obtained permission to absent himself from a scene so painful to him. The Duc de Chevreuse had been appointed by the bridegroom to act as his proxy on account of relationship, although actually they were not close kin. The duke and king were respectively the great-grandson and great-great-grandson of Claude, Duke of Guise, who had died in 1550. The brief ceremony at the church door took place in sunshine. Henrietta renounced all rights to the French throne, received the homage of the English ambassadors and passed into the darkness of Notre Dame. She did not communicate at the ensuing mass as it had been decided that if she had to fast so long she might faint. The Duc de Chevreuse acted the part of the Protestant bridegroom with such realism that he did not accompany the Catholics into the cathedral, where the service lasted for two hours. So the day drew to a close with a banquet at the archiepiscopal palace and bonfires and fireworks in the streets. And all through the night Colonel Sir George Goring, who had left the cathedral square directly the giving of rings had taken place, pressed on the road to Boulogne, bearing to England the news that Charles I was at last a husband.[1]

IX

When the King of England's bride saw the sea for the first time in her life she was so excited that she must needs go out upon it at once in a little boat. She took as cavalier her brother Gaston, a low-statured, heavy-featured youth of eighteen. He was not to prove a noble character, but to the end of their lives he possessed two passports to Henrietta's favour—good manners and strong artistic tastes.

A month had passed since her marriage at Notre Dame and she was still in France enjoying queenhood, which her mother had taught her to regard as the summit of earthly desire. England meant exile and a husband of whom she knew no more than could be gathered from the descriptions of courtiers, court portraits and a few courtly letters. The arrival of the magnificent Duke of Buckingham to hasten her departure had caused some consternation in Paris. An indisposition of Louis XIII—no uncommon occurrence—had been the excuse offered for her delay in setting out, but neither the king's mother, wife nor sister had felt obliged to stay at the Louvre on an evening when Cardinal Richelieu had offered an entertainment at the Luxembourg. May had slipped into June before Henrietta left

[1] *L'ordre des cérémonies observés au mariage du roy de la Grande Bretagne et de Madame, soeur du roy*, Paris, 1625. Dodd; Brienne.

the capital, in a litter with curtains and cushions of scarlet velvet embroidered with gold, drawn by two mules in scarlet housings, wearing white aigrettes. All the way to the coast her slow progress had been interrupted by pageants and illnesses. Her brother, the king, had been unable to take her further than Compiègne, where a stay of two days had been made. At Amiens the Queen Mother had fallen sick. There had been some hushed-up scandal, some midsummer madness, during the fortnight that Amiens had entertained three queens. Anne of Austria had been advised by the Comte de Brienne to stay with her ailing husband, but the unloved young queen, in unusual beauty, had insisted upon accompanying her little sister-in-law as far as possible. One warm night, while the vigilant Queen Mother lay abed and the court wandered in a Picardy garden by the banks of the Somme, Anne's equerry had heard a cry in a voice that he had recognized. He had rushed up to the spot from whence it came, to find his mistress pale and trembling, the English duke, her sole companion, tense and glowering. Neither could speak the other's language efficiently, but ever since his unwelcome arrival the jealous French had recognized the bold language of the dark eyes of *"cet étranger présomptueux"*.[1] It was agreed that the Queen of England need not wait on in Amiens until her mother was recovered. Marie de Medicis said farewell to her daughter and gave her as parting gift a letter of immense length, full of sage advice couched in the most elegant style. The fiction was that it came from her own pen, but the actual author was the Father Bérulle who was going to England as the bride's confessor.[2] So Henrietta had made on to the coast attended by nobody of her family except her younger brother, and at Abbeville the English duke, who had been sent to escort her to his master, had suddenly left her. He had posted madly back to Amiens, saying that he had another message to deliver

[1] Brienne; de Motteville.   [2] D'Avenel.

there. He had rejoined Henrietta again at Montreuil, but now the weather was unsuitable for a passage to England.

The news that "the Lady" was close at last reached the Mayor of Dover, who wrote to Lord Conway on June 9th (O.S.) that "a mariner of England", who had slipped across the Channel between storms, reported that the queen had reached Boulogne about five o'clock the night before, in good health and very merry. The man had seen her little majesty standing on the shore looking out to sea, so rapt that she had not observed how boldly the waves were approaching to kiss her feet, until she had sunk overshoes in the sands.[1]

Some days previously Charles, too, had been gazing across the waters. He had stayed up on the leads of Dover Castle for two hours on a cold night, to the discomfiture of the lords that were with him. Now he had been persuaded to retire to Canterbury until certain tidings of his wife's landing should come. His first Parliament was awaiting his presence and was preparing to be importunate on the subject of enforcing the penal laws against recusants. The Puritans of England said that their Papist queen had been commanded by the Pope to stay a fortnight at Amiens doing penances for having married a heretic.

A number of English ladies and gentlemen had gathered at Boulogne to pay their respects to the bride. Amongst them was a much-travelled Sir Tobie Matthew. Descriptions of Henrietta's appearance as infantile had been so widespread that he was surprised to find her well grown. "Whatever they say, believe me, she sits already upon the very skirts of Womanhood." Tobie was lyrical in the account that he sent to Buckingham's mother, but then Tobie was a convert to the new queen's religion. "Madame", wrote he, "upon my Faith, she is a most sweet, lovely Creature. Believe me she is full of Wit . . . I dare give my Word for her that she is not afraid of her own Shadow." Her attire, he had noticed, was very plain, a fashion

[1] *Cal. S.P.D.*, 1625.

which he hoped English ladies might follow. She had given most gracious greetings to all presented to her.[1] So she may have, but not in their own tongue. Marie de Medicis, upon her first arrival in France, could speak and understand her husband's language so well that she had interrupted a congratulatory speech at Amiens to associate herself "energetically" with the hope that before the year was out she might become a mother. It is extraordinary that she let her daughter dep rt, after such long preparation, mistress of an enormous and carefully chosen trousseau but not one sentence of English. Henrietta, however, was a spoilt child and a bad linguist, and the King of England, like every well-educated gentleman, would be able to speak French. Another new subject was equally well impressed by her. "For we have now a most noble new Queen of England, who in true Beauty is beyond the long woo'd Infanta; for she was of a fading flaxen hair, big-lipp'd, and somewhat heavy-ey'd; but this Daughter of France, this youngest Branch of the Bourbon (being but in her Cradle when the great Henry her Father was put out of the world) is of a more lovely and lasting complexion, a dark brown; she hath Eyes that sparkle like Stars; and for her Physiognomy, she may be said to be a Mirror of Perfection."[2]

At length came a promising morning, and the port of Boulogne echoed to the salvoes of artillery as the English ships, sent to fetch home the King of England's bride, put out to sea. Henrietta's qualifications for being queen of a Protestant country were, beyond her welcome dowry of 800,000 crowns, that she was "sweet" (an unanimous opinion) and that she could dance and sing exquisitely.

"Mam's bad luck at sea" was to become notorious amongst the children whom she was destined to bear in England. Her first voyage from Boulogne to Dover occupied twenty-four hours.[3]

---

[1] Tanner MS. 74. 40.   [2] Howell.
[3] As the narrative has now reached England, the dates are, unless otherwise stated, henceforward given in Old Style.

X

Seven o'clock on a wet Sunday evening is admittedly not a propitious hour for foreigners to gain a happy first impression of England. The sumptuous-minded Lord Carlisle had written home anxiously hoping that suitable arrangements were being made to greet the French by whom he had been entertained so long and lavishly. A chair was waiting for Henrietta on the quayside, but no husband; a few people cheered but no expensive pageant was set in motion. The chilled and astonished guests were assisted up a steep and forbidding-looking ascent towards a fortress built for defence not delight, with 21-foot-thick walls, black, tortuous newel staircases and a well 293 feet deep. Lord Carlisle did his best to play the host, taking the Duc de Chevreuse and other noblemen out for a stroll in the town when it had been ascertained that the queen was going to bed directly after supper; the Comte de Brienne, always the courtier, noticed the comfortable sight of a royal crown on the furniture of Henrietta's apartments and found his first English meal "magnificent", but the Comte de Tillières denounced the English crown furtniture as lamentably antique and considered his mistress shabbily lodged. His countrymen, he says, began early to be of the opinion that they had been misled as to the riches and splendours of England. Various reasons were suggested for the bridegroom's non-appearance, the charitable asserting that feelings of the most delicate consideration withheld him from introducing himself to a weary and dishevelled bride, or that Marie de Medicis had expressly begged him to allow her daughter a night in which to recover from her journey.

Charles arrived at ten o'clock the next morning. Hearing that the queen was still at breakfast, he announced that he would wait, but she, rising from table, hastened downstairs to meet him. The great moment had come at last, and found her childishly incompetent. She attempted to kneel at her husband's feet and kiss his hand, but Charles gallantly "wrapt her up in his arms with many kisses". Henrietta then began the lovely archaic speech prescribed by etiquette for a royal bride: "Sire, I am come into your majesty's country to be made use of and commanded by you . . ." but excitement and nervousness overcame her. The princess of France whose "smart discourse, gallant carriage and extraordinary accomplishments" had been so much advertised, lost her head and burst into tears. Charles, himself struggling against overmastering nervousness, played the man. He kissed the terrified and terrifying girl again, saying that he should continue to do so until she left off weeping, and told her gently that "she was not fallen into the hands of enemies and strangers, as she apprehended tremblingly, but into the wise disposal of God, who would have her leave her kindred and cleave to her spouse". He added in the most soothing courtier's vein "that he would be no longer master himself than whilst he was a servant to her".[1]

They stepped aside and looked upon one another. Henrietta, through her tears, saw a troubled young man of five-and-twenty who had not yet come into confident possession of considerable good looks. She recognized the regular features and heavy-lidded eyes to which court painters had mendaciously imparted an attractive vivacity. His complexion was not as settled as had been depicted. In childhood Charles's legs had been weak. He was now a good horseman and tennis-player and his carriage was dignified, but only in the saddle could he be represented as majestic. Like her own elder brother he suffered from a hesitation in his speech. He was not intimidating. His manner, like his dress, was quiet and easy. She brightened and, seeing him, as she thought, looking down to discover if her height had been increased by stilt-heeled slippers—for he was not a tall man; after all, she reached to his shoulder

[1] H. M. de B.

—she impulsively swept aside her skirts to show him her shoes. "Sire, I stand upon mine own feet; I have no helps by art; thus high am I; neither higher nor lower."[1]

Charles, who had come eager to be a good husband to his long-looked-for princess, found much to captivate him. The neck and wrists protruding from her stiff, rich attire were thin. She was sallow, and had a pathetic look of adolescence about her. But her long curling dark hair and her large eyes, tragic with tears at one moment and sparkling with merriment at the next, would by themselves have given her a claim to beauty. She was nimble of wit and gesture, and evidently all desire to please. Before dinner she presented her servants to their new master, naming each person correctly in order of rank, and at dinner she ate heartily of the pheasant and venison carved for her by her bridegroom, although her confessor (who stood throughout the meal immovable by her side) had warned her that she must fast, because it was the Eve of St John. Her first request when she found herself alone with Charles was that he would not be angry with her if through youth and ignorance of the customs of his country she made some mistakes. She hoped that he would himself tell her if she offended, and not employ any third person to do so.

An occasion for dispute at once presented itself, for when the royal coaches came round to carry the court to Canterbury, the daughter of Henrietta's old *gouvernante* insisted upon occupying a seat in the same equipage as her mistress and the king. A tiresome little scene took place, during which Henrietta vivaciously explained the rights of her beloved "Mamie St George", and the French ambassadors officiously suggested that this lady had doubtless received instructions from the Queen Mother of France that such a position was her due and she must not cede it to any "Huguenot" English lady, even of equal rank. Charles, coldly disgusted, gave way, and the Comte de

[1] Harl. MS. 389, f. 460.

Tillières maliciously noted that his doing so was due to the ambassadors' representations, not his wife's volubility. Charles, not unnaturally, conceived a violent dislike for Henrietta's favourite attendant from that moment.

Eventually they drove off, between lanes of cheering people, and on Barham Downs were brought to a halt by a pretty spectacle. A number of country ladies had assembled themselves upon the bowling-green to pay their court to their new mistress. They had ranged themselves in two rows on the greensward, and the Queen of England, who had not one word of English with which to accept their greetings, was led down their ranks by her husband. One native observer thought that his country-women in their simple attire much outshone the French *élégantes*, whom another wrote down "a poor lot, not one worth the looking after, save herself and the Duchesse de Chevreuse, who though she be fair, yet paints foully".

In the Great Hall of St Augustine at Canterbury, on the evening of Monday, June 13th, 1625, Henrietta was married for the second time to Charles, a much less magnificent affair than the Notre Dame ceremony, but superior in that the bride-groom attended in person. A banquet followed, after which the queen retired to her bedchamber, attended by the amorous and wordly-wise Duchesse. Charles presently appeared, and, driving everyone out, shut all the doors and drew seven bolts with his own hands. He let in two of his gentlemen to undress him, but when they had done their duty bolted them out also.[1] Next morning the court set out for the Duchess of Lennox's mansion near Gravesend; Charles was reported "jocund", but Henrietta "very melancholy".

As the plague was raging in London, no state entry by road could be attempted. An inspection of the Fleet, lying at anchor, was made the excuse for a passage by barge to the capital. In spite of "vehement showers", the bridal couple kept the win-

[1] Harl. MS. 389, f. 461.

dows of their craft open, and some of the thousands of spectators who had crowded onto the river and its banks were able to ascertain that both the king and queen were wearing green, and that the queen was waving her hand to them. One crowded vessel turned turtle and precipitated over a hundred loyal subjects into the Thames; however, nobody was drowned. Fifty good ships and the garrison of the Tower discharged ordnance, and the Londoners complacently surmised that the little Madam would never have heard the like of such a peal before. A popular story passed from mouth to mouth, that when someone had asked her whether she could abide a Huguenot, she had replied with aplomb: "Why not? Was not my father one?"[1]

Unfortunately the influences which were to postpone and nearly wreck one of the most perfect royal romances in English history were already at work. From the hour of their arrival, Henrietta's French attendants had disparaged England and everything English. After her first interview with Charles—at which she had acquitted herself so poorly and he so well—they had dampingly opined that she had been disappointed by his appearance and his understanding. They had all been painfully struck by his "*triste mien*". He had presented himself a day late, poorly dressed and worse attended. Since Charles had inherited three-quarters of a million of debt from his father, a plain dress and a pensive air were excusable. His apparent virtues were, unluckily, of a somewhat negative quality. A bachelor monarch of five-and-twenty, thrifty, diffident and so chaste that he blushed whenever an immodest word was used in his presence, would be rather an object of derision than admiration to the courtiers of France.

Henrietta, exiled and only fifteen, at once began to think what she was told that she must think. Furthermore, between her and her bridegroom stood the figure of an Englishman who

[1] *Ibid.*

eclipsed his master in stature and prestige. Buckingham, alarmed by the attractiveness of Charles's bride, took every opportunity of aggravating the troubles occasioned by the tactlessness of her suite. Mischief was easily made between so inexperienced a couple. Charles found Henrietta cold and perverse, while she, under-developed and overwrought, conceived an hysterical aversion from him, which was to preclude for over three years all prospects of a Prince of Wales.[1]

[1] De Tillières; de Brienne; Howell; H. M. de B.; Harl. MS. 389, ff. 460, 461.

CHAPTER II

OBERON AND TITANIA

I

As far as outward appearances went, the England in which Henrietta had arrived still bore many traces of having been the Merrie England of Queen Elizabeth. English men and women of no more than middle age could clearly remember the defeat of the Spanish Armada. Only nine years ago William Shakespeare had died at Stratford-on-Avon.

Whitehall, the chief royal palace in London, had undergone little alteration since Tudor days. Its grounds stretched between the Thames and St James's Park, and through it ran a public highway from Charing Cross to Westminster, spanned by two archways, added by Henry VIII after his seizure of the official London mansion of the archbishops of York. Royal Whitehall was an irregular collection of buildings, mostly accomplished in narrow Tudor red brick, and very loosely strung together. On the east, facing the river, rose a ramping mass of state apartments, with privy stairs to the Thames, a chapel and a Great Hall. Privy gardens occupied the space between them and a rambling set of buildings on the west, reached by galleries and grouped around a cockpit and a tilt-yard. Of all the designs for a stupendous new palace in the Italian style submitted to the late king by the fashionable architect, Inigo Jones, only a banqueting-hall, urgently needed to replace one demolished by fire, had been completed. This admired pearl-grey building of Portland stone, a product of the school of Andrea Palladio, who had imitated ancient Roman monuments with-

out regard to classical principles, was destined to have a dreadful significance for Henrietta. Of the other royal residences
awaiting her in London, St James's, ordered by Henry VIII
as a hunting-lodge, presented in its plan essential features which
had been common to all large country houses in England for
five centuries. It was built around courtyards, a relic of the days
of fortification, and its principal entrance was guarded by a
fine gate-house with four octagonal towers. Denmark House,
formerly Somerset House, unfinished when the Lord Protector
Somerset had been hurried to the block, had been renamed
in honour of the last queen consort.¹ Charles I followed his
father's example, and presented it to his wife, but the formal
notification of this grant was not made until eight months
after Henrietta's arrival in England. However, the London
palace which was to be her own, and in which she was to
experience many joys and sorrows, was the first in which she
set foot, for she landed from Gravesend at the steps of Denmark
House at 5 P.M. on the evening of June 16th, 1625. Its water-
gate and garden front had been rebuilt two years before by
Inigo Jones. Around London clustered a collection of country
palaces, of which Hampton Court, Nonesuch,² Oatlands,³
Theobalds,⁴ Sheen,⁵ Greenwich⁶ and Windsor were to be most
frequented by her.

¹ In the reign of Charles II it was again generally known as Somerset
House, but to avoid confusion it is described throughout this biography by
the name by which it was known in the reign of Charles I.

² At Ewell. Given by Charles II to Lady Castlemaine, who dismantled it.
Only a lime avenue now remains to mark the site.

³ Near Weybridge. Built by Henry VIII. Destroyed during the Civil War.
Another mansion was built in its park in 1794.

⁴ Near Cheshunt, Herts. Given to Anne of Denmark by Lord Salisbury
in exchange for Hatfield. Dismantled by Cromwell in 1651. Its gallery was
112 ft. long. Fragments remain on the west side of the road from London
to Cheshunt.

⁵ At Richmond-on-Thames. Built by Edward III, rebuilt by Henry V
and Henry VIII. Sold in 1649, and allowed to fall into disrepair. Only a
gateway and part of one courtyard remain.

⁶ The Queen's House, Greenwich, built for Henrietta Maria by Inigo

Some confusion had reigned as to how the new queen should be called. In May she had been prayed for "in the king's chapel by the name of Queen Henry, for Henrietta, but since, the style is changed everywhere to Queen Mary",[1] "which 'tis said, the king rather chose to have her called by than her other".[2] The choice was luckless. People began to remember that "French queens never brought any happinesse to the English; some kind of fatality too, the English imagin'd to be in her name of Marie".[3] The only previous queen to bear this name in England had been Mary Tudor, of the Marian persecution.

Henrietta's first stay in her husband's capital was short and unsatisfactory—three weeks of bustle, dispute and continual entertainment in an overheated atmosphere. Charles gave a banquet in honour of his French guests, and the Duc de Chevreuse outshone all present. On the next night a feast as magnificent as any ever seen in France was offered to the foreigners. The host was the Duke of Buckingham. The queen and her train would have preferred that some of the "prodigal plenty" expended upon these shows could have been diverted to another quarter. Although Inigo Jones had been entrusted more than two years past (when the expected bride had been the Infanta) with the preparation of chapels for the use of a Roman Catholic queen, that at St James's was not yet ready. Only in her own apartments could Henrietta attend services of her own religion. In answer to the importunities of her many priests, the king was said to have replied coolly, "that if the Queen's Closet, where they now say Masse, were not large enough, let them have it in the Great Chamber; and if the Great Chamber were not wide enough, they might use the Garden; and if the Garden

Jones, was completed in 1633. All its principal rooms were on the first floor, attained by a singular circular staircase, and it had no passages or corridors. The old Greenwich palace of "Placentia", built for Humphrey, Duke of Gloucester, 1433, had been a favourite residence of the Tudor sovereigns.

[1] Brewer. Letter of J. Chamberlain to Sir Dudley Carleton, May 4, 1625.
[2] Hutchinson.   [3] *Ibid.*

would not serve them, then was the Park the fittest Place". "On Friday last", reports the same indignant news-writer,[1] "the Queen was at her first Masse in Whitehall, which was mumbled over to her majesty at eleven of the clock, what time she came out of her bedchamber in her petticoat, with a veil upon her head, supported by the Count de Tilliers, her lord chamberlain, and followed by six women. Whilst they were at Masse, the King took order that no Englishman or woman should come near the place."

On the following morning Charles opened his first Parliament wearing his crown, although he had not yet been crowned, and Henrietta sat on a throne by his side. All the principal statesmen of her husband's reign were present at a ceremony which even her compatriots admitted to be striking and dignified, but Henrietta knew nothing of English politics. Since she was not yet in her husband's confidence, no speculations troubled her when she heard that he had adjourned the assembly, and the court was moving out to a country palace. Unknown to her, the deserted and plague-stricken capital, where bells tolled every day for the funerals of fresh victims, had already decided to be unfavourably impressed by her. The complaints of her were many, and some were unfair. She had taken no pains to make herself agreeable to eminent Londoners. She had scowled at the loyal subjects pressing in to watch her dine. She had established her bosom friend, the much-painted French duchess, in her dower palace of Sheen. (Here Madame de Chevreuse gave birth to a third daughter, and, before the summer was out, scandalized the inhabitants of Richmond-on-Thames by swimming across their river.)

From Hampton Court Charles took his bride to Nonesuch and Woodstock. At Oxford he dissolved his first Parliament. With early autumn, perfectly in accordance with the Elizabethan tradition, the king and queen set out on a progress "to

[1] Harl. MS. 389, f. 464 B.

several parts of their kingdom". Before Henrietta returned to Hampton Court in November she had visited Lord Southampton's splendid mansion of Titchfield, from which Charles went hunting in the New Forest, and had been left for over three weeks at Wilton while her husband went on to Plymouth. From her progress the fifteen-year-old bride sent to her parent a handsome gift. How the ponderous and afflicted Queen Mother of France appreciated the arrival of several spirited English beagles is not recorded.[1] Meanwhile, the volume of gossip inimical to Henrietta followed her persistently, and swelled. At Titchfield there had been a shouting-match at the dinner-table one day between a Protestant chaplain and her majesty's confessor, both determined to say the grace before meat. On another morning the queen and her ladies, whilst a Protestant service was being held in the hall of the house, had twice promenaded ostentatiously through the assemblage of worshippers, loudly laughing and talking.

King Charles and Queen Mary returned to Whitehall, and the queen began rehearsals for a pastoral to be performed at Denmark House. Inigo Jones was designing the costumes and scenery. The dialogue would have to be all French, since the queen, who intended to take the chief part, spoke no English. She had gone secretly one afternoon for a day's shopping in the Exchange, and passed nimbly from stall to stall buying any pretty knack that took her fancy. On being recognized, she had fled by water to Hampton Court. "A French trick", muttered her husband's subjects. Christmas came, and the queen had her pastoral. Early in the New Year she went "in her embroidered carosse" to the Tower, where a banquet was given to her and ordnance was shot off. Londoners, watching the procession return by torchlight, noted furiously that the coach of their queen's confessor preceded that of their queen.

On Candlemas Day, a date deemed sinister by those that

[1] *Cal. S.P.D.*, Oct. 23, 1625.

looked for omens, Charles I went alone to his coronation, a ceremony so shorn of its usual trappings that gentlemen did not consider themselves justified in undertaking the expense of coming up from the country to see it.[1] The queen, with her ladies "frisking and dancing", watched from an upper window of the gate-house of Palace Yard, while the young king, clad in white satin instead of the customary royal purple, went by under dark and overcharged skies. Since his wife could not receive her crown from the hands of a clergymen of her own religion, and would not attend a heretic service, she would never be crowned.[2] She was the first queen consort of England to dissociate herself from her husband's coronation, and his Protestant subjects, noticing that even the latticed chamber set ready for her in the abbey, so that she could be present unofficially, remained unoccupied throughout the ceremony, henceforward regarded her as a declared enemy.

II

Charles I at the age of twenty-six was a most unhappy being. His first Parliament, ignorant of the fatal secret clauses in his marriage treaty, had insisted upon his enforcing the laws against recusants, and voted him utterly insufficient supplies with which to aid his sister Elizabeth of Bohemia in the Low Countries. He held that the executive government of the Crown was independent of parliamentary control; nevertheless, before meeting his second Parliament, he took the precaution of making all the chief speakers of the opposition Sheriffs, so that they would not attend at Westminster. His ruse to save his unpopular minister, Buckingham, was unsuccessful, and when he sent the two members who had taken the chief part in the duke's impeachment to the Tower, the House refused to sit until they were released. On June 15th, 1626, he dissolved his second Parlia-

[1] Harl. MS. 390, f. 8 B.   [2] *Ibid.* ff. 10, 11.

ment, and set about getting money by other means. War with his wife's country was impending, and he was not sorry. For his marriage, too, had been a failure. His wife wanted to return to her mother.

Henrietta was, in fact, so disappointed and disgusted with her brief experience of queenship and marriage, and so homesick, that she had actually been indulging in a little schoolgirl effort at secret diplomacy. She had brought herself to propose to Buckingham that if he would influence her husband to allow her to visit France, she would get her mother to agree that the duke should be her escort. That Buckingham desired nothing more than to see Paris and her sister-in-law again she was precociously aware. Unfortunately for her first attempt to move pieces upon the chequer-board of Europe, she was entirely unaware that her mother was now a mere cipher at the French court. Richelieu sent a definitive refusal to receive the duke, and Henrietta dejectedly returned to nursing her toothache, her homesickness and her dislike of her husband's favourite.

According to her devoted chamberlain, de Tillières, Buckingham, with brief intervals of condescending patronage, behaved towards Henrietta with unparalleled insolence. The *parvenu* duke, not content with criticizing the little queen's taste in dress, proceeded to offer her advice as to her relations with her husband. When Henrietta repelled his impertinence with scared dignity, he resorted to menacing allusions as to the fates of unsatisfactory queen consorts in England, and terrified the hysterical girl by a vague threat that he could make her the unhappiest woman in the world.[1]

Contemporary accounts of the differences between Charles I and Henrietta Maria during the first three years of their married life are irresistibly reminiscent of the quarrels of Oberon and Titania. The young king and queen accused one another of the worst offence in Fairyland—bad manners. Certainly both were

[1] Tillières; Clarendon, *Hist.* I. 82, 83.

justified. Charles, with extraordinary ill-taste, spoke and even wrote to Buckingham about his wife's shortcomings.[1] Henrietta contradicted her husband in public, and made acid comments on the customs of England.[2] Eager gossip-mongers described at length a series of trivial squabbles, unworthy of record, save for the light that they throw upon the characters of the combatants.

There was a storm in a tea-cup when the queen failed to appear at the house of Buckingham's mother to watch the procession passing to the opening of Charles's second Parliament. Henrietta unconvincingly pleaded a sudden shower of rain as her excuse for having failed to keep a disagreeable engagement, and Charles tactlessly sent the slighted host as his messenger, bearing haughty commands and reproaches to his errant consort. Tears and kisses ended that misunderstanding, but it was soon succeeded by another, detailed by Charles himself in a document unpolluted by a single gleam of humour.[3] Henrietta chose as a propitious moment to present to a weary husband an unwelcome subject, the hour after they had retired to bed. The matter in question was the appointment of persons to profitable posts connected with her revenue lands. Charles, scenting trouble, announced that he would give the list she proffered his attention in the morning, adding that any suitable English persons suggested in it should be appointed. Of course all the plums in Henrietta's list had gone to her own countrymen, and she persisted that she had the right to advance officials chosen by her mother to attend her. Upon Charles's indignant denial that the Queen Mother of France had any power to make appointments in his country, Henrietta told her husband "plainly" that if she could not have the people she chose put in charge of them he might keep his lands, and Charles awfully bade her "remember to whom she spoke". "Then she fell into

---

[1] Harl. MS. 6988, f. 5.   [2] Tillières.
[3] D'Israeli, *Commentaries on the Life and Reign of Charles I*, vol. i. p. 205.

a passionate discourse, how she is miserable. . . . When I offered
to answer, she would not so much as hear me, but went on
lamenting that she was not of such base quality as to be used
so! But", concluded the stiff young husband, "I both made her
hear me, and end that discourse."

If Buckingham was the arch mischief-maker between Charles
and Henrietta, two members of her French suite must be held
chiefly responsible for her bad behaviour. "Mamie" St George
continued upon every occasion to thrust herself into the royal
coach and take precedence of English ladies. Charles believed
this person to have such absolute influence over his wife that
even when Henrietta appeared anxious to please he nervously
attributed the improvement in her manner to some interested
counsel of the *gouvernante*. At the head of Henrietta's ecclesiastical retinue came the Bishop of Mende, a connection of Richelieu, an aristocrat, less than thirty years of age and possessed of
a dangerous tongue. At the time of the coronation he had wished
to crown the queen. His offer had met with an indignant refusal,
and popular opinion attributed Henrietta's absence from the
ceremony to his advice. A third much-reported scene of royal
disagreement took place when the French bishop contested
with Lord Holland for the stewardship of the queen's dowry.
Years after the death of the Bishop of Mende, Charles, a long
and cold hater, still remembered the young foreign prelate's
infuriating habit of striding into the queen's private apartments
whenever he chose.

III

As long ago as the previous November Charles had written
to Buckingham that he hoped shortly to find reason to "cashier
my Monsiers", as he contemptuously called his wife's French
followers.[1] Eleven days after he had dismissed his second Parliament, at three o'clock on the afternoon of June 26th, the king,

[1] Harl. MS. 6988, f. 1.

attended by the Duke of Buckingham, presented himself unexpectedly in the queen's chamber at Whitehall. A number of
her attendants were "unreverently dancing and curvetting"
before the listless girl of sixteen, whom Charles abruptly desired
to retire with him. Henrietta, either alarmed by his mien, or
because she had become accustomed to offer opposition to everything he suggested, replied that if he had anything to say to her,
he could say it here. Charles's answer was that he would do so,
if she would send away her women. After their fluttered exit,
he locked all doors of the room, and advancing towards his
wife, announced to her that as her compatriots had invariably
given her bad counsel, and encouraged her to neglect her duties
towards her husband and her new country, he was sending them
all back to France. Utterly taken aback, Henrietta sobbed
throughout his lecture. When she had recovered sufficiently
she flung herself on her knees and begged him, if he was in-
flexible about "Mamie" St George, whom she knew that he
disliked, at least to leave her Madame de Tillières, against whom
nobody could find cause for complaint. Charles answered that
all were going. Henrietta, between screams, demanded to be
allowed to say farewell to her unhappy servitors. Her screams
failed to move Charles, but they brought into the courtyard
below a number of the persons on whose behalf they were
undertaken. She rushed to the window, and breaking several
panes of glass with her bare fists prepared to call to the in-
quisitive audience gathering below. Charles pursued her and
removed her from the casement with such force that the hands
with which she clung to its metalwork were bruised and torn
and her gown was rent. At last, at the cost of breaking his word
to his wife and treating her with physical violence, he was
master. Henrietta, hurt and astounded, wept so uncontrolledly
that her unseen auditors prophesied that she would cry herself
to death.[1]

[1] Tillières.

They did not depart without some show of resistance. The Bishop of Mende began by declaring that it was not in his power to retire from a country to which he had been accredited, almost as an ambassador, unless the King of France should send for him. "But he was told again that the king his master had nothing to do here in England, and that, if he were unwilling to go, England would send force enough to convey him away hence. . . . The women howled and lamented as if they had been going to execution, but all in vain, for the yeomen of the guard, by that lord's appointment, thrust them and all their countryfolk out of the queen's lodgings, and locked the doors after them."[1]

The dismissed foreigners were removed to Denmark House, and Henrietta found some means to convey to the bishop a distracted note in which she described herself as a prisoner allowed to speak to nobody, and called on her God and her mother to succour her.[2]

Over a month later, although their wages, amounting to eleven thousand pounds, and gifts of jewels estimated as worth twenty thousand pounds, had been delivered to the French, they were still in London, finding one pretext after another to delay their departure. Charles, whose wrath had not abated, sent instructions to Buckingham to get them out of England by fair means if possible, "otherways force them away, dryving them away lyke so manie wyld beastes, untill ye have shipped them, and so the Devill goe with them".[3] Their embarkation was eventually attended by bloodshed, for a hooligan amongst the angry mob assembled to see the last of them, threw a stone which knocked off the head-dress of "Mamie" St George, and a zealous young English gallant who had been leading the lady to the barge drew his sword and ran the man through on the spot.

[1] Harl. MS. 383, f. 33.
[2] *Affaires Etrangères Angleterre*, tome 41, Bibliothèque Nationale.
[3] Harl. MS. 6988, f. 11.

An English news-writer declares that with her servants went the whole of Henrietta's famous trousseau. One old satin gown was sent back to her in answer to a demand from the Lords of Council. Before its arrival her wardrobe had been reduced to two smocks and one gown.[1] "Mamie" St George, in a torrential letter which makes Charles's feelings towards her explicable, says that the gowns removed had been presented to her friends by Henrietta, but adds that since the keys of her majesty's wardrobe, silver and jewellery had been seized by the English, and the trunks of her banished suite broken open at Dover, they can safely assert anything.[2] It seems indisputable that the outraged *menie* pilfered their distressed mistress royally. When her servants claimed further that she owed them many sums for goods bought by them at her dictation Henrietta herself denied to Charles that she had contracted any such debts.

He had taken her down to Nonesuch, and her spirits were optimistically described in London as "very jocund". The English weather, as if determined to increase her poor opinion of her new country, was doing its worst. Rain fell "every day more or less" from June 10th to July 7th this summer. Presently Charles made a slight alteration in his original sentence of wholesale banishment. The queen was, after all, to be allowed two priests—one an Englishman, the other a Scot—and three female attendants who could speak her own tongue—her nurse, "Madame Pantelet that dresseth her," and the Duchesse de Thouars.[3] When Charles sent to St James's to order apartments to be made ready for the duchess the housekeeper sent back triumphant answer that her majesty's French retinue "had so defiled that House, as a week's worke would not make it cleane".[4]

---

[1] Harl. MS. 383, f. 34.   [2] Tillières.
[3] This lady was acceptable on account of her Protestant connections. She was the daughter of William the Silent, Prince of Orange.
[4] Harl. MS. 383, f. 37 B.

IV

The English Ambassador in Paris, when consulted as to the probable effect of a dismissal of Henrietta's suite, had answered that in his opinion France was at the moment too deeply engaged elsewhere to make serious reprisals. His forecast was correct. The only immediate result of Charles's drastic action was a series of letters. Marie de Medicis wrote to her daughter that she had not been so upset since the assassination of Henri IV. But the Queen of England's urgently repeated desires to visit her mother received no encouragement. Last year, when Charles had broken his word with regard to the recusancy laws, the Marquis de Blainnille had been sent over to protest. France now despatched another Ambassador-Extraordinary to London. The poor gentleman departed very unwillingly, as well he might. The Marshal de Bassompierre, brother-in-law of the Comte de Tillières, had been wounded by the side of Henrietta's father on the field of Ivry. He was an elegant Alsatian of forty-seven. Five years later Richelieu sent him to the Bastille, where he lay for twelve seasons occupying himself by writing his memoirs. He records that on the eve of his arrest he had to spend a whole day destroying the more than six thousand love-letters sent to him by infatuated females. His account of his Embassy to London is full of unconscious humour, and his shots at English words fully justify his reputation for intrepidity.[1] His first efforts to fulfil his mission were not met in a conciliatory spirit. "He hath gotten no audience as yet, nor shall have, very suddenly", reports a writer, who adds that the ambassador was having to pay for his own lodgings in London. Charles only consented to accord the marshal a public reception on the condition that he made no mention

[1] Kensington is his worst stumbling-block. It appears as "Inhimthort" and "Stintinton", but he is also in perpetual difficulty over his trips to the Duke of Buckingham's residence of "Jorschaux" (York House).

of the business on which he had been sent. The king, explained the ubiquitous Buckingham, would be unable to contain his passion if the subject were broached in public, and the queen "might commit some extravagance and cry in the sight of everybody". Bassompierre, although duly horrified at the prospect of such a breach of etiquette, insisted that he could not honourably abstain from some attempt to convey his sovereign's messages. Finally, upon an agreement that the king should interrupt him with a promise of a future private interview, he accompanied the duke to Hampton Court, where he found Charles and Henrietta seated in state upon a dais. "The company was magnificent and the order exquisite." The pre-arranged dialogue passed off without mishap, but tears welled in Henrietta's eyes as she spoke her few formal words of greeting to her countryman, and although the audience was brief, the queen, overcome by emotion and supported by the Duchesse de Thouars, was obliged to retire before the ambassador.

Bassompierre remained in England for over two months, gallantly struggling, at least, to bring about a better understanding between Charles and Henrietta. He attempted an Olympian impartiality, and on more than one occasion accused Henrietta of having "pick'd a quarrel" with her husband, in his presence. The king took the ambassador aside on the excuse of displaying his collection of jewels, "which are very fine", before he began his complaints against his wife. After weeks of travail, just when the marshal was beginning to congratulate himself on having effected a reconciliation between the royal pair, Henrietta provoked another scene and the exasperated peace-maker trod from her presence declaring that he would return instantly to France and tell her mother and brother that she, not her husband, was to blame for their continued estrangement. Henrietta sent after him but he sulked for two days, at the end of which time they found themselves seated at the same supper-table in the house of the Duke of Buckingham.

York House, like Whitehall, had once been a London palace
of the northern archbishops, but Buckingham had razed the
original structure to the ground and erected on its site a mansion
described by Bassompierre to be "extremely fine" and "the
most richly fitted up" that he had ever seen. Only the water-
gate of the house, where Bassompierre came by torchlight on a
November Sunday evening to sup with Buckingham and
Charles and Henrietta, still stands at the foot of the street bearing the duke's name. Its moulding is coarse, for it was designed
to produce an effect when seen from the river. The entertainment provided by the favourite that night was found worthy
of record by several pens. It was estimated to have cost between
five and six thousand pounds; "all things came down in clouds"
and every course was accompanied by a ballet. "One rare device
was a representation of the French king and the two queens
with their chiefest attendants, and so to the life that the queen's
majesty could name them." At four o'clock in the morning,
when the guests had exhausted themselves in country dances,
their host led the way to "the vaulted apartments", where five
more collations awaited them.[1]

Bassompierre walked in "the Moorfield" and was taken by
the queen to see the Lord Mayor's Show. While waiting for
the procession to pass down "Shipside" Henrietta made the
ambassador play a card game with her, in her coach. He
swallowed much London fog and lost his voice, so that he
was "in a bad state for a discussion" when "the Earl of Dor-
chets" arrived at seven one morning, heralding the lords of the
council, eager to comment on his reply to their Memorial of
the king's reasons of complaint against the queen's French
domestics. The Memorial was of portentous length and contained all the old grievances and some that were new to the
ambassador. Most concerned the Bishop of Mende and his
priests, who were accused of having intrigued amongst English

[1] Bassompierre.

subjects, converted the queen's house into a rendezvous for
Jesuit fugitives and imposed upon Henrietta as penances "base
and servile acts" not only unworthy of her dignity but actually
dangerous to her health. A contemporary news-letter throws
further light upon the supposed penances, declaring that the
queen had been obliged to go barefoot, to spin, to eat her meat
out of wooden dishes and wait upon her own servants at table.
On "a foul morning" she had been condemned to "dabble
in the dirt", walking on her own feet from Denmark House to
St James's whilst "her luciferian confessor"[1] rolled by in his
coach. Her suite were further denounced by the lords for
having "discovered what was passing in private" between her
and Charles, and "laboured to create in the gentle mind of the
queen a repugnance to all that his majesty desired or ordered".
Even Henrietta's inability to speak English was put down to
the account of her French followers, who "have endeavoured by
all means to inspire her with a contempt for our nation and a
dislike of our habits . . . as if she neither had, nor wished to have,
any common interest amongst us".[2]

Before he could reply to one point in the document, Bassompierre had to seek elucidation from Henrietta herself. The
Memorial stated that on St James's Day she had walked to
Tyburn to lead a public prayer for the souls of the political
malefactors exposed on the gallows there. Exaggerated accounts
of this story asserted that she had gone barefoot and fallen on
her knees under the gallows with her rosary in her fingers.
Henrietta empowered Bassompierre to say that on an evening
within a month of her arrival in England she had walked
from the Park of "St Gemmes" into "the Hipparc", an expedition which she had often undertaken accompanied by her
husband, but that she had led a public procession to the gallows
or even approached within fifty paces of them she utterly
denied.

[1] Harl. MS. 383, f. 34.   [2] Bassompierre.

Bassompierre left England on December 18th in a storm, and on his arrival at Calais had to spend a day there recovering from sea-sickness. His servants, who had preceded him, were tossed in the Channel for five days and obliged to throw overboard both his coaches and forty thousand francs' worth of clothes purchased by him in London. He had not failed altogether in his mission, for he had obtained promises that Henrietta should be allowed sixty French attendants in place of her original train of three-score which, before dismissal, had swollen to four hundred. Charles had engaged to treat his Catholic subjects with all possible leniency and nineteen priests had been released from English prisons as a compliment to the departing ambassador. But Bassompierre's efforts were poorly requited at the Louvre. Louis XIII refused to accept the conditions obtained after so much effort and continued to besiege his Protestant subjects at Rochelle. Three months later all the marshal's work seemed to have been undertaken in vain, for the long-threatened war between England and France broke out.

At Whitehall, Henrietta celebrated Twelfth Night by a masque which seems to have broken the record even for amateur theatricals, since its performance lasted from three in the afternoon till four in the morning. A thousand yards of taffetas and satin had been employed for its costumes and scenery. The prisons of London were filling with gentry who had refused to subscribe to her husband's forced loans towards the war. On a March day a dinner was given in her honour aboard the *Neptune* at Blackwall, and a gentleman who met her procession returning on horseback to Denmark House noted that the queen and her ladies were all wearing masks and little black beaver hats, Henrietta's being distinguished by a white plume. The forty or fifty gentlemen attending her rode bareheaded. The only males in her train to retain their headgear were her Papist majesty's four priests.

V

Henrietta was now in the miserable position of a wife whose adopted country is in arms against the land of her birth, but the war cloud had for her a silver lining. In command of the English fleet of a hundred vessels, sent to relieve Rochelle, went Buckingham. His wife and mother had gone upon their knees in their endeavours to dissuade him from exposing himself to such unnecessary peril, but to the bold "Steenie" the role of laurell'd captain had proved irresistible. He had gone to war in the grand manner, giving four farewell banquets to the friends who might never see him again. The last of his entertainments, on board the *Triumph* at Portsmouth, had been more expensive to the chief guest than to the host, for during it the chest containing the king's plate had fallen into the sea and there remained in spite of all the attempts of "the Dutch diver" to locate it.

The duke was away five months, during which time Charles, deprived of his usual confidant, turned to the wife whom he had always at heart admired. His obtuseness is illustrated by the fact that he wrote to the absent duke, happily describing his improved relations with his queen. Henrietta's heart was still in France. During de Bassompierre's visit she had written to de Tillières declaring that she had wept for two days on learning that stories wickedly misrepresenting her behaviour in England were being transmitted to her mother. Her beloved but dreaded parent had chosen for her the advisers who had encouraged her to treat her heretic and inadept husband with contempt. Suddenly bereft of their daily counsel she waited in growing anxiety for instructions direct from headquarters, and Marie de Medicis, for the first time, sent her youngest child advice productive of happiness. The bewildered Henrietta found herself commanded to complete obedience to her husband, "matters of religion only, excepted". Marie de

Medicis, whose sole hold over her own husband had been through their children, had not any intention, even if she had possessed the power, of welcoming home an unhappily married daughter. The incompetence of the younger generation was driving her to distraction. Her eldest daughter the Queen of Spain, although continually pregnant, appeared incapable of producing a healthy infant. Unrelaxed enquiries failed to discover that her other two daughters, married for respectively eight and two years, had even shown any symptoms of making her a grandmother. Her elder son's wife claimed a history of two miscarriages, but the streets of Paris were placarded with declarations that its inhabitants would suffer no kings that could not beget heirs. Of all the promising children that the ambitious Marie had borne to a consistently unfaithful husband, only the one for whom it was not of first importance to raise a family had performed that duty punctually. The heiress-bride of her younger son Gaston, whose intrigues against the Crown were a menace to the peace of France, died four days after giving birth to a daughter. This first child of her favourite brother was to play a conspicuous part in Henrietta's after-life. Henrietta's court went into three months' mourning for a princess against whose country England was at war, a sister-in-law whom their queen had never greeted, and departed with their mistress for several weeks of high summer to a peaceful English watering-place. Wellingborough, an ancient market town of the abbots of Croyland, pleasantly situated in the centre of an agricultural district on the north bank of the river Nene, possessed chalybeate springs.[1]

[1] Tradition asserts that the queen and her attendants encamped in tents round the Red Well, in a field half a mile to the north-west of the town, and that in the following year both Charles and Henrietta stayed at an inn called the White Swan, burnt in the Great Fire of Wellingborough in 1738, when all streets except Sheep Street and Gold Street were demolished. The little Northamptonshire town, whose staple industry (before the development in the early nineteenth century of the leather trade) was handmade lace, has been rebuilt, almost entirely in the local ironstone. Only the

With autumn the queen returned to London. In spite of obedience to her mother and her physicians she still had no prospect of improving her position by the birth of an heir. On November 1st, 1627, she employed her undirected leisure by consulting a soothsayer. The Lady Eleanor Davy, a daughter of Lord Castlehaven, had been twice unhappily married to gentlemen who had failed to share her own respect for her psychic powers. Both had thrown her books of prophecies "behind the fire". By her first husband, of whose approaching demise she had been so convinced that she had ordered widow's weeds several days before it took place and communicated the fact to him, she had become the mother of a bright little girl and one son, "a perfect idiot". At the time of Henrietta's summons to her she was about twenty-six and at the height of her reputation "amongst the ignorant people". She conceived herself to be a reincarnation of a prominent Scriptural character, claiming that the letters of her name made an anagram of the words "Reveal O Daniel!" A member of the privy council called upon to rebuke her for spreading provocative political rumours, subsequently declared, equally incorrectly, that the letters of her name also made an anagram of the words "Never so mad a lady".

After mass on the evening of All Saints' Day was the hour appointed by the impatient young queen for the prophetess's attendance, and although Henrietta arrived upon the scene accompanied by courtiers, amongst whom was the dapper Lord Carlisle, her first question displayed no false modesty. According to Lady Eleanor's autobiography, Henrietta opened

names of Cheese Lane, Hog Hill and Silver Street retain the picturesqueness which endeared it to "the Queen", whose visits are still proudly related by its inhabitants. Henrietta evidently enjoyed her first stay at the Northamptonshire spa, for she returned there twice. Archbishop Laud noted in his journal a visit to the king and queen at Wellingborough in 1637. In 1645, on their road to Naseby, Cromwell's Ironsides were, according to local legend, refreshed by ale brought out to them in buckets from the hostelry called the Hind, then in the course of construction.

the séance by asking point-blank "when she should be with child". Needless to say the prophetess gave her royal client an answer satisfying in matter, though inexact as to date. The nobleman who four years past had gone to Paris to treat for "the little Madam's" marriage with his king, translated this utterance, which was couched in Latin, as "Soon" or "In a short time". Henrietta then proceeding to the next matter nearest her heart, made an enquiry as to the Duke of Buckingham's success in the present war, to which Lady Eleanor replied as agreeably as possible "that as for his honour, of that he would not bring much home, but his person should return in safety with no little speed". Henrietta anxiously reverted to her earlier subject and was assured that her first child should be a son and that "for a time she should be happy". Unfavourably impressed by this second vagueness as to date, she persisted "But how long?" to which Lady Eleanor awfully replied: "For sixteen years; that was long enough". At this point, the thrilling interview was brought to an end by the entry of the king, who, after demanding coldly of Lady Eleanor whether she was not "the person" who had foretold her own husband's death with fatal consequences, withdrew his credulous wife from her company. Lady Eleanor, writing after this event had come to pass, adds that she then further divulged to the queen's ladies that "although it was indeed true that the queen should shortly have a son . . . it would be born, christened and buried all in one day".[1]

Buckingham landed at Plymouth ten days later. His scheme to regain popularity by a successful foreign campaign had been a failure. England had not sent him the reinforcements he had demanded for his siege of the fort of St Martin, and the bodies of two thousand Englishmen strewed the narrow causeway along which he had been obliged to retreat towards his ships. Charles, eager to despatch a second expedition to repair this

[1] Ballard.

disaster, had no choice but to summon a new Parliament. It met in March of the following year. The restive Commons had found a leader in the swarthy and taciturn Sir Thomas Wentworth, but before they had forced the Petition of Right upon their humiliated king this statesman had dissociated himself from their action. Henrietta, always unable to appreciate honest worth unaccompanied by outer graces, afterwards described this great man "of all the king's servants the most able and faithful", as "though not handsome . . . agreeable enough" and the possessor of "the finest hands of any man in the world".[1] Charles was again giving all his confidence to the duke and she was still utterly uninstructed as to the political situation. She stood sponsor, by proxy, to Buckingham's infant heir, a ceremony which Charles attended personally, clad "in a long soldier's coat, all covered with gold lace". Purchases of "rare and outlandish flowers" by the queen are recorded of this season,[2] and a lady of her court noted that "she interferes with nothing and thinks only of how to kill time".[3] The writer of this pathetic admission was a fellow exile, now the wife of an English nobleman. The widowed Duchesse de Thouars, who had gone back to France during Bassompierre's stay in London, had made a match between her very plain but very amiable and richly dowered daughter and the son and heir of Lord Derby. Young Lord Strange had but seventeen years to his bride's twenty-four and, in spite of having finished his education abroad, spoke no French. However, he was a docile son. Unfortunately for Henrietta's comfort his tastes were those of a country gentleman; he detested court life. As soon as his wife's pregnancy could be made the excuse he withdrew her from London. Charlotte de la Trémoïlle, Lady Strange, departed with her husband to spend sixteen years living quietly at Knowsley or Lathom House, and to bear nine children. Henceforward her appearances at Whitehall were few.

[1] de Motteville.   [2] *Cal. S.P.D.*, 1627–8.   [3] de Witt.

Henrietta's first choice of a friend amongst the English ladies, of whom she had been originally doubtful "whether they were set to watch her as a prisoner or wait upon her as a princess",[1] was almost inevitable. Lord Carlisle's wife was of unexceptionable birth and the most effective woman at court, where her name had been coupled with that of every gentleman whose admiration could add to her prestige, including even Buckingham. Her father had passionately opposed her decision, at the age of seventeen, of throwing herself away upon one of James I's handsome young men with a rise in him, pointing out that a Percy "could not endure that his daughter should dance any Scotch jigs". At seven-and-twenty, Lucy Hay, having long outgrown her first romance, was remarkable for her strongly developed acquisitive sense, amusing conversation and striking good looks. She had far more self-confidence than Henrietta, and soon made her company indispensable to the impressionable girl ten years her junior. When "Lucinda" caught smallpox in the late summer of this year, courtiers forgot politics in their anxiety lest her famous charms should be impaired, and the queen, regardless of infection, visited her new great friend's sick-chamber. Henrietta never feared infection, and although smallpox proved fatal to many members of her family there is no record that she ever contracted it. Lady Carlisle recovered and reappeared in society wearing a mask, which when removed disclosed enhanced beauty. "The ladies of Buckingham" naturally viewed her promotion with disgust, and jealously prompted the story that she had taught the young queen to paint. Henrietta, whose youth had been spent in circles where ladies, especially those of Spanish origin, laid on rouge in such unconvincing quantities that nervous Englishmen mistook their intention for humour, could hardly have needed such instruction. Close companionship with the Duchesse de Chevreuse must have shown her every possibility of this art

[1] H. M. de B.

years before. However, the queen's new complexion coincided with the queen's new friendship and may have been responsible also for the rumours, widely repeated, that she was pregnant. Close observers said that if this were so it could not yet be sufficiently advanced to be declared with certainty. Actually Henrietta's painted cheeks and haggard air were inspired by hopes deferred. The most renowned physician in England could do no more for her than recommend a second visit to the waters of Wellingborough.

Theodore Turquet, son of a French Protestant historian of Piedmontese origin, had been born at Mayerne, near Geneva, studied medicine at Heidelberg, Montpelier and Paris, and been brought to London early in the last reign by a grateful patient, an English peer, who had introduced him to James I. Sir Theodore de Mayerne, or Mayerne as he was now universally called, had become first physician to both Charles's parents and had attended every influential sick-bed in England for the past twenty years. He had seen Sir Robert Cecil's tumour, and Lord Rochester's dyspepsia, and Lord Monteagle's daughter's epilepsy, and King James's colic, and melancholy and jaundice, and bad arm after a fall in the hunting-field, and prescribed again and again and again for his late majesty's gout. He had been present at the autopsy on the present king's elder brother, and had studied Charles's constitution from childhood. The medical attendants banished with Henrietta's French train had left their ailing mistress with a bill for drugs amounting to eight hundred pounds. In their place had come to her the bluff and benevolent Sir Theodore, who, judging by a Rubens sketch,[1] must have borne a close resemblance in appearance and manner to the popular conception of Father Christmas. He had a venerable beard, and silver hair thinning on a redoubtable forehead, blue eyes sparkling with omniscience under bushy white brows, a high colour, and already, at five-and-fifty, a figure indeed

[1] In the British Museum.

comfortable. He reported imperturbably after a professional visit to the palace of Nonesuch in June of this year: "The King and Queen are well, and live together with a satisfaction which all their true servants and honest people ought to wish"[1].[2]

Henrietta's departure for Wellingborough, where she was to stay while Charles assisted at the embarkation of the second Rochelle expedition, was postponed twice during the month of July owing to the duke's unreadiness, and eventually Charles set out towards the coast alone, leaving Buckingham to follow him. Leaflets distributed in the streets of London were asking "Who rules the Kingdom? The King. Who rules the King? The Duke. Who the Duke? The devil."[3] At midsummer, when Buckingham's portrait had fallen down in the High Commission chamber at Lambeth, his death by assassination had been openly predicted. But the lady upon whose shoulders had descended the mantle of the prophet Daniel had informed her circle of believers that "his time is not till August".

VI

On Tuesday, August 19th, 1628, a morose unemployed officer of thirty-odd years, called John Felton, whose left hand was useless owing to an old wound, borrowed a small sum from his mother, who lived over a haberdasher's shop in Fleet Street, and announced his intention of going to Portsmouth, where the second Rochelle expedition was mustering. He had applied twice last year for the command of a company, and on one occasion at least his application had been refused by the Duke of Buckingham, who, in answer to his desperate plea that without such a command he could not live, had replied that in that

[1] *Cal. S.P.D.*, 1628.
[2] Mayerne occupied his leisure hours with chemical experiments and first won Henrietta's favour by giving her prescriptions for cosmetics. In a curious little contemporary volume of recipes, entitled *The Queen's Closet Opened*, several of Mayerne's prescriptions are included.
[3] Harl. MS. 390, f. 415.

case he would have to hang. Felton now bought a tenpenny dagger-knife from a cutler on Tower Hill, fastened it to his right-hand pocket so that he could draw it without using his crippled left hand, and set out on foot for Portsmouth. Arriving there before nine o'clock on the following Saturday morning he made his way to the house in the High Street where the duke was lodged [1] and entered its crowded hall without hindrance. The duke's horse was waiting at the door but its owner was still breakfasting. Presently Buckingham appeared and stopped for a moment to speak to an officer of low stature. Felton approached the pair, and with the words "God have mercy upon thy soul", leant over the shoulder of Colonel Sir Thomas Fryer and stabbed Buckingham in the left breast. Lord Cleveland, who had just turned his back, was close enough to hear "the thump" as Felton's tenpenny knife went home into Buckingham's heart. The duke tore out the weapon and made an effort to draw his sword, but after staggering a few steps fell heavily against a table, crying "Traitor! thou hast killed me!" His duchess, hearing a commotion, rushed in her nightdress to the gallery which overlooked the hall, but the duke had already expired in the arms of his surgeon.[2, 3]

For the second time in her short life of less than nineteen years the knife of a fanatic had affected the destiny of Henrietta Maria.

[1] Now No. 10, on the east side near the north end of Portsmouth High Street.

[2] Felton gave himself up, narrowly escaped lynching on the spot, and was carried prisoner to the Tower. Popular sentiment hailed him as a national deliverer. At his trial in the Court of the King's Bench on Nov. 27 he pleaded guilty, but said that he had acted "not maliciously, but with a love to his country". He was hanged at Tyburn the next morning and his corpse was subsequently suspended in chains at Portsmouth.

[3] Ellis; Clarendon, *Hist.* 1. 52-60; Howell; *Cal. S.P.D.*, 1628-9; Gardiner, *Hist. of England*, vol. vi.

VII

Charles was at morning prayers with his household when the news of Buckingham's assassination was brought to him. The royal chaplain brought the service to a pause as the startling message whispered to the king spread amongst the congregation, but with a dreadful composure his master desired him to proceed. Not until he had retired to his private chamber did Charles fling himself on his bed and burst into tears.[1] Never before in his life had his emotions been so roused, and he turned instinctively, as he had done when Buckingham had been only temporarily removed from him, to the consolations of Henrietta. She hurried south and he took a day's journey towards her. A new energy inspired him. In spite of its commander's death the expedition must sail. "The King, they say," wrote a clergyman at Oxford,[2] "in fourteen days after the duke's death, despatched more business than the duke had done three months before." Henrietta's attentions to the bereaved Buckingham family were "kindly taken" by her husband. Public opinion declared that her display of grief could not be sincere. Up to this time her efforts to please her ungenial consort had certainly been prompted by self-interest, but now that he came to her stricken and unmanned, strong maternal instincts stirred her.

The writers of news-letters, looking round this autumn for some gentle pastoral matter with which to refresh readers sated with the murdered duke's obsequies and the starvation in Rochelle, found just what they needed in an unexpected quarter. A delicious comedy was succeeding tragedy in court circles and the entertainment was rendered the more amusing by the fact that the chief performers were both shy amateurs. The king was falling in love with his own wife and she with him. They were not quite aware, as yet, what was happening

[1] Howell; Clarendon, *Hist.* 1. 62.   [2] Harl. MS. 390, f. 437.

to them, but the affair was proceeding apace attended by all the correct symptoms—exchange of gifts and portraits, deep melancholy during short separations. "The White King" grew *"more galant"* every day.

Meanwhile Sir Theodore Mayerne was prescribing for a new patient. On a September day he was consulted by a country gentleman, a Fenland squire, Member of Parliament for Huntingdon, eight years married and the father of five children; a long-bodied, short-legged, heavy-featured man with blue-grey eyes and a conspicuous mole below his under-lip. Mr Oliver Cromwell, who was rather uncouth, complained of nightmares and depression and the fashionable doctor wrote him down as "valde melancholicus".[1]

Christmas week came and the queen slept ill while her husband had to be away at Theobalds for four nights. She erected his portrait by her bedside. On Christmas Eve a letter-writer stated cautiously, "We are here putt in some hope that the queen is with child, she shewing some signs thereof, but a little longer time will make it better knowne".[2]

This time the hopes were well founded.

VIII

Oxford University and city rang joy-bells and lit bonfires, when the queen's pregnancy was formally announced,[3] but in London persons who had spoken against her were under examination, and a glorious clown's dialogue was being solemnly reported. One unwary babbler was accused of having wished

---

[1] Sloane MS. 2069, f. 92 B.   [2] Harl. MS. 7010, f. 107 B.
[3] In the prayer "for the safe Child-bearing of the Queen's Majesty", drawn up by Archbishop Laud in the winter of 1628-9, thanksgiving is offered "for Thy great mercy and loving-kindness ... in giving her Majesty hope of her long-desired issue". "Be with her in soul and in body", runs the finely worded supplication; "preserve her from all danger, keep her safe to, and in the hour of travail ... and make her a joyful mother of many children."

her hopeful majesty at the bottom of the sea, and another of having suggested the addition of a mill-stone about her neck.[1]

In Paris, the Queen Mother's bliss at the "joyful assurance" brought to her by one of Henrietta's French household[2] was only disturbed by the realization that both her tardy daughters had now chosen the same month in which to perform their duty, and the best *sage-femme* of France, long held in readiness for such occasions, could not be in Turin and London simultaneously. Marie de Medicis' decision was characteristic. The younger daughter, whose child would inherit a kingdom, had first claim on the services of the redoubtable Madame Peronne.

But on May 12th, a much humbler character was hurriedly summoned to Greenwich Palace, whose inhabitants were vociferous with contradictory reports of disaster. The queen had been frightened by the fighting of two large dogs, one of which had snatched at her dress in the midst of their feud. . . . She had never felt well since her return by water from attending an Ember Week service in London last Monday, when her barge had moved away from the landing-place just as she had been about to step ashore. . . . She had been taking far too much exercise, and, what was fatal, walking uphill. . . . Whatever the cause, the fact was that she was in labour about ten weeks before her time, and without any skilled person in attendance. "The poor town midwife of Greenwich" swooned when she found herself in the royal bedchamber, and had to be carried forth. A surgeon called Chamberlaine arrived on the scene, and prepared to act as male midwife. The case proved to be one of breech presentation. Charles, making continual appearances at the bedside, commanded that the mother's life must be saved at all costs, and after much difficulty the queen was delivered. The child, the hoped-for heir, was born alive, about three o'clock on the following morning, but was so undersized and

---

[1] *Cal. S.P.D.*, 1629.

[2] Madame de Vantelet. Two de Vantelets were still in Henrietta's service at the time of her death, forty years later.

feeble that its christening was considered of immediate import-ance. Henrietta, directly her sufferings were relieved, dropped into an exhausted sleep, while Charles in the adjoining chamber disputed with her confessor, who desired to admit the child into the Church of her own faith. The infant, "likelie' in a few months to have proved a hopeful prince", was baptized "Charles-James" by the king's chaplain, died an hour after its christening, and was carried the same night to Westminster Abbey, where Dr. Laud officiated at its burial by the side of its grandfather, James I.[1] Mayerne, who arrived too late to be present at the birth, found the queen "full of strength and courage". Hen-rietta's spirits always rose in adversity. He added to his flowery report of the tragedy a brief professional note that an express should be sent to France to stop Madame Peronne, who would now be at liberty to attend the Princess of Piedmont.[2]

Both Henrietta's sisters bore living children this year—the Princess of Piedmont a daughter, and the Queen of Spain a son.

Charles had dissolved his third Parliament this spring amongst scenes of violence, and declared that in future he meant to reign without one. By good fortune, not good management, the succeeding eleven seasons while he did so happened to be years of material prosperity. Peace with France was concluded in 1629 and with Spain in 1630. Scotland was "growing into a combustion" but the land of his birth was not very present in his mind. His chief immediate anxiety was for his wife's recovery, which had been retarded "by throws of another nature", occasioned by pamphlets in which she found herself "reviled as a daughter of Heth, a Canaanite and an idolater". The prospect of their Papist queen providing England with an heir had been resented by "mutterers" who had complained that God had better provided for them in the hopeful progeny of the Protestant Queen of Bohemia.[3]

---

[1] Harl. MS. 7010, ff. 117 B, 119; Laud.
[2] *Cal. S.P.D.*, May 13, 1629.　　　　[3] H. M. de B.

A French Ambassador arrived in London, and sent home glowing descriptions of the King of England's devotion to his wife. Charles, after kissing Henrietta "a hundred times" in the course of an hour, said to the Marquis de Chateauneuf, "You do not see that in Turin, nor", lowering his voice, "in France". Henrietta, who confessed to the ambassador that she had felt a little jealousy of her successful sister Christine, now courageously announced herself, "Not only the happiest princess, but the happiest woman in the world".[1] "Thank God, the danger is past, and as to my loss, I wish to forget it."[2] "Your mother is sending you a governor", said Charles, when he heard that Chateauneuf had been empowered to suggest that a bishop from France should supersede the queen's present confessor, Father Philip. "I am no longer a child", said Henrietta, and no bishop came. She seemed accustomed to her English ladies, and rather indifferent as to the appointment of the sixty French attendants promised to her before the outbreak of the late war. A single lady of the bedchamber, who could go to church with her, would, she said, suffice for her needs. She went to Tunbridge Wells to complete her convalescence, but found herself so bored apart from the king, that she cut short her visit, and returned "suddenly, by great journeys," to Oatlands, where Charles, having heard of her intention, had repaired to give her a surprise by greeting her.[3] The result of this lovers' meeting in August 1629 was Charles II.

Already by mid-October rumours of the queen's pregnancy were current in the streets of London. A servant of her household had been seen running all about the town trying to buy mussels. Her majesty had expressed a sudden irresistible craving for shell-fish.

[1] Aff. Etr. Ang. t. 43, Bibl. Nat.

[2] Everett-Green. Letter to the Prince of Piedmont, Aug. 15, 1629, dated "Henley".

[3] Letters and Despatches of Thomas, Earl of Strafforde. Letter of Lord Cottington to Lord Wentworth, Aug. 5, 1629.

When Marie de Medicis heard that her daughter was so promptly at work again, she determined that no lack of warnings should be responsible for another tragedy. She sent over, accompanied by volumes of advice, the gift of a chair which Henrietta pronounced so beautiful that only to look at it made one long to go out in it. Charles wrote to his mother-in-law, assuring her that her daughter was being so careful of herself this time that the only authority he needed to exert was that of love. "The sole dispute between us being which shall vanquish the other by affection." Madame Peronne was again engaged, and as early as March Henrietta's favourite dwarf, Jeffery Hudson, and her dancing-master, were sent over to France to fetch the *sage-femme* and her assistants. To the delight of disgruntled English, who had considered their country slighted by this importation of foreigners to preside over the birth of a Prince of Wales, the odd party fell into the hands of pirates, by whom they were detained until their services were no longer necessary. Ten Capuchin friars, however, arrived safely, and were attached to the queen's chapel at St James's, which was at last ready. Protestant opinion was mollified by the news that all the attendants of the royal nursery were to be of the established religion of the realm, and that a French doctor, despatched by the Queen Mother of France, had not even been allowed an interview with Henrietta.[1] Lady Eleanor was, of course, prophesying again. Charles sent her a message, "to leave off her predictions", but undeterred, she amiably assured his messenger that the next baby should be "a son and a strong child".[2] Both prospective parents were nervous. "On this new hope that God has given us", wrote Charles to his mother-in-law, "depends my content." Henrietta wore round her neck a little heart, sent to her by her mother. She believed so firmly in the powers

[1] Harl. MS. 7000, f. 292.
[2] Eventually her "beam of a divine knowledge of future things proved extreamly unfortunate" to her, "for on account of four prophecies which she got printed, she went to prison for two years". Ballard.

of this trinket to avert miscarriage, that if she found herself without it, she began to tremble.[1] The weeks wore on; she passed the date which, last year, had been fatal to her, and arranged to avoid the scene. After some discussion, Greenwich was decided against, and Henry VIII's old red-brick hunting-lodge of St James's chosen as the place most agreeable to both their majesties, for the queen "to attend the happie hower for herself and us". A set of pleasant apartments, with a peaceful view of the terrace and deer-park, were made ready, and a new and magnificent bed with hangings of embroidered green satin, valued at £675, was installed in the future birth-chamber.

At last all the preparations were completed, and this time the confinement was perfectly normal. Henrietta fell into labour about four o'clock on the morning of May 29th, 1630, and before noon had become "the happy Mother of a Prince of Wales". As Charles rode in state to St Paul's on the same day, to return thanks for the birth of a remarkably healthy heir, a star was observed shining in the midday heavens.[2] He had already taken care to send word to his wife's Capuchins "not to trouble themselves about the baptism of his son, as he would attend to it himself", and Prince Charles was christened at St James's, though not in the queen's chapel, by Dr. Laud. A silver font presented by the Lord Mayor of London was used, the king gave the prince's nurse a thousand pounds, and the Duchess of Richmond, standing as sponsor proxy for the Prince Palatine, brought the infant a jewel worth seven thousand pounds. Henrietta, although distressed at the rites employed, had a secret source of amusement. The Prince of Wales, whose arrival London was celebrating with fireworks, versification and bonfires, did not look the part. The exiled queen had borne an unmistakable French baby. His skin had a warm tint; when he looked at his vivacious little mother with his enormous black

---

[1] Everett-Green.
[2] H. M. de B.; *Cal. S.P.D.*, 1630; Harl. MS. 7000, f. 294.

eyes, she had an uneasy feeling that he was already far wiser than she. She had his portrait painted for her mother, and the result convinced her that "this monsieur" was a strikingly ugly person. But she comforted herself that he had "no ordinary mien", and his size and fatness made up for his want of beauty. He grew so fast that at four months, said courtiers, he was already as big as a child a year old. "As soon as he is a little fairer", said Henrietta, she would have him painted again.[1] Charles grew larger and larger, and darker and darker. Beside his small-boned parents, the swarthy giant baby looked a changeling. He may have got his inches from his Stuart ancestors. His great-grandfather, Darnley, had been remarkable for his height, and his uncle, Prince Henry, over six feet at sixteen. Charles II's colouring and features have been attributed to his mother's Medici blood, but portraits of his illegitimate uncle, César, Duc de Vendôme, to whom he bore a remarkable resemblance, prove that it came through Henri IV.

When her son was less than a year old, Henrietta wrote to her beloved Mamie St George, asking for thirteen pairs of French gloves and the rules of all the latest games "now in vogue" in France. She apologized for not having written before, but she had been feeling very idle. She was ashamed to say so, but she believed that she was already "again on the increase".[2]

A career of unbridled maternity was indeed opening before her. Ere Prince Charles was eighteen months old, he had a sister. The Princess Mary proved a regular Stuart child, with chestnut hair and eyes and delicate features. Before the Princess Mary could talk, James, Duke of York, a fair and lusty infant, had arrived in the royal nursery, and two years later came the Princess Elizabeth, equally fair and blue-eyed. The Princess Anne followed the Princess Elizabeth by less than two years; then came a set-back. The Princess Katharine, first of Henrietta's five surviving children to be born elsewhere than at St James's,

¹ Everett-Green.   ² Strickland.

died less than half an hour after her birth at Whitehall. Next year, however, her loss was repaired by the arrival, at Oatlands, of Henry, Duke of Gloucester.[1]

There seemed, to the ingenuous observer, no reason why Charles and Henrietta, whose chosen mode of life imitated so faithfully that led by many country gentry of their realm, should not, like them, succeed in raising a family of a dozen or more.

[1] The Harleian MS. 6988, ff. 220-1, contains the following list of the places and dates of birth of all Henrietta's children, in the handwriting of her second daughter:

Prince Charles,	borne at Greenwich,	May 15, 1629	
Prince Charles,	,, St James,	May 29, 1630	
Princesse Mary,	,, ,,	Nov. 4, 1631	
James, Duke of Yorke,	,, ,,	Oct. 14, 1633	
Princesse Elisabeth	,, ,,	Dec. 29, 1635	
Princesse Anne,	,, ,,	March 17, 1636	
Princesse Katharine,	,, Whitehall,	Jan. 29, 1639	
Henry, Duke of Gloster,	,, Otlandes,	July 8, 1640	
Princesse Henrietta,	,, Exeter,	June 16, 1644	

The princess has made three errors. She has antedated her sister Anne's birth by a year. All contemporaries agree that her own birth took place at 10 A.M., on Dec. 28, 1635, during a snowstorm. Henrietta's first child was born and died on May 13, 1629.

CHAPTER III

THE·HAPPIEST WOMAN IN THE WORLD

I

THE happy years promised to the queen by the soothsayer had come, and although they were not to number sixteen, they were to be practically cloudless. "I was the happiest and most fortunate of queens," said Henrietta, tearfully looking back on them, "for not only had I every pleasure the heart could desire; I had a husband who adored me."[1]

None of the children ever ousted Charles from the sovereignty of her heart. She had resented her years of sterility from motives of ambition, and even before her first disastrous attempt at maternity her wish for an heir had been dictated by Charles. Her household included a train of dwarfs,[2] negro servants, monkeys and dogs of all sizes, to whom she was more indulgent than to errant princes and princesses. She enjoyed exchanging locks of hair, portraits and anecdotes with the nurseries of her brother and sisters, but providentially for England she was not,

---

[1] de Motteville.

[2] Her favourite dwarf, Jeffery Hudson, was the son of a Rutlandshire butcher. When he was about nine years old, and scarcely eighteen inches high, Jeffery was brought onto the dinner-table, concealed in a pie, at a banquet given to the king and queen by Buckingham. He passed into Henrietta's service, and appears in several paintings as one of her attendants. He was yellow-haired and his expression was not unamiable. He was "though a dwarf, no dastard", and in 1644 had to fly overseas on account of having shot dead a gentleman who had insulted him. He was captured by a Turkish ship and sold as a slave into Barbary, where the miseries he endured caused him, he asserted, to grow to a height of over three feet. He returned to England, and after the Restoration received payments from Charles II's secret service fund.

like Marie de Medicis, a passionately possessive parent. She made rather a strict little mother, and her family did her credit. Both the elder boys had plenty of spirit and needed a firm hand.

"Charles," wrote the queen to her "deare sone, the Prince",[1] "I am sorry that I most begin my first letter with chiding you, because I heere that you will not take phisike. I hope it was onlei for this day, and that tomorrowe you will doe it, for if you will not I most come to you, and make you take it, for it is for your healthe. I have given order to mylord Newcastell to send mi worde tonight whether you will or not, therfore I hope you will not give mi the paines to goe. . . ."

To which the prince, in laborious round hand between ruled lines, answered to his governor:

My lord,

I would not have you take too much Phisick, for it doth all waies make me worse, and I think it will do the like with you. I ride every day, and am ready to follow any other directions from you. Make hast to returne to him that loves you.

Charles P.[2]

Already, at eight years, Charles P. was a wag. His mother's spirits were volatile, and she had an appreciation of the ludicrous. His father was absolutely humourless. The queen had the portrait of her eldest son (whom she secretly confessed to be her favourite child) painted for her palace of Denmark House. For "Le Prince Carlos en armes" she paid £40. She was learning English at last. No other language was spoken in her nurseries, and when the Prince of Wales arrived in Paris at the age of sixteen, he was lamentably unable to make himself agreeable to French ladies. To perfect herself in her husband's tongue the queen took an English tutor, and ordered English poets to write the plays in which she loved to act. She learnt by heart screeds of courtly trash, of which she made no complaint,

[1] Harl. MS. 6988, f. 95.   [2] Ibid. f. 101.

except regarding length. Ben Jonson plied his pen for her in vain. The old broken-nosed crony of William Shakespeare wrote one masque for her, and then was commanded no more. She preferred the saccharine products of a little Mr Montagu, who, in addition to being the son of a peer, showed signs of conversion to her faith, and the songs of another young gentleman of good birth, Mr Edmund Waller, who could turn out melodious verse on such subjects as her insomnia. In her defence it must be remembered that she had as secretary a veteran Scots poet,[1] whose cast-iron elegiacs were enough to confirm any young princess in a preference for such lines as "Go, lovely rose". As far as the bulk of her subjects could judge, all her artistic sense seemed to have gone into dress and decoration. Attendants who overheard her singing lullabies to her children claimed that her voice was divine. Its charms had been much advertised when she was fourteen, an age at which it is unlikely to have been of surpassing quality. Etiquette forbade that she should sing in public, and since for twelve years she had been almost incessantly pregnant, she had been debarred from the regular practice essential to produce a great artist. Her patronage of music was limited to enthusiastic attendance at court concerts, and charming amateur performance in private. In dress, however, she proved a beneficent deity to her new country, and indeed to Europe, for although the people who made her clothes, and some of the materials used by her, came from France, neither her mother nor her sister-in-law could claim the credit of having set the new fashions. With relief courts and countries abandoned the ornate and artificial costume of the last half-century. Wires came out of neck-gear and hoops, lace collars lay down instead of encircling throats like pie-frills or rearing up behind heads like peacock's tails, and skirts reverted to classical dignity. Instead of a pound of dead dyed false hair and a bushel of warring jewellery, ladies wore a string or two of pearls, a few fine

[1] Sir Robert Aytoun, 1570–1638.

stones simply set as clasps and bracelets, and a *coiffure* composed of a knot, high on the back of the head, and some ringlets on the brow. Gentlemen, like their king, adopted a dress that was serviceable and manly. The little pot hat or muffin-shaped cap gave place to the graceful wide-brimmed beaver, and the padded doublet and skin-tight hose to coat and breeches, silk stockings and shoes with ribbon roses, or long close boots. Wasp waists vanished, even for ladies. The continually hopeful queen could not attempt them. In the end of 1630 she wrote to Mamie St George, complaining that the last petticoat waist sent to her from Paris was so heavy and narrow that she could not wear it.

The only criticism unfavourable to her looks in her teens had been that she was somewhat thin and sallow. With her twenties, her family and her happiness, she blossomed, and all women hastened to imitate the choice in dress of a queen who was also a beauty. The improvement in colour was as great as that in line. The Queen of England suited her brunette complexion with gowns and shoulder-draperies of the fashionable russet shades, "*feuille morte et couleur de feu*", and shadowy blues. When she chose a primitive colour, she let it make its effect unchallenged. Amongst the many portraits of her in her prime, she is shown wearing glowing amber, oyster white with scarlet ribbons and carnation. For formal occasions she always had a Frenchwoman's appreciation of the value of black, and her black satins had the blue gloss of a raven's wings. The new simplicity in dress called for better materials. The ladies and gentlemen of Henrietta's England attired themselves in satins, taffetas, velours, petuanas, camlets, paduasoys and damasks. For informal occasions they had busyarns, durance, grograms, mohair cloths (mockadoes), serges and tobines. The manufacture of fine linen in Ireland became a thriving industry, and lace-making developed. The royal ladies of Elizabethan days had been famous for their crewel-work and plain sewing. King

Charles's saddle, of blood-red velvet, patterned with a leaf-and-stem design in gold galloon, his white kid gauntlets stitched and fringed with silver, his cambric shirts stiff with drawn-thread work and his skull-cap of cloth of gold, sewn with azure and carmine roses, all extant, are all masterpieces of needlecraft, but there is no evidence that Henrietta was responsible for any one of them. Her chief embroiderer, Charles Gentile, a Frenchman, received her lavish and detailed instructions, set to work a hive of underlings, and in an extraordinarily short time produced marvels. But he had to wait for his payments. Although she had not yet settled the bill for the green satin bed in which the Prince of Wales had been born, Henrietta, the next summer, ordered another, of tawny velvet, in preparation for the arrival of the Princess Royal. Gentile, eight years later, was still presenting his account of £1500 for the pair.[1] The education of the daughters of Marie de Medicis had not included close acquaintance with the homely needle. Henrietta delivered her orders to professionals, and occupied her leisure with card games, billiards and letter-writing, particularly to the Princess of Piedmont. The sisters, who began to fill their nurseries at the same time, gradually drifted into a correspondence and a friendship which was to be lifelong. Although they never met, they felt that they knew one another, for between them passed favourite courtiers, bearing portraits, presents and long intimate messages. The princess and the queen confided in one another their hopes of pregnancy before they were certain.[2] On several occasions they were expecting children about the same time. Once Christine produced twin daughters in November, and Henrietta a daughter in the following March. A full-length painting of the three eldest children of Charles I was ordered for the Princess of Piedmont. According to tradition, when their formal father saw the delightful result, he was horrified to discover that his

[1] *Cal. S.P.D.*, March 1638.   [2] Ferrero.

offspring had been depicted wearing their pinafores. Henrietta kept it, and a duplicate, without the offending garments, was was sent to Turin, where it is still to be seen.

The new fashions in dress extended to the nursery. Charlotte de la Trémoille had been shocked by the archaism of her adopted country, which persisted in swaddling infants and then short-coating them prematurely. Henrietta's children were attired in long-clothes of fine linen and white satin, followed by three-quarter length robes. Like every good French mother of her day, she dressed babies in white.[1] Her boys and girls alike, until they attained an age of about four years, wore simple gowns, with aprons, collars and round caps, all lace-trimmed. After that the boys got jackets with lace collars, and breeches, and the daughters square-necked tabbed bodices and full skirts often looped up, as much for ease of movement as to display the petticoats below. Both sexes began to grow long hair, and judging by portraits of the little princesses before and after their promotion to this imitation of adult costume, they also got curl-papers.

Unlike her great predecessor, Queen Elizabeth, Henrietta did not possess hundreds of jewel-sewn dresses. For her theatricals she was always wantonly extravagant, commanding thousands of yards of perishable tinsels, satins and gauzes, but she preferred to have a limited wardrobe, and once having settled upon a style of dress which was becoming to her, she stuck to it. Her majesty's perfumer, Jean Baptiste Ferine, and an army of clear-starchers and laundresses were kept busy with details of her *toilettes*, but she would wear a favourite garment a couple of years. Her largest debts were incurred on behalf of furniture of fine quality, redecoration of her apartments and single magnificent precious stones. For a pendant diamond a Portuguese received a hundred pounds more than the famous Le Sueur for his larger-than-life-size bronze statues of both their majesties,

[1] de Witt.

designed to grace gate towers at St John's College, Oxford.

The picturesque new fashions and the stately new architecture demanded new interior decoration. All furniture that was reminiscent of the hutch disappeared from the houses of the rich. The old gate-leg and refectory tables were superseded by ones "square with leaves to draw out, or round, or oval with falling leaves". Tables and chairs received coverings of velvet or stamped leather, edged with shaggy fringe. The curtained four-poster and the carved coffer were still essential features of the bedroom, but they had for companions now, in luxurious homes, a full-length couch and mirror, a silver ewer and basin, and a dressing-table, fitted with drawers, on which stood a toilet-box. The queen had a toilet-set of silver-gilt, which included "great" and "small" hair-brushes, powder-boxes and bottles, and two pin-boxes bearing the royal arms of France.[1] Amongst the royal plate which the Parliamentary Commissioners attempted to recover in 1649 was "a folding table covered all over with silver plate, ingraven" and "four large hanging wall-candlesticks"—silver sconces, fitted with reflector plates. The use of goldsmith's work for purposes unconnected with eating and drinking was increasing. Two cabinets of lignum vitae, owned by Henrietta,[2] bear exquisite silver furniture containing her monogram, and tradition attributes to her the ownership of a book-cover of South German workmanship, gold enamelled, representing on one side the Creation of Eve, and on the other the Fountain of Youth.[3] On the dining-table the salt was decreasing in impressiveness, and the bowls of spoons were tending towards the oval in shape. The first recorded silver table-fork made in England—a two-pronged, square-handled affair—was designed when the queen was three-and-twenty. Large fruit-dishes, silver-gilt, and crystal beakers,

[1] S.P.D. foreign, France, 78.128, P.R.O.
[2] Now in the Vandyck Room, Windsor Castle.
[3] Now in the Victoria and Albert Museum.

received the piled-up green grapes, striped flowers and shell-fish beloved of the Dutch still-life painters. Silver and pewter standing cups, and tankards with lids, had not yet, however, been ousted by table glass, though from Staffordshire was coming a black-glazed table-ware and from Lambeth every variety of Delf. Tea was being drunk by merchants in the Far East, but mainly for medicinal purposes. It had not yet become the excuse for a fourth meal. Dinner and supper were the elaborate meals of the day, and the courses served at them were many and various. The old mediaeval love of towering edifices of sugar-work, birds roasted in their feathers with beaks and claws gilt, and monster fish, had not yet died out for festal occasions. The penurious Charles made some unsuccessful attempts to reduce his household expenses.

The rush-strewn floor was now to be seen only in small country places. Stone floors were sanded or scrubbed, and floors of polished wood sometimes bore carpets. Amongst Henrietta's *trousseau* had come two large Turkey carpets, but such treasures were often used to fling over couches and tables. Rooms were wainscoted, with large wooden panels, and decorated by pictures, tapestry and classical busts. Charles was accused by indignant contemporaries who did not share his erudite taste, of "squandering away millions of pounds upon old rotten pictures and broken-nosed marbles" [1], and of "causing a whole army of foreign Emperors, Captains and Senators, all at once, to land on his coasts, to come to do him homage and attend him in his Palaces of St. James's and Somerset House". The Emperors, Captains and Senators complained of came from the collection of the Duke of Mantua, which he purchased outright for twenty-five thousand pounds, and from "that noble and absolute complete-gentleman, Sir Kenelm Digby, Knight," he

---

[1] *The Non-Such Charles, his character, extracted out of divers original Transactions, Dispatches, and the Notes of several public ministers, as well at home as abroad*, 1651.

acquired marble columns and altars from the ruins of Apollo's temple at Delos.[1] Amongst his other "curiosities" were "The Temple of Jerusalem, made of ebony and amber", "a fountain of silver for perfumed waters, artificially made to play of itself", "a chess board, said to be Queen Elizabeth's, inlaid with gold and pearls", "a conjuring drum from Lapland", "a Saxon king's mace", and "several sections, in silver, of a Turkish galleon, a Venetian gondola, an Indian canoe, and a first-rate man of war".[2] The comment of a foreign visitor that the King of England's twenty-four palaces were all "very elegantly and completely furnished" seems justified. Charles patronized the manufacture of tapestry in England, and on hearing from "Sir Peter Paul Rubens that exquisite Painter of Antwerp" that seven enormous Raphael cartoons were lying in a neglected condition at Arras, he bought them to be copied at Mortlake. Rubens had decorated the ceiling of Inigo Jones's Banqueting House, and received three thousand pounds for the undertaking. Charles prized the result so highly, and was so nervous of possible damage to it that, when Henrietta proposed to present a Great Masque there, he dissuaded her, and gave her instead, for her single performance, a temporary building erected within the precincts of the palace of Whitehall.

In his breakfast-room the king kept the portraits of his three favourite painters, Rubens, of course, Daniel Mytens, now an old man, and a young artist, Antoon Van Dijck, who had first visited London at the age of one-and-twenty. In March 1632 this young man returned to England at the invitation of its ruler, and, within four months of his arrival, had completed a full-length of Charles, a half-length of Henrietta, and a family group of the king and queen with the Prince of Wales and the Princess Royal. He received knighthood, and was henceforward styled "Sir Anthony Vandike, principalle Paynter in Ordinary to their Majesties at St James's". He was five months older than

[1] Peacham, *Complete Gentleman*, 1634.   [2] Harl. MS. 4898.

his royal patron, and no taller, the son of an affluent Flemish burgher, an amusing companion when he was not brooding over the possibilities of discovering the philosopher's stone, and, with his dashing military moustache and wild head of auburn curls, a great breaker of hearts. All the principal nobility hastened to commission him, and he duly portrayed Sir Kenelm Digby's lady as Prudence, the Duchess of Richmond as Venus, the Duke of Hamilton's son as Love and the Countess of Portland and the Duchess of Aubigny in the habits of nymphs. The Earl of Pembroke, who was rebuilding Wilton, was amongst his most regular employers; even that country-loving gentleman, Lord Strange, who cared nothing for fashion, sat to him thrice and obtained a family group representing his beloved Charlotte, placid and enormous in sky-blue satin, one limp small daughter, and himself with the expression of a decent child called upon to recite. For the next eight years Sir Anthony spent most of his time depicting delicate sheep-faced English mothers in pale satins and corkscrew curls, hirsute English fathers, noble in blue-black armour or defiantly drawing cloaks across black taffeta shoulders, and scores of demure English children, fringed or ringleted, attended by solemn mastiffs, shivering greyhounds or fatuously adoring spaniels. In his leisure moments in his studio he worked upon a Holy Family for the queen, and for the king a Dance for the Muses, Apollo flaying Marsyas, and Bacchanals. Between her twenty-third and her thirty-first year Henrietta sat to her ideal court painter at least twenty-five times, so there cannot have been many weeks during her months in London when Sir Anthony's easel was absent from her apartments. His memorandum of arrears due from the Crown in 1638-9 mentions thirteen portraits of "la Reyne"—"dressed in blue, price thirty pounds"—"dressed in white, price fifty pounds"—"for presentation to her sister-in-law, the Queen of Bohemia"—"for presentation to the Ambassador Hopton . . ." The prices of five out of seven portraits intended as gifts to friends and relatives are cut down, probably by the Lord Treasurer Juxon, much in her majesty's favour. Two "pour Mons. Barnino", for which Sir Anthony asked twenty pounds a head, were reduced by ten pounds.[1] This was hard on Sir Anthony, whose debts and gout were increasing, but times were growing hard. In the following year he received a more bitter blow. His sketches for a series of paintings representing the history of the Order of the Garter, destined for the walls of Inigo Jones's Banqueting Hall, were returned to him with an intimation that his estimate was exorbitant. He left London for his native Antwerp, taking with him the Scottish lady of Henrietta's household with whom Charles had provided him in the fond hope that a sensible wife might induce him to a more equable existence. Although he returned to England to die at the age of forty he never painted Henrietta again, but neither did any other artist of anything approaching his calibre.

II

Out of doors during the happy years of Charles's reign the change in taste was as noticeable as within. The small utilitarian herb, fruit and flower gardens of old Merrie England began to give place to gravelled terraces and vistas of sward and clipped trees, interspersed with fountains, wrought-iron work, vases and statues.

The garden of St James's Palace boasted "half a dozen bronze Statues, rare ones, cast by Hubert le Sueur, His Majesty's servant", of which the finest was "the Gladiator, moulded from that in the Borghese Villa". Henrietta sent to France for fruit trees and plants. She was a great lover of flowers, and once took a train of lords and ladies, filling no less than a hundred and fifty coaches, on a Maying expedition. When she spied a bush loaded with the blossoms, held in England to be unlucky if plucked, she sprang from her carriage and gaily decorated her

[1] Carpenter.

hat.[1] In 1629 John Parkinson, Apothecary of London, and the King's Herbalist, dedicated to her, "knowing your Majesty so much delighted with all the fair flowers of a garden", a volume called *Paradisi in sole Paradisus Terrestris; or a garden of all sorts of pleasant flowers, which our English ayre will permitt to be noursed up*. The title is a pun on the author's surname—Park-in-son's Earthly Paradise. The Queen's Book of Paradise contains descriptions of nearly a thousand plants, and woodcut illustrations of seven hundred and eighty varieties. Amongst the flowers in "this speaking Garden, that may inform you in all particulars of your store as well as wants, when you cannot see any of them fresh on the ground" are "the Primrose Peerelesse" (*Narcissus medio lutens vulgaris*) "of a sweet but stuffing scent", and "The Franticke or Foolish Cowslip".[2]

"It is an ancient custom in England," wrote one of the Capuchins of the queen's chapel,[3] "that soon after Easter, when the weather is fine, the court sets out on progresses; that is to say the King, the Queen, and all the courtiers leave London and go into the country to various royal residences in the provinces, staying six weeks at one, two months at another; the whole kingdom thus having the satisfaction to see its sovereign."

Henrietta, in a coach and six whose design differed little from that in which her father had met his death, covered hundreds of miles of English countryside every summer. May Day was the date against which her new equipages, adorned with gold and silver fringe, were ordered. Her Coachman and her Yeoman of the Leash rejoiced in the excellent English names of Easenwood and Mogridge, and in her caravan went a selection of her inevitable dogs, dwarfs, blacks and monkeys.[4] The royal children spent the summer months settled in one of the

---

[1] *Gazette de France*, June 4, 1632. Such Maying expeditions had been the custom in the court of France since mediaeval days.

[2] It is styled by the great eighteenth-century botanist, Pulteney, as the first book which "separately described and figured the subjects of the flower garden".   [3] de Gamache.   [4] *Cal. S.P.D.*, 1636.

country palaces which she visited during her tour. The best roads on which she travelled were bad. Most of the lesser ones were too narrow for her lumbering vehicle. Country ladies of the mid-seventeenth century were perfectly accustomed to abandoning their coaches and finishing their journeys on pillion behind a groom, while their luggage was brought on by packhorses. Occasionally even the royal transport broke down. The king and queen arrived in London one night, *en route* from James I's old hunting-lodge at Royston in Hertfordshire to the palace of Oatlands in Surrey, to discover that they had outstripped their bedding. Whitehall was not expecting them and was undergoing spring cleaning. Their majesties were obliged to go down to St James's "to try what hospitality the prince kept". Their capital boasted some fine noblemen's houses in the districts of Drury Lane and the Strand, and some of its tortuous dark streets were being rebuilt, but one of the complaints of the Parliament of 1625 had been of "the building of all houses in London in one uniform way, with a face of bricks towards the streets". In 1630 the king had to take stern measures to check the erection of fish-stalls almost exactly opposite the entrance to his consort's palace, "lest in short space they might grow from stalls to sheddes and then to dwelling-houses, as the like was in former time in Old Fish Street and in St Nicholas Shambles". Out in the country, wattle and daub were still usual in villages; for cottages and churches the Gothic tradition persisted. Even for gentlemen's houses, the picturesque Elizabethan style, with its rich plaster ceilings, heavily carved mantelpieces, groups of chimneys, and diamond-paned casements, continued with some changes. Only a few connoisseurs such as Lord Pembroke, who provided Wilton with an Italianate south front on his king's advice, were attempting to impose the new architecture on a rustic background. Two great Derbyshire houses, Bolsover and Welbeck, whose owners entertained Henrietta with masques, incorporated respectively a Norman keep and a Premonstratensian abbey of the twelfth century. Kew Palace, Raynham Hall, Norfolk, Broom Park, Kent, and Swakeleys, Middlesex, all built during her happy years, were all of brick. The Dutch gable style, as it was called, sometimes allowed stone dressings and generally wooden mullions.

The landscape through which she travelled was largely uncultivated. Between the deer-parks of the gentry and the neighbouring county towns stretched great tracks of waste ground—moors, heaths, fens and marshes. Their best parts were used by adjacent villagers as common pasture. Agriculture was certainly advancing, for farmers were learning of the rotation of crops from Flanders, where "after the flax is pulled, immediately they sow turnips, and presently after, their rye; what they do not eat themselves they give unto their cattle".[1] This obviated the old wasteful custom of slaying and salting down at Michaelmas all stock that could not be housed, and on root crops the beasts of England grew "so fat withal that you would wonder at it". But the fields of these farms were undivided except by the outlines of their crops, and hedges were rare except in the immediate vicinity of rich villages. Still England, with its fair orchards and cherry gardens, its gravel walks by the river-sides in provincial towns,[2] its sleeping village greens, ancient churches and gabled manor-houses, appeared to the queen's literary Capuchin "an abundant country", whose inhabitants led a luxurious life. They had, he states comfortably, no taxes. His mistress, who was on bad terms with my Lord Treasurer Weston, knew better than this, but she too was blissfully unconscious of impending storm.

The happy years slipped by, bringing to her no worse trials than might have befallen the humblest of her subjects. One of her eight experiences of labour was inordinately painful. "As she had always been brought up in very great devotion to the

---

[1] Sir R. Weston's "Legacy to his sons", 1645.
[2] T. Gerard, *Description of Somerset*, 1633.

Blessed Virgin, and was singularly attached to her, she had recourse to her powerful intercession. With great humility and fervour, she prayed in this extreme necessity, for her assistance, and she received immediately an extraordinary ease, which was followed by a very happy delivery and perfect health." [1] Her chief anxieties were connected with Charles. When he had to leave her for a few weeks in order to go to Edinburgh for his long-deferred coronation she became "a perfect mourning turtle". She was expecting a child, and in any case would not visit Scotland, "that nation being infected with perfidious men, that pretended an honest animosity, and specious plain dealing". [2] Charles, having lost the heart of his northern subjects by his tactless insistence on a form of ceremony abhorrent to them, made back to her in such haste that he took her by surprise. When separation owing to illness threatened she refused to be parted from him. Charles, having felt unwell for several days in the winter of 1632, sought to throw off his malaise by playing a hard game of tennis. The exercise brought out a rash on his breast and brow, which he discovered just as he was about to go to bed. Attendants were horrified to observe the royal couple retire together as usual. Charles's illness proved smallpox, but so slight an attack that he was able to sit up "in a warme roome, with a furr'd gowne on his back", very merry, playing parlour games with his wife, who was never out of his company. [3] Even a hint of danger to Charles terrified Henrietta. Perhaps unwisely, considering her condition, her attendants divulged to her one autumn day that a gentleman called Rochester Car, of Lincolnshire, who had been "mad all this summer and kept up", had escaped his keepers and broken loose into the streets, announcing that he was off to court to kill the king and marry the queen. The wife of Charles I swooned. Cold steel had already twice altered her destiny.

[1] de Gamache. [2] H. M. de B.
[3] Harl. MS. 7000, f. 344; Laud's Diary, Dec. 2, 1632.

Her fondness for theatricals never ceased to give offence to many of her subjects. The profession of actress did not as yet exist. All women's parts in the theatre were still played by boys. Unfortunately for a "Mr Prinne, an Utter-Barrister of Lincoln's Inne", his pamphlet demanding how "any Christian woman" could be "so more than whoreishly impudent as to act, to speake publiquelie on a Stage (perchaunce in man's apparel and cut haire) in the presence of sundrie men and women", was published the day after the queen's appearance in a superb pastoral at Denmark House.[1] Henrietta attempted without success to save the Puritan pamphleteer from the barbarous punishment of losing his ears in the pillory. He had attacked the Church as well as the court and Laud was implacable.

One more continual source of annoyance during these years must be mentioned. The Plague raged intermittently, and scarcely a season passed when the queen was not obliged to postpone or forgo some expedition owing to an outbreak in the locality she intended to visit.

Such were her troubles. Her occasions for enjoyment were manifold and varied. Unlike most ladies, even of noble birth, when the attractions of the country began to pall upon her she could always depart to the pleasures of the town.[2] Henrietta and Charles went to Bedlam to see the mad people and were rather frightened. They shopped together on Ludgate Hill, were presented with three comedies by the University of Cambridge, visited Newmarket repeatedly and were feasted by Lord Pembroke "after his extraordinary good winnings at a horse race at Winchester". To their court came such interesting characters as the Muscovite and Persian ambassadors, and

---

[1] Harl. MS. 7000, f. 464 B.

[2] They did apparently pall; witness a letter of Lady Hatton to her husband: "Pray, dear, let Smith buy a Westphalian ham, two or three neats' tongues, and *do* remember the pickles". After thanking him for the oysters, "but for God's sake hasten home, my dear, for I am weary of my life until you come".

"Johannes Albertus Racouski, Treasurer of the Great Dukedom of Lithuania, of a comely presence and promising countenance, and able exactly to speak five or six languages". A French inventor presented himself, with a project for enlivening the view from the windows of her majesty's dower palace by the construction of "a floating bathing-palace, to be placed in the Thames opposite".[1] Lord Arundel brought up to London for their inspection, Thomas Parr, aged 153, born in the reign of Edward IV.[2] From further afield arrived colonists, who had "seen Indians besprinkle their paintings with powder of gold", and reported "rare precious stones among them, and plenty of black fox, which is, of all others, the richest fur". New England still attracted a leavening of excellent settlers, worthy successors of the Elizabethan heroes, but was tending to become the dumping-ground for the family ne'er-do-well. The transport of African negroes, to be used as slaves on the plantations, had begun, and a "black boy" whose swarthy skin formed a telling contrast to the ivory complexion of a lady of quality, was already a popular adjunct in a fashionable portrait.

The court of Charles I was admitted, even by his Puritan subjects, to have a far higher moral tone than that of his father. In the days of James I, says a severe critic, the court "was a nursery of lust and intemperence . . . and every greate house in the country became a sty of uncleanesse. . . . The face of the court was much chang'd in the change of the king; for King Charles was temperate, chast and serious. . . . The nobility and courtiers, who did not quite abandon their debosheries, had yet that reverence to the king to retire into corners to practise them."[3]

III

All through the winter of 1632–3 the Queen of Bohemia was daily expected in London. Charles, who was devoted to the

[1] *Cal. S.P.D.*, May 1635.   [2] Laud's Diary, Sept. 1635.
[3] Mrs Hutchinson.

beautiful only sister whom he had not seen for twenty years, sent messengers, directly he heard of her husband's death, pressing her to return to her old home and settle in England. The valiant "Queen of Hearts" eventually refused his "kind and brotherly invitation" on her own account, but three years later sent over on a protracted visit to their uncle, her two eldest surviving sons. Charles Louis, disinherited heir to the Palatinate, and Rupert, youths of seventeen and fifteen, were the "hopeful progeny" mentioned by the Puritan pamphleteers of England at the time of Henrietta's first frustrated pregnancy, as infinitely preferable to any child that might be borne by her. However, since then she had produced two healthy male heirs. She kissed the shy and solemn Prince Elector Palatine on his arrival, and prepared to take part in a series of gaieties in his honour, one of which had to be postponed at a few hours' notice. Her elder daughter, the Princess Mary, had made her appearance in the world several weeks before expected. On the birth of this second daughter, Elizabeth, doomed to be as fair and unlucky, but much shorter-lived than her namesake, the Queen of Bohemia, Henrietta received a special embassy of congratulation from the States of Holland. She had herself ordered a *layette*, valued at nearly £2500, for her fourth addition to the royal nursery. The ambassadors brought her, besides "a massy piece of amber-grease, two fair and almost transparent China basons and an exquisite clock of curious art", "four admirable pieces", paintings by Titian and Tintoretto.[1] She made a quick recovery; the deferred fireworks display, two masques and a great banquet took place six weeks after her confinement, and on the Wednesday before Lent she went merrily, attired as a citizeness, to an entertainment offered to Charles Louis by the Middle Temple. "Mistress Bassett, the great lacewoman of Cheapside", led the disguised queen foremost into the hall. Henceforward, the two tall Protestant princes were

[1] H. M. de B.

chief guests at all court festivals. Vandyck painted them dressed alike in best suits of unrelieved black. They were as diverse in character as in appearance. Charles Louis, fair-complexioned, with straight, light-brown hair, a square, solid countenance, wary grey eyes and a pursed mouth, wrote long letters to his mother, expressing his delight in English hospitality, and subsiding cautiously into rows of cipher figures when politics had to be discussed. A scheme to marry his eldest sister to the King of Poland, which he somewhat cold-bloodedly referred to as "the Polish business", would not, he believed, be furthered by Henrietta, although the first condition of the match was that the bride should become a Papist. "The queen is so discreet that she will not meddle in it." [1]

For Rupert, narrow-browed, dark as night and already, with his impetuous friendships, a care to his precise elder brother, a dashing military career was intended. A confidential old friend assured the Queen of Bohemia that King Charles took great pleasure in the "unrestfulness" of her younger son.

In August the king and queen visited Oxford, accompanied by their nephews. Laud, Chancellor of that university, leading a procession of doctors, proctors, masters and citizens, met them two miles outside the city. The queen was left at her lodgings to repose herself, while the king attended evensong in the cathedral. In the evening they witnessed a play in Christ Church Hall, described by an authority as the worst he ever saw, only excepting one at Cambridge. Next morning the two princes received scarlet gowns and masterships of Arts, and their names were, by his majesty's leave, entered at the Chancellor's college. After Convocation Charles joined Henrietta in her coach, and they proceeded to St John's, where they saw the new buildings and were greeted as they ascended the library stairs by "a fine short song". At dinner, baked meats in the shapes of archbishops, bishops and doctors, were served. Laud, who had recently sup-

[1] Bromley.

plied the funds for the rebuilding of the second quadrangle[1] in his old college, was their host. Its colonnades had classical pillars of greenish marble from a local quarry discovered by Bishop Juxon when hunting in the neighbourhood. Over the new gate-towers presided le Sueur's majestic six-foot bronze figures of King Charles and Queen Mary. They had cost four hundred pounds, and five shillings had been paid in the previous April for their carriage from London to Oxford.[2] After the banquet a play, acted entirely by members of St John's, was offered. It took place in the hall, where windows had been shut and candles lighted, but the air was perfectly fresh and cool, as no person had been allowed to enter until after the king and queen had been enthroned in their seats. The play, which was "merry and without offence", lasted till six o'clock, with an interval for supper.[3] Later the same evening a third theatrical entertainment took place, at Christ Church, and the queen was so much pleased with *The Royal Slave* that she borrowed its costumes and scenery in the following November for a performance at Hampton Court. Before nine o'clock the next morning the royalties left Oxford for the palace of Woodstock. They were further entertained on the Woodstock–Chipping-Norton road by a visit to the waterworks of a Mr Bushell, at Enstone. Here they wandered amongst skilfully contrived grottos, islands and lakes. The attractions of the waterworks included a rustic banqueting-hall, fountains with which practical jokes could be played, and a pond on which an artificial spaniel chased an artificial duck. This combination of the ingenious and the natural exactly hit the French-born queen's taste, and before she left the waterworks she graciously ordered that a certain rock over which poured a foaming cascade should be known by the name of "Henrietta".[4]

Some other foreigners, not nearly so grateful to English eyes

---

[1] Persistently attributed to Inigo Jones.
[2] *Cal. S.P.D.*, 1633, 1636.   [3] Laud's Diary.   [4] Falkner.

as the Palatine princes, had become prominent in her circle. In the spring of 1634, Gregorio Panzani, a canon of St Peter's, had arrived in London. His ostensible mission was to compose the eternal strife between the secular and regular Roman Catholic clergy resident in England. He brought to Henrietta an odd selection of gifts from Italy—"artificial flowers and fruit, a bottle of oil of Cedrino, a rarity not seen in England before, an extraordinarily fine relic case, with one side covered by a large crystal of the mountains and within it a bone of S. Martine, virgin and martyr (whose body was a little before found under the Capitol)", a summary of the saint's career and a volume of Roman archaeology. The King of England's tastes were well known in Rome, and Charles's interest in Panzani was instantly aroused by the beauty of the relic case. Presently the canon was deputed to act as agent for the King of England in the business of procuring paintings, statues and curiosities for the royal collection. Aided by his powerful patron, Cardinal Barberini, nephew of Pope Urban VIII, Panzani began to strip his native country of artistic treasures. In one quarter only did he meet a repulse. Charles had expressed a desire to possess a celebrated statue of Adonis, property of the Duchess of Fiano in the Villa Ludovisia. This sensible woman resolutely refused to part with her heathen deity on the chance of converting the king of a nation of heretics. That such was Barberini's hope is unquestionable. He wrote to one of his countrymen, a rising cleric, Giulio Mazarini, lately appointed nuncio-extraordinary to the court of Louis XIII: "The statues go on prosperously, nor shall I hesitate to rob Rome of her most valuable ornaments, if in exchange we might be so happy as to have the King of England's name amongst the princes who submit to the Apostolic See".

Panzani remained in England for over two years. He failed in his ambitious object of effecting a union between the Church of England and that of Rome, but he succeeded in obtaining permission for a permanent nuncio from the Vatican to be appointed to the Queen of England's court.[1] "These nuncios", reports the queen's literary Capuchin triumphantly, "had their chapels open to all Catholics, to the great discomfort of the Puritans, who, filled with animosity and fury against the Pope, were enraged to see ecclesiastical prelates sent from Rome so well received by their King, with permission to profess publicly what they called Popery. From morning till noon masses were continually said in their chapels . . . they were known to everybody. Their carriages rolled about the streets of London, without anyone daring to say a word against them."[2] Cardinal Barberini was so delighted by this great step towards the re-establishment of the old faith in England, that he sent Henrietta a superb gift of paintings by ancient and modern Italian masters. "Works of Albani, Corregio, Veronese, Stella, Vinci, Andrew of Sarto, Juilio Romano and other artists of the first repute" were unpacked in the queen's bedchamber where she was recovering after the birth of the Princess Anne. Charles, hearing of the arrival of the boxes from Italy, hurried to attend their opening. None of the pictures were of devotional subjects, at which Henrietta expressed naïve disappointment and surprise.

The first nuncio to her court was as skilfully chosen as the gift of secular pictures to the Papist wife of a Protestant king. George Conn, whose manners were charming and whose understanding was strong, was a canon of St John Lateran, and of the same nationality as the queen's confessor. He led that amiable and saintly old man to gossip in a manner that should have cost him his appointment. Conn, who had an excellent verbal memory, reported weekly to Rome, and fortunately for Henrietta's biographers, details of her inner life, which should never have been disclosed, were carefully preserved. No queen had ever less to fear from such indiscretion.[3] At twenty-six, although eleven years a wife, and already six times a mother, "her in-

[1] Panzani.   [2] de Gamache.   [3] Add. MSS. 15389-92. B.M.

nocence" was, according to these two elderly celibates, "incredible". She blushed like a virgin in the presence of strangers. No courtiers were ever admitted to her bedchamber. When she arrived to confess or communicate, her earnestness surprised even her confessor, but the sins of which she was so eager to unburden herself proved to be entirely trifles of omission. Father Robert Philip, who professed himself a great enemy of such, averred that he did not spare correction. He was positive that she was never troubled by carnal desires. Her religious faith was equally serene.[1]

Conn followed the court into the country, and brought with him, on his first introduction to Henrietta, several gifts, including a picture of St Catherine. This he had intended merely to show to her, as it was not yet framed, but "declaring that she would take that trouble upon herself, she took away from me the tin case and the packthread with which it was tied, and gave orders that the picture should be fastened to the curtains of her bed". This scene took place in a red-brick Elizabethan manorhouse in Northamptonshire.

The much-travelled Scottish canon quickly won the confidence of the whole royal family, and sent to Rome many anecdotes of their domestic happiness. The queen had taken the Prince of Wales to mass, but desisted at the request of her husband. The Princess Mary was delighted to possess a little rosary, which she produced from her pocket when sure that no Protestant eyes observed her. The king had at first refused to play at a game in the queen's apartment, seeing that some of the prizes were medals, crucifixes and relic cases. Henrietta had suggested with a smile, that if he won any of them he could give them to her elder daughter, to which Charles had answered, "No, no, I will give them to George here," pointing to Conn, "and he shall give me such of the other things as he wins".

---

[1] Conn to Barberini, Add. MSS. 15389, f. 196. B.M. Roman Transcripts, 9. 124, P.R.O.

During an absence of her husband, the queen had taken all her children to vespers at Hampton Court. The service was long and the Princess Elizabeth became fractious. To quieten her, she was given an illustrated prayer-book. Hearing sympathetic murmurs of "Poor man! poor man!" the queen's attention was drawn to her younger daughter, whom she perceived bestowing many kisses upon a picture of Christ scourged. But when her majesty reported this incident to her husband, he merely replied "She begins young!"[1] Rightly despairing of conversion in that quarter, Conn turned his attention to Henrietta. Four years had passed since she had "with her own hands helpt to lay the two first square corner-stones" of the chapel to be built in the tennis courtyard of her dower palace of Denmark House. The occasion had been one of great magnificence, the proposed site being entirely enclosed by a tent made of arras and silks, its floor strewn with flowers and its temporary altar garnished with silver-gilt chandeliers and vases "worthy of being compared with those of Solomon's Temple". At the conclusion of mass, the queen, descending from a dais on which she had been kneeling on a cushion of crimson velvet, had been presented with a trowel "the handle of which was covered with fine fringed velvet. . . . And taking mortar from a large glittering basin . . . with a grace which imparted devotion" to her audience of over two thousand, she had cast mortar thrice upon the silver foundation stone, in which was encased a silver plate suitably inscribed. In the short space of three months her chapel, a "Paradise of Glory", replete with "Angels larger than life", "Hidden lights" and gold plate, was ready for consecration. "A very learned, very eloquent and very pathetic" sermon, on the text "This is the Lord's doing and it is marvellous in our eyes", was preached after the first mass attended by the queen, and tears were observed to fill her eyes as she knelt in devotion.[1] Her strongest passion, she declared, was the advancement of the

[1] Harl. MS. 7000, f. 336; de Gamache.

Catholic religion in her adopted country, but Conn now took her to task for lethargy, and stirred her up to unceasing effort to ameliorate the lot of English Catholics. His insistence on the proper observance of fasts roused the wrath of the queen's doctor, the great Sir Theodore, and some too-spectacular conversions achieved by him brought Henrietta into collision with Laud, now Archbishop of Canterbury. Laud urged Charles to enforce the laws against Catholics, but Henrietta's pleadings influenced her husband so effectively that his proclamation, as eventually issued, was in the mildest of terms. Had the zealous Scottish nuncio been allowed to stay longer in England, where he, almost alone of his kind, was clear-sighted enough to detect signs of coming trouble,[1] he might have effected more. But his health was breaking. After three years' occupation of his post, he retired to Rome, to die. His successor, the Conte de Rosetti, a noble young Ferrarese of under thirty, was charmed on his arrival by the lenience shown to English Catholics. Rosetti caught the storm.

It came, appropriately, heralded by a stormy petrel. The Duchesse de Chevreuse, who had only escaped Richelieu's vengeance by flying over the Pyrenees in the disguise of a cavalier, had found Madrid an unsuitable place from which to carry on her political intrigues. England, although dull, was a comfortable country. In May 1638 she appeared in London, uninvited and unexpected. Her assets consisted of her birth, her looks, at which time had struck a blow, an un-eugenic scheme for a double marriage between the two eldest children of England and Spain, her escape story, and all her old talent for discovering entertainment. Charles, who could never outgrow a belief that Spain was romantic, gave her proposal serious consideration; Henrietta, always faithful to old friends,

---

[1] "God only knows how long this calm will last." "The queen thinks little of the future, trusting entirely in the king." Conn to Barberini, Add. MSS. 15389, f. 196, B.M.

particularly those down on their luck, received her with open arms. Nevertheless, during the past twelve years the Queen of England had naturally formed other close ties. The duchess had to make up her mind at once whether she was going to be an admirer or a declared rival of the most important woman at court. Lucy, Countess of Carlisle, was now a widow and forty, but her *salon* was still thronged, not only by politicians, but by literary celebrities and foreigners of eminence. She openly preferred the conversation of gentlemen to that of ladies, though she condescended to "talk on the fashions" with females. She was actually several months older than the duchess, but her charms had not been exposed to such trials. The two energetic women, who had so much in common, took the wisest course. They struck up an ostentatious friendship.

Among the gentlemen in Henrietta's circle, two of Lady Carlisle's brothers were prominent. Algernon Percy, Earl of Northumberland, was haughty, gained by portentous silences a reputation for wisdom, and had undoubted good looks of the high-nosed type. Henry, his younger brother, equally supercilious and handsome, had a fascinating manner with ladies. Lord Holland, the duchess's old flame, was sadly reduced in prestige. He sat sulking in his Kensington house, wrapped, said the spiteful, in a very fine embroidered smock that had belonged to his mother, and with ample leisure to indulge in the fashionable game of writing "characters" of his acquaintance, or to visit "Madam Chevreux". The post of Lord High Admiral, to which he had aspired, had gone to Northumberland. Holland was a dandy of past fifty now.

"Mr Harry Jermyn, the Queen's prime servant", although not so distinguished by birth as the Percy brothers, was another of the younger men who must not be overlooked. His career so far had been perfectly conventional for a courtier. He was the son of a simple knight, but several years' residence in Paris, as a gentleman attendant on the Embassy, had taught him ideas

H

of comfort irreconcilable with his fortune. They had also taught him to be present when he was needed, inconspicuous when he was not, agreeable to preposterous people, and always ready with a plan, however bad, to avoid possible unpleasantness. He was a large, heavy, fair young man, with a sleepy eye, the shoulders of a drayman, not many brains and a mordant vein of humour. His success at court had been immediate. At the age of twenty-four he had found himself Vice-Chamberlain to the Queen, and Member of Parliament for Liverpool. At the age of twenty-seven he nearly got into trouble for brawling with another young gentleman, who had "bandied balls on purpose" at him in the gallery of the tennis-court at Whitehall.[1] Since then he had suffered a short term of imprisonment for carrying a challenge from Lord Holland to Lord Treasurer Weston, and a long period of banishment for seducing one of the queen's maids of honour. Unfortunately for Mr Jermyn, Eleanor Villiers had been a niece of the late Duke of Buckingham, and the king had taken a stern line. Mr Jermyn considered his disastrous situation. An alliance with the Villiers family presented no advantages that he could see. The late duke's widow and mother had never been liked by the queen, and were now entirely eclipsed by Lady Carlisle. The present duke was a pallid little boy of five, in a satin suit, who was asked to play games with the royal children because their father had been fond of his father. It would be years before he could be of use to anyone with his way to make. Besides, Mr Jermyn was not a marrying man. He was a born gambler. He pleaded his lack of fortune, and firmly refused to enter upon so improvident a match. His last argument may have appealed to Henrietta's Gallic common sense; she may have felt contempt for her languishing maid of honour, who admitted that she had never received any offer of marriage from Mr Jermyn, and had loved him too much to make conditions of surrender. Whatever the queen's reasons,

[1] Harl. MS. 7000, f. 315.

she supported her Vice-Chamberlain in his ungallant resolve; he left the court, and Eleanor Villiers duly became an unmarried mother.[1] Old Sir Thomas Jermyn sent a midwife to assist at the birth of a child declared by its mother with "deep oaths" to be that of Harry Jermyn and no other man. Charles's sentence had been eternal banishment, but within four years Jermyn was back again at Denmark House, certainly not a sadder man, and except in avoidance of maids of honour, not a wiser one. He was appointed Master of the Horse to the queen.

Madame de Chevreuse charmed the queen's circle by inventing a new full-length sleeve, discussed politics with Lady Carlisle, and annoyed the king by taking the Princess Mary to mass. She was costing Charles two hundred guineas a week, but worse guests were to come. His mother-in-law was to come.

More than seven years had passed since her carriage had thundered over the Picardy frontier into equally flat, but blessedly Spanish, Hainault. Richelieu might have driven her out of France, but she had fled to a quarter from which she could still vex him. English writers had sneeringly expected Henrietta's mother and younger brother "to have kept a brave Christmas here at London"; Louis XIII had suggested to his parent that she should retire with dignity to her native Florence. But the old lady, described by Pope Urban VIII as one of the most obstinate persons in the world, had chosen to stay in the Low Countries, a district haunted by refugees and, what was more to the point, secret agents of all nations. The cardinal could not last for ever. His cough was growing worse. Everybody said so. But the slow months dragged by, and still the pale sickly man, sitting wrapped in furs before a blazing fire in his study in the Palais Cardinal, continued to sip his favourite strawberry syrup and weave his webs. Henrietta's marriage had been one of his few failures. He could not have foreseen that a child of Henri IV and Marie de Medicis should provide Europe with a model

[1] *Cal. S.P.D.*, Jan. 1639; *Strafford Letters*, i. 174.

of wedded happiness. There was no hope of getting her to engage in any business useful to France. When he sent a special envoy to London, he had to give the man instructions not to deliver the cardinal's letter to the queen if her expression seemed hostile. He regretted infinitely that her heart had not remained in her old country. He knew that the Queen of France's letters to her relatives got to Madrid via London.

Spain could not help her any further. Marie de Medicis moved out of the Spanish Netherlands into Holland. At the Hague she was accorded an expensive reception, but given to understand that her presence would not long be tolerated. Her daughter Christine was, like herself, a widow, and beset by troubles. The Pope confined his answers to her stormy letters to expressions of sympathy. When the English Ambassador in Paris, prompted by Henrietta, endeavoured to soften the heart of Louis XIII, he was politely told that he was interfering in "*une affaire domestique*" and, further, that if the Queen Mother were invited to England, France would regard the action as an insult. A new and unexpected situation, full of possibilities, had arisen. Madame Peronne, who had superintended the births of royal children in London and Turin, was at last to find employment in her native capital. After twenty-three years of matrimony, Anne of Austria was in hopes of, was expecting, had actually given birth to a Dauphin. Marie de Medicis' mind was made up. The astrologers by whom she surrounded herself assured her that her ailing son was soon to die, and she would again be Regent for an infant king of France. Sending before her a gentleman of her suite with the announcement that she hoped, if welcome, to land at Harwich the same night, she sailed for England. She was not as bad as her word, for storm delayed her, giving Charles the opportunity to close his ports against her, but she had judged rightly that he was far too devoted a husband to take so drastic a step. "She brings with her six coaches, seventy horses, and a hundred and sixty in her train; by this you will easily decry her", wrote one unhappy English official to another, ordered to make hasty preparations for her arrival.[1]

IV

The future Martyr-King set out in state for Chelmsford, to welcome upon a visit of indefinite length a mother-in-law of elaborate tastes, with a grievance. Henrietta hurried to St James's, to prepare fifty of the best apartments in the children's palace for their grandmother. This meant that the next child, expected in four months' time, would have to be born at White-hall, but no personal considerations could be allowed to inter-fere with the comfort of the queen's afflicted and aged mother. Charles had allotted a hundred pounds a day for his self-invited guest's expenses. Henrietta, determined that English hospitality should produce a splendid first impression, spent another three thousand on re-decoration and new furniture for her mother's rooms. Her efforts were not wasted, for the Sieur de la Serre, a gentleman of Marie de Medicis' household, left a detailed ac-count of the flattering reception given to his mistress.[2]

The Queen of England was in no condition to linger on an October afternoon in a draughty courtyard of St James's. When a flourish of trumpets announced the appearance of the procession from the coast, she descended from an upper cham-ber. A chair had been set for her at the foot of the grand stair-case, and around it were already grouped her children, so oddly described by her court painter in his celebrated group of them as "Le Prince Carles, le ducq de Jarc, la Princesse Maria, la Prin-cesse Elizabet et la Princesse Anna". But when the coach con-taining her husband and mother swept into the great quadrangle, Henrietta could not contain her feelings. She rose from her seat, breaking up the carefully arranged tableau, and hastening for-

[1] Cal. S.P.D., 1638; Sir H. Vane to Sir J. Pennington.
[2] Histoire de l'entrée de la reyne, mère du roy très-chrestien, dans la Grande Bretaigne, par le Seigneur de la Serre; 1639.

ward, endeavoured with trembling fingers to open the coach
door. Someone more efficient assisted her, the Queen Mother
of France dismounted, and the Queen of England, falling on
her knees, implored the blessing of the massive lady to whom,
she believed, she owed everything of her present happiness.
Marie de Medicis wept, Henrietta wept. The four children, following her example, knelt around her. According to de la
Serre, there was not a dry eye in the vicinity of St James's.

   Marie de Medicis was now in her sixty-sixth year, and
had never been a beauty. The chief emotions stamped on her
visage by the events of the past thirteen years were rage and
chagrin. Henrietta admitted in a letter to her sister Christine
that she had found their parent a little altered at first, but she
attributed this to the trying effects of a sea passage.[1] She did not
admit that, on hearing of her parent's intended visit, the words
·"Farewell, my liberty!" had escaped her lips. She helped Marie
de Medicis by buying from her some of the tremendous jewellery amassed by a Queen Regent, and insisted that her mother
must sit to her court painter. Marie de Medicis duly sat to Sir
Anthony, who charged Henrietta £50 for the result. At the
sale of the royal collection by order of Parliament after the execution of Charles I, this evidence of daughterly devotion was
valued at £3. Fortunately the nursery at St James's formed a
great common interest between the queen and her mother. The
children were beginning to grow up—Charles, Prince of Wales,
a slightly frog-faced boy of eight, with the blackest of fringes
and eyes, had his own governor and tutor now, and the wooden
toy which he was accustomed to take to bed had been removed.
The Princess Mary, aged seven, breakfasted alone off manchets
of fine bread, beer and ale, mutton or chicken. The three elder
children sometimes supped with their parents and grandmother,
but the Princess Elizabeth did not sit up for that meal. For this
gentle little girl, whose shower of silvery ringlets and pale,

[1] Ferrero.

flower-like face reminded beholders that she had been born on Holy Innocents' Day, when nothing but snow had been visible from the windows of the queen's bedchamber, her grandmother had come primed with an offer of marriage. During her stay in Holland she had officiously discussed with the Prince of Orange the propriety of a match between his only son and the second of her English granddaughters. Charles, however, considered such an alliance beneath the dignity even of a younger princess of his family, and Henrietta was averse from any Protestant overtures. Marie de Medicis had to let that affair drop, and turned her attention to advising her daughter on more urgent problems. For Charles, the continued residence in his country of a person deemed by the superstitious to bring ill-luck wherever she went, and by the most level-headed to be an inveterate old mischief-maker, was a personal as well as a national disaster.[1] Henrietta, whose health did not permit that she should accompany her husband on many expeditions, gave up all her usual occupations so as to spend as much time as possible in her mother's apartments. Simultaneously her good fortune began to wane.

V

The King and Queen of England had now attained the appearance made so familiar by the most famous of their court painter's many portraits of them. Both had improved considerably in looks since the date of their marriage. Henrietta, who had been over-thin and neurotic-looking in her teens, gained assurance and presence with her twenties. In the first pictures of her as a proud mother, her features and forearms are rounded, her mien is complacent, her general appearance can only be described as blooming. As she approached her thirties, her looks began to alter again, subtly and almost imperceptibly. Her

[1] The Thames watermen dubbed the week of gale and flood which ushered in Marie de Medicis' three years' visit to England "Queen Mother's weather". Laud's Diary, Oct. 1638.

figure became a model of elegance, her lively mouth more sympathetic, her eyes a little watchful, her whole air more spiritual and pensive.

Charles, like most royal Stuarts, found silver threads in his chestnut hair before he was thirty. As a happy parent he too gained in assurance and elegance, but his years of content brought no corresponding cheerfulness into his countenance.

Marie de Medicis had arrived in England within a month of her daughter's twenty-ninth and her son-in-law's thirty-eighth birthday. The luxurious apartments assigned to her in the palace of St James's overlooked the deer-park and the terrace, the favourite promenade of the court. Here the royal children, slightly exhilarated after their midday meal of Gascony wine, white fish, roast chicken and custard tart, took their airing on fine afternoons, often accompanied by their parents, a brilliant train of visiting ladies and courtiers from Whitehall, and a troupe of vociferous pet animals. Charles was at his best in a pastoral scene surrounded by his family, Henrietta never more attractive than when enjoying herself with a few light-hearted companions. She was more lucky in her humble than in her noble friends. Amongst good mistresses she must receive honourable mention.[1] Her husband told her laughingly that she was a careless and extravagant housekeeper, but her servants were attached to her because they knew that her interest in all their personal concerns was unaffected. In the days of her tribulation they did not desert her.

The King and Queen of England in 1638 were a couple of whom any nation might have been proud. Unfortunately, most of their subjects could not see behind the scenes at St James's, Whitehall, Denmark House or the country palaces. On public occasions Charles suffered from a return of his youthful diffidence, his stammer became pronounced, he could not muster a shade of geniality. His wife, on the other hand, was

[1] *Cal. S.P.D.*, 1639–41.

voluble in a tongue she spoke most imperfectly, and displayed
abundant un-English gesture. She appeared to her critics alter-
nately arrogant, and too sweet to be wholesome. On her passages through their streets she was always attended by a flight
of quick-eyed chattering foreigners. The courtyards of her
London palace were haunted by black-hooded birds of ill-
omen.

Amongst the many commissions undertaken for Henrietta
by Panzani was one to obtain, from the celebrated Bernini,
busts of her husband and herself. The haughty Roman sculptor,
who had refused to take any interest in an order from Cardinal
Richelieu, condescended to portray the handsomest royal
couple in Europe. The "Princippale Paynter in Ordinary to
their Majesties at St James's" prepared for the sculptor's guid-
ance three portraits of his master—a profile, a three-quarter
face and a full-face—all on one canvas; and two of his mistress.[1] When the triple likeness of Charles I was unpacked in
Bernini's studio, the artist's attention was instantly and power-
fully attracted. After a prolonged, silent contemplation of the
features of this unknown English gentleman, he exclaimed that
never had he beheld a countenance so unfortunate.[2]

[1] The Bernini bust of Charles I was either destroyed or stolen at the time
of the great fire at Whitehall in 1698. Whether that of Henrietta was ever
accomplished is unknown, but by the time that the portraits for it reached
Rome her troubles had begun.
[2] Panzani; Bulstrode.

CHAPTER IV

GENERALISSIMA

I

TWELVE years had passed since the Queen of England had made a single amateurish effort at political intrigue. Shortly after the arrival of her mother, she began to take a belated but feverish interest in the troubles thickening around her. It is possible to judge exactly how much she grasped of their causes and effects, for many seasons later, in the sunset of her life, she dictated to a sympathetic lady of the French court [1] a graphic break-neck narrative entitled *Abrégé des Révolutions d'Angleterre*.

Henrietta's effort as an historian is remarkable for its omissions, and valuable for its many personal touches. That its style is confused is not surprising. From the moment that her husband left her to enter upon his first campaign against his subjects, until the fall of an axe on a scaffold outside Whitehall made her a widow, she scarcely knew a moment's peace of mind. For ten years she existed in an atmosphere of alarm, ceaseless intrigue and insecurity. Her disasters crowded upon her with no more warning than those announced by the messengers of a Greek tragedy. She took vigorous action directly she realized that her husband's happiness was threatened, but months passed before she was dolefully convinced of the magnitude of the approaching storm, and that it would not pass over like others before it, to give place to further days of sunshine occupied by the masques, the progresses and the *fêtes champêtres* in which her gay and innocent soul delighted. Her narrative of the revolution

[1] Madame de Motteville.

reads like a nightmare, and so, beyond doubt, these years of her life did appear to her when recollected in sorrowful tranquillity.

Scotland, a country for which she felt instinctive dislike, had already for two years been aflame. Charles, she relates, brought to her in her apartments, on an evening in 1637, a copy of the new prayer-book which he intended to impose upon the Scots. He asked her to study it with him, so that she might appreciate how little it contained that was not to be found in her own books of devotion. The queen's opinion of the volume destined to be known to history as "Laud's book" was fully as unfavourable as that of Jenny Geddes. To "this fatal book", and to the villainy of Richelieu, whom she accuses of having fomented disaffection in London by the distribution of large sums of money, Henrietta attributes the first struggles of her husband's subjects to revolt against the monarchical system.

The time came for her to bear her seventh child. She had, as never before, the benefit of her mother's presence and sympathy. No apprehensions vexed her. But her luck was out. After extraordinary agony, she was delivered of a daughter who died within half an hour, and before "his jewel" had fully recovered from this unexpected trial, her husband had to deliver her into the safe keeping of the Lord Admiral. Charles set out to war. The king, whose figure, clad in blue-black armour, was familiar in so many court portraits, seemed likely to see service at last. Since his last Scottish expedition, the occasion of his coronation, he had never been separated from his queen for more than a few days. Henrietta bore Scotland a grudge, as the ungracious country that took her husband from her when she was unable to accompany him. She did not realize that this parting was to be the first of many, and that each successive absence was to be for a longer period.

Only a formidable army could have enforced Charles's will in Scotland, and he was too impoverished to raise one. Henrietta took the ill-advised step of calling upon the Catholics of

England for financial assistance. She was proud of the response made by her friends. An appeal to the ladies of England was less successful. Further, with a view to cutting down expenses and relieving her husband of an unpopular guest for whose presence she felt herself responsible, she sent the ingratiating Jermyn to Paris to negotiate there for the return of the Queen Mother. She added that she herself would like to pay a visit to France. Louis XIII replied unfavourably to both proposals, and by June Charles had signed the Treaty of Berwick, by which his "strangely united" northern subjects nominally obtained everything for which they asked. He returned with a lover's devotion to his queen, covering two hundred and sixty miles in four days. She, inflamed by the histrionic Duchesse de Chevreuse with a romantic notion of sharing a soldier's life, regretted the hasty peace. Her anxieties for that year, however, were not over. The Prince of Wales broke his arm, and became suddenly, for a short time, seriously ill. The peace with Scotland proved to be a peace only in name.

A champion not at first welcome to her now appeared upon the scene. Although no two men could have been more dissimilar than the suave little cat-faced Archbishop of Canterbury, who had been primarily responsible for driving the moderated Protestants into the arms of the Puritans, and the tactless and taciturn Wentworth, Lord Deputy of Ireland, Henrietta disliked both for the same reason. Her husband would follow their advice. Her tragic dark eyes always looked over Charles's shoulder for the figure of a second Buckingham. Wentworth arrived from Dublin, full of fire and force. "The Great God of battels long and long preserve your majesty."[1] He was informally appointed Charles's chief counsellor, and created Earl of Strafford. He advised his master to call a Parliament, and meanwhile suggested that privy councillors should offer him a loan to raise an army. Henrietta, nervous lest the

[1] Harl. MS. 7379, f. 103 B.

forthcoming Parliament should insist on enforcing the recusancy laws and demand the dismissal of Rosetti, papal nuncio to her court, overcame her feelings sufficiently to beg the new earl to use his influence in her interests. She was childing again, but so eager to reassure herself that her happy days were not yet at an end that she would not suffer the Shrovetide court gaieties to be abandoned. Her masque this New Year was written by the laureate D'Avenant. Inigo Jones designed the costumes and scenery, and Lewis Richard, Master of the King's Musick, composed the songs. Henrietta herself took part, attired in an Amazonian habit of carnation, silver-embroidered, with a plumed helm, and "an antique sword hanging by her side, all as rich as might be".

This was the last comedy to be played at Whitehall in the reign of Charles I. A year later a tragedy was being performed daily in Westminster Hall, and the king and queen were anxious-eyed spectators.

II

One of Charles's expensive foreign guests left London this spring, but her departure was prompted by purely personal considerations. Madame de Chevreuse had heard that her husband was coming to England.

On April 13th, 1640, the new Parliament met. In it sat, as one of the members for Cambridge, Oliver Cromwell, the Fenland squire who twelve years earlier had complained to the queen's chief physician of nightmares and depression. The Short Parliament lasted three weeks. According to Henrietta's account, it was dissolved not by Charles's desire, but because "a secretary of state" who hated Strafford had treacherously and falsely told the House that nothing less than the full subsidy demanded by the king for his war against Scotland would content him. On the morning of the dissolution Strafford, who had been raised to the dignity of Lord-Lieutenant of Ireland, offered to bring over an army from that country. Within two days of his proposal, the rumour that "Black Tom Tyrant's" army was to be used against rebellious English as well as Scots, was current in London. The Archbishop of Canterbury fortified his house. A sinister anonymous placard announced that Whitehall was to let. At the palace, which she shared with the royal children, old Marie de Medicis refused to go to bed for fear of being murdered. The king had received a letter threatening to "chase the Pope and the Devil from St James's, where is lodged the Queene, Mother of the Queene". Little Prince Charles was reported to have wept for five days. At nights he was troubled by bad dreams. When his father came to ask the cause of his distress, the boy answered mournfully, "My grandfather left you four kingdoms, and I am afraid your Majesty will leave me never one".

Henrietta chose a country palace for her eighth confinement. Her last experience of childbirth had shaken her nerve, and she prepared to die. But since that tragedy at Greenwich, which had been occasioned by an accident, she had never found any difficulty in bringing a male child into the world. It was only with daughters that she was unlucky. Henry, Duke of Gloucester, born at Oatlands on July 8th, 1640, was christened there privately without any of the customary rejoicings, and the only royalties available, his two elder brothers and his eldest sister, were his sponsors. Henrietta, always high-spirited in time of danger, declared herself "never so well after a child",[1] but before the end of the month she had been bitterly disappointed by the news that the Pope, to whom she had applied for help, would do nothing until her husband became a Catholic. In that case six or eight thousand soldiers would be despatched to England.

The Scots were over the border, and Charles again went north. His funds were almost exhausted. The great council summoned by him at York insisted upon opening negotiations

[1] *Cal. S.P.D.*, July 1640.

with the rebels. He announced his intention of calling another Parliament, and in order to endear his wife to his listeners, added that his decision was due to advice in a letter from her.[1]

Henrietta was soon in need of sympathy. Two of her infants had died at birth, but she had never before lost a child old enough to have been a character and a companion. The Princess Anne, a particularly bright little girl, just about to enter her fourth year, had for some time been weakened by a feverish cough. Being reminded by her nurse to say her prayers, " 'I am not able', saith she, 'to say my long prayer ("Our Father") but I will say my short one—Lighten mine eyes, O Lord, lest I sleep the sleep of death.' This done, the little lamb gave up the ghost."[2] Henrietta and Charles, overcome by grief, ordered a post-mortem. Mayerne, who superintended it, pronounced that no accidental circumstance had been responsible for this sudden death. The child had been consumptive.[3]

As Strafford had expected, the first act of the new Parliament was to attack him. He was impeached, and thrown into the Tower, where Laud soon joined him. Henrietta was now her husband's chief counsellor, and foreign aid was the foremost idea in her grief-crazed brain. She wrote to France, again offering herself upon a visit, and to the Pope's nephew, specifying five hundred thousand crowns as the sum she required for the purpose of corrupting Members of Parliament. When Cardinal Barberini received this amazing document, he was at first inclined to believe it a forgery, but investigation convinced him that it was written in the queen's own hand.[4] She had begun upon the long series of tortuous intrigues which, undertaken with no object but her adored husband's re-establishment, were to be principally responsible for his death. When fighting for him she would stick at nothing. She humbled herself to send to Parliament a message, explaining that in raising a subscription

[1] Clarendon, *Hist.* 2. 107.   [2] Fuller.
[3] ⌐The Princess Anne is the beautiful baby in the group reproduced in the arts section.   [4] Roman Transcripts, 9. 92. P.R.O.

from the Catholics she had been moved "merely out of her
dear and tender affection for the king. . . . She was ignorant of
the law." She apologized for "the great resort to her chapel",
and promised that in future she would be "careful not to exceed
that which is convenient and necessary". As she believed that
the presence of "one sent from the Pope" was resented in England, she would dismiss the nuncio as soon as possible.[1] Rosetti
did not go immediately, but Walter Montagu, once her masque-
writer, now a zealous Catholic, was reluctantly banished by her.
Naturally those of her religion who had helped her so generously less than two years before were chilled and astonished
by her abandonment of them. She proceeded to stretch out a
friendly hand towards a Protestant power. The Prince of
Orange's offer, so scornfully and repeatedly rejected, was now
abruptly accepted. By a secret condition in the marriage treaty,
the prince engaged to send money, and if necessary troops, to
Charles's aid. But the prince, too, made his conditions. He
demanded for his son the eldest daughter of the King of England, having heard, he said, that the health of the Princess Elizabeth was somewhat infirm. Charles, although taken aback, was in
no position to haggle. He announced to the Parliament destined
to bear the title "Long" that a Protestant marriage for the Princess Royal had been arranged by him. All Europe was startled
by the poverty of the match, and in Spain and France especially,
its sudden conclusion gave rise to much scornful speculation.

The weeks immediately preceding the first wedding in her
family were painful and exhausting ones for Henrietta. Daily
Strafford was defending himself in the House, watched from a
latticed gallery by the king, the queen and their two eldest
children. Nightly, according to Henrietta's narrative, she was
giving secret audiences to leading members of the Opposition,
with the object of saving the earl.

[1] Message sent by the Queen's Majestie to the house of Commons, by
the Master Comptroller. Feb. 5, 1639–40.

It would be interesting to know who were the sinister figures summoned by her in the ingenuous hope that the blandishments of a royal lady would change their hearts. None apparently refused her invitation, and she states that she saw "the most wicked". She lighted her steps by a single taper, and descending alone by a little back staircase, met her enemies in a room belonging to a lady of the court now in the country.[1] Like her husband, she regarded his opponents as actuated by purely factious or the basest personal motives. She made no attempt to understand their point of view. The only recruit gained by her was a nobleman, Lord Digby. Unfortunately for Strafford, she was also, during these chill nights of early spring, engaging in the Army Plot.

The undoing of the Army Plot consisted in the fact that it was a two-handed engine. Four aristocratic young Members of Parliament, Henry Percy, Henry Wilmot, Hugh Pollard and William Ashburnham, all army officers, believed that the troops were so discontented with the leaders of the Opposition that they would declare for their king against his Parliament. They brought their project to Charles. Simultaneously, George Goring (a son of that Goring who had ridden post-haste from Notre Dame sixteen years before with the news of the wedding of Henrietta Maria to Charles I) brought to the queen a far more violent scheme which included the seizure of the Tower and a march of troops from the north upon London. His confederates included a couple of poets, Sir William D'Avenant and Sir John Suckling. The moment came for the two sets of conspirators to be informed of each other's existence, and invited to collaborate. Henrietta details the lively argument she had with her husband, who suggested Jermyn as the most suitable person to be entrusted with so ticklish a business. She affirmed with reason that her household was already regarded as a centre of intrigues. If Jermyn fell under suspicion, she would lose one

[1] de Motteville.

of her most valuable servants. Charles, however, carried his point, Jermyn received his instructions, and the result was confusion. Goring, chagrined at the prospect of playing a secondary part, betrayed both plots to Parliament. He was commanded to proceed, as his friends expected, to Portsmouth, of which valuable place he was Governor, and keep in touch with them as if all were well.

Meanwhile the Prince of Orange, bringing his son to be married to the Princess Royal, arrived in London. The Protestant princes received an enthusiastic welcome from the populace, but the streets through which their fifty carriages passed towards Whitehall were lined by armed guards conspicuous for their numbers. The wedding took place in the chapel at Whitehall on Sunday, May 2nd, 1641. The bridegroom, an upstanding and frank-faced boy of fifteen, wore a costume of satin and velvet, the colour of a raspberry. The bride's procession presented a perfect example of Henrietta's faultless taste in matters of dress. The ten-year-old princess, whose chestnut curls were tied up with silver ribbons, wore a simple gown of silver tissue. Her wreath, necklace and chain were of pendant pearls. Her long train was carried by sixteen nobly-born damsels, all attired in the colour of innocence. Henrietta, with her mother and her remaining daughter Elizabeth, on whom she now pinned her hopes of a brilliant Catholic alliance, watched the ceremony "incognito from a gallery because of the Difference in Point of Religion". The ensuing banquet was marred by the absence of Charles Louis, Prince Palatine, who considered himself slighted by the preference of William of Orange as his cousin's mate.[1]

Ignorant that the Army Plot had been betrayed, Charles chose his daughter's wedding-day for an attempt to gain, by a ruse, military possession of the Tower. The Lieutenant of the royal fortress in which Strafford was confined refused admission

[1] Breval.

to a body of troops ostensibly intended for service in Holland, and next morning a wild rumour that a French fleet was on its way to invade England united a London mob, who howled for the blood of Strafford outside the House of Lords, and paid a destructive visit to Westminster Abbey.

Two days later Pym revealed the Army Plot to Parliament; Strafford's attainder was immediately decided upon, and a request was sent to Charles that no person of the queen's household should be permitted to quit Whitehall. Henrietta replied that she was a daughter of Henri IV. He had never fled in the face of danger, nor was she about to do so. Jermyn, however, made off for Portsmouth, where he met Goring, and having no idea who had played the traitor, warned him that their plot had been betrayed. Goring had the decency to put in his pocket the order for Jermyn's arrest and see his friend on board ship, before informing the special messenger who had brought this document that it had arrived too late.[1] Suckling and Henry Percy also escaped, but Northumberland now ranged himself amongst the Opposition, and sent to the House his conspirator brother's farewell letter.

From the Tower Strafford urged Charles not to hesitate to sacrifice him. On the same day that the bill for the earl's attainder passed its third reading, a tale that French ships had captured Guernsey and Jersey roused the mobs of London to fresh fury. Henrietta, hearing that she and her husband were to be committed to the Tower, ordered her coach, with the intention of joining her friends at loyal Portsmouth. The French agent, Montreuil, the Bishop of Angoulême and her confessor were successful in dissuading her whilst her carriage waited at the doors of her palace. Her enemies, determined to represent her character as entirely despicable, had even subjected the ladies of her bedchamber to an inquisition regarding her friendships and habits. The midnight rendezvous given by the queen

[1] de Motteville.

to unknown strangers in an empty set of apartments could not have passed unobserved in a court, and anybody but Henrietta might have been prepared to treat calumnies with the contempt they deserved. But throughout her career she was unable to consider any commiserating circumstances in cases of female inchastity. When it was broken to her that a flight to Portsmouth would confirm a widely believed scandal that she was Jermyn's mistress, she became as frantic as her worst wisher could have desired.[1] Forty-eight hours later the Catholic inhabitants of Whitehall made their last confessions, in momentary expectation that the mob shifting outside was about to storm the palace and proceed to their massacre. The new Constable of the Tower had announced that he was prepared to execute the earl without legal warrant. Henrietta says that a procession of bishops, who represented to Charles that it was better one man should perish than the realm of England and the whole royal family, shook his resolution, but actually, of the four bishops consulted by the distracted king, only one urged him to yield. She adds that "no sooner had the barbarous revolutionaries the king's signature than, without heeding the royal commandment to the contrary, they hurried their victim to his death. . . . The king suffered extreme grief; the queen shed many tears. Both anticipated that this death would, sooner or later, deprive the one of life, the other of all solace in this life."[2] She repeats several times that she and her husband were now servantless. Parliament had dismissed the existing royal household. For the second time in her life Henrietta was left without a single familiar attendant. Her confessor was arrested and, after a severe cross-examination, sent to the Tower. Father Philip was released after a short period of imprisonment, but the news of his detention aroused unfavourable comment in an unexpected quarter. Cardinal Richelieu expressed disgust at this further manifestation of the madness of the English. His

[1] Add. MSS. 27962, f. 232. B.M. Montreuil to de Chavigny, Fr. tr. 3. 72. P.R.O.   [2] de Motteville.

sources of intelligence were still particularly efficient, and
although he had never seen Strafford, he was able to announce
with authority that "the English were so foolish that they
killed their wisest man".

III

The Prince of Orange, who fully realized that he had bought
while the market was cheap, was anxious not to lose sight of
his bargain. All that he had beheld in London had convinced
him that the sooner he gained possession of the Princess Mary
the better. His son, who had been impressed by the splendour
of the match made for him, had moreover found his bride an
attractive and amiable little creature. He had been provided with
a key to the garden of her mother's palace, and had visited her
every day during his stay in England. When the time had come
for him to return to Holland, he had begged her parents to let
her accompany him. The marriage treaty provided that she
should not leave home for another two years, and his ardent
entreaties had been refused. In July of the same year, however,
Henrietta began to see advantages in acceptance of the Prince
of Orange's insistent invitations.

Her husband was going north again. He hoped, by conceding
everything that his Scottish subjects asked, to win their support
against his Parliament. Her mother also was at last making a
move. Marie de Medicis had sadly decided that St James's had
ceased to be a desirable residence. Whenever the rabble of
London had nothing better to do, it assembled outside the
palace in which she abode. Parliament had afforded her the
protection of an armed guard, but her representations that her
son-in-law was no longer giving her a sufficient allowance had
been answered by a request that she should take herself and
"all her chaggraggs" out into the cold world. She had been
Charles's guest for three years, and that she was at least partially
responsible for his wife's wild essays in intrigue is proved by

the fact that she was now prepared to carry overseas with her a document signed by him, offering to the Pope, in exchange for money and arms, liberty for the Catholics of England, Scotland and Ireland, and the extirpation of Puritanism. Henrietta determined to make an effort to leave England with her mother. The waters of Spa in Lower Lorraine had a European reputation. She announced that she was proposing to take a course of them, after leaving her daughter in the Low Countries. She sent for Mayerne, who supplied her with a long list of diet prescriptions, but refused to jeopardize his professional conscience by saying that without Spa waters she would die. Parliament objected strongly to both her projects. Broken health was certainly not her sole reason for desiring a continental trip. The disadvantages of delivering the princess to her husband before she was of an age for the consummation of her marriage were equally obvious. Parliament demanded Sir Theodore's opinion of her majesty's condition, and the great doctor replied at length and cautiously. The gist of his report was that the queen believed herself to be dangerously ill. Her sickness was as much of mind as body. He did not himself consider Spa waters would be efficacious in her case, although they were preferable to any waters obtainable in England. The Commons accordingly prohibited the queen's journey, and sent her an address assuring her that nothing should be left undone to promote her peace of mind at home. Henrietta sent an equally fulsomely worded reply, thanking them for their tender care of her. "I hope I shall see the effect of it."

In the second week of August her husband left for Edinburgh and her mother for Antwerp. Two days before parting with Charles, she wrote to her sister Christine, now Duchess of Savoy: "I swear to you that I am almost mad with the sudden change in my fortunes. From the highest pitch of contentment I am fallen into every kind of misery, which affects not only me, but others. Imagine what I feel to see the King's power taken from him, the Catholics persecuted, the priests hanged, the persons devoted to us removed and pursued for their lives because they served the King. As for myself, I am kept as a prisoner, so that they will not even permit me to follow the King. . . . You have had troubles enough, but at least you were able to do something. . . . We have to sit with our arms folded." [1]

To Mayerne also she confided her fear that she would go mad. "Do not fear that, madam," was the tonic reply of her exasperated physician. "You are already so." [2]

She took herself down to peaceful Oatlands, but her shattered nerves allowed her no peace. A complaint was made in the House of Commons that the Prince of Wales, who should have been residing at Richmond with his governor, Lord Hertford, visited his Papist mother far too often. Henrietta construed this into a design to separate her from all her children. She sent Parliament "a very wise and discreet answer" that the princes had the instructors chosen for them by their father. "Moreover she knew it was not the will of the king that they should be brought up in her religion." [3] So as to avoid further accusations of tampering with her children's faith, she moved from Oatlands to an adjacent country house. Her description of her stay there contains an extraordinary story. In order to drive her out of the country, she says, her enemies now led her to believe that they intended to capture her person. A magistrate living near by received a mysterious order from Parliament to muster militiamen, and bring them at midnight into Oatlands park, where they would be met by a large body of cavalry whose officers would give them further instructions. The magistrate, being of royalist sympathies, brought his orders directly to the queen. She calmly bade him follow them, but she sent hastily to such friends as she still possessed in London, begging for their protection. Every servant of her household

<hr>

[1] Ferrero.   [2] de Motteville.   [3] Evelyn.

capable of bearing arms, even her scullions, prepared to defend
their mistress. When they were all ready, she walked boldly
into the park to await events. Nothing happened. All that
night the only strangers to present themselves in the vicinity
of Oatlands were some twenty horsemen, very ill-mounted,
whose probable prey was his majesty's deer.[1]

Nevertheless she warned Goring, whom she had unaccountably restored to her favour, that he must not be surprised to see
her arrive at Portsmouth, and she engaged relays of horses on
the Portsmouth road. Presently she moved again, this time to
Hampton Court, and applied herself to securing the allegiance
of some valuable waverers. With the Lord Mayor of London
she was so successful that when Charles returned from his
fruitless expedition into Scotland he received a civic welcome.
Henrietta, with her three eldest children, met the king at
Theobalds. They set out for Whitehall, all riding in the same
coach. At Stamford Hill the sheriffs of London and Middlesex
joined their procession towards Moorgate, where the mayor,
pompously attended, gave the royal family welcome and
received from the king the honour of knighthood. Charles and
his eldest son were invited to mount two richly caparisoned
steeds, presented to them by the City, and Henrietta and the
younger children to mount into a magnificent coach. They
were cheered all the way to the Guildhall, where they were
entertained with a banquet.

This gleam of popularity was the last enjoyed by them in
London. It proved entirely delusive. Most unluckily for Henrietta, reports of an appalling massacre of Protestant colonists
by the natives of Northern Ireland horrified England this
winter. The revolt became known by the name of "The Queen's
Rebellion". On January 3rd, 1641, believing that his wife was
in imminent danger of being impeached by Parliament, Charles
determined to get his blow in first. He ordered the Attorney-

[1] de Motteville.

General to impeach five leading members of the Lower House
and one of the Upper, whom he knew to have been in communication with Scotland. Next afternoon he went down to
Westminster attended by three or four hundred armed men.
Before leaving Whitehall he embraced Henrietta and told her
that in an hour he hoped to return to her, master of his enemies.
When her watch told the impatient and nervous queen that the
fatal hour had safely elapsed, she could not resist crying to
Lady Carlisle, who had just entered her cabinet, "Rejoice with
me, for by now the King is, I hope, the master of his state!"
She added the names of the five members whom he had gone
to arrest—Pym, Hampden, Holles, Haselrig and Strode. The
faithless Lucinda, who even in these times of discontent took
pains to be acquainted with every prominent man in the
country, had, soon after the execution of Strafford, become an
admirer of "the Ox", as court ladies called the stout and shaggy
Pym. Scandal declared that she had been the mistress of both
politicians, but it almost certainly accused her of too much
generosity. Although her friend had now become "such a she-
saint" that she frequented Puritan sermons and took notes of
their most moving arguments, Henrietta still trusted her. Indeed
she believed that Lady Carlisle mixed in Opposition circles
only so as to betray their secrets to her mistress. Without
betraying any emotion but surprised at the queen's news, her
best friend now withdrew and quickly scribbled a note to Pym.
Charles, who had been detained by the presentation of supplica-
tions by several poor persons on his journey to the House,
entered it to find his birds flown. There is little doubt that
other warnings besides that sent by Lady Carlisle had reached
the intended victims, but Henrietta's narrative imputes the
failure of the *coup* to herself alone. On her husband's return,
she says, she confessed her *"malheureuse indiscrétion"* with passionate penitence. The saint-like man gave her no reproaches.[1]

[1] de Motteville.

Six days later he left Whitehall, never to return again until the morning of his execution. The coaches carrying the royal family to Hampton Court had to make their slow way through a threatening crowd of several thousand persons, all holding staves to which were attached placards inscribed with the single word "Liberty!" When the king and queen reached their destination they found that no apartments had been prepared for them. They had to bed down for the night with their children in a single chamber. Two days later they moved on to Windsor.

To Henrietta's surprise, all the objections raised last year to her project of going abroad were now suddenly withdrawn. Resolved to take her opportunity before her enemies changed their minds, she set off with her daughter for the coast "in such post haste", complains a court official,[1] "that I never heard of the like for persons of such dignity". Charles, who intended, as soon as his wife was safely out of the country, to make for Hull, which contained all the military stores collected for the Scottish campaign, accompanied her to Dover, the port at which he had first set eyes on her sixteen years ago. In order to give colour to his announced intention of several weeks' hunting, he took with him equipage for the chase.

Hasty though the queen's journey had been, the glad news had been carried to Holland and the Prince of Orange had sent for her escort a squadron of fifteen Dutch ships commanded by Admiral van Tromp. The parting of the royal family drew tears from spectators. As Charles said farewell to the narrow-browed, soft-featured little princess who resembled him so closely, he expressed the fear that he might never see her again. He took Henrietta in his arms for a last kiss, not once but many times. His last promise to her was that he would not let himself be persuaded during her absence into making a peace disadvantageous to his family. In his pocket he had the key to the cipher in which they were to correspond, and in her baggage she had

[1] Sir T. Smith to Admiral Pennington.

the crown jewels. The wind proved favourable for coasting, and after the fleet had put out to sea, the king, attired in his simple hunting-dress, rode for four leagues along the coast, waving his hat repeatedly to the vessel that carried his wife and child from him.[1]

IV

Henrietta's bad luck at sea was to become proverbial. On this, her second voyage, she came in sight of Flushing after fifteen hours; here however, contrary winds sprang up, and when she eventually reached Helvoetsluis, the ship containing the vessels and plate for her chapel foundered and sank before her eyes in the entrance to the port. Prince William was waiting to welcome his bride. His instructions had been to escort the royal ladies by water to Rotterdam in the royal yacht, but they showed strong disinclination to put out to sea again. Accordingly they crossed the island of Voorne to Brill, where the Prince of Orange greeted them, and, sailing across the mouth of the Maas, landed at Hounslerdike.[2] At a little distance from the Hague their procession encountered that of Charles's only sister, Elizabeth of Bohemia. The two queens mounted into a red velvet state coach, where they sat side by side, faced by Prince William and his bride. In the "boots" of the vehicle were accommodated the Prince of Orange, Prince Rupert, second son of the Queen of Bohemia, and a couple of her daughters. It was a close pack, even for close relatives, and the two queens, who had never seen one another before, had few tastes in common. They presented a complete contrast in types.

Elizabeth of Bohemia knew not the meaning of nerves. Her health was naturally robust. At forty-five she would not have looked out of place amongst her brother's collection of battered, but eternally noble, classical deities, for her celebrated fair beauty had braved many storms. She had long ago, as much from choice as necessity, abandoned any effort at elegance in

[1] de Motteville.   [2] Breval.

dress. For eleven years she had been familiar with every shabby contrivance by which fallen royalty could obtain credit. Affliction had sharpened her witty tongue but failed to daunt her spirit. She had especial reason to regret her brother's recent reverses (for which, in her opinion, his wife was largely responsible), for she had always hoped to place at least two of her eleven surviving children in a country of which she never forgot that she had been Princess Royal. To her now was presented a sister-in-law, *chic, petite, difficile* and *dévote*. All Henrietta's salient characteristics were best described by words that have no English equivalents.

The procession began to lumber across a frieze-like background in stormy March weather, and the beholding crowds noted with edification the extreme graciousness with which the stranger queens conversed. On their entry to the capital, fireworks were discharged, eighty pieces of cannon sounded a triple salute, and an assemblage of the principal citizens, fully armed, prepared to accompany them to the New Palace in the Staedt-Straat, which had been reserved for the sole use of the Queen of England and her train. The Prince of Orange could not sufficiently show his "great affection" for his new relatives. Frederick Henry, Stadtholder of the Dutch Republic, was a full-blooded, dark-moustached man of fifty-three. His marriage had been a love match. His wife had been a maid of honour to Elizabeth of Bohemia. He now commanded his attendants to follow his example in appearing bareheaded in the presence of his son's bride; further, to distinguish between her and his own princess, she must be addressed as the Princess Royal. His republican subjects were disgusted by this homage to "greatness of birth", and his wife, Amelia of Solms, who was in delicate health, conceived a jealousy of her unoffending little daughter-in-law which only death was to end.

Henrietta had come to Holland intent upon raising money to assist her husband in the shortest possible time, but she found herself obliged to attend a series of entertainments given in her honour, before she could settle to business. The manners of her worthy hosts were noted by her with secret amusement. Unaccustomed to reverencing royalty, the burgomasters of the Hague kept their hats on in the Queen of England's presence, sat down without being accorded permission to do so, talked to her as if she were an equal and, when they had stared their full at her, slouched away without farewells.[1] The tall, handsome Dutch Ambassador, newly accredited to the court of St. James's, when paying a formal visit before setting off for London, kissed the hands of Jeffrey Hudson, the queen's dwarf, mistaking the twenty-two-year-old pigmy for one of her majesty's sons.

Seventeen days after her arrival, Henrietta got her first news from her husband since their parting. They had never before been separated by the sea, and a fleet under the command of an officer appointed by Parliament was beating up and down the North Sea and the Channel, eager to capture messages and supplies sent by the queen to England. Nevertheless, over forty letters from Henrietta to Charles reached their destination, and contemporary copies are available to her biographers to-day.[2] She wrote most of them with her own hand, and in French. The passages quoted in italics denote cipher in the originals. The principle of the code used by Charles I and Henrietta Maria was not new. Giovanni Michiel, Venetian Ambassador to the court of Mary Tudor, had employed it in his despatches over a hundred years before. It consisted of a table of numbers and letters in which each number and letter stood for a word or a syllable.[3] Henrietta used two varieties during her stay in Hol-

[1] de Motteville.
[2] In the British Museum, Harl. MS. 7379. The devil who transcribed them has contrived that scarcely two consecutive letters appear in order of date. Some are cut in two, or joined to others with which they have no connection. The spelling is as wild as the arrangement of this valuable series, first deciphered by Everett-Green, 1856.
[3] An article, entitled "Dark Words", by R. Hill, *Cornhill Magazine*, Feb. 1936, gives some interesting information as to seventeenth-century cipher letters and their messengers.

land, that of the second six months being more complex than its predecessor. The obvious objections to it were that all parties using it must possess a manuscript key, and should a letter interlarded with numbers fall into enemy hands it could not possibly be mistaken for an innocent document. Many of her letters were intercepted, but their captors were either quite inexpert in the business of decipherment, or lacked time to forward them to professionals. The "Tabula Cryptographica" of the king and queen gained the reputation of being completely mysterious, and became a family possession. Charles II and his friends used it during the Protectorate to communicate with royalists in England. Pseudonyms appear frequently in Henrietta's letters from Holland. "*Les malheureux*" in the first series always means the Catholics, and "Isabelle" probably either Lady Roxburgh or Lady Denbigh. "189" in the second cipher signifies Charles I and "ooo" Henry Percy, who rejoined her about the same time as Jermyn, "187". Letters written in English by the hand of a secretary generally contain a French postscript from the queen herself, adding some personal news and apologies such as "My dear heart, I pray you to excuse me if I do not write with my own hand; I have such a severe headache that I cannot see a bit".

Henrietta also despatched letters, in English and without cipher, designed to fall into the hands of her enemies and mislead them. In one of these she acknowledges messages from Pym with the object of bringing him into suspicion with his own party. Her handwriting is large, slanting and spidery; her use of capital letters and her spelling of proper names is entirely arbitrary. Jermyn is often Jermin and Bridlington is also Birdlington within a few consecutive lines. Her own name never gets a capital but "*le roy Monseigneur*" always does. For punctuation a double colon served her in every emergency. The heads and tails of her letters carry long tremulous loops; her signature, "henriette-marie", is invariably run into a single word. To her sister she signed herself with a monogram and scribbled abominably. Blots and crossings-out abound in her letters to members of her family, and her opening words "My dear heart" are always on the same line as the first paragraph.[1] A great difference is noticeable when she is writing formally to some peer or cardinal ("*mon Cousin*") and taking pains. Yet the impression produced by a page of her unmistakable script is that the use of the pen was a pain and grief to her, a pathetic reflection considering that for two-thirds of her life the writing of letters was one of her chief occupations.[2] Until her widowhood, when her orgy of mourning included black sealing-wax, Henrietta Maria's letters bore small scarlet seals with an impression of the royal arms of Great Britain and France, *party per pale*.[3] She was continually in a fever lest Charles should lose the key to their "mystical lock of numbers", which he always carried in his pocket. On one occasion she declares that she has been "driven well nigh mad" by the difficulty of making out his meaning because he has introduced blanks unknown to her, and used their cipher incorrectly.

After the battle of Naseby, when Charles's cabinet was captured, the royal correspondence was published in order to

[1] Her haughty niece, Mlle de Montpensier, once complained of the Duke of Savoy's incivility in beginning letters in such a fashion. Henrietta replied that she always did the same herself and she "believed Mademoiselle was not of a better house".

[2] Dozens of the thousands of letters penned by Henrietta Maria have survived, and, yellowing in museums throughout Europe, are available to her biographers. A comparison of the fine series in Lambeth Palace Library, with other contemporary letters in the same collection (Lambeth MS. 645), displays convincingly that the queen was no scholar. Her second daughter, and her sons, could write neatly, and spell and punctuate creditably, and a page of her husband's handwriting produces a beautiful effect. The princesses Mary and Henrietta Anne, however, were even more unblushingly illiterate than their mother. The following specimen from a letter of Henrietta Maria, written in English, gives an idea of her mastery of that tongue. "Maistre Nicholas : I have reseaved your letter and that which you send me from the king which writes me word that he as been veré well reseaved in Scotland and that both the armi and the people have shued a creat joy to see the king." Evelyn, iv. p. 7.

[3] An excellent example is to be seen in the Museum of the Public Record Office, Pedestal: Exhibit 70.

arouse popular indignation. Until that time, their majesties' enemies had been obliged to concoct forgeries for this purpose, and the style imagined by them to be suitable for a queenly Delilah is ludicrously unlike that actually used by Henrietta. In a spurious letter purporting to have been sent by her from Holland in February 1643, she is made to address Charles as "Most royal and illustrious monarch of Great Britain, my great, my good and worthy liege, the most regal object of my loving heart, best affection and utmost endeavours", and sign herself, after pages of high-flown incitement, "your most dutiful wife and liege woman, Henrietta Maria R." In fact, her invocations to her husband are far from remarkable for Oriental submissiveness. She points out his past errors and recurs to his besetting sins of procrastination and ductility with an insistence that must have driven a stronger-willed man homicidal. Her letters always begin "My dear heart" and, when they have a formal conclusion, end either "Adieu, my dear heart!" "Entirely thyne" or "Absolutely yours".

v

The Queen of England arrayed her wares and the Dutch merchants arrived to appraise them. Not all of the Dutch merchants had been born in Holland. Several of them had hooky profiles, deep in colour and warm in tone, and wore their black furred garments in a manner which brought a whiff of the Orient into her majesty's presence chamber. Some of the crown jewels of England, and all the ornaments lavished by a doting king upon a beautiful consort for seventeen years, made a startling appearance in a room of the New Palace on the Staedt-Straat on an early spring day in 1642. The two most remarkable pieces displayed were a couple of collars, the lesser of which contained rubies indeed worth a king's ransom.

The merchants made their examination slowly. They seemed to have no idea that time was money to the little French lady

who awaited their decision with eyes as sparkling as her
diamonds. The merchants' situation was very awkward. At
heart many of the solemn Hollanders sympathized with the
republicans of her husband's country. Moreover, considered
the golden-skinned old gentlemen whom Rembrandt loved to
paint, agents from London who had arrived at the Hague soon
after this lady, said that these jewels did not really belong to her.
They were the crown jewels of England, state property, and
the English Parliament would shortly be issuing a proclamation warning foreigners that no legal traffic could be carried on
in them. Besides, the lady wanted specie, immediately, the
hardest saying. The merchants looked uninspired; the lady enquired their difficulty. When she thought that she understood
such part of it as they could explain, she offered eagerly to
show them her husband's signature to a document empower-
ing her to pledge his property. It was true that she possessed
at the moment no such sign of her authority, but she could
easily obtain it. But the merchants all reflected silently that
formidable sums would have to be given in receipt of either of
those collars, and if they were never redeemed they would
represent money locked up for a long period. Not five people
in Europe could afford to consider their purchase. To break
them up and sell their stones separately would be bad business
as well as barbarism. Part of their value lay in the fact that they
were so perfectly matched.

The merchants with one consent refused to show any interest
in the large pieces. They turned to the smaller jewellery. What
had so recently been bought by a fashionable woman would
still be marketable. After much deliberation, they began to
offer for the queen's little chain, and the cross which had
belonged to her mother. But they would prefer to buy outright, not to take anything in pledge. The sums suggested by
them were insultingly small, less than half what her jewels were
worth, said the queen. She means less than half what she had

paid for them. The flat-faced, Dutch-born merchants took their
unceremonious leave, the regretful Jews melted away incon-
spicuously as snow in April, and with them vanished the queen's
smiles. She set herself down to write to her husband. The wind
which was preventing her letters from reaching him had
driven news of him in to her, but not news from him. The
damp air of this low country was giving her aches in her bones.
She hoped she was getting nothing worse than a cold. She wrote
unhappily:[1] "A report is current here that *you are returning* to
London, or near it. *I* believe nothing of it, and hope that *you* are
more constant in *your resolutions*; you have already learnt *to
your cost* that want of *perseverance* in your *designs* has *ruined* you."
Now she thought she saw why her enemies had suddenly withdrawn all their objections to her leaving England. Charles, the
peace-loving, would agree to almost anything if his wife was
not by his side. Directly he was out of her sight, he had been
persuaded not to go to Hull, a place which "must absolutely
be had". Well, if he did not intend to make a stand in defence
of his wife and children, she was finished with him. "If it be so,
adieu!" she wrote frantically, and added an old threat with
which she was wont to torment herself as well as him. She
would retire into a convent in France and spend the rest of
her days praying for him. "For I can never *trust myself* to those
persons who would be *your directors*, nor to *you*, since you would
have broken your promise to me. If you had wished to make
an accommodation you could have *done* it as *well* at *York*, and
more to your *advantage* than near *London*. As you had decided on
this *at my starting*, I cannot believe any other, although I confess
I am *troubled* almost to *death*, for fear *of the contrary*; and I have
cause, for if you have *broken your resolutions* then there is nothing
but *death* for *me*. I am afraid it is a trick of *H*. and *L*. together, for

[1] The spelling and punctuation of the following extracts from letters
of Henrietta Maria, all of which are to be found in Harl. MS. 7379,
follow the 1856 translations and decipherment of Everett-Green.

it is very public here that *L* is *betraying you*. I pray God it be not so. If all that is said is true, *you* are lost and *I* too. . . ."

While she was writing, a letter from Charles was brought in to her. It was dated from Newmarket, *en route* for York. Partially satisfied by the reasons he gave for his delay, she added some sheets to what she had already written. Her unjustified reproaches would do no harm.

The merchants came again, and finally agreed to take all her personal jewellery in pawn. Charles's mother had been a princess of Denmark. She determined to try and pledge the larger of the great collars to the King of Denmark. She, with whom fine stones were a passion, saw "all my little ones" go without comment. The only loss that moved her to speech was the sale of Charles's pearl buttons. She had been told that they would be saleable if removed from their settings, and so they had proved. "You cannot imagine how handsome the buttons were when they were out of the gold and strung in a chain, and many as large as my great chain. I assure you that I gave them up with no small regret. Nobody would take them in pledge, but only buy them. You may judge, now that they know that we want money, how they keep their foot on our throat."

Knowledgeable people told her that Amsterdam and Antwerp were more suitable places than the Hague in which to market big jewellery. She would have preferred to visit the Jews of Amsterdam quietly, but the Prince of Orange "holding on his wonted nobleness in cheering her" prepared to accompany her. They must make a state entry. She had "such a bad toothache that I scarcely know what I am doing", but she could not afford to annoy her host. While the merchants of the Hague had kept her waiting, she had thought to have gone up to Cologne to comfort her mother, who was sick and sorry there, but the Prince's republican subjects, anxious to keep on good terms with their brothers in England, had opposed her journey. They had also issued a proclamation, forbidding royalist refugees to visit her, "on pain of imprisonment and sending back into England under strict guard". All the same, two "wonderfully well disguised" cavaliers had adventured to kiss her hand, and the prince had kindly turned a blind eye during their stay.

Bad weather had again deprived her of news from Charles for a fortnight. His last messenger had been driven back three times by storm. She knew now that her husband had reached York, and before she set out on her journey she wrote again, urging him not to make any agreement with his enemies. "My whole hope lies in your firmness and constancy, and when I hear anything to the contrary, I am mad." She had, at last, some money to send him, but only a little as yet. "I send you this man express, hoping that you have not *passed* the *militia bill*. If you have, I must think about retiring for the present, into a convent, for you are no longer capable of protecting anyone, not even yourself." Before this letter was despatched, she heard that Hull had declared against her husband. Its governor had shut the gates of the town in the face of her ten-year-old son, James, Duke of York, who had been sent up in charge of his cousin, the Prince Palatine, to occupy the city in the king's name. All the money she had so painfully collected in the last eight weeks would not suffice to make good this loss. As usual her spirits rose to meet disaster, and she added in a postscript that she wished she had been in her little son's place. "I would have flung the rascal over the walls, or he should have done the same thing to me. . . . Courage! I never felt so much; it is a good omen. . . . May heaven load you with as many benedictions as you have had afflictions, and may those who are the cause of your misfortunes, and those of your kingdom, perish under the load of their damnable intentions!"

The Queen of England, bringing with her "the great collar", came in sight of Amsterdam at six o'clock on a still, clear May evening. The dykes on either side, as she approached the town, were lined by armed burgesses mustered under twenty banners. Three triumphal arches spanned her path. In the Boulévard de Velour she was assisted from her coach into "a most rich and costly barge, in which her majesty being entered, without help of oars or sails, she was conveyed into the city by divers living swans, which were fastened to the foresaid barge". Watersports were performed to entertain her as she passed down the canal, and when she set foot on land again, pageants were awaiting her in the streets. With dusk she reached the palace, where, after the presentation of a complimentary address from the senate and a march-past of the twenty companies of burghers who had lined her route, she was permitted to retire to her own apartments. "For cost and magnificence," stated an eye-witness, "the like of this day's festivities was never seen in Holland before."

Four days later she was back at the Hague. The Dutch court had been plunged in mourning by the sudden death of one of the Prince of Orange's daughters. Henrietta began to think that "the great collar" had some malediction upon it. Although the prince himself had offered to stand guarantee for its redemption from the merchants of Amsterdam, "nobody in the world will have anything to do with it". The funeral of the little princess took place at Delft, without much ceremony. Amelia of Solms was to present her husband with another daughter before the season was out, and he was in a hurry to join his army and open his annual summer campaign against Spain.

Henrietta wrote to Charles at eleven o'clock on the night of June 2nd, telling him that to-morrow she must rise at six to undertake a journey as far as from Newmarket to London. She was taking her daughter to witness a great review in the camp between Gouda and Utrecht. Four days later she and her child stood in the entrance of the Prince of Orange's tent while the Dutch army marched past, presenting arms to them. Their host led the foot, his young son the cavalry. The princes

were away three months, and during their absence life at the
Hague moved slower than ever. Henrietta and her daughter
walked in the hall of the prince's palace, which was nearly as
large as Westminster Hall, and hung with trophies captured
from the Spaniards. They spent breathless summer afternoons
in precise Dutch gardens, rich in gravelled paths, fountains,
marble statues, grottoes, flowering shrubs and show plants.
The queen's brain was occupied with the purchase of barrels of
powder and hundreds of pairs of pistols, firelocks and carbines.
The merchants of this country seemed to be infected by the
example of their landscape, in which, owing to the continual
presence of water, the quickest way to get to a destination was
often to turn one's back upon it. They moved as slowly as the
traffic on their canals. "The more they are hurried, the less
they do." Lord Digby and Jermyn had sent to ask if they
might join her, and she told Charles that she had replied "this
will give *me* great pleasure, for I have nobody in the world
in whom to trust for *your* service, and many things are at a
standstill, for want of some one to serve me". They came
and she sent Digby to the Prince of Orange to ask that preoccupied gentleman what further assistance he was prepared
to give to her husband. Digby, who since his defence of
Strafford had enjoyed a reputation for emotional eloquence,
addressed the prince as if he were a recalcitrant House of
Commons, and her long-suffering host informed Henrietta
that he disliked her messenger, and found him "violent".
Jermyn slipped back into his old post of confidential adviser,
and her preparations went forward. In mid-July she heard a
piece of news which would, a couple of years before, have driven
all other considerations out of her mind. Marie de Medicis'
existence, since her retirement from England, had been increasingly miserable. The malice of Richelieu had driven her from
Antwerp to a small house in Cologne, where, for the last months
of her life, she had been living in utter destitution, deserted by

most members of a household whose wages she was unable to pay, and obliged to break up the furniture of her apartments to serve as firewood.[1] In the last paragraph of a long screed of advice and exhortation to her husband, Henrietta explained: "Excuse my letter being so badly written; I am troubled about my loss of the queen my mother, who died a week ago, but I only heard the news this morning. You must put on mourning, and all your suite also, and all the children."

In spite of the States' declaration that they would not assist the King of England against his subjects, arms and money were beginning to pass quietly out of the mouth of the Maas, across the North Sea, to anchor in the Humber. Webster of Amsterdam had advanced her majesty 140,000 gilders on her rubies and her pendant pearls, the burgomasters of Rotterdam 40,000 gilders, and Fletchers of the Hague another 129,000.[2] She had found a merchant who promised to deliver whatever she chose, wherever she directed. Civil war in her husband's country was now a certainty, and she began to pine for England. "For, since I have been in Holland, I have almost always pains in the eyes, and my sight even is not so good as it was. I know not whether it be the air of the country, or the writing, which is the cause of it, with the tears that are weighing them down sometimes." Her nephew Prince Rupert, "very *young* and *self-willed*", set off to join in the forthcoming fray. As soon as she heard that war had been declared, she would follow him. She had heard that her enemies had "made a declaration against me, and that I am not to be spared in any fashion in the world", but that only increased her desire to rejoin her husband. At the thought of seeing him again, "in spite of all the wicked people who would wish to separate us", her brain was almost turned. She could think of nothing else. "Since it is the only pleasure which remains for me in this world; for, without you, I should not wish to remain in it an hour."

[1] Dreux du Radier.   [2] H. M. de B.

Two days before she wrote this, Charles I had unfurled his standard at Nottingham. With him under its heavy and glittering folds were grouped his two elder sons and two of his sister's sons. The evening of August 22nd, 1642, was wet and windy, and the king's proclamation was haltingly declaimed by a herald who could not read his master's last-minute corrections. During the night a gale blew down the royal standard.

VI

"Send me word where I must land", wrote Henrietta on August 30th. "I shall have eighteen ships to go with me to England." She sent Jermyn to conclude her arrangements with the Prince of Orange, who was lending her experienced Dutch officers to serve under the younger Goring. But with autumn, the seas that divided her from England became impassable for days together, and over them now hung the impenetrable clouds of war. She was twice left for six weeks without news from her husband, and her letters to him were detained by the States, at the request of the new parliamentary agent at the Hague. Strange figures were admitted to the queen's apartments during these dark days. "There is a poor man arrived here, who had come to seek birds, who says that he left the place where you are, a fortnight ago. He has comforted me much by his relations, simple though they be." . . . "There is a poor woman, whom I had employed for Intelligence at Portsmouth, who has come to me to Holland, out of England. . . ." Her news had not been comforting, for she had hurried to warn the queen that she had overheard some captains of Essex's army discussing a plot to seize the king.

Newspapers reported that the first battle of the Civil War had taken place. The king was a prisoner and his army scattered. Other accounts of the engagement declared that the king and Prince Rupert had fallen, and the Prince of Wales was a prisoner. Persons who swore that they had touched the dead bodies of the two Palatine princes gathered eager audiences at the Hague. Everyone seemed convinced that, whoever else had survived, Prince Rupert must be dead. He was obviously a young man doomed to an early grave. They little foresaw that in the background of every ceremonial occasion in England a quarter of a century later, the saturnine features of his majesty's aged bachelor uncle were to be noticeable. An agitated foreign lady enquiring in a Dutch bookseller's shop for the latest English news, made an exit as precipitate as her entry. The Queen of England in disguise, whispered onlookers.

A rumour that his adherents were complaining to her husband that she was either ill, or not using her best endeavours to forward money and arms, penetrated to Henrietta. The thought that anyone could imagine that she was wilfully lingering in this lethargic little country, whose heavy, handsome houses and inhabitants, and sleek landscape, drove an impatient Frenchwoman nearly melancholy mad, roused her to fury. She wrote, in no docile spirit, a detailed account of all the difficulties against which she had struggled from the moment that she had left Dover. Until she had heard of the fall of Hull, she had never understood that she was meant to buy arms. Directly she had received such instructions, she had obeyed them to the letter. The first ship bearing them to England had been prevented by storm from reaching its destination. She had augmented its cargo, and after much labour, engaged a Dutch convoy. "This little boat" had returned to her, complaining that it had insufficient information regarding the disposition of the enemy fleet, and contradictory orders as to its landing-place. The French-born queen discoursed familiarly of such tongue-twisting places as Scarborough, Newcastle and Holy Island, and gentlemen called Strachan, Ruthven, Knowles and Withipole, ready to adventure in the *Lion* and the *Swallow* for her. As to money, she had never for one hour relaxed her efforts to pledge the jewellery, but the more you pressed for specie, the less you got. "People here are so Parliamentarian." "Extremely disheartened", she enquired whether her husband would prefer her to go to France or join him. If he was proposing to agree to anything dishonourable, "*Adieu* Royalty!" She would go and hide herself "in some place where I shall fancy myself a country girl". Her Almoner, whom she had sent with "a compliment" to her brother, had come back with a civil assurance that "entertainment" would be offered to her in France, if she could obtain none in England. She addressed friendly letters to Cardinal Richelieu, whom she had always disliked, and another cardinal, Mazarin, whom she had never seen, but knew to have become influential. Leaves began to flutter from the trees that lined the long canals of Holland: the queen woke to frosty mornings. "I do not wish to remain in this country", became her cry. "I need the air of England, or at least the air where you are." In a letter written in October, she alluded to her enemies for the first time by the nickname of "Roundheads". She knew their nicknames for her and her husband. "I'll go pray for the Man of Sin that has married the Popish Brat of France, as the preacher said in London."

On November 20th she was ready to sail, but the wind proved contrary, and a message from Lord Newcastle, whom she had been preparing to join in the north, begged her to defer her arrival. He had been attacked at York and driven back to Durham. From Paris came news of the death of Richelieu. She sent Walter Montagu to plead her husband's cause anew with her brother, but even now that the cardinal was removed, she got little encouragement. Louis XIII had his hands full in his own country, where the first mutterings of the storm which was to break five years later were already audible. On January 9th the Queen of England wrote what she hoped would be her last letter from Holland, not a long one, for she would give her husband all news by word of mouth at their joyful meeting. She sailed from Scheveningen ten days later in the *Princess Royal*. The little lady after whom the man-of-war had been christened, wept bitterly at parting from her mother, but by her side stood someone who was to be a second mother to her—Elizabeth of Bohemia, whose comments on her sister-in-law's activities during the past year had been, "I hear all and say nothing" and "I am not curious to ask what I see is not willingly to be told". Her host and his wife also attended Henrietta's embarkation, which, judging by the production of a contemporary Dutch artist, must have been a stirring scene. Eleven transports packed with men and ammunition accompanied the *Princess Royal*, and her convoy, under the command of Van Tromp, fired a salute which was answered from the shore. The banks behind the tent where the queen sheltered until the moment came for her to go aboard, were black with seated spectators. The quay was thronged by processions of coaches, market carts, horsemen, countrywomen with baskets on their heads, and sympathetic dogs. In the background rose a little church and a windmill. Sea and sky alone were calm. Henrietta, after "expressing the Obligations she lay under to the Prince, Princess and the States, in a most courteous and pathetick manner", kissed her little daughter "with infinite tears", and stepped aboard.

The voyage which followed was destined to imprint itself indelibly on her memory. Soon after she left the Dutch coast, the aspect of the heavens changed. She settled herself resolutely in "her little bed", and her attendants, including the Duchess of Richmond and the Ladies Denbigh and Roxburgh, disposed themselves similarly close around her—over-close, as events were to prove. A north-east gale began to blow, and the ladies to suffer. As darkness fell, the fury of the tempest increased, and they gradually realized that they were about to tryst with "the greatest storme that hath been seene this many a year". The first days of this experience, says Henrietta, were the worst.

During them she had no prospect of survival, but her only regret was that her death might discourage her husband and delight his enemies. When she found herself unexpectedly still alive, her spirits rose, and she could not help laughing at anything ridiculous that occurred. Several of her Catholic officers, shaken out of their usual reticence, insisted on shouting their most secret sins to her faithful confessor and two Capuchins. Days and nights passed without the possibility of her moving from where she lay, except in so far as she was flung by the motion of the vessel, and the efforts made to bring her food and drink were attended by many ludicrous accidents. The only person who kept his sea-legs was that one of her Capuchins who had been a Knight of Malta. "His constitution had become so habituated to a naval life, that he received no inconveniences from it and employed his health in charitably assisting all the sick and particularly the queen." At one point in the voyage they came within measurable distance of Newcastle-on-Tyne, and Henrietta arose. But there was no hope of effecting a landing. Suddenly she remembered that no queen of England had ever been drowned. "Comfort yourselves, my dears!" Distracted by considering this piece of historical information, her ladies checked their lamentations. Nine days later they found themselves back at Scheveningen. A fishing-smack took Henrietta ashore. One of her priests had to be supported under both arms while he pronounced a benediction; none of her ladies could walk, owing to giddiness and bruises. The clothing of the whole party was in such a condition that it was only fit to be burnt.

The Queen of England had lost two of her valuable transports, but she had gained "what she can never lose", a reputation for indomitable courage. She proceeded to justify it. Within eleven days, which she spent profitably, increasing her armaments, scolding the Dutch for having arrested and searched one of her ships, and collecting some money advanced by the King of Denmark, she prepared once more, "O admirable

resolution! to trust herself to the furie of the ocean and to the
winter's rigour". Her friends attempted to dissuade her, with
dark mariners' warnings of "a strange conjunction of planets
which will happen when I am at sea, which has never taken
place since the birth of Our Lord". Henrietta replied "God is
above all", and sailed. She was rewarded with a perfect passage
until within about fifteen hours of Newcastle, when the wind
veered to the north-east and forced her into Burlington Bay.
Here the *Princess Royal* anchored, and her passengers remained
on board until a troop of a thousand cavaliers came into sight
on the shore.[1]

VII

After a year's absence, the Queen of England was back in
her husband's country, and safe, surrounded by friends. She
lay, on the night of her landing, in a little thatched house on
the quay of the Yorkshire fishing village in which she had
come to rest after so many trials. Snow covered the sands and
roofs of Bridlington; the night was one of hard frost, and there
was fog at sea. Across the foot of her weary majesty's bed lay
another exhausted traveller. Mitte was not as young as she had
been, and was becoming a very plain old lady, but she had
proved herself a faithful companion, sharing her mistress's
adventures uncomplainingly. During their first horrific experience of the North Sea a fortnight ago, no person attendant
upon the queen had obtained sleep for nine days and nights.
Mitte, her majesty's favourite hound, now slumbered deeply.
In token of her gratitude for having been preserved from ship-
wreck, the Queen of England resolved to send into Picardy, to
the famous shrine of Our Lady of Liesse, the model of a ship,
fashioned in silver. . . .

She was awoken by the sound of flying footsteps. Jermyn
dashed into her room. She was not safe, even in England and

[1] de Gamache; de Motteville; de la Fayette; Bossuet; Breval; Clarendon,
Hist. iv. 267.

surrounded by friends. Four parliamentary vessels had arrived
in the bay where her ammunition transports still lay unloaded.
She was, for the first time in her life, under fire. She replied
gaily that she would lead a defence in person, though a little
small to act as a captain, but before she could get out of bed,
her chamber was crowded by persons urging her and all
women to leave the village to the military, who were prepared
to repulse an attack with vigour.

The shot which had woken her was the first of a bombardment. Before she had shrugged into her smock, balls began
to whistle about her lodging. It was five o'clock on a February
morning, quite dark and bitterly cold. In the middle of the
village street, to the dismay of her attendants, the queen turned
about, and began running back. She had forgotten something.
But on her majesty's bed Mitte lay still deeply asleep.

The party set out again, and a sergeant was shot dead,
within twenty paces of the queen, before she reached shelter.
The ditches up behind the village in which she crouched
for two hours, whilst balls played over her head, sometimes
sending spurts of soil into her face, reminded her, she said,
of those at Newmarket.[1] With daylight came peace. Van
Tromp had sent word to the Parliamentarians that unless they
ceased attacking the queen's fleet, her neutral escort would
open fire in return. With the comment that his action had
been a little tardy, the daughter of Henri IV returned to her
lodgings, through which two balls had passed from roof to
basement. She would not have it said that her enemies had
driven her from her first position.[2] Spalding's account of this
adventure deserves quotation. "Her Majesty, having mind of

[1] The river under whose banks the queen sheltered was the Gypsey
Race, also known as the Woe and War Water of the Wolds. This stream,
which disappears for years together, has been famous since the twelfth
century as a presage of disaster. According to local tradition, it heralded
the Great Plague, the landing of William of Orange, and the late
European War.

[2] H. M. de B.; Harl. MS. 7379; de Motteville; Bossuet; Spalding.

no evil, but glad of rest, now wearied by the sea, is cruelly assaulted, for these six rebels ships sets their broadsides to her lodging batters the house and dings down the roof or she wist of it herself. . . . She gets up out of her naked bed, in her night waly-coat, bare-foot and bare leg, and with her maids of honour (whereof one, through plain fear went stark mad, being one nobleman of England's dochter) she gets safely out of the house, albeit the stanes were flirting about her head . . . and by providence of the Almighty she escapes, and all her company, except the foresaid maid of honour, and goes to ane den, which the cannon could not hurt, and on the bare fields she rested, instead of stately lodgings clad with curious tapestrie." On the quayside, opposite her windows, Englishmen laboured throughout the short winter's day, unloading the stuff brought by her for the destruction of Englishmen. She sent an account of her welcome to her husband, ate three eggs and took a little rest. "As soon as I have arrived at York," she wrote, "I will send to you to ascertain how I can come and join you; but I beg you not to take any resolution till you have tidings from me." Another five months were to pass before she met Charles, and during her enforced stay in Yorkshire although she never ceased to add to the series of letters to her husband, which are the most reliable source of information as to her movements and intentions at this highly romantic period in her career, the fourteen which survive prove that many more were intercepted. In one she speaks of having written four times this week. Traditions of her life as Generalissima in the north are many and picturesque.

Boynton Hall, three miles from Bridlington, is denoted as the spot to which she retired whilst awaiting the arrival of waggons to carry her baggage and armaments south. There was poetic justice in the fact that this house was the property of a brother of Walter Strickland, the parliamentary agent who had done his utmost to hinder her mission at the Hague. She carried off her absent host's plate to be melted down for her husband's service, and left as a pledge of her intention to refund its value, a portrait by Jansens of herself in a white gown with green ribbons. She had brought with her from Holland a supply of trinkets—rings, lockets and bracelet clasps—for presentation to loyalists who would make her loans. Any haunter of antique shops who finds amongst a tray-load of undistinguished-looking trifles a crystal cut as a table-diamond, enclosing in a gold setting a scrap of red velvet on which reposes the monogram H.M.R. in gold filigree, may know that he has happened upon one of the tokens given by the wife of the Martyr-King to some adherent, whose family, in time, forgot the significance of a pledge that was never redeemed.

"Tell me now by what road I may come to join you", wrote Henrietta on February 22nd. "I will not repeat that I am in the greatest impatience in the world to join you", and Charles replied eight days later, "I am making all the haste I may, to send my nephew, Rupert, to clear the passage between here and York". A belt of country held by Parliament, and including the towns of Leicester, Coventry and Northampton, lay between the queen in Yorkshire and the king at Oxford. In Holland, Henrietta had heard every day of a fresh disaster to her husband's arms. Now that she was able to obtain unlimited first-hand news, she discovered that his situation was by no means so desperate as had been represented by his ill-wishers. Actually only two major engagements had taken place as yet, and neither had been decisive. His cavalry was far superior to that of his enemies, and cavalry at this date was the most important part of any army. Colonel Oliver Cromwell, realizing this, was at this moment at work in his native fen country raising troops of horse which, when they were put into the field, were to startle their opponents. The troopers chosen by him were mostly young yeomen farmers of splendid physique and strong character, and several of their officers were of gentle birth. This war was not wholly one of religion, nor one of class. Most of the great peers and all of the young courtiers had rallied instinctively to the king, but on the parliamentary side were many nobility and gentry who mistrusted Charles personally, and had been moved to take up arms against him from patriotic motives. A number of prominent men who had great possessions were, and were to continue, coquetting with both parties. Henrietta had no notion of being conciliatory to such characters, although she was always ready to be chivalrous to a fallen foe. When she met, on his road to execution, a parliamentary officer who had been captured and convicted of taking part in the bombardment of her Bridlington lodgings, after calling him up to her side to receive an exhortation not to persecute a mistress who bore no malice towards him, she ordered his release.[1] When, however, Sir Hugh Cholmely, Governor of Scarborough, came to kiss her hand after relinquishing the fortress held by him against his king, the queen turned her back on the ex-rebel.

At the time of her landing her husband's power lay in the north, the west, the cathedral cities and the Universities. Up and down the country, a band of female hawkers organized by Richard Royston, Bookseller to His Majesty, were carrying despatches between the royalist garrisons. Industrial towns were strongholds of Puritanism but many of their inhabitants had no more martial or revolutionary ardour than the worthy Ambrose Barnes of Newcastle, who hoped he should be saved, "for I never make visits on Sundayes, but keep within doors and read Dugdale's Baronage of England". Parliament held a large portion of the Midlands and all the south-east including the capital. Moreover, Parliament could impose any reasonable tax with the assurance that it would be paid, and commanded the Fleet and every valuable port with the exceptions of Newcastle and Chester, whilst Charles's financial sources were as precarious as his communications with the Continent.

[1] Bossuet.

From Boynton Henrietta moved westwards across wolds on which rose against stormy skies, the dark sentinel shapes of standing stones. This countryside, rich in menhirs and tumuli, had seen marching men before. In its bosom, under close-cropped grass, from which winds from the North Sea had pinched all colour, lay the bones of marauding Danes, British weapons of bronze and stone and Early Saxon beads of amber and rock crystal.

The queen left garrisons at Moulton and Stamford Bridge. Her background for three thrilling months of spring weather was to be an ancient and loyal city whose stately minster and crooked by-streets were guarded by mediaeval walls pierced by frowning Bar gates.[1] To her in these surroundings flocked all loyal Yorkshiremen, and several peers from Scotland anxious to discuss the situation in their country. Her principal adviser was an excellent and industrious man of studious and aristocratic tastes and no military imagination. One of the Scottish gentlemen who had accompanied her from Boynton, also a peer and a poet, bore a name destined to shine like a star in the firmament of history.

William Cavendish, Earl of Newcastle, was already well known to the queen. He had entertained her royally in happier days at Welbeck and Bolsover. His influence and wealth in the north were tremendous. His "Whitecoats", as the tenantry put into arms by him were nicknamed owing to their stout clothing of undyed wool, were the most formidable foot soldiers

[1] The queen's letters are simply dated "York", and no local tradition appears to exist as to the quarters occupied by her. The old Abbot's Lodgings of St Mary's Abbey (now the Blind School) became, after the Dissolution, a royal palace, and was the official residence of the Council of the North. Alternative places are the Deanery, or one of the residentiary houses, such as the Treasurer's House. Before the Dissolution, travelling royalties were usually entertained by one of the canons. Margaret Tudor was lodged in Minster Yard as guest of the Archdeacons of Richmond and the East Riding. Wherever Henrietta was accommodated she had a garden, for the Marquis of Hamilton put an end to a dog-fight "in the queen's garden at York" by slaying the Earl of Newcastle's dog. Napier.

fighting in the king's name. His notions of war were chivalric. Shortly before the queen's arrival he had written to Lord Fairfax, challenging the rival commander "to follow the example of our heroic ancestors, who used not to spend their time in scratching one another out of holes, but in pitched battles determined their doubts". In appearance he was a man of middle size and middle age, with somewhat narrow, strongly marked features and a ruddy countenance. He had not his sorrows to seek while he was rallying Yorkshire, skirmishing with the enemy and advising the queen, for Charles, disapproving of their policy, sent condemnatory messages highly resented by Henrietta, which arrived unfortunately at a moment when the earl had been summoned to his wife's deathbed.

James Graham, Earl of Montrose, was at this date one and thirty, a slight, active man, with penetrative grey eyes, chestnut hair and a stately carriage. He had come to England to warn his king that the Scottish army was likely to join the enemy. He desired to be allowed to raise the loyalists of his country while there was yet time. Interested persons tried to prevent Henrietta from reposing confidence in a leader whose wholehearted adoption of the royalist cause was less than three years old. They did not succeed. Montrose's personality, "the generosity of your character", made an impression upon her which was to be lifelong. His warnings, however, were represented to her as alarmism, and he failed in his mission. After his departure she wrote to him regretting that, owing to her husband's wishes, she had not been able to follow his counsel, and adding that for her part she would send him every possible assistance. She told him frankly of the aspersions on his loyalty brought to her, and ended her letter, "But my trust in you, and the esteem with which I regard you, are not built upon so slippery a foundation as mere rumour, nor to be shaken by an event which, if it be as reported, could only have been occasioned by your zeal for his majesty's service. Be assured, moreover, that neither shall I fail in my promise to you, and that I am and ever will be, your very good friend." [1]

While she waited at York, longing to join her husband, yet aware of the desirability of achieving some considerable success in the north with the reinforcements which she was bringing to him, she had her successes and her sorrows. She rode into Scarborough with Montrose at her side, she all but won Hull and Lincoln owing to the defection of their governors, and she composed many differences between touchy local royalists. On the other hand, from Paris came news of the death of her brother and regency of her sister-in-law, whom she had no reason to count her friend, and from London terrible accounts of the persecution of her priests and pillaging of her chapel. Her correspondence at this time drove her, she lamented, nearly crazy. "When I see you", she wrote to Charles, "you will say that I am a good little girl, and very patient, but I declare to you that being patient is killing me, and were it not for love of you, I would, with the greatest truth, rather put myself into a convent than live in this manner." [2] By early June the path was clear for her to set out for Newark. At last, also, her enemies had declared her guilty of high treason. On May 23rd Archbishop Laud had entered in his diary, "This day the Queen was voted a traitor in the Commons House". Since she had never been crowned queen consort of England she was no-where in their impeachment given that title. She left loyal York in the first week of June and proceeded by Tamworth and Pontefract to Newark, where she waited for a fortnight, hoping hourly to hear of the capitulation of Hull and Lincoln. Scandalmongers, still busy with their fruitless attacks upon her moral character, declared that when the handsome twenty-three-year-old Lord Charles Cavendish had escorted her to Burton, which he took by assault, she parted from him with

[1] Henrietta Maria to the Marquis of Montrose, dated York, May 31, 1643. Wishart.   [2] Harl. MS. 7379, f. 10.

extreme reluctance. "She was fonder than it was right for a
virtuous woman to have shown herself." A letter of her own
to her husband disposes of this slander. Cavendish, she says, had
desired extremely to accompany her south, but since "gentlemen of the country" had desired her not to deprive them of his
presence at Newark, of which place he was governor, she had
left him behind "for the safety of Nottinghamshire and Lincolnshire". The gallant young cavalry officer, who may well have
conceived a romantic devotion for the little royal lady whose
close companion he had been for three weeks of English midsummer, fell within the month at the siege of Gainsborough.

Henrietta was alive to the picturesqueness of her situation.
She herself relates that she always rode on horseback at the head
of the fine army she was bringing to her husband, and that she
shared her soldiers' fare in open country in the heat of the sun,
without any ceremony. She treated them as brothers and she
believed that in return they all loved her.[1] Her camp life
resembled a little, she imagined, that of the great Alexander.
"I carry with me", she wrote in high spirits, "three thousand
foot, thirty companies of horse and dragoons, and two mortars.
Harry Jermyn commands the forces which go with me, as
colonel of my guards, and Sir Alexander Lesley the foot under
him, and Gerard the horse, and Robin Legg the artillery; and
her she-majesty Generalissima over all, and extremely diligent
am I, with a hundred and fifty waggons of baggage to govern
in case of battle."[2] "She styles herself Generalissima", sneered
her enemies. They gave her "the prodigious title Mary, by the
help of Holland, Generalissima".

She expressed anxiety, now that her happiness was almost
within her grasp, lest any troops of Essex's army should "in-
commodate" her progress. No troop did so. Sir John Meldrum,
sent expressly to intercept her, let her slip through his fingers.
Travelling by short stages she passed through Ashby-de-la-

[1] de Motteville.   [2] *King's Cabinet Opened*, p. 33.

Zouch, Croxall and Walsall, to King's Norton. At Stratford-on-Avon she was met by Prince Rupert and was entertained in the finest house of that town by Mistress Judith Hall, "witty above her sex". Charles I, who had annotated in his own fine hand his copy of the works of William Shakespeare, would have been more appreciative than his queen of the interest of sleeping under the roof of New Place as the guest of the greatest English dramatist's only surviving child. Two days later, on July 13th, 1643, a scene of pageantry in which Shakespeare would have rejoiced, took place. The king, attended by the stripling Prince of Wales and Duke of York, rode out of Oxford towards his faithful wife. His procession met hers in the leafy vale of Kineton, below Edgehill. A medal struck to commemorate this auspicious hour optimistically represents Charles and Henrietta seated on thrones under a firmament containing the sun, the moon and many stars, while the dragon Python, symbolizing rebellion, lies dead at their feet.

VIII

Now followed those months of mingled gaiety and anxiety when a University city was the refuge of a brilliant court.

Oxford celebrated the queen's safe arrival with peals of bells, and she was escorted in triumph through cheering crowds to Merton College. Its Warden, Sir Nathaniel Brent, having sided with Parliament, had absented himself eight months before when the Town had become royalist headquarters. Throughout her stay in Oxford Henrietta occupied a fine set of apartments in the Warden of Merton's lodgings. A large and light room, attained by a heavily carved oak staircase, with a mullioned south window overlooking the Great Quadrangle, and a smaller window looking west, is still known as the Queen's Room.[1] Out of it opens a chamber built over the archway

[1] Now Merton Senior Common Room.

leading into the Great Quadrangle. When the Emperor Alexander I of Russia visited Oxford he was assigned Queen Henrietta Maria's bedchamber. From it a staircase of eleven steps gives access directly into the Hall of the college. One of the reasons for choosing Merton as the queen's residence was that the king, who was lodged in Christ Church, could visit her without going out into the streets. His "private way" was through a door which can still be seen in the east wall of the garden belonging to the Professor of Pastoral Theology, by Corpus gardens to the Grove, Chapel, and Sacristy of Merton, and thence across the bridge over Patey's Quadrangle into Merton Hall. The Chapel, one of the finest in Oxford, was given up to the queen for the exercise of her faith. Her suite was accommodated in rooms overlooking the Fellows' garden, where an ancient mulberry tree planted in the days of her father-in-law still exists, and from a path above one of the bastions of the old wall of Oxford, she could see the towers of the college where her husband was lodged, outlined against the westering clouds at sunset.

In her light and lofty reception chamber, with its noble view of the new buildings of the Great Quadrangle, she gave audience to prominent royalists, including Montrose, played her lute and frisked with her favourite spaniels, eagerly awaited the visits of her sad-faced king and two tall sons, and wrote in the large spidery handwriting, which she laughingly alluded to as "my little hand", letters to Cardinal Mazarin and her allies in the north.

The weather that summer was very warm and spirits in Oxford were high. Pastoral plays were performed for the queen's amusement in college gardens and the figures of Charles I and Henrietta Maria became familiar in sunlit quadrangle and shadowy cloister. Trinity Grove, on a fine afternoon, might have been mistaken for Hyde Park so many notabilities thronged it. Royalist gentlemen, bringing their families, crowded into the town, and thought themselves lucky if they could obtain a

couple of rooms over a shop in a back street. The loyal colleges
had melted down their plate for the king's service: Magdalen,
whose bell-tower was loaded with stones to be cast down on
rebel invaders, headed the list of donors with a gift of over two
hundred and ninety-six lbs. The Mint was in New Inn Hall.
In the Astronomy and Music Schools a hive of master tailors
cut out thousands of uniforms, which were tied up in bundles
and carted over dust-dumbed high-roads to seamstresses in
neighbouring villages. The old city walls had been strengthened,
a great earthwork was being flung up to the north, and the
University bell-man paraded the streets calling upon Town
and Gown to assist at the trench-digging, while troops drilled
on the flats of Port Meadow and in the new gun-parks.

Ladies attendant upon the queen set a fashion of going to
morning service in Trinity chapel, where they presented themselves in becoming *déshabilles*, "half-dressed, like angels". The
President of Trinity, Dr. Ralph Kettel, "had a terrible gigan-
tique aspect, with his sharp grey eies", and lively Lady Isabella
Thynne suggested to "fine" Mistress Fanshawe that frolic
might be got out of a surprise visit to this character, famous
even in Oxford for eccentricity. But the eighty-year-old
misogynist, quickly perceiving that "they came to abuse him",
drove forth his fair guests with a homily startling even to court-
bred ears.[1]

Amongst Henrietta's new ladies-in-waiting was a serious-
minded girl of literary aspirations who found herself regarded
as "a natural fool" by her gay companions. Margaret, daughter
of the late Sir Thomas Lucas, after a short experience of royal
service which she had entered full of romantic zeal, begged her
mother's permission to return home. She was commanded to
stay where she was, soon followed Henrietta into scenes of

---

[1] "Madam, your husband and father I bred up here, and I knew your
grandfather; I know you to be a gentlewoman, I will not say you are a
whore, but get you gone for a very woman."

anguish, and was rewarded two years later by winning the heart
of the widower Lord Newcastle. According to a cynical contemporary she did her worthy husband a great disservice by her
pen. She represented him as a pattern paladin.

Outside Oxford, during the last summer weeks of 1643,
leafy lanes resounded to choruses of "Troop along, troop along!"
and "Which nobody can deny!" At sleepy Oseney, the old
abbey mill was making gunpowder. The north of the county
was almost entirely parliamentarian in sympathy and Puritan
ministers complained bitterly of the incursion of roystering
cavaliers who turned them out of their rectories and made
the short nights hideous with blasphemous drinking-songs.
Prince Rupert and his followers made long, mysterious expeditions after the line of festal lights had died in Oxford town.
With dawn they were surprising enemy outposts at Thame,
at Aylesbury, at Reading. With midday, weary and bedraggled
prisoners would be marched by them into the streets of Oxford,
to be lodged in the castle or any church that might serve as a
temporary gaol. The rustics of the Oxfordshire hamlets who
saw the dark, hawk-faced young general flash past in the moon-
light, called him "Robert". Tales of devilish barbarities committed by troops led by one who had learnt his business in the
wars of the Low Countries, were spread by the Puritans, who
saw in the Palatine prince and his followers, the Assyrians described by the prophet Ezekiel. Royalist ladies, however, were
not repelled by a hint of brutality in these "captains and rulers
clothed most gorgeously, horsemen riding upon horses, all of
them desirable young men". Naturally, with so much inflammable material to hand, there were romances and quarrels
in the little court. Rupert, sumptuously lodged in Laud's college,
of which he was a member, refused to obey orders from anyone
but the king. The seventy-year-old archbishop, who was responsible for the colonnaded cloister of greenish marble pillars,
and stately east front overlooking vistas of turf and trees across

which the light feet and light voices of court ladies now flickered and echoed, still lay in the Tower, awaiting trial.

Henrietta's narrative of her adventures during the Great Rebellion devotes only a few lines to the eight months spent by her in Oxford. They were her last months as wife of Charles I, and their pattern of sun and shadow was as vivid as any flung across the quadrangle over which presided deceptively large effigies of herself and her king. While she had been absent from him overseas, and even in Yorkshire, the invisible chain always drawing so devoted a couple towards one another, had fretted her perpetually. She had been like an ivy torn from its oak. Now that she had him again in her embrace, she was still uneasy. Too many of his best friends considered her attachment to their king indeed that of ivy in its effects.

Her majesty's first request on meeting his majesty, had been for recognition of the invaluable services rendered by the colonel of her Guards. His majesty transformed Colonel Harry Jermyn into Baron Jermyn of St Edmondsbury, and no peerage ever gave more heartfelt satisfaction to the recipient. Charles then proceeded to the siege of Gloucester, and Henrietta, left behind in Oxford, after only one month of reunion, wrote disconsolately to her northern ally, Newcastle. Everyone here, she said, had been dissatisfied at the king's sudden decision to attend the siege in person. The counsels followed by him had been those of his nephew, young Rupert, not his wife. The jealousy learnt by Henrietta in the days of Buckingham's ascendancy was a terrible thing, but she knew better than anyone the fatal ductility of the gentle, bewildered, impressionable man whom it was her fortune, and the fortune of England, to call master. While Charles was away three earls—Northumberland, Bedford and Holland—showed signs of repentance for having joined the parliamentarians, or at least of wishing to return to their old allegiance. Holland, graceful as ever, and apparently in no doubts as to the warmth of his reception, actually presented himself at Oxford. Charles paid a flying visit to his disturbed court, and removed Holland and Bedford to serve in his unsuccessful siege of Gloucester. The first battle of Newbury, in which her husband failed to prevent the return of Essex to London, was hailed by Henrietta as "a very great victory". After it, Holland dropped into the irritating habit of calling upon her at Merton at hours when her husband was accustomed to visit her. Jermyn advised a conciliatory attitude, but she could not bring herself to make her manner cordial. When Charles bestowed the post of Groom of the Stole, previously held by the earl, upon the Marquis of Hertford, Holland made a midnight flitting. In London he explained that his efforts to negotiate a reasonable peace had been repulsed. Other waverers who had been waiting to see how he prospered, now decided definitively for Parliament.

Autumn settled upon the garrison town, bringing fog and flood, and a bad outbreak of typhus amongst the troops. The many loyal families who had packed into sordid lodgings in attendance upon their sovereign, deprived of the *al fresco* entertainments which had made the summer so agreeable, and all "as poor as Job", began to find themselves "like fishes out of the water" and fear that they were doomed to end their days in tents.[1] Prospects were not as bright as they had been earlier in the year, and Henrietta never ceased to regret that her husband had failed to march upon London while he had been in a position to take the offensive. Time was upon his enemies' side. In early October she wrote to Newcastle, "A misfortune has happened to me in which I believe you will sympathize". Her hopes of support from France had been raised by the recall of an ambassador of parliamentarian sympathies, and the appointment, at her request, of the Comte d'Harcourt. The useful and adroit Walter Montagu had made an attempt to slip into England in Harcourt's train, "in a disguised habit, his

[1] Fanshawe.

face all besmutched, and having on a very great perriwig".
At Rochester he had been recognized and arrested. He was
carried to the Tower of London, where he lay for four years.
The new ambassador protested in vain.

Henrietta began to feel unwell. She had one of the best
physicians in Europe within call. William Harvey, famous as
the discoverer of the circulation of the blood, a cultivated man
of five-and-fifty, was in attendance upon Prince Rupert's
younger brother, Maurice, who had caught the prevalent
typhus. But the symptoms which troubled her were all too
familiar. Exactly fifteen years ago she had experienced them
first with thrilling rapture. Now she recognized their development with utter consternation. Her reunion with an adored
husband after eighteen months' separation had brought its
almost inevitable physical fulfilment. She, who had already
provided so amply for the succession, was to bear at this most
unpropitious moment a ninth and quite unnecessary child.

On wild wintry days, when the view from the Fellows' garden
in Merton was of bare, rook-haunted elm avenues and gleam-
ing water-meadows, and the bells of Oxford sounded with
insistent melancholy, bad news began to arrive. The Scots were
over the border, and Lord Newcastle had sent to ask for reinforcements, which could not be spared. On a March day Montrose rode out of Oxford, at last provided with the commission
to raise the loyalists of his country, for which he had pleaded a
year before. At the beginning of the war, the royalists had possessed a strong circle of guardian outposts around Oxford. One
by one during the early days of 1644 these fell, and the name
of the now-famous general of horse, Oliver Cromwell, became increasingly menacing. In February, proposals for a peace
were offered to the king, but their terms were inadmissible. A
desperate attempt to provoke a royalist insurrection in London
failed. In London, Prince Rupert's elder brother, the careful
Charles Louis, was negotiating with his uncle's enemies for

the continuation of his pension. In Oxford the poet laureate was ending an adulatory poem to the queen, "But what, sweet Excellence, what dost thou here?" Chester and Bristol, both ports from which she could, if necessary, make an escape from England, were discussed as her destination. Eventually Bath, with its curative waters, was decided upon, when she was within eight weeks of her confinement. Accordingly, on April 17th, a doleful procession of travelling coaches, strongly guarded by armed horsemen, climbed a southern hill out of Oxford, from which on a spring morning may be seen an unforgettable view of towers and spires lit by fleeting sunshine. The Generalissima, who had ridden into the city glowing with vigour and happiness, left it broken in health and spirits, coughing incessantly as she crouched in the corner of a lumbering vehicle, every lurch of which she had reason to dread. A new and frightening internal pain, during the visitations of which she could not bear the least movement even in her vicinity, now vexed her. She thought that the damp airs of Thames-side were responsible for "my rhume", which was presently to become sadly familiar in her letters as "my old disease". Sir John Wintour, her physician in attendance, said that her disorder was hysterical.

In the little town of Abingdon, from which in summer days of drowsy heat the young king and queen with their lovely children had taken barge for Oxford, the procession halted for the night.[1] Next morning the travelling carriages, escorted by Lord Jermyn, set out westwards, into the Vale of the White Horse, and a small band of cavaliers, led by the melancholy-faced king, turned back silently to threatened Oxford. Charles and Henrietta had said their last farewell.[2]

[1] Dugdale.
[2] A letter preserved in the Bibliothèque de l'Arsenal, Paris, written in Italian, and purporting to be a translation of one sent by Henrietta to Charles II on the death of Charles I, declares that after this parting she fell into a swoon from which she did not recover until she was ten leagues distant from her husband.

CHAPTER V

LA REINE MALHEUREUSE

I

FROM various points on her journey Henrietta sent back messengers and baggage waggons to her anxious husband. A terror of being captured by the enemy in her present condition haunted her. After a few days' stay in Bath, although travelling manifestly increased her sufferings, she pressed on west. From Exeter, on May 3rd, alarmed by the violence of her symptoms, she sent a note to old Mayerne, imploring his assistance in her hour of need. Her letters to her husband gradually ceased to be concerned with anything but her physical distress. Charles wrote to the old doctor, "Mayerne, for the love of me, go find my wife".[1]

Mayerne was past three-score years and ten, but for love of Charles he set out instantly from his house in St Martin's Lane on a journey of over a hundred and seventy miles, taking with him a second opinion in the person of Sir Matthew Lister, also a royal physician, a gentleman of about his own age, perhaps a few years his senior. Anne of Austria, with characteristic generosity, now sent her distressed sister-in-law a complete *layette*, every object that could be needed in the confinement, Madame Peronne, still the best midwife in France, and a gift of fifty thousand pistoles. Retaining the smallest possible portion of the money for her own immediate needs, Henrietta at once forwarded the bulk of it to her husband. Newspapers were reporting the death of the Queen of England, after being delivered of a still-born child. Mayerne and Lister found their

[1] Sloane MS. 1679, f. 72.

most difficult patient still alive, but in the lowest possible spirits, and completely unnerved by the prospect of a worse ordeal than she was already enduring. After their arrival, she sent her husband the last letter she would be able to write before her confinement, "perhaps it will be the last letter you will ever receive from me". The cruel pains which she had suffered since she had parted from him, too severe to be understood by anyone who had not experienced them, made her believe that the time had come for her to think of another world. "If it be so, God's will be done." Jermyn and Father Philip would give him further messages from her. If she were to die, writing this letter had brought her great comfort. "Let it not trouble you, I beg. . . . Adieu, my dear heart." Her last wish was that she might see him again "in the position in which you ought to be".

At Bedford House, Exeter,[1] on June 16th, 1644, she gave birth to a living child, a daughter. De Sabran, an agent of inferior rank, despatched to England by Anne of Austria on the failure of Harcourt's mission, penetrated to Exeter eight days later and reported that he found the queen very weak and partially paralysed. Her child was of exceptional beauty. Henrietta's fears of death had not been realized, but to her dismay, instead of finding relief with her delivery, she was now prostrated by such agonies that she only wished for death. To add to her afflictions, the town in which she lay helpless was threatened by her enemies. She sent de Sabran to ask the invading general for a safe-conduct to Bath, to which Essex replied that her safety was no concern of his, and that he refused to say whether or not he intended to bombard Exeter. Henrietta arose from her sick-bed with the intention of making her way to France. She has been blamed for her desertion of her husband and children at this point in her career, but her letters to

[1] Bedford House, a mansion belonging to the Russell family, and built on the site of the convent of Black Friars, was demolished in 1773. The locality is now marked by Bedford Crescent.

Charles, describing her symptoms in great detail, present a classic case of puerperal sepsis.[1] The Generalissima was vanquished.

Fifteen days after her confinement, disguising herself in a humble dress, and taking with her only Sir John Wintour, one lady and her confessor, she stole from the city. About three miles outside Exeter, according to an almost incredible account of this escape,[2] she was obliged to take refuge in a hut, where she lay for forty-eight hours, without nourishment, crouched under a heap of litter. As the soldiers advancing on the town passed her hiding-place, she heard them swearing that fifty thousand crowns would be the reward of the man who carried the head of Henrietta to London. At length all "the Lobsters", as the Devon people nicknamed the parliamentarian infantry, passed by, darkness fell for the third time, and the distressed queen arose to hurry to a rendezvous on the Plymouth road, where "in a cabin in a wood" a perfect fairy-tale group awaited her. It included her massive chamberlain, her faithful dwarf and her favourite spaniel.

Six days later she reached Pendennis Castle, near Falmouth, carried in a litter, by the side of which, reports Wintour, he "walked most of the way into Cornwall".[3] A Cornish gentleman who encountered Henrietta, wrote to his wife that the poor queen, who did not look to him as if she had many hours to live, was the woefullest spectacle he had ever set eyes upon. Even Mayerne had pronounced that he believed she would die this time. In Falmouth Bay lay a little fleet of friendly Dutch vessels. On the night before her embarkation Henrietta sent her husband a letter commending several of her servants to him by name and expressing the hope that by God's grace she might recover her health in France, so as to serve him further. "I am giving you the strongest proof of love that I can give. I am hazarding my life, that I may not incommode your affairs. Adieu, my dear heart.

---

[1] Harl. MS. 7379, ff. 92, 96, 98, 99.
[2] Quoted in the sermon preached by Bossuet at her funeral.
[3] Ellis, series 3, vol. iv. p. 303.

If I die, believe that you will lose a person who has never been other than entirely yours, and who by her affection has deserved that you should not forget her."[1]

Her troubles, however, were not yet over. No sooner had she put to sea than she found herself pursued by enemy craft, which opened fire upon her. She forbade any return to be made, and begged the captain to crowd on all sail. If he considered escape impossible, she desired him to ignite the powder he had on board and sink his vessel. She afterwards regretted having given so selfish and un-Christian an order. Alone of the women on board she uttered no sound as the cannonading continued. When they were nearly in sight of Jersey a shot hit their boat, and all gave themselves up for lost. Their rigging was damaged, and they were forced to slacken sail. But at this moment some ships from Dieppe hove in sight, and the enemy abandoned the chase. Unfortunately, before the Dutch fleet could make Dieppe harbour, a storm sprang up, scattering their escort. Hours of misery followed, before the queen came in sight of the wild Breton shore near Brest, where the natives mistook her party for pirates and prepared to oppose their entry. Henrietta herself explained her identity, and the fisher-folk helped her to scramble ashore between rocky coves, up a precipitous path to a thatched hut. From this humble refuge she despatched Jermyn to announce her arrival to her sister-in-law and Mazarin, and beg that doctors might be sent to meet her at Angers. During the night the news that the daughter of Henri IV, who had been given in marriage to England, had returned to France "more like a miserable heroine of a romance than a true queen", spread in the neighbourhood, and next morning the obscure spot was crowded by Breton country gentlemen, arriving with carriages to offer her majesty every assistance on the next stage in her long journey.[2]

[1] Harl. MS. 7379, f. 96.
[2] de Motteville; de Gamache; de la Fayette; Bossuet; de Montpensier.

II

Bourbon l'Archambault, in the very heart of France, was a lovely place in which to repose a broken mind and body. It had a mouldering, ivy-hung castle with red-roofed turrets the shapes of witches' hats, a small grey church dating from the twelfth century, and a peaceful lake in which were mirrored the reflections of crowding green trees. Over the hedgeless roads that encircled the little town, sleek white oxen of the Bourbonnais dragged carts of primitive design towards fields heavy with harvest and cheerful with bright-coloured wild-flowers. The thermal springs of Bormonis had been famous in Roman times. Four hundred years ago, that formidable ruin on the wooded hill had been the scene of festivities to which the whole court of France had travelled. In August 1644 Bourbon was still very fashionable. The appearance of the most distinguished invalid taking the waters was eagerly observed by other summer visitors.

Nobody would have guessed that the Queen of England was not quite five-and-thirty. She walked bent double, helped along by two attendants. Only one of her wild dark eyes had vision. Her face was haggard and tiny, her figure, alas! shape-less. She was continually in tears for no reason, or at any rate no new reason. Her compatriots decided that this daughter of Bourbon had returned to the cradle of her race only to die. Instinctive antipathy against the perfidious island which had reduced a young and beautiful Frenchwoman to such a state, flared forth. When they had exhausted their expressions of indignation and sympathy, her fellow patients returned with gusto to discussing what exactly were the relations between their own Queen Regent and her chief counsellor.

"I have been everywhere received with such honours and marks of affection by everybody, from the greatest to the least

... I am so well treated everywhere", declared the lachrymose Henrietta.[1] Her sister-in-law, the Queen of France, had sent her, besides ten thousand pistoles and the patent for a pension of thirty thousand livres a month, one of her own favourite ladies-in-waiting to act as guide and companion. Françoise Langlois, Madame de Motteville, was suitable in every way for such a post. Her manners were particularly gentle. She was the daughter of a Gentleman of the King's Bedchamber, and a niece of the bishop-poet, Jean Bertaut. Her mother, a nobly born Spaniard, was a close friend of Spanish-born Anne of Austria. Although only twenty-three, Madame de Motteville had already been a widow for two years. She had been given at the age of eighteen to a bridegroom of eighty. She was a pretty, pensive, elegant woman, not intellectual, but full of intelligent interest in the wicked world about her. She was able to explain, in the most tactful way, that it would perhaps be inadvisable for the Queen of England to pursue her scheme of inviting the Duchesse de Chevreuse to join them in this retreat. The Duchesse, who had been joyfully recalled to court on the death of Cardinal Richelieu, had returned in too ebullient a mood. She had given offence to her old mistress and the new adviser, Cardinal Mazarin, by boasting of the unbounded influence she would now enjoy and her intention of using it on behalf of her late benefactors in England. The cardinal had considered that her somewhat tarnished figure was not suitable at the side of a widowed Queen Regent. In fact, the Duchesse was now back in banishment again. Henrietta sadly but instantly resigned herself to the abandonment of a friendship which might prejudice her husband's interests. She had travelled through half-remembered scenes by slow stages, for a month, in pelting heat. In the bustling provincial towns of Tours, Orleans and Nevers she had been received in state. Half crazy with pain, insomnia and excitement, she had returned ingratiat-

[1] Harl. MS. 7379, f. 99.

ing answers to influential people. On her arrival at Bourbon the
Jesuits had presented her with a copy of verses, expressing their
hope that both her arm and her heart would here be relieved.
"This is very well done; but do still more", said she, meaning
that she hoped for financial assistance for her king.

She then collapsed, and lay for three weeks, unable even to send
a line to Charles. Her heart-muscle was affected, an abscess had
formed in one of her breasts, a toxic rash covered her body. She
complained of numbness in all her limbs, especially one of her
arms, and of such drowsiness that she could not make any mental
effort. Not until September 7th did she take up her pen to
write to her husband. "I begin to hope that I shall not die. . . .
Now that I am better, I may tell you that I have been very ill,
and that I never expected to see you again." With her first
flickering hopes of recovery came emotional thoughts of her
first-born son. The Prince of Wales was now fourteen, and
growing fast. She sent a message asking for his measurements,
so that she could have a suit of armour made for him in France.
No news from England, or rather "nothing in the world" from
the king of that disturbed country, penetrated to this remote
paradise, but "I would not add to the ills I suffer that of suppos-
ing that you think no more about me".[1] It was as well that she
could not see some of the evidences of her unpopularity now
current in the kingdom from which she had fled. *The Great Eclipse
of the Sun, or Charles, his Waine, overclouded by the Evil Influences
of the Moon*, published in London this month, bore upon its title-
page, besides the words "Thy subjects' blood, with fire and
sword, cries Vengeance, Lord!" an insulting caricature of
Charles, pointing with unsheathed blade at his chief adviser,
the baleful moon, grinning down upon scenes of murder and
arson.

Even while in peril on the sea, according to one of her Capuchins, the queen had suffered "violent apprehensions for her

[1] Harl. MS. 7379, f. 90 B.

infant, abandoned to the fury of those tigers". She did not yet know that, twelve days after her flight from Falmouth, her distracted husband had entered Exeter, and Lady Dalkeith, a Villiers by birth, to whom she had entrusted her fortnight-old daughter, had placed in Charles's arms the one of his children who was to resemble his wife most closely. He had caused his chaplain to baptize the infant princess by the name of her mother.[1]

At first Madame de Motteville could do little for her unknown royal charge. The eminent physicians sent from Paris held sway. Henrietta's breast was lanced, she began to take the waters and, as soon as she had strength, the baths. She regained the use of her eyes, her head became less painful, and the size of her body diminished. But as her physical condition improved, terrible memories crowded upon her brain. She could think and speak of nothing but the revolution in England. Madame de Motteville ministered to a brain diseased, and by the time that the physicians could do no more for her, the queen had regained enough of her natural courage to face the prospect of returning to the world with some of her old courage and vivacity. She had also gained a friend far more valuable than the one whose companionship she had denied herself. Madame de Motteville noted with enthusiasm that, although her mental and physical distresses had prematurely destroyed the beauty attested by portraits of the Queen of England during the days of her prosperity, she possessed points that were not dependent upon youthful freshness. Her eyes and her complexion were admirable, her nose was well formed. Since her face had become so emaciated, her mouth, always her worst feature, appeared unduly large, but there was something so sweet in her expression, and so gracious in her manner, that she would continue to win hearts to the end of her days. Her temperament natur-

---

[1] The name of Anne, out of compliment to her aunt, the Regent, was apparently added after the princess's arrival in France.

ally inclined towards gaiety, and in the middle of a tragic discourse, if suddenly reminded of some ludicrous incident that might amuse her audience, she would suspend her narrative to explain it, even while tears rained down her cheeks.[1]

October winds from the neighbouring mountains drove away most visitors from the fashionable watering-place. The pathetic figure of the little Queen of England, attended by the large English peer who was the head of her household, her sympathetic ladies, her dwarf, her pet dogs, was amongst the few silhouetted against the melancholy vacancy of a popular resort out of the season. At last even her tottering daily promenade towards the curative baths was discontinued. She had taken as much of the Bourbon waters as her physicians considered advisable in her present weak state. She wrote to her dumb and distant husband that she did not feel much better as yet, but that, she was assured, was the way with this treatment. It was not until several weeks after you had left this place that you suddenly began to feel yourself marvellously strong and well.

She now had to brace herself to meet members of her own family whom she had not seen since she had left France as a bride. A small olive-skinned gentleman with restless black eyes, pursed lips and arched eyebrows, wearing a fiercely upturned moustache, a tuft of beard, and garments cut in the last extreme of fashion, arrived to conduct her to Paris. This was "Monsieur" —Jean-Baptiste-Gaston, Duke of Orleans, her only surviving brother. Sixteen years spent in political intrigues fully as unsuccessful as those in which she had recently engaged herself, had marked his features with a permanent expression of surprised disgust. He was already beginning to discover that he was not to enjoy much more influence under the new cardinal than under the old one.

Brother and sister set out together, and at Nevers, the first important town on their route, Henrietta was greeted by

[1] de Motteville.

enough news from England to convince her that she was again in touch with a world in which work was awaiting her. Three letters from her husband, the first of which bore a date nine weeks old, told her of the safety of her children, his successes over the army of Essex in Cornwall, and his hopes that she would be able to send him support from France. Excitement gave her the strength to walk alone to interview and question the messenger who had brought such a packet of good tidings, but the effort proved too much for her. She had to employ Jermyn's pen to send her husband an answer in a new and intricate cipher. Her own effort at a short personal note, assuring him that she would never be really happy or well apart from him, produced a blinding headache. High fever followed, and an abscess developed in her crippled arm. Her state entry to Paris had to be deferred. After an interval of three weeks, her physicians, enjoining her to continue to drink asses' milk every morning, pronounced her fit to move again. She wrote to her sister Christine, regretting that she had not been able to come up to meet her at Chambery, as she had hoped. Still, now that she had become so great a traveller, she considered their plan for a reunion only postponed.[1]

Ten miles outside the French capital, on an early November day, she was met by the important lady who was to ride by her side in a royal coach to the Louvre. Her brother Gaston's only daughter by his first marriage (to the heiress of Montpensier) appeared already, at seventeen, as fully developed in mind and body as she was ever likely to be. Anne-Marie-Louise d'Orleans bore no resemblance to her father's family. She was a tall ash-blonde, with a big aquiline nose, prominent blue eyes, a long brightly coloured mouth full of bad teeth, and an air of ineffable condescension. The blooming, spoilt girl, whose chief sources of pride were her wealth, her birth and her high spirits, looked at the small, *passée* figure installed beside her, and determined

[1] Ferrero.

to note in her *mémoires* that although her unknown aunt had evidently taken great pains over her appearance for this occasion, the result could inspire no emotion but pity. On the outskirts of the city their *tête-à-tête* was interrupted by the approach of more relatives. The Queen Regent of France and the Queen of England met upon an enormous carpet spread over the miry high-road at Montrouge. Anne of Austria was attended by her two sons, the King of France, aged six, and the Duke of Anjou, aged four. Both children were very dark, and the younger, whose eyes and hair were jet-black, was really too beautiful for a boy. The sisters-in-law embraced, and wept at the changes wrought by sixteen years. Anne of Austria had grown unattractively stout, but was still vain of her peerless white hands. Henrietta, who had no illusions as to her own ravaged looks, declared that she had perceived their departure when she was two-and-twenty, and did not believe that the beauties of most ladies lasted much longer.[1] Anne, large in heart as in body, showed no signs of remembering the petty malices to which she had been subjected by a sparkling and much-courted Daughter of France, at the instigation of Marie de Medicis. The whole royal party embarked together in the same coach, and drove through decorated streets over the Pont Neuf to the palace in which Henrietta had been born. Here she was installed in apartments which were to be hers for eight years. Court mourning for her sister, the Queen of Spain, whose death, after child-birth, had actually occurred nearly a month before, was now announced.

III

Henrietta paid a state visit of thanksgiving to Notre Dame, and received congratulatory deputations upon her safe arrival, from the city of Paris and many old friends. The most important man in France, who performed no act without tortuous

[1] de Motteville.

calculation, had absented himself from the scene of her arrival.
He visited her quietly on the morning succeeding her entry.
As in the days of her youth, France was being ruled in the name
of a Queen Regent, for an infant king, by a cardinal. Anne of
Austria, however, had no intention of disputing the power
wielded by the man whom she had raised to his present position,
and Jules Mazarin, once Giulio Mazarini, Intendant to the noble
house of Colonna, who had gained his influence over a long-
neglected woman by expressions of romantic admiration, dutifully continued the treatment which had produced such satisfactory results. Henrietta wrote to her husband, asking him to
note that he must begin his letters to the Cardinal "My cousin",
and end them "your affectionate cousin". The polished rouged
Italian of forty-two, whose regular features gained significance
and dignity owing to the presence upon them of a slight perpetual frown, had shown himself "most obliging" at their first
interview. She had since sent Jermyn to talk business with him.
She felt optimistic and almost herself again, although only the
sight of her husband—for which she hoped with the spring—
could restore her to complete health. He must not think that
she was so well treated here that she did not wish to return to
England. But for the thought that by her hourly endeavours
in this court she was serving him best, she would take no
pleasure in her present comfort.

Jermyn also was finding comfort. Many acquaintances of his
Paris Embassy days were delighted to discover an old friend in
the large and amusing Englishman who now occupied so conspicuous a position in the household of their distressed princess.
His continual presence at Henrietta's side, which had caused so
much scandal in England, was here accepted without a shrug or
the raising of an eyebrow. He was "le favori", and there was an
end of the matter. Even Madame de Motteville, a model of
propriety, calmly gave him this title. She added that, in her
opinion, although honest and very good-humoured, he was not

a man of parts, and that his advice was not always followed by his queen. Jermyn, with the pleasure-loving man's genius for deputing work, had discovered a willing secretary in the shape of a stern young singer of humble birth. While Mr Abraham Cowley worked all days and three or four nights of every week transcribing letters from the queen to the Prince of Orange, the Duke of Lorraine, and the new Pope, Innocent X, asking for pecuniary and military assistance, and, further, putting into a scarifyingly complicated cipher, volumes of advice, propositions and complaints to his king, Baron Jermyn of St Edmondsbury, in charge of her majesty's finances, rolled to every entertainment in mid-winter Paris, in his new coach, spattering noblemen of ancient lineage who had reduced themselves to penury in the royalist cause. There were many fierce hatreds amongst the band of refugees that gradually collected around Henrietta at the Louvre. Several of them bore names which showed that they were a direct legacy from the courts of the Tudor sovereigns. Amongst the families who followed her into exile were Careys, Denhams, Crofts, Killigrews and Berkeleys.

The Duke of Newcastle, "transported with passion and despair", after the destruction of his beloved northern army at the battle of Marston Moor, had thrown up his commission and retired to Holland. Many royalists regarded his action as treachery, but Henrietta, who sympathized with his complaints of the rashness of her nephew Rupert, answered his letters of explanation with unchanged friendliness, and when he arrived to join her little court, welcomed him warmly. She had begun to realize that money was raised in Paris no quicker than at the Hague, and communication with England was even more difficult. Weeks multiplied themselves into months without bringing news from her husband, and the "Flying reports" and "London prints" current in Paris all described defeats to his arms. Still she laboured indefatigably. She lent an ear to a Jesuit called O'Hartegan, who came as mouthpiece of the confederate

Catholics of his country, with a scheme for landing in England an Irish army, to be financed by the cardinal. Her Grand Almoner, the Bishop of Angoulême, applied in her name to the Catholics of France for a loan, to be repaid by instalments. The bishop, who was a popular preacher, delivered in the month of February to the General Assembly of French clergy in Paris, a moving oration in which he described his mistress's zeal in forwarding the interests of her Church during the days of her prosperity, and her piteous "fall from a kingdom to slavery". His stirring account of the persecutions she had endured in England made a hopeless confusion of her Bridlington and Falmouth escapes, but fortunately few who heard him were aware of his inaccuracy.

Spring, to which Henrietta had looked forward with such hope, brought her a train of disasters. The Dutch refused to allow the troops raised for service in England by the Duke of Lorraine, to pass through their territory; the papal nuncio despatched from Rome to Ireland was not the man that she would have chosen for the post; O'Hartegan was unmasked as a complete rascal; the sum raised by her Almoner's appeal was "fitter to buy hangings for a chamber than prosecute a war". Rumours that Charles was exposing himself to unnecessary dangers, and about to offer his enemies a peace upon bare and unsafe terms, drove her to distraction. "Be kind to me, or you kill me", she wrote to her husband, and suggested a fresh cipher to be employed by themselves alone, and not even communicated to Jermyn. She caught a chill, and suffered a relapse. The best doctors of France hastened to bleed the enfeebled woman, but for the third time in twelve months she made an unexpected recovery from "within two fingers of death". The invisible chain binding her to England and Charles was as strong as ever. The following letter is the last of the series captured and published after the battle of Naseby.[1]

[1] Harl. MS. 7379, f. 83.

MY DEAR HEART,

This letter is only to assure you that God has still pleased to leave me in this world to do you some service, and that excepting a severe cold which my fever has left, and my old disease, I am tolerably well. The physicians give me to hope that the spring will cure me perfectly, which I the rather wish that I may see you again before I die, than for any love I have for the world, for all that troubled me during my illness was that I was dying far from you; otherwise I did not care about it much. I hope He will yet again give me this joy (which I wait for) with much impatience. I refer to Jermyn to write many things to you, not yet being able to do it myself.

Adieu, my dear heart.   PARIS, May 17th, 1645.

The crushing defeat of her husband at the battle of Naseby[1] two months later, put an end for the moment to her hopes of rejoining him, but as usual she refused to bow to misfortune. She declared that this disaster should hasten French assistance, and took comfort in the continued kindness of the Queen Regent and the cardinal, and the series of splendid victories achieved in Scotland by the gallant Montrose. On the very day that she ordered a Te Deum to be sung in celebration of the conquest of Scotland, Montrose was vanquished at Philiphaugh. Two days earlier Prince Rupert had delivered up Bristol to the enemy, an act for which Charles never really forgave him.

With the approach of the dead season in Paris, Henrietta had moved out to the château of St Germain, which Anne of Austria had munificently presented to her as a summer residence. During the minority of Louis XIV the French court never occupied the Louvre, so the Queen of England had possession of all the royal apartments of two palaces. The monthly pension

[1] A biography of Henrietta Maria cannot pretend to give any detailed account of the Civil Wars. The queen was present in England for only seventeen months of the conflict, and for over six months of this time she was a complete invalid.

assigned to her was large, but so were her expenses. Since she sent more money than she could comfortably spare to her husband, many of the royalist refugees who crowded to her for relief found the only support offered them sympathetic words and trifling souvenirs. Discontent grew in her mimic court, and on one occasion she had to come out of her chamber to command the cessation of a noisy dispute about money between members of her suite, who had actually drawn their swords in her antechamber. For a few months after her arrival, says her niece, Mademoiselle de Montpensier, "she was attended as a queen should be, with a full number of ladies in waiting, maids of honour, running footmen, coaches and guards. Little by little, however, all these disappeared, and soon nothing marked the loss of her dignity more than the appearance of her retinue." This year was very dull, adds Mademoiselle, and she visited her aunt assiduously. "In her miserable condition her greatest pleasure was to talk in an exaggerated manner of her past prosperity—the sweetness of the life she had led in England, the beauty and excellence of that country, the entertainments she had which she had been given—above all the splendid qualities of her son, the Prince of Wales. She showed such desire that I should see him that I guessed her intentions, and what follows will show that I was not mistaken in my conclusions."

Henrietta was indeed considering the advantages of a match between her purse-proud niece and her beloved eldest son, entirely with a view to utilizing Mademoiselle's fortune in the royalist cause. Mademoiselle, with equal materialism, was occupied with the possibility of becoming Queen of Spain. Philip IV was now a widower. He was mentally unbalanced and vilely unhealthy, but, leaving the man himself out of the question, a splendid match.

Henrietta was becoming extremely nervous for the safety of her eldest son, who for the past seven months had been

separated from his father. The loyal west to which he had been
sent was now threatened. She wrote to the king, urging him
to order the prince to join her in Paris, and at the same time
sent word to Lady Dalkeith at Exeter, asking that her youngest
child should be brought to her. The vessel carrying these letters
was captured near Dartmouth. The captain, to whom they had
been entrusted, made an effort to cast them overboard, but
they were rescued from the waters and the gist of them appeared
in February 1646 in the *Weekly Intelligencer*. Towards the
gloomy close of 1645 even the dauntless Henrietta admitted to
her brother, the Duke of Orleans, that "the state of my affairs
in England, as you know, are in so bad a condition that I
expect nothing but entire ruin unless France assist us". She
suggested that the duke should use his influence with the Regent
and the cardinal, now that French troops engaged against Spain
were retiring to winter quarters, to detach some for service in
England. Mazarin, however, although as pleasant as usual, had
no men or money to spare for her. Early in the New Year
she turned in despair to a plan which she had hitherto rejected,
of an alliance with the Scots, and Charles, at Oxford, began
the negotiations which were to end in his taking the fatal step
of delivering himself into the hands of his northern subjects.

Not one of the many letters despatched by Henrietta to her
husband between January and October 1646 has survived, but
no fewer than sixty-four received by her from him during
that year are extant. Copies of them came to light in 1855,
when a gentleman living in Bath bought from an antique-
dealer of that city a small quarto parchment-covered volume,
containing eighty-eight manuscript leaves, entirely in the hand
of a single transcriber, probably of the early eighteenth century.
The antique-dealer had obtained the book from an auctioneer's
porter, who sometimes amused himself with picking up odd
lots at the many sales which he attended. Further than that the
history of the little book could not be traced. The generally

accepted theory is that after the king's letters to Henrietta had been deciphered they were copied into a book for purposes of reference, and the existing manuscript is a transcription of such a collection. Much of the royal correspondence at this time was transmitted by means of a friendly Portuguese agent, Souza de Macedo, who continued resident in London throughout the Civil Wars.[1]

Charles I was a good letter-writer. His style, which is elegant, but tends to become flowery and involved, is a model of clarity when he is moved. Similarly, at his trial he overcame his habitual stammer. His vocabulary is an interesting mixture of the English of old Merrie England and that of to-day. When he finds himself "strangely and barbarously threatened", condemns the Scotch treaty as "fourbery" or grieves that his sweetheart had been "juggled withall", Richard II or Othello might be speaking. On the other hand, his statement that a proposal to go to London will be "the best put-off" that he can give the Scots, and his gloomy postscript "I owe Jack £9,200", strike a startlingly modern note. Montrose, whose name occurs repeatedly is always "Mountrose" and the future Lord Clarendon "Ned Hide".

The court of the Queen Regent aimed at a decorous tone. A succession of gaieties was not the rule during the months that Henrietta received these letters. Still, there were grand ceremonial occasions, such as the visit to Parliament of the boy king, and the ball given in honour of the Queen of Poland, in the theatre of the Great Saloon at the Palais Royal. At Mardi Gras a comedy with music was performed, and a concert of twenty violins in a small chamber was a common occurrence. The Queen of England could not absent herself from any entertainment to which she was invited, nor present herself with a hanging countenance. The best for which she could hope, as her aching head and her wasted frame were dressed

[1] Camden Society, vol. 63.

for the ball or the comedy at the Palais Royal, was that during her absence Mr Cowley might be deciphering another long letter, gently pointing out the differences between the creed of the Scots rebels and that of the Church of England, and that the weary man who had brought this treasure all the way from Oxford, and seen its writer, might be awaiting her torrent of questions in some quiet corner of the shuttered Louvre. The names of the audacious and untiring men who crossed and re-crossed the Channel in these days—Pooly, Elliott, Progers, Seymour, Talbot, Bennet and Legg—become as familiar in the letters as the name-days of the week; and not all of them were lucky. "William Prettyman, employed three years in the Heat of the War, conveying letters from the Queen to the late King", presented, over twenty years later, his humble petition for some compensation for his imprisonment and ransom.

Charles indulged the maddening habit of quoting his wife's own words to her with such disarming preambles as "I am doubly grieved to differ with thee in opinion, though I am confident that my judgment, not love, is censured by thee for it". Now he was the resolute one, she the party bent upon making concessions. "For the Scots", he says, "I promise thee to employ all possible pains and industry to agree with them, so the price be not giving up the Church of England, with which I will not part upon any condition whatsoever. . . . For I assure thee, I put little or no difference between setting up the Presby-terian government or submitting to the Church of Rome. Therefore make the case thine own. With what patience wouldest thou give ear to him who should persuade thee, for worldly respects, to leave the communion of the Roman church for any other? Indeed, sweet heart, this is my case." Early in the year he still hoped "by the blessing of God, to overcome all my misfortunes and that we shall live together again as we have done". Henrietta, to whom the Presbyterian and the

HENRIETTA MARIA
The Bride

CHARLES I, AS PRINCE OF WALES

The Bridegroom

CHARLES II, AS PRINCE OF WALES
"Mi Deare Sone, the Prince"

FIVE OF THE CHILDREN OF CHARLES I

HENRIETTA MARIA
after Vandyck

HENRIETTA MARIA
by Vandyck

HENRIETTA ANNE
"Minette"

HENRIETTA MARIA

"The Widow of the Martyr"

Episcopalian faiths were alike heresy, did not foresee the appalling danger into which he was running. Few letters, however,
are more clearly marked by a sense of approaching doom than
those written by Charles as he prepared to leave Oxford for the
north. On April 4th he wrote that the Scotch were to send their
horse to meet him at Harborough, "where I shall be on Wednesday next, resolving to go from hence the night before. I
will trouble you now with no more cyphers. . . . No misfortune can take away the contentment of our mutual constant
affections." Two days later he is still confident "by the Grace
of God to join with the Scotch on Wednesday, at Harborough".
He sends a message of thanks to his wife's French hosts, and
the curious phrase "if I should miscarry" makes its first appearance. Still his only fear is lest he should be captured on his
journey. Nearly three weeks pass before mistrust of the Scots
becomes suddenly acute. They are "abominable relapsed rogues".
They have retracted almost every promise made by them to
him, advisers are crowding around him to dissuade him from
his journey. "The dispatch of the greatest importance and the
saddest that ever I sent thee", after unfolding various plans for
an escape in disguise, ends, "In the meantime, I conjure thee,
by thy constant love to me, that if I should miscarry (whether
by being taken by the rebels or otherwise) to continue the same
active endeavours for Pr. Charles as thou hast done for me, and
not whine for my misfortunes in a retired way, but, like thy
father's daughter, vigorously assist Pr. Charles to regain his
own".

Five days later, very early in the morning, the king with two
companions only, quitted Oxford. After wandering for another
five days apparently in a condition of utter irresolution, he
entered the Scots camp at Newark on May 5th, 1646.

IV

In France the summer of 1646 was excessively hot. The Queen
Regent retired early in the season to Fontainebleau, where she
and her ladies spent their days entirely in the cool depths of the
forest or the waters of the Seine. The dust which they collected
on their passage through the woods was soon washed away,
says Madame de Motteville, by the solacing river. Everyone
immersed themselves in the Seine for several hours of every day.
The massive queen and all who had the honour to attend her
wore bathing costumes of grey linen, which trailed on the
ground. The little king and his governor, who joined in their
sport, were similarly attired, so "modesty received no wound".
Except for the officers of the household and a few courtiers who
happened to be ministers of state, no gentlemen were present
at these aquatic revelries worthy of the brush of Rubens. All
able-bodied men over sixteen were away fighting Spain in
Flanders. The news that the Prince of Wales had arrived safely
at St Germain, and that the Regent had invited his mother to
bring him upon a three-days visit, caused excitement in the
small and almost wholly female court at Fontainebleau. Before
he could present himself, however, there were serious matters to
be settled. The Queen of England sent to ask if her son ought
to take precedence of his host, the boy king. Such had been the
etiquette on the occasion of his father's visit, when Prince of
Wales, to the King of Spain. The Regent replied that her
brother had yielded precedence then because his guest had been
travelling under the name of the King of Scotland. An armchair would be accorded to the Prince of Wales in her drawing-
room, but upon the entrance of the consort of a reigning
sovereign, even though in this case she happened to be his
mother, he must exchange his armchair for a joint stool. When
they happened to meet in the promenade or the dance the
eight-year-old king would, of course, apologize profusely before

taking precedence of the sixteen-year-old prince. At last all the formalities on which the Spanish-born Anne of Austria set such store were arranged, and on a July day the little Queen of England, attended by the big eldest son who was, she secretly admitted, her favourite child, set out for delicious Fontaine-bleau.

Their visit-opened inauspiciously. No dazzling group of ex-pectant courtiers was assembled at the entrance of the palace to greet them. In fact, the palace was empty. Although the cardinal had encouraged the removal to France of the Prince of Wales he did not wish to offend the ruling powers in England by identifying himself with the interests of their rejected rulers. This visit must be made to appear a mere friendly meeting of a few close relatives, devoid of any political significance. Hen-rietta tactfully failed to notice any studied neglect in her re-ception, enquired into what direction the Regent had driven, and ordered her coach to take the same route. On one of the many dead-straight roads that cut through the solemn aisles of the royal forest of Fontainebleau, the guests came up with the French court. Anne of Austria's suite watched with eager interest the descent from a dusty equipage of the familiar figure of the Queen of England, followed by a tall, strange young man. Henrietta presented her son first to the King, then to the Queen of France. His hostess, after kissing the prince, presented him to the foremost lady of her court, her heiress-niece. Both "La grande Mademoiselle" and Madame de Motteville have left on record their first impressions of the future Charles II. He was well made, says the elder lady; his brown complexion accorded excellently with his fine black eyes; his mouth was large and ugly, but his figure was very good. Mademoiselle says with less enthusiasm, "he was only sixteen or seventeen, but quite tall for his age. His head was noble, his hair black, his complexion brown, his person passably agreeable." After the exchange of a few compliments the royalties packed into the Regent's coach for return to the palace, and short though their journey was, it was long enough for all parties. The voluble Henrietta's much-vaunted son appeared to be a deaf-mute. He either could not, or would not, reply to a single remark. He looked the part of a grandson of France well enough. With dismay the ladies who were to be his close companions for three days realized that "he neither spoke nor understood French, a most inconvenient thing". On arrival at the palace the little king gave his hand to Henrietta, and the prince, in solemn silence, offered his arm to the Regent. The guests were deposited in their apartments without the slightest delay. Luckily at Fontainebleau, even at short notice, hunting-parties could always be arranged. Formal morning calls by the prince upon every princess of France, were, however, ceremonies that could not be evaded. He presented himself in the Regent's drawing-room, and was accorded his armchair. Hard on his heels arrived his mother, and he gladly withdrew to stand amongst a group of courtiers. The three-days visit passed off as well as could be expected, and Henrietta poured into her niece's ear some soothing flatteries. The Prince of Wales found his cousin exactly the type that he most admired. If his mother had not prevented him he would have been presenting himself in Mademoiselle's chamber at all hours. He was in despair at the death of the Empress, because he anticipated that Mademoiselle might be given in marriage to the Emperor. "I guessed her designs from the moment that she told me that he talked of me incessantly", commented the haughty blonde. "I listened to all she said, but I did not put all the faith in it that perhaps she desired. I do not know whether the prince might have fared better had he spoken for himself." Charles, however, did not speak for himself. His counsellors, even his father's wise old Secretary of State, Sir Edward Nicholas, had been against his joining his mother at the French court. They had considered him safer in Jersey, where he had spent the last two months. But his mother had sent him a letter which he could not ignore—a command from his father to obey the queen "in everything except religion, concerning which I am confident she will not trouble you; and see that you go no whither without her, or my particular direction". He had no choice but to show himself "a dutiful son and a careful one". Henrietta, convinced that a penniless prince of sixteen in Paris ran less risk than one who possessed even a little money, appropriated the pittance allotted to him by his French hosts, told him that the Princess Louise of Orange and the Infanta of Portugal had been decided against as possible mates for him, and ordered him to occupy his time by courting his large heiress-cousin.

The Scots army had taken the king to Newcastle. His letters complained that he was neither allowed to choose his servants nor communicate with his friends. He still enjoyed a semblance of freedom, "both he and his train having liberty to go abroad and play at Goff in the Shield Field, without the walls", but this would only continue so long as his captors had hopes that he would sign the Covenant. He was doing his best to gain time, for he believed that so unruly a body of men must, if given opportunity, fall out with the English rebels.

Over four years ago Henrietta had written from Holland to her husband, "I wish that you would send and fetch away the children, who are at London, for, if affairs get to an extremity, they are not well to be there".[1] Four of her children, James, Duke of York, aged thirteen, Henry, Duke of Gloucester, aged six, and the Princesses Elizabeth and Henrietta, aged ten and two, were now in the hands of her enemies. Her worst anxieties were on behalf of her infant daughter. When she had heard that Exeter was besieged she had sent reproachful messages to Lady Dalkeith, to whom she had entrusted her baby. This lady, however, had been doing her best. She had been totally unable to escape from the city. After its capture she had been allowed to

[1] Harl. MS. 7379, f. 61 B.

go with her charge to Oatlands. She had been in communication, on behalf of the child, with parliamentary generals, the Speaker of the House of Commons, and the Committee for the County of Surrey. At length she had been informed that she was to be dismissed and the princess was to be brought to London to share the captivity of her brothers and sister. Determined not to be deposed, Lady Dalkeith decided upon a bold step. On Friday, July 25th, 1646, she dressed herself in a tattered and patched gown, stuffed out her back with linen, so as to disguise her stately figure, and set out on foot for the coast. She passed as the wife of her *valet de chambre*, who was her only attendant, and the heavy, twenty-five-months-old child, who was carried in turn by them all the way to Dover, was addressed by them as "Pierre". At the port, the English authorities were only too glad to see a family of French beggars stagger aboard the Calais packet. Henrietta's Capuchin, Father Cyprien de Gamache, who was with his mistress when the news of her child's escape arrived, tells the end of this romantic story. The queen, he says, immediately sent carriages to fetch to St Germain the heroic *gouvernante* and "her precious deposit which she had so happily preserved amidst so many awful dangers. O, the transports of joy! O, the excessive consolation to the heart of the queen! She embraced, she hugged, she kissed again and again, that royal infant. . . . Many thanksgivings did she render God for this mercy; and, regarding the Princess as *un enfant de bénédiction*, she resolved with the grace of God to have her instructed in the Catholic and Roman religion, and to use her efforts to obtain the consent of the King her husband."[1]

Henrietta now had the companionship of the only two amongst her six surviving children whose looks gave strong evidence of their French blood. Her namesake Henriette-Anne, who, when she had last seen her had been a fifteen-day-old baby suffering from convulsions, had grown into an active little

[1] de Motteville; de Gamache; de la Fayette.

girl of two, with a glowing complexion, a head covered with golden-brown curls and a pair of dark-blue eyes sparkling with intelligence. Her precocity indeed had been a cause of some anxiety to her supposed parents during her escape, for she had plucked contemptuously at the wretched clothes in which she had been dressed and announced herself shrilly, "Not Pierre. Princess!" The large, solemn, silent Prince of Wales found this piece of quicksilver an amusing plaything during these depressing days. He gave her the nickname of "Minette", "little puss". Their harassed, scolding, loving, eternally letter-writing little mother was "Mam" to them. Henrietta, less lonely and in better health than she had been for over two years, was busier than ever.

She sent the accomplished Sir Kenelm Digby to Rome, but his extravagant eloquence failed to move the new Pope, who merely commented that he thought the Queen of England's agent slightly mad. Another of her friends, the Prince of Orange, was certainly now suffering from delusions. These had taken the unfortunate shape of extreme jealousy of his son and heir.

In October a new terror began to assail Henrietta. "We hear from London that the Scots are resolved to deliver you up into the hands of Parliament." [1] She considered leaving the security of France to adventure with her son into Ireland. He, meanwhile, was performing the only duty allotted to him, in his own way. The winter season of 1646 was unusually gay in Paris. The Prince of Wales followed *la Grande Mademoiselle* like a shadow. Before an entertainment given in her niece's honour Henrietta herself helped to dress the heroine of the evening. The swarthy prince, attired in Mademoiselle's colours of carnation, white and black, held a torch near by her, while the last touches were given to her *toilette*. When she arrived at the house where the assembly was being held, he was waiting on the doorstep to hand her out of her coach. He followed her into a

---

[1] *Clarendon State Papers*, ii. 271.

chamber where she rearranged her hair before a mirror, and again held a torch to cast a light upon her. He had now provided himself with an interpreter in the shape of his cousin, Prince Rupert. While Mademoiselle beautified herself, the hawk-faced Palatine prince informed her that the Prince of Wales understood everything that she said to him. She gravely noted this in her *mémoires* as an extraordinary thing, considering that he was supposed to know not one word of her language. His gallantry finally achieved its highest peak at a fête given at the Palais Royal, where an Italian comedy was followed by a ball. "My gown", announces Mademoiselle, "shimmered all over with diamonds, and was trimmed with tufts of carnation, black and white. I had upon me all the crown jewels, as well as those which the Queen of England still owned then. No one was more magnificently dressed than I that day, and I did not fail to find many people to tell me of my splendour and to talk about my beautiful figure, my graceful bearing, the whiteness of my skin and the sheen of my blond hair. These, they said, adorned me more than all the riches which glittered upon me." A throne raised by three steps and covered by a canopy overlooked the dancing-floor. Neither the little king nor the Prince of Wales would occupy it, so Mademoiselle sat there in state, alone. The prince, who was to become the most famous lover in Europe, stretched himself beneath her and lay like Hamlet at the feet of Ophelia during the play scene. Mademoiselle looked down upon him "with my heart as well as my eyes", and decided that he was an object of pity. "The thought that I should marry the Emperor was foremost in my mind. . . . I realized that the Emperor was neither a young nor a gallant man, but the truth was that I cared more for my establishment than for the person of my suitor. . . . I must not forget to say that at this ball of which I have just spoken, the Queen of England noticed that I looked at her son somewhat disdainfully. When she learned the cause of it she reproached me, and said that my head was full of nothing but the Emperor. I defended myself as well as I could, but my face disguised my sentiments so poorly that one had only to look at me to discover them."

v

On the second day of the New Year that was so gay in Paris, Charles I wrote to his wife:

DEARE HART,

I must tell thee that now I am declared what I have really beene ever since I came to this army, which is a prisoner.[1]

The Scottish Parliament, having discovered that he had no intention of taking the Covenant, had no further use for him. On January 30th their army turned homewards from Newcastle, and shortly afterwards received the first instalment of the sum agreed upon with the English Parliament in exchange for the person of their king. Charles was conducted by a party of English commissioners to Holmby House, Northamptonshire.[2] Here he resided for four months, whilst his enemies, as he had hoped, quarrelled amongst themselves. He read much, and was better treated than he had been at Newcastle. Henrietta could picture him at Holmby, for she knew the large Elizabethan house well. There, eleven years before, George Conn, papal nuncio, had brought her the picture of St Catharine which she had fastened to the curtains of her bed. But she now had no regular means of communication with her husband. In May, a Major Bosvile was arrested in the disguise of a rustic, and charged with having carried messages from the queen to the king.[3] On being questioned about the contents of the letters, which he had succeeded in delivering, the gallant officer declared

[1] *Clarendon State Papers*, ii. 324.
[2] It had been rebuilt by John of Padua for Sir Christopher Hatton, the Elizabethan Chancellor, and bought in 1607 by James I.
[3] Tanner MS. 58. 44.

that in such parts of them as he had been able to read, her majesty had desired his majesty "to seek his own privileges and rights, and secure his friends and settle the kingdom in peace, though she never came over into England again". He added that she had deplored the troubles in Ireland and asked permission for the Prince of Wales to accompany his uncle the Duke of Orleans to war against Spain. A few weeks later, "a handsome lady and wondrous bold", suspected of having visited the king, was seized and searched. She managed to slip behind some hangings in the chamber in which she was interrogated, a letter which was only discovered after some days, and even then proved useless to its captors, since it was entirely in cipher.

On the morning of June 2nd, a Cornet Joyce, who had been a tailor, arrived at Holmby with five hundred horse. Two mornings later, on the lawn outside the house, Charles asked to see the cornet's commission, and Joyce in answer silently pointed to the troopers behind him. Charles with his slow smile replied that it was as fair a commission as he had seen in his life. The military party was now in the ascendancy. He was removed south, and at Caversham, in Berkshire, was allowed to receive a visit from the three of his children, who were, like himself, prisoners. His meeting with his little daughter and two sons, the younger of whom did not recognize him, made a mournful impression upon General Cromwell, who was a spectator of the scene. By August the king had been established at Hampton Court.

Henrietta, full of hope at the transference of power from Parliament to the army, despatched to England Sir John Denham, the poet, and Sir Edward Ford, a brother-in-law of General Ireton, to act as intermediaries between her husband and the new masters of his country. A third cavalier, Sir John Berkeley, late Governor of Exeter, believed to have influence with the military party, followed them. All gained permission to see Charles, who was again deep in intrigues with Scotland.

But while the king believed that he was playing off his enemies against one another, they came to a complete understanding, much facilitated by the discovery of his intentions. Some extremists clamoured that he should be brought to trial, others began to plot his assassination. Realizing the increased danger of his position, he made an escape from Hampton Court to the Isle of Wight. He apparently expected that the Governor of Carisbrooke Castle would put no obstacle in the way of his further flight to France. Colonel Hammond, however, who was a connection of General Cromwell, detained him, and there he stayed for twelve months negotiating ceaselessly with the several parties of his realm, none of whom now put the faintest confidence in his promises. Henrietta wrote to him repeatedly, but got no answers. Her letters, which she directed "to a gentlewoman in the castle, or in her absence to Mistress Mary, to be conveyed to Captain Mildmay, who is in ordinary attendance upon the king", were intercepted. But as all the interesting parts of them were in "her cabalry and mystical lock of numbers", their captors, as usual, could make nothing of them.

Meanwhile all was far from well in her court at the Louvre. The Prince of Wales, relieved by the temporary retirement of Mademoiselle into a convent, from the necessity of making love in dumb show, was bitterly disappointed at being baulked in his desire to serve in the French army. He suffered for several months from an agueish fever. That Mazarin was well satisfied to keep England weak and divided while he settled his account with Spain, was now obvious to most English refugees. Those who could afford to do so, relieved their tedium by indulging in spectacular quarrels, and during this year a man whose tact and gentleness had endeared him to everyone was removed by death from the queen's household. Her old confessor, Father Robert Philip, retired to die in the Oratorians' House in the Rue St Honoré. Henrietta, deeply moved at the prospect of her loss, visited him there several times during his last illness. His successor, Walter Montagu, though a more intellectual man, was much less fitted to reconcile her fiery adherents. Lord Digby received challenges from both Lord Wilmot and Prince Rupert, and fell out with Lord Jermyn for attempting to play peacemaker. The Queen's Guard had to be summoned to arrest both principals and seconds in the impending duels. Henrietta herself had given offence to the house of Stanley. Her old acquaintance, Charlotte de la Trémoïlle, was now Countess of Derby, and had held one of her husband's houses against siege by the parliamentarian troops. Upon the death of the Comte de Laval, brother of Charlotte, a Mademoiselle Orpe of Henrietta's household came forward with a tale that, since she had been secretly married to the Comte, she was entitled to succeed to his property. To the indignation of Lady Derby, Henrietta interfered on behalf of this person, who, unfortunately for the queen's prestige, lost her case.[1]

Montrose, who had laid down his command in Scotland in obedience to his king, arrived at the Louvre, and was repulsed by its atmosphere. The ignorant, most unjustly confounding with its dominant political party the whole of his gallant nation, were vocal against "the Scots", who had sold their master. Henrietta was as friendly as ever,[2] but a suggestion that his niece, Lilias Napier, should become a maid of honour to the queen was quashed by him in uncompromising language. "There is neither Scots man nor woman welcome that way; neither would any of honour or virtue, chiefly a woman, suffer themselves to live in so lewd and worthless a place."[3]

[1] de Witt. A "Henriette Orpe" was in Henrietta's service twenty-two years later. The name is also given by contemporaries as la Harpe and Orme.
[2] "When she was allowed to follow her own inclination she was greatly disposed to encourage and advance this noble friend . . . but being deluded by the artifices of her court, who vaunted of the power and riches of the Presbyterians in a cajoling, and at other times in a menacing, manner, she was forced into opposing measures, and perplexed Montrose with various and contradictory sentiments."—Wishart.
[3] Napier.

In the spring of 1647 the Prince of Orange died, and Henrietta decided to approach Holland again. On her last visit to that country she had disliked it intensely and quitted it with relief, hoping never to see it again. It was, as she said herself, not the place for someone who had scarcely any patience. She soon had an excellent excuse for offering herself upon a visit. Her daughter Mary, aged fifteen and a half, was hoping to make her a grandmother. But in October the Queen of England received an intimation from the States of Holland that if the sole object of her journey was to be present at the Princess of Orange's confinement, she might spare herself the trouble. Her daughter was making a good recovery after a severe miscarriage.

The year 1648 opened inauspiciously in Henrietta's place of refuge. The civil war, known as the Fronde, "the sling", because during it the windows of Cardinal Mazarin's adherents were pelted with stones by the Paris mob, broke out on January 7th (N.S.) with a stormy meeting of indignant merchants resolved to resist an illegal house-tax. There was no real likeness between the revolution in France and that in England. The origin of the Fronde was the desire of the people to be restored rights granted to them by Henri IV, but gradually extinguished by Richelieu and his successor. The struggle, which was to last for four years, degenerated into a factional contest between the discontented princes of the blood, all eager for Mazarin's overthrow. Henrietta, unalarmed by reports of disturbances in the streets, came to Paris from St Germain in July, but did not stay at the Louvre. With her last jewels she had raised the sum of thirty thousand pounds, to assist her eldest son in an effort to regain his father's country. He had gone off for Helvoetsluis, where his brother, the Duke of York, who had escaped from England, and a portion of the English fleet which had declared against Parliament, were awaiting his orders. For some months past there had been signs of a reaction in favour of the romantic figure of the prisoner of Carisbrooke. In May the Scots had sent a formal invitation to the Prince of Wales to head an army for the conquest of the south. Carlisle and Berwick were in royalist hands, and Kent and Wales were in arms. Lord Holland had returned to his allegiance, and was taking the field in command of the English troops, whose rising was to coincide with the Scots' invasion. Even Lady Carlisle, always hitherto on the winning side, had pawned her pearl necklace to further a second civil war, and had been sending messages to her old mistress.

Henrietta had gone into retreat to pray for the safety and success of her son. Madame de Motteville and a younger lady, Mademoiselle de Beaumont, visited her on a July afternoon in the Carmelite convent in the Faubourg St Jacques, where, nearly a quarter of a century before, she had spent the day before her wedding in prayer and repose. They found her now in a little room, extremely busy, scribbling and sealing letters which, she assured them, were of the first importance. When she had despatched her business, she turned to them with characteristic vivacity, and holding out a little gold cup from which she was accustomed to drink, asked them to believe that this represented all the gold that she possessed in the world, and that her anguish in parting from her son had been interrupted by the arrival of all the officers of his household to announce that unless she could pay their wages, they must beg leave to retire from his service. Since she was no longer receiving her pension from the French Government, and had just parted with the last of her jewels, she had been obliged to send them away empty, and she knew that their wants were not exaggerated. However, she related with satisfaction, they had behaved much better than the officers of her mother, Marie de Medicis, who, when her husband had been unable to give them their salaries punctually, had caused him great distress by proceeding to bombard his Parliament with their demands.

Henrietta's "lively apprehensions" that the campaign towards which her son was hastening might not prove a success were

justified. Already by the time she was confiding them to visitors
in the guest-room of a Parisian convent, Lord Holland was a
prisoner. The prince was met on his arrival in the mouth of
the Thames with the news of the Duke of Hamilton's capture.
After taking some prizes and issuing a proclamation calculated
to conciliate the Scots and the Londoners, he returned to
Holland to endure one of the gloomiest winters of his life. His
little fleet of nineteen ships gradually dispersed, and while he
lay stricken by smallpox, tidings of the defeat of the Scots at
Preston, at Wigan and at Warrington, trickled in. The beautiful ruined royalist girl, to whose blue eyes he had fallen a victim
before setting out on his luckless high adventure, declared
herself with child. . . .

Since August, when the cardinal had suddenly arrested all the
leaders of the French Parliament, Paris had been in open revolt.
Henrietta came from St Germain to the capital to offer her sister-
in-law moral support and counsels of peace, but the Regent was
entirely under the influence of her unpopular minister. Henrietta was experiencing the greatest difficulty in keeping up any
communication whatsoever with England. For months no letter
of hers had penetrated to her husband, and the only one of his
which she had received had produced such an effect upon her
that her alarmed ladies had hurried to implore the Regent to
repair to their mistress, whom they believed to be dying of
shock. Charles I had written to his wife that he was now convinced that he was not destined to remain much longer in this
world, and was preparing himself to enter a better one. He told
her not to continue her efforts to save him, for they would be
useless. "Struck to the heart with amazement and confusion
upon the report of what the Parliament intended",[1] Henrietta
sent him answer by a servant of the ingenious Major Bosvile,
who alone had been successful last year in conveying word
from her to the captive. She said that she shared her husband's

[1] Clarendon, *Hist.* II. 216.

sorrow, that she wished to die with him, that she would not live without him, and that she would continue "to do her utmost in all possible ways and means to help him".[1]

Christmas 1648 was a season of black frost in London. The king had been brought from grim Hurst Castle to Windsor in preparation for his trial. Paris, at the same date, reports Madame de Motteville, resembled Venice. The Seine was in flood, and people were going about the streets in boats. Henrietta passed the festival in the Carmelite convent. The *Moderate Intelligencer*, under the date of December 26th, reported her return to the Louvre after several days spent in devotion. "She seems not dejected at the present state of the King her husband, in England, yet, say her ladies, her nights are more sad than usual."

On one of the last mornings of the old year, the future Cardinal de Retz, one of the leaders of the Frondeurs, went to the Louvre to see how the Queen of England was faring. He found her seated by a bedside in a room lacking a fire, although snow-flakes were flying past its windows. The dark-blue eyes of a bright little girl of four peeped at the caller over the edge of her coverlet. "You find me keeping my Henriette company", said the queen composedly. "I would not let the poor child rise to-day, as we have no fire." The horrified Liberal immediately sent faggots and food to the palace from his own house, and the same day made an impassioned propagandist speech in Parliament, describing the condition to which he had found a daughter and granddaughter of Henri IV reduced, while within a stone's-throw of the Spanish-born Regent and her Italian adviser.[2] A grant of forty thousand livres was made to the distressed queen and her starving but faithful attendants, and "you will do me justice to believe", announces de Retz in his

[1] H. M. de B.

[2] de Retz was himself of Italian origin. His family had come to France with Catherine de Medicis. But it had acquired great estates in Brittany and allied itself to some of the noblest houses in the kingdom. He always spelt his name "Rais".

Mémoires, "that the Princess of England did not keep her bed the following day for lack of a faggot".

Anne of Austria, however, was hardly to blame for being occupied with her own troubles at the moment. She was preparing for a midnight flight from the danger zone. At St Germain, as Marie de Medicis had once said, one seemed to have one foot in Paris. This palace, situated in a commanding position, overlooking the flood-waters of the Seine and guarded on its flank by a forest of thirty miles, was considered the most suitable place in which the Regent could wait for the tumults in the city below to resolve themselves. Obliged to re-assume the gift which she had made to her sister-in-law, she desired the Queen of England to take possession instead of any other royal residence. Henrietta stayed at the Louvre. The capital of France, however disturbed, got the latest rumours from London. She had already sent a long document offering proposals of peace to the men who were preparing to bring her husband to trial. On the very day that Paris woke to discover the flight of its royalties, and vent its rage in riots and street-fighting, the queen, who four years earlier had fled half across England in physical terror of falling into the hands of revolutionaries, wrote the following letter:

To M. de Grignan, French Ambassador in England

MONSIEUR DE GRIGNAN,

The state to which the king my lord finds himself reduced, will not let me expect to see him by the means he heretofore hoped. It is this that has brought me to the resolution of demanding of the two chambers (both Houses of Parliament) and the general of their army, passports to go and see him in England.

You will receive orders from the Cardinal to do all that I entreat of you for this expedition, which will be to deliver the letters that I send you herewith, according to their addresses.

I have specified nothing to the Parliaments and to the general, but to give me the liberty to go to see the king my lord; and I refer them to you, to tell them all I would say more particularly.

You must know then, that you are to ask passports for me to go there, to stay as long as they will permit me, and to be at liberty all the time I may be there, and likewise all my people; in regard to whom it will be necessary to say, that I will send a list of all those that I wish shall attend me, in order that if there are any in the number of them that may be suspected or obnoxious, they may be left behind.

There are letters for the Speakers of both Houses, and for the general. You will see all these persons, and let me know in what manner they receive the matter, and how you find them disposed to satisfy this wish. I dare not promise myself that they will accord me the liberty of going; I wish it too much to assure myself of it at a time when so little of what I desire succeeds; but if, by your negotiations, these passports can be obtained, I shall deem myself obliged to you all my life, as I shall (whatever may happen) for all the care you have taken, of which I make no doubt.

I shall add no more, except to assure you that I am, Monsieur de Grignan, most truly

Your very good friend

HENRIETTE-MARIE R.

From the Louvre, this 6th January 1649.[1]

A curious fate awaited the three carefully worded enclosures scribbled by the wife of Charles on this day of dire happenings in Paris. De Grignan duly did his duty, but after a debate in the House of Commons it was decided that the documents forwarded by the French Ambassador should be left unopened. Their contents were already known by his accompanying requests. Their writer had, six years ago, been voted guilty of

[1] Strickland.

high treason. Thirty-five years later, Henrietta's last appeals to the executioners of her husband were discovered, still sealed, by a clerk going through a bundle of waste papers thrust into a desk of the parliamentary office at Westminster.

As the black winter days passed without bringing her answers from any of the persons to whom she had applied, Henrietta persuaded herself that the blockade of Paris by the Regent's troops was responsible for this ominous silence. She would, after all, be more likely now to get news at St Germain than in a besieged city whose inhabitants were too much engaged with their own troubles to "care much of what may happen to the King of England". The queen of England's few remaining possessions were soon packed, and she and her little daughter cloaked and hooded for their difficult expedition through the barricaded streets and cold winter countryside. But when it had got no further than the garden of the Tuileries, her little *cortège* was stopped by Frondeur guards, and given no choice but to return to the Louvre.

Actually sinister rumours of the tragedy that had already happened in London were reaching the queen's attendants from Holland. Madame de Motteville, although by her own declaration far from valiant, was still in Paris. On one of the first days in February she arrived to pay a call at the Louvre. She found Henrietta in a piteous condition of mingled horror and relief. A report had just reached her that her husband had been led from prison to execution. With floods of tears, she related that at the very foot of the scaffold, the London mob had risen and saved their king. Madame de Motteville believed that Jermyn was responsible for this fable, designed to prepare his mistress for the blow that was now inevitable.

On the morning of February 8th, Henrietta despatched a trusted messenger to the French court to ask for news. His journey might not be an easy one, for he had to pass and re-pass through both the Frondeurs guarding the town and the royalists besieging it. During dinner that day, which he attended for the purpose of saying grace, Father Cyprien de Gamache received a whispered intimation that his duties this afternoon would not be concluded with returning thanks to God at the close of the meal. He would be required further to offer spiritual consolation to her majesty, upon the sad tidings that were likely to be brought to her. "Shuddering all over", he remained in attendance. The large and comfort-loving Jermyn, a man by nature and habit averse from any painful scene, had taken upon himself the task of breaking the bad news. He was, of course, the principal officer of the exiled queen's household. He did his business much as might have been expected.

After dinner, a dreadful hour passed in uneasy conversation on indifferent matters. Henrietta, entirely preoccupied by the prospect of her messenger's return, was the only person present unaware of her attendants' nervous and prompting glances at her miserably silent chamberlain. The short February afternoon drew in. At last she uttered a weary complaint of her messenger's tardiness. Taking his courage in both hands, Jermyn began to suggest in a circumlocutory manner "that the gentleman she had sent was usually so prompt and so faithful in executing her Majesty's commands that he could not have failed to come quicker had the news he brought been good...." [1]

[1] de Gamache; de Motteville.

CHAPTER VI

THE WIDOW OF THE MARTYR

I

ON January 27th, 1649, sentence of death had been passed upon Charles I. The scene of his trial had been Westminster Hall, in which, eight years previously, he had been a daily spectator at the trial of Strafford. He was hurried from the hall while struggling to speak in his defence, and soldiers broke off shouting "Justice" and "Execution" to puff tobacco smoke in his face as he passed. On the same night he asked that his dogs might be removed, and sent to his wife in France. Two days later, his request for a farewell interview with his children having been reluctantly granted, they were brought up to St James's by coach from Syon House, the residence of Lord Northumberland, who had been granted their custody. The Princess Elizabeth, a delicate girl with a profusion of flaxen curls, and eyes which appeared over-large in a small heart-shaped face, was just thirteen. The Duke of Gloucester, a sturdy boy of eight and a half, had chubby cheeks, light brown hair and a determined mouth. When they caught sight of their father, whom they had not seen for fifteen months, both children began to cry. His hair had become almost grey; his beard and his dress had a wild and neglected appearance. The king took his daughter on his knee and asked her to listen carefully, as he had not much time for the things of importance which he must say to her, and he wished her to write them down afterwards. "What the king said to me on the 29th January, 1648-9, being the last time I had the happiness to see him" was accordingly transmitted to history by the pen of the little princess, whose premature gravity had won her the name of "Temperance".

Charles told his children not to grieve for him, for he was to die a glorious death in defence of the laws and liberties of his country and the Protestant religion. He had forgiven his enemies, and hoped that God would forgive them. He commanded all his children to do the same. He recommended to his daughter various books which "would ground me against Popery. He bid me tell my mother that his thoughts never strayed from her, and that his love should be the same to the last. Withall, he commanded me, and my brother, to be obedient to her. . . . Then, taking my brother Gloucester on his knee, he said, 'Sweetheart, now will they cut off thy father's head'. Upon which the child looked very steadfastly upon him. 'Heed, my child, what I say; they will cut off my head, and perhaps make thee a king. But mark what I say. You must not be a king so long as your brothers Charles and James do live; therefore, I charge you, do not be made a king by them.' At which the child, sighing deeply, replied, 'I will be torn in pieces first'."

After various other exhortations, only some of which, says the princess, she is able to remember at present, he gave each of his children some of the jewels he still possessed, and called upon Bishop Juxon to lead them away. He was leaving the room for the adjoining bedroom, when a wail from the princess brought him back for a last kiss.[1]

About the same hour Cromwell and his friends were signing the king's death warrant. When Cromwell had written his name, he playfully smeared with ink the countenance of Colonel Harry Marten, late Governor of Aylesbury, and Marten returned the compliment.

Charles slept calmly that night, but before dawn was woken by the sighs and moans of Sir Thomas Herbert, who was sleep-

[1] *Reliquiae Sacrae Carolinae.*

ing near by him on a pallet. By the pale light of a cake of wax burning in a silver basin, the king perceived that his Groom of the Bedchamber was vexed by a nightmare. He spoke; Herbert woke, and announced that he had been dreaming that Archbishop Laud, executed four years since, had entered this room, dressed in his pontifical habit, "had knelt to the king—that they had conversed together—the king looking pensive . . ." Charles decided to sleep no more, although the hour was not yet five o'clock. Herbert's hands trembled so that he could scarcely assist the king to dress. Charles said, "Herbert, this is my second marriage day. I would be as trim to-day as may be." He attired himself in black, but not mourning, and placed in the pocket of his doublet a fresh handkerchief and an orange stuck with cloves. He wore two shirts, lest the cold this sharp morning should cause him to shake on his passage to the scaffold. "I would have no imputation of fear, for death is not terrible to me. I bless my God I am prepared. Let the rogues come whenever they please."

They came at ten o'clock to attend him from his palace of St James's to his palace of Whitehall. Ten companies of infantry formed a double line on either side of his route, and a detachment of halberdiers preceded him, with colours flying and drums beating. On his right hand walked Bishop Juxon and on his left a Colonel Matthew Thomlinson. In the park there was early mist and a bone in the earth. Charles called to his guard, "Come, my good fellows, step out apace". An officer asked him the extraordinary question, "If it was true that he had conspired with the Duke of Buckingham in causing his father's death". The king answered, "My friend, if I had no other sin than that, as God knows, I should have little need to beg His forgiveness at this hour". A little further on, he pointed at a tree in the park, and said that it had been planted by his brother Henry. On arrival at Whitehall, Colonel Thomlinson, who had been in charge of him throughout his trial, delivered him to Colonel Hacker, bearer of the death warrant, but at the king's request Thomlinson did not retire. Charles refused the spiritual assistance of two independent ministers, and received the Sacrament in a bedchamber, from Juxon. Dinner had been prepared for him. At Juxon's instance he took a glass of wine and a morsel of bread, lest he should faint. "Now", when he had finished, "let the rascals come. I have forgiven them and am quite ready."

Not until half-past one, however, were they ready for him. Led by Colonel Hacker he walked through galleries lined by people, most of whom were praying, and through one of the windows of the Banqueting House, passed out into the cold open air. In case of his resistance, staples had been driven into the floor of the black-hung and black-railed scaffold, so that he could be secured with ropes. The two executioners awaiting him were dressed in coarse, tightly fitting woollen clothes and black masks. One of them had disguised himself in a grey wig and beard; the other wore a black peruke and a wide-brimmed black hat fastened up in front; both were muscular men. All windows of houses overlooking the scene, and even their roofs, were packed by spectators, but there was little colour or movement amidst the crowd that had waited since dawn of this bitter day to see a king's passing. The cold fitted like a mask to upturned faces, whose breath hung upon the air, and the loudest sound was the fretting of the cavalry chargers beneath the sombre platform on which could be distinguished six figures. As only the foremost ranks of the massed troops guarding the scaffold were within earshot, the king addressed his farewell speech to Juxon and Thomlinson. The black-wigged executioner advanced, and, kneeling before the king, asked his forgiveness, to which Charles replied firmly, "I forgive no subject of mine who comes deliberately to shed my blood". He gathered his hair under a cap, and enquired from the man, "Is any of my hair in the way?" "I beg your majesty to push it more under your cap", said the man, with a bow. Juxon helped his master to do so, saying, "There is but one stage more which, although turbulent and troublesome, is yet a very short one. Consider, it will carry you a great way—even from earth to heaven." Charles answered, "I go from a corruptible to an incorruptible crown". He took off his black cloak and doublet and gave the George, which he had been wearing with the ribbon of the Garter, to the bishop. Pointing to the block he asked the taller of the two executioners to place it so that it should not shake. "It is firm, sir," the man assured him. "I shall say a short prayer", said the king. "When I hold out my hands thus—strike."

As he stood a moment, erect in shirt and breeches, taking his last look at the heavens above him, some spectators could see that the shirt worn by the figure silhouetted against skies dark with unshed snow had its embroidery tied up with narrow ribbons of red and blue. The king's lips moved. He was speaking soundlessly. He knelt and laid his head upon the block. After a short interval his wrists shot out and the grey-wigged executioner raised his axe. A single blow did the deed. The short, stout executioner ran forward, and nipping up the severed head by its faded hair displayed it to the swaying multitude below. Some persons wept, others turned their faces away, several fainted. The groan that went up was echoed throughout Europe.[1]

II

When Henrietta gathered from the faltering sentences and stricken look of the large jolly man, drooping horribly before her, that the invisible chain binding her to England had been severed by a single blow, she seemed at first incapable of understanding her loss. She had never believed that such could be the end of her eleven years of frantic, unceasing, nerve-racking

[1] Ellis; Sir T. Herbert; *State Trials*; de Motteville.

travail on behalf of "the most virtuous of men". Jermyn's words brought her to her feet, but she stood transfixed, as if turned to marble. "A great philosopher", observes her Capuchin, "says that moderate afflictions permit the heart to sigh and the mouth to lament, but that very extraordinary, terrible and fatal accidents fill the soul with a stupour, which renders the lips mute and prevents the action of the senses. Such was the pitiable state to which our queen was reduced. The words, the arguments that we employed to rouse her, found her deaf and insensible. At last, in awe, we were obliged to desist and remain grouped about her in profound silence." Alarmed for her reason, her attendants sent a summons to a lady to whom she was much attached, the wife of her illegitimate brother, César, Duc de Vendôme. Françoise de Lorraine, "a saint and the mother of the poor", arrived after dark, in floods of tears, and finally succeeded in gaining Henrietta's attention. The widow began to cry.

For the whole of the next day "her grief rendered her invisible" to callers, and when Madame de Motteville saw her on the following morning, her conversation, which was feverishly repetitive, was interrupted by wild bursts of weeping. "Having obtained by means of some friends, a pass to go and join my mistress at St Germain," says Madame de Motteville, "I went to say good-bye to the afflicted queen. As soon as she saw me she told me to come and kneel beside her bed, and she did me the honour of giving me her hand while she spoke." Henrietta began to ask her visitor to report to the Regent in what condition she had found her, but tears choked her utterance. While she had been lying here in the solitude which would now be eternal, she had been looking back over the past, and she had become convinced that the king, her lord, whose death had made her the most unhappy person in the world, had perished because nobody had ever told him the truth. She had an important message to send to her sister-in-law. Unless the Regent had the power to enforce her will she must never irritate "the people". That ferocious beast, once aroused, was insatiable, as her husband's fate had proved. If Madame de Motteville was a true friend of her mistress she would speak to her clearly on the state of her affairs. The queen prayed to God that the Regent might be luckier in France than she and her husband had been in England, but with prophetic urgence repeated that Madame de Motteville must persuade her mistress to listen to people who would tell her unpleasant truths, and struggle to discover them. All the troubles of kings and queens, leading to the loss of their empires, came from ignoring such opinions. She then sent her compliments to her sister-in-law and begged that her eldest son might now be recognized at the French court as King of England, and her second son, the Duke of York, as his heir. "Wringing my hand with renewed tenderness and sorrow, she said that she had lost in the king a husband and a friend for whom she could never weep enough, and that the rest of her life must be unrelieved torment."[1]

Madame de Motteville departed from her visit of condolence, deeply moved and astonished by the message of solemn warning which she had been called upon to deliver. "Nor did I ever forget the discourse of this princess, who, enlightened by adversity, seemed to presage for us such disasters. Heaven averted them, but God knows that we deserved them." Heaven averted them from the royal house of France for another hundred and forty-odd years.

Henrietta confided her four-year-old daughter to the care of Lady Dalkeith and Father Cyprien, and retired to her favourite convent in the Faubourg St Jacques. Here was brought to her a farewell letter written by her husband after sentence of death had been passed upon him. On this occasion she behaved as everyone had expected her to do when Jermyn had unfolded his news. After reading a few lines, she fell fainting into the arms of two nuns.[2] The first days of her bereavement, spent

[1] de Motteville.   [2] Cotolendi.

amongst distracted servants in a half-empty palace surrounded
by revolutionaries, had seemed interminable. The regular
routine of convent life was a merciful anodyne. She devoted
herself resolutely to exercises of the faith of which she had always been so good a daughter, and, in the words of an unknown
nun, "by degrees her mind returned to God. But she could not
resign herself to His Will until she had many times offered up
this orison, 'Lord, thou hast permitted it, therefore will I submit myself with all my strength'."[1] She expressed surprise that
she had survived a blow which she would have expected to be
mortal, and admitted how glad she would have been to have
exchanged her pompous apartments at the Louvre for permanent residence in some humble monastery.[2]

On an early spring day her call from the world reached her.
It arrived, inappropriately, by the mouth of an ingenuous and
discursive priest clad in a shabby *soutane*. The good Father
Cyprien, full of the importance of his mission, disclosed to her
"that the affairs of the king, her son, and of her whole family
and household were in such a bad state that they required her
immediate attention, counsels and intervention". The voice was
that of an elderly Capuchin, but the words were those of her
departed saint. "Continue the same active endeavours for Pr.
Charles as thou hast done for me, and whine not for my misfortunes in a retired way, but, like thy father's daughter,
vigorously assist Pr. Charles to regain his own." The widow of
the martyr-king emerged from the Carmelite convent clad in
the mourning costume which she was to wear for the rest of
her life. Her black robe, not unlike that of a nun, had full skirts
which swept the ground and, except that its bodice came to a
point in front, paid no tribute to prevailing fashions. Its cuffs
and its collar, which fastened up to the chin, were of linen edged
by lace and veiled by transparent muslin. On her head she wore

[1] Strickland, from an inedited MS., K 1381, Secret Archives of France,
Hôtel de Soubise.   [2] Ferrero.

either a cap with a widow's peak and a long dependent veil, or a cap edged and bordered with black lace, the scallops of which were arranged to shade the brow. Her side hair was visible, dressed in ringlets. In March 1649 she would have heard with incredulity that her figure, so attired, was to be a familiar sight to the inhabitants of Paris for another twenty years.

As far as her household was concerned, Father Cyprien's summons may have been necessary. Her son, the king, however, was now rising nineteen. Her husband's injunctions concerning him had been written three years ago. The only intrigues in which she was henceforward to be permitted to engage herself were those connected with her children's marriages. But she did not yet realize that her political career was over. She took up her pen and sent long dictatorial instructions to a gentleman who was to visit King Charles II in Holland. He must also visit the Prince of Orange and the Danish Ambassador. She favoured the idea of the king going to Ireland. She had managed to recover three or four rubies which were in pawn here. As soon as the king let her know the date of his remove towards Paris she would despatch Lord Jermyn to meet him and advise him as to the best manner of approaching the Queen Regent.

The inimitable Mademoiselle paid her aunt a visit of condolence. "I went down to the Louvre, where the Queen of England is lodged. I found her not so deeply affected as she should have been, considering the love the king her husband had borne her and that she had been perfectly well treated by him. She was completely mistress of herself, although the manner of his death must have added greatly to her affliction. She must possess great strength of will. Perhaps God gives an extraordinary amount of strength for such occasions in order that one may submit with resignation to His Will. Sometimes the continuation of sorrow and the despair which accompanies it so accustom us to grief that we become insensible to it."

Several weeks after Mademoiselle had received this impression, Henrietta had to apologize to the Duchess of Savoy for a badly written letter. The truth was that her hand was shaking so that she could not control her pen. Somebody had reported to her a rumour that some people representing "the murderers in England" had been received at the French court. "My spirits are a little upset. I don't believe it, but that does not prevent it from torturing me a little."[1] Madame de Motteville, a far better psychologist than Mademoiselle, asserts that Henrietta was never the same woman after her husband's death. "She wore a perpetual widow's mourning for him on her person and in her heart. This lasting sadness, those who knew her well were aware, was a great change from her natural disposition, which inclined to gaiety rather than seriousness." Between this and her earlier description of Henrietta laughing at something ridiculous even whilst tears of sorrow ran down her cheeks, the explanation of Mademoiselle's impression may be found. The little widow had only one manner for the entertainment of guests. All her life she had been accustomed to welcome them with vivacity and amuse them to the best of her ability. That she still chattered of plans, accompanying her eager speech with extravagant gesture, did not for a moment mean that her heart was not broken. Prolonged tragic silence would have been for her a physical impossibility. When Anne of Austria and she first met after the tragedy, the two widows fell into one another's arms and wept their fill. After that occasion, however, by tacit agreement, they never alluded to Henrietta's bereavement.

Mademoiselle found with her aunt an unknown cousin. The Duke of York had arrived from Holland, where he had been staying with his sister, the Princess of Orange, since his escape from confinement in St James's Palace. He was very pretty, thought Mademoiselle. He had a slight figure, fair hair, a bright complexion and refined features. His manners, like those of his

[1] Ferrero.

brother, were excellent. All the sons of Henrietta Maria were remarkable in this respect, for having "observed often the great defects of the late king's breeding and the stiff roughness that was in him, by which he disobliged very many and did often prejudice his affairs very much", she had given "strict orders that the young princes should be bred to a wonderful civility".[1] Mademoiselle wrote down the duke as thirteen or fourteen, but he was in his sixteenth year. He spoke French well, which made him more attractive than his brother. "In my opinion nothing detracts from a person as the inability to converse." Nevertheless, she was beginning to entertain the notion of marrying his brother. After all, neither of the widower monarchs of whom she had nourished such high hopes had made her an offer. The King of Spain had preferred to marry a mere child, the daughter of his own sister, that Infanta whom Charles I had wooed in vain. The Emperor had inexplicably condescended to choose one of his cousins, a Tyrolean archduchess of remarkable beauty. Mademoiselle realized that she was past her twenty-second birthday and that never in her life had anyone made love to her. Her exalted rank could hardly be the reason, for she had heard of queens having lovers. She began to consider what kind of a lover Charles II would make. He was a king, at any rate in name, now, and she knew that his mother was still eager for the match. The queen had sent Lord Jermyn to make a definite offer on her son's behalf. But the interview between the Chamberlain and the heiress had not been satisfactory. Mademoiselle disinclined to commit herself to an intermediary, had said that if the King of England was so deeply in love with her he would change his religion to please her. That, Lord Jermyn had replied, was not in his majesty's power, and had added that such a step would exclude his majesty for ever from his kingdom.

The new King of England arrived in France with midsummer. Everyone at St Germain said that he had come to make

[1] Harl. MS. 6584, f. 26.

love to Mademoiselle. Even the Regent chaffed her niece about
his approaching visit. Their meeting was to take place in a
pleasant country setting—the picturesque old château of Compiègne. Mademoiselle had her hair curled, "a thing that did not
happen often", and set off early in the queen's carriage, distinctly fluttered at the prospect of having to listen to "sweet
nothings" from the first king to make her a firm offer of marriage. She arrived at her destination in time for dinner. The
King of England, very tall, very black in his deep mourning,
greeted the Regent and her son, then his cousin. He was distinctly good-looking. The court proceeded to dine. King Louis,
aged eleven, conversed with King Charles about dogs and
horses, the Prince of Orange, and hunting in England. King
Charles answered in French. Then the Regent began to ask him
about the state of affairs in his country. He fell silent. She continued her questions, really wishing to know how serious he
considered the troubles in his country. He excused himself from
entering upon so knotty a problem in a tongue which he understood very imperfectly. The most delicate birds—ortolans—had
been set upon the table. The King of England helped himself to
a piece of beef, followed by some shoulder of mutton. He would
never do, decided Mademoiselle. His refusal to talk about English politics could only mean that he was ignorant of them. In
spite of his curiously attractive looks he must be quite stupid.
After dinner worse followed. The queen carefully left him alone
with her niece. Quarter of an hour passed before he uttered a
word. He stared at her with his great black eyes, to be sure, but
she could not be certain of what he was thinking. When the
hour for his departure arrived he had not made her one compliment. He took his leave of the King of France, and then coming
to stand stiffly before her, said that he was her obedient servant.
He believed that Lord Jermyn, who spoke better than he, had
been able to explain his sentiments and his offer.

The widowed Queen of England's favourite son, whom she

understood least of her children, returned to tell his little Mam that he had done his best in the matter on which her heart was set. Jermyn was afraid that the affair would never march. Weeks passed without a further move being made by either party. Then news arrived that the Emperor's bride had died suddenly. When next Henrietta met her niece, she could not resist a scratch. "We must congratulate you on the death of the Empress, for if this affair failed on a former occasion, it is sure to be successful this time." Mademoiselle replied loftily that she did not give it a thought. "Here", said Henrietta, "is a man who is persuaded that a king of nineteen is preferable to an Emperor of fifty, with four children." The Emperor was six months older than she—forty-one—but she was in no mood for accuracy. The king of nineteen listened in grave silence to his female relatives enjoying themselves. He detested women's quarrels, especially when he was their subject, and he was beginning to be their subject. Henrietta persisted for some time, then said sharply, "My son is too poor and too miserable for you". Presently, pointing out an English lady in attendance, she told her niece that her son was attracted in that direction. "He is afraid that you should know it. Look, how ashamed he is that you should meet her, lest I should tell you!" Charles left the room abruptly. He did this nowadays when his mother became impossible.[1] Henrietta asked her niece to come with her into her cabinet. When they were alone together she said that her son was wishing to ask his cousin's pardon if the proposal he had made at Compiègne had displeased her. But he was in earnest—in despair. Personally, she believed that Mademoiselle was wise to refuse him. "You would be miserable. I am too fond of you to wish that." Well, he was leaving France now, and all he wished was that in future his cousin would think kindly of him.

But they were not to part without a farewell. Hearing that Mademoiselle was going to visit her half-sisters in a convent

[1] Clarendon, *Hist.* 12. 59.

school at Poissy, both the king and the Duke of York offered to accompany her. Mademoiselle accepted the duke's escort, but drew the line at the king. He was, as she truly said, no longer a child. The Queen Mother stepped into the breach. She would chaperone the young party. A superb scene followed. Having got her victims firmly enclosed with her in a coach for a country drive, Henrietta proceeded to paint a rosy picture of the happiness of any woman who became her eldest son's wife. His queen would indeed reign supreme in his heart. Her previous and more interesting portrait of a gallant monarch who looked in the direction of attractive ladies in waiting was remorselessly expunged. Charles rather overdid his part in the conversation. How any man in possession of a reasonable wife could ever think of another woman was, he said, beyond his comprehension. From the moment that one was a married man, such sentiments should perish.

After her visit to the convent, which she cut very short, Mademoiselle was led to her carriage by her suitor with his usual grace, but in his usual silence. In any case, she reflected, sweet nothings would have been thrown away upon her. She had decided for the Emperor. No suspicion that her aunt and her cousin had been at pains to reassure her, appear to have entered her brain. Yet many people must have known that Charles's household now included a handsome young mother and a four-months-old baby. The English Ambassador's respectable son-in-law had travelled out to St Germain in Lord Wilmot's coach, with "a browne, beautiful, bold, but insipid creature", who passed by the name of Mrs Barlow.[1] Charles's mistress accurately represented the state of his fortunes. She filled the eye and would not, as far as appearance went, disgrace him in any company, but she was a poor man's choice. She was the daughter of a gentleman whose Welsh castle had been destroyed by the parliamentarian forces. But there was an

[1] Evelyn.

awkward hiatus in her story between her flight from her ruined home and her reappearance at the Hague. When Charles had taken Lucy Walter under his protection, he had injured no faithful royalist family, except, perhaps, that of Sidney. Colonel Robert Sidney had himself received the lady as a parting gift from his brother Algernon on his recall to his regiment. When Henrietta first realized that her son was a true grandson of Henri IV is unknown. Her code of morals had always been lenient to gentlemen. Since Lucy Walter was undoubtedly at St Germain at this date, it is even possible that she was the lady pointed out in the hopes of arousing jealousy in the breast of Mademoiselle. The Princess of Orange certainly accepted her brother's mistress under her roof. But fourteen months later, Henrietta at least affected to believe that the arrival of her daughter Mary's son made her a grandmother for the first time.

III

"The king lives with me", wrote Henrietta to her sister, "in the greatest affection possible. You, who have a son who treats you in the same manner, can judge what this means to a mother." [1]

Every word of this was true. Charles was invariably affectionate. With James it was possible to quarrel. The fair, sensitive Duke of York was always game for a fight. He would defend himself when attacked, give sour answers to sharp questions, and sulk for days together. Both her growing sons had inherited their father's obstinacy. But Charles went his own way imperturbably. Her first urgent letter to him after her husband's death, telling him to join her instantly and not to admit any person to be a member of his Privy Council without consulting her, had arrived too late. The young king had already acted. The Queen Mother's messenger had been obliged to

[1] Ferrero.

translate her requests as a mere desire to inform his majesty of his late majesty's intentions. And when at last Charles had joined her it had been in a mood of distressing reticence. The late king had refused to appoint a gentleman of the bedchamber without his consort's approval. The new king showed absolutely no desire for assistance from an adoring mother, the best qualified person in the world to advise and act for him. He would not discuss his affairs with her, and he would not quarrel with her. When he discovered that she was "passionate" upon a point, he dropped it and sent to her as his mouthpiece a person she already disliked.[1]

Sir Edward Hyde, the "Ned Hide" of her husband's letters, was an able lawyer and her husband had trusted him; but he was not nobly born, and his appearance and manners did not prepossess Henrietta in his favour. He had ridiculous pink cheeks, treacle-coloured hair and moustaches, and a fat paw. Sir Edward, empowered by his master "to speak freely", arrived to her upon what he himself described as "no pleasant business". The king did not wish the Princess Henrietta to be reared in the Roman Catholic faith. By the articles of her marriage treaty, said the Queen Mother, taking fire, she was allowed complete control of her children until they reached the age of twelve. She had, further, the late king's consent that her youngest child should be of her religion. Besides, what "preferment" did her brother think that the princess would have unless she was of the accepted religion of the country in which she was a guest? Sir Edward could only "conjure her not to think of putting the princess in a nunnery". To that the queen gave a ready assent. A splendid marriage was her ambition for her darling. His majesty's mouthpiece retired, defeated, and his majesty comforted himself with the reflection that for three or four years his sister would "be capable of knowing very little in religion". By that time, perhaps, he would have a home to offer to her. Sir Edward departed on his

[1] *Clarendon State Papers*, iii. 10.

master's business to Madrid, and the Queen Mother's dislike concentrated itself on other of the advisers who had gathered around her son in Holland. None of them appreciated the invaluable Jermyn. They actually called her friends "the Louvre party", and hinted that nothing could be more injurious to the young king's prospects than the suggestion that his mother had any influence with him. Charles, looking grim in his deep mourning, rode protectively by the side of his mother's coach as she passed through the streets of Paris to St Germain. The Louvre had become impossible as a residence. The Frondeurs believed her to be in sympathy with their oppressor, the Regent, and her creditors had threatened to arrest her on her journey.

By August she was back again, accompanying the Regent and the young King Louis on their triumphal re-entry into their capital. The revolution appeared to have petered out. In September Charles left her. He sailed for Jersey, taking the Duke of York with him. His designs to land in Ireland had been frustrated by the arrival of Cromwell in that island. Henrietta took the road to Bourbon, where nothing ever happened. In spite of the presence of her favourite child, her first summer of widowhood had been unrelieved misery. She returned to Paris, to spend a very quiet winter. For the second year in succession she passed Christmas in the Carmelite convent of the Faubourg St Jacques. Visits to religious houses were her only relaxation. Having now an excuse that nobody could question, she avoided, as far as possible, any entertainments at her sister-in-law's court. Soon few were being offered. The Fronde had broken out again, with a new name and a new complexion. It was now called "the Princes' Fronde". The Cardinal, having come to an understanding with the Duke of Orleans, had suddenly arrested the princes of Condé and Conti, and the Duke of Longueville. Marshal Turenne was leading the rebels.

Charles kept his mother ill-supplied with news of his intentions, but she continued to work for him. Montrose, upon hearing of her husband's death, had fallen into a death-like swoon from which he had arisen to swear that he would avenge his slaughtered king, or die in the attempt. Henrietta wrote to him, urging an impossibility—"to unite with all your country-men who entertain a just indignation against that murder, and to forget all former differences".

In February the appearance of the parliamentary fleet at Ports-mouth decided Charles to move to the Netherlands, where he could confer with the Scots commissioners. Henrietta insisted that she must see him, and he obediently took France on his route. At Beauvais they met and "conversed together three or four days". The king listened to his mother politely, went off to Breda, and even before he had heard of Montrose's defeat, accepted the commissioners' terms, which imposed the Covenant upon him-self and all his dominions, and demanded the extirpation of Papistry. One immediate result was a letter from his mother, informing him that although she would never cease to love him as a son, never again would she offer him political advice. Late in May he sailed for Scotland in a frigate provided by the Prince of Orange and commanded by the young Van Tromp. Spain had refused him help. Some money raised in Muscovy and Poland arrived, characteristically, too late. A punishing twelve months awaited the grandson of the king who had thought Paris worth a mass. His figure vanished into the darkness and dangers of his northern kingdom. To London and Paris presently came rumours that he was sick or dead. Henrietta, racked by anxiety and unable to exist without any other occupation than admonish-ing her fretting younger son, turned her energies in a direction where they were to be welcomed and successful.

Forty years before, St Francis of Sales had founded the Order of the Visitation for women of gentle birth and good education, who desired to embrace a religious life unattended by austerities beyond their capacity. There was a house of this Order in Paris in the Rue St Antoine. Henrietta was attracted towards the Filles de Sainte Marie for several reasons. She could remember St Francis. At the marriage of her sister Christine to the heir of Savoy, he had prophesied for her, then a child of ten, a more glorious destiny. The Mother Superior of the house in Paris, Louise de la Fontaine, was a woman of remarkable talents, who had been educated as a Protestant. Amongst the nuns was Louise de la Fayette, whose youthful beauty had attracted Louis XIII much to the alarm of Richelieu, and a Scottish lady, Mary Hamilton, whom Henrietta had last seen at her own court at Whitehall. The queen was introduced to the community by Madame de Motteville, whose younger sister had just entered it as a novice. Nothing could be more appropriate than for a royal widow to make a religious foundation. Moreover, the idea of extending the Order by the establishment of a daughter house had already occurred to one of its senior members, Mother Lhulier. Henrietta, with an income entirely dependent on charity, and already unequal to her expenditure, began to drive about the environs of Paris, looking at desirable properties.

At the end of the tree-lined Cours de la Reine, one of the most fashionable avenues in the capital, rose the little village of Chaillot, already almost linked to the Faubourg de la Conférence. The château of the late Marquis de Bassompierre, that elderly gallant who had arbitrated nearly a quarter of a century before at the quarrels of Oberon and Titania, was for sale. Since he had died deeply in debt, his creditors had leased the handsome house with its "gardens, terraces and rare prospects" as a place of entertainment. Nobody lived in it. For years nothing had been spent on repairing it. Naturally it looked a little dejected. People merely came out from Paris to gamble and amuse themselves here. The place had, in fact, acquired a very dubious reputation. Nothing deterred, Henrietta alighted from her coach and entered into her second kingdom.

Her quick eye at once detected the possibilities of Chaillot. She need look no further. Her mind was made up. On the next appearance of the Queen Mother of England's shabby-genteel equipage at a retreat shady in every sense, three black-robed visitors dismounted, to tour faded saloons and tangled gardens. Her majesty had brought a couple of nuns from the Rue St Antoine to inspect the place which was to be their home, and, for at least several months of every year, hers too. She had chosen her rooms—those with a view of the high-road, the Seine and Paris. If she and her ladies occupied the front portion of the building, they would cause no disturbance to the sisters, whose quarters should all look out on the gardens beside and behind. She swept her two guests from room to room of the lordly pleasure-house built by Catherine de Medicis, watching with child-like enjoyment their expressions of dismay and delight. The only objection found by the holy women was that it was all too beautiful, too splendid, for their purpose. Henrietta, however, saw herself Foundress of Chaillot and no other place. The nuns gave way to her, and she proceeded to battle against a seemingly inexhaustible succession of opponents. First the Archbishop of Paris, whose assistance was indispensable, pointed out that there were already three houses of the Visitation in the capital. He was inclined to be disagreeable to the Queen of England, for he had never forgotten the slight put upon him at the time of her wedding. The marshal's creditors were asking only six thousand pistoles, the property was an absolute bargain. Henrietta might have no money, but she still had influence, and Mother Lhulier was possessed of a determination equal to her own. The future prioress appealed to all her acquaintance, and in the nick of time was rewarded by the offer of a wealthy friend to guarantee the entire sum required. Henrietta enlisted the sympathy of the Regent, and the Regent conferred with the archbishop. At last Chaillot, the foundation of the Queen of England, was the property of the Filles de Sainte Marie.[1]

[1] MS. 2436 Bibl. Mazarine. Add. MSS. 12186, ff. 264-5-6, 280. B.M. S.P.D. Fr., 3. 90. P.R.O.

Months must elapse before it could be ready for their occupation, but meanwhile the widow had found an absorbing interest. Two or three times a week her carriage passed along the Cours de la Reine towards "her inchoative nunnery". She knew that she had a talent for interior decoration. She began to plan what furniture she would bring from the Louvre. The nuns, of course, would be bringing some pieces from the Rue St Antoine. . . . She chose for her country parlour a tapestry of "verdure", for her bedroom black and "Isabelle" brocade, and stools worked with flower designs. Her little cabinet, in which she would say her prayers and write her letters, got furniture of "walnutt tree", hangings "with flower pots and greate pillars", and stools of "flow'red Turkey work". [1,2]

Her first prospect of consolation and peace of mind since the death of her husband was shattered by heart-breaking news from overseas. All her immediate anxieties had been for her first-born. She heard now that she had lost a child in England, but not Charles. The Princess Elizabeth, a delicate girl of thirteen, exposed to all the terrors and trials of adolescence unsupported by a single person of understanding, had never recovered from the shock of that last interview with her doomed father. On hearing of his execution she had "fallen into great sorrow, whereby all the other ailments from which she suffered were increased". Her illness had brought one old friend to her side. Sir Theodore Mayerne, who had presided at her birth, reported

[1] Chaillot was destroyed in the Revolution. Its site is now occupied by the Trocadéro. Napoleon I had its foundations cleared away, intending to build a palace there for the King of Rome. In 1867 the work undertaken for the Great Exhibition completely changed the appearance of the ground on which Henrietta's nunnery once stood.

[2] "Isabelle" was a "dirty white" or light buff, traditionally named after Isabella of Castile, who swore to the Virgin not to change her shift until Granada fell into her hands. It has also been associated with Isabella of Austria, daughter of Philip II, who made a similar vow in the siege of Dieppe in 1601. But Queen Elizabeth possessed "a rounde goune of Isabella-coloured sattin" in July 1600.

that the princess's frame was wasted, her pulse was rapid, and she was unable to digest any but the smallest quantities of his medicines. He prescribed fomentations for a tumour, and as much gentle exercise as she was able to bear. After the retirement of Lord Northumberland, who had made a formal protest against the sentence passed on Charles I, Parliament had found great difficulty in appointing a guardian for the two royal children in their possession. Nobody cared for an onerous post insufficiently and unpunctually remunerated. At last it was accepted by Lord and Lady Leicester, and during twelve months spent in their peaceful country home of Penshurst in Kent, the ailing princess recovered some measure of health. She was by far the most scholarly of her family, and had occupied her neglected and unhappy childhood by learning Greek and Hebrew. The landing of their brother Charles II in Scotland had brought a disastrous change in the fortunes of "Bessy and Harry Stuart". A commission directed to enquire into their state, decided that the peace of the realm was endangered by the presence of two of the late king's children in England, and recommended their removal to the Isle of Wight. When she heard that she was to be taken to gloomy Carisbrooke, the imaginative girl was horror-stricken. Within a week of her arrival there she caught cold from getting wet through while playing bowls with her brother. The governor was not particularly alarmed when his elder prisoner, whose sickly look was enhanced by the little black robe which she wore as perpetual mourning for her father, complained of headaches and refused her food. When, however, she took to her bed and developed high fever, he did all that he could. He summoned the best doctors in Newport, and sent an express to London, asking for the assistance of Sir Theodore Mayerne. The old royal physician at the age of seventy-one had set out for Exeter at the command of his king. At the age of seventy-seven he did not set out for the Isle of Wight at the command of the governor of Carisbrooke. The substitutes whom he sent, armed with a host of prescriptions, arrived too late. The death of the Princess Elizabeth was officially attributed to "a malignant fever", but her mother declared passionately—"She died from grief at finding herself brought to the same castle where her father had been imprisoned, and in a place where she had no assistance in her malady".[1]

Actually the death in captivity of a virgin princess, renowned for her attachment to the Protestant religion, was an unfortunate circumstance for the present rulers of her country. According to her father's instructions, she had applied repeatedly to be allowed to join her sister, the Princess of Orange, in Holland. Three days before her death, Parliament had decided to grant her request. A wave of sympathy swept England for the daughter of the Martyr-King, who had fallen into her last sleep with her wasted cheek lying upon a Bible open at the text "Come unto me all ye that travail and are heavy laden and I will give ye peace".[2]

"The hawks of Norway," commented a contemporary,[3] "where a Winter's day is hardly an hour of clear light, are the swiftest of wing of any Fowl under the firmament, Nature teaching them to bestir themselves to lengthen the shortness of the time with their swiftness. Such was the active piety of this Lady, improving the little life allotted to her, in running the way of God's commandments."

Henrietta, after shedding many tears, announced that it had pleased God to visit her with another affliction, and comforted herself with the thought that, as far as her child was concerned, "she is very happy, to be out of the hands of those traitors". In a letter purporting to be from her pen,[4] she had appealed to her eldest son as long as eighteen months ago—"yet my real

¹ Ferrero. ² de Gamache; Sloane MS. 2075, f. 33; Ferrero. ³ Fuller.
⁴ Preserved in the Bibliothèque de l'Arsenal. It has suffered translation from French into Italian and from Italian into an English very unlike the queen's usual style.

afflictions do not make me forget your brothers, and that unfortunate Elizabeth. Oh! if before my death I could see her
out of the hands of the traitors, I would die content. To this,
at least, I will exhort you to employ every force, to use every
artifice, to withdraw so dear a part of my own heart, this innocent victim of their fury, your worthy sister, from London." [1]

Charles was now in no position to help anybody. Five days
before the death of the Princess Elizabeth, Cromwell had defeated the Scots at Dunbar.

The next bereavement which Henrietta was to suffer was to
have less personal, but more political significance. By November of this year she was looking eagerly towards Holland, where
her elder daughter Mary had for the first time achieved nearly
nine months of pregnancy. News came from the Hague, but it
was tragic. The Prince of Orange had been stricken with smallpox. He had died after a few days' illness, and an attempt to
conceal her loss from his wife until after her confinement had
been unsuccessful. Mary, however, like her small and fragile
mother, had a far more vigorous hold on life than was justified
by her appearance. On her nineteenth birthday, eight days after
she became a widow, she gave birth to a living child. The posthumous prince, who was not at first expected to live, was baptized William. Mary, although she had been devoted to her
young husband, desired that their child should receive the name
of her father and brother, but her old foe, the Princess Dowager, won her point. The death of the Prince of Orange could
not have come at a more unfortunate time for his wife and all

[1] In 1793 the coffin of the Princess Elizabeth was identified in a vault,
close to the communion table in Newport Church, but until Queen Victoria
ordered the erection of a monument to this most unfortunate child of
Charles I and Henrietta Maria, only the initials E. S. cut in the nearest wall
indicated her place of interment. The result, by Marochetti, is singularly
successful. It represents the fourteen-year-old girl, lying at full length, in a
gown of Puritan simplicity, with her fair hair sprinkled over the Book which
was her father's last gift to her. A shattered portcullis above her figure signifies the victory of Death over prison bars.

her family. He had just failed in an attempt to raise the Stad-holderate at the expense of the provincial liberties. Henrietta wrote to Turin: "It seems that God wishes to show me that I should detach myself altogether from this world, by taking from me those who would lead me to think of it. The loss of my son-in-law makes me see this, for in him were placed all my hopes for my son's restoration." She hoped that the little Prince William might live to be a comfort to her daughter. "For my-self I am too old to see him grow up."

The sister to whom she wrote was engaged in a happy busi-ness this winter. Her youngest daughter was to be married to the Duke of Bavaria's young heir. The Princess Adelaide-Henrietta's trousseau must be Parisian. Duchess Christine had asked that her sister's eye might direct the choice of the Savoyard Comptroller-General. Henrietta put her own troubles in her pocket and drove off to inspect satins and *pannes*. She wrote a little pathetically that her own knowledge in matters of dress was little, but she was going to consult Mademoiselle. Her pleasure in the beautiful gowns being prepared was as great as if they had been for her own daughter. They were actually for a girl a year younger than the daughter who had just died at Carisbrooke.

Anxiety for two absent sons was now tormenting her. James had gone off to Flanders a couple of months ago, refusing to disclose his intentions. In December a rumour that the Duke of Lorraine was going to hand over eight regiments to the Duke of York was current in Paris. The Duke of Lorraine, having been driven out of his own country by France, had re-tired to Brussels, where he hired his troops to Spain. Henrietta had been obliged to write to Mazarin, disclaiming all authority for her son's actions. She pinned her hopes to a farewell promise he had given her that he would not, at any rate, fight against the country which was sheltering his mother. James did not find employment in Flanders, and to her mortification his sister

Mary was prevented by her subjects from offering him a home. He had no money. His brother's horses, some "much pris'd by His Majesty", were having to be sold "to pay for their meat". He took himself to Rhenen, where his aunt, Elizabeth of Bohemia, gave him a hearty welcome to her threadbare, crowded, untidy house. In June he returned to his mother, who received him "without reproaches". His first attempt to escape from her apron-strings had been a sufficiently enlightening experience. She had also enough quarrels on her hands at the moment. Anne of Austria saw herself saddled for life with her widowed sister-in-law. For Henrietta herself she felt sympathy, but the presence of dozens of English Protestants in her capital was beginning to get on her nerves, and she was missing her cardinal, who had fled into Rhineland when the citizens of Paris began to hang him in effigy at their cross-roads. She came to Henrietta to announce, with great solemnity, that she believed all the troubles by which France was afflicted had been sent by God as a punishment because heretical worship was countenanced at the Louvre. An exiled Protestant cleric, Dr. Cosin,[1] held services there in "an under-room" set apart for his ministrations. No good Catholic, said Anne, could permit such a state of affairs. She added that she considered her sister-in-law backward in the business of converting the Prince of Wales and the Duke of York. When Sir Edward Hyde arrived in Paris from Madrid, he found himself appointed spokesman of a deputation of injured Protestants. Henrietta treated this matter with tact. As a guest of France she could offer no opposition to the Regent's desires. Dr. Cosin would have to go. But she would continue to pay his salary, and arrange that her servants should attend the chapel in the English Ambassador's residence. She asked Hyde to speak to the Abbé Montagu, whose zeal she was afraid had prompted the Regent's action. She regretted that death had deprived her of her old confessor, Father Philip, a person who

---

[1] Afterwards Bishop of Durham.

had never allowed her to take part in any "passionate undertakings", but always done all in his power to maintain good relations between her and her Protestant subjects.[1] A disappointment in which they could not be expected to share was now threatening her—no less than the loss of "her beloved and most delicious retiring place at Chaillot". Marshal Bassompierre's principal heir had appeared unexpectedly upon the scene, and was declaring that his late relative's creditors had proceeded illegally in disposing of his house during his absence. The Comte de Tillières, like many persons whose property has lain long in the market, suddenly discovered with the advent of a purchaser that he had always meant to live there himself. He was, however, gallantly prepared to grant a lease of it to the Queen of England, on the understanding that she reserved it for her own private use. The magistrates of Chaillot, who had found that the existence of a place of entertainment in the largest house of their village brought them custom, shared the Comte de Tillières' objections to the transformation of his château into a nunnery. The law appeared to be upon the Comte's side, so Henrietta determined to secure nine points of the law. On June 21st she "did suddenly transport her nuns to take possession of Bassompierre's house". She was waiting on the threshold to welcome the ten or twelve holy women who arrived shortly after herself at the place over whose beautification she had taken so many pains, and before they retired for the night she conducted them personally over the entire premises, pointing out to them every charm and convenience of their new home. It was a little damping that after this they all elected to spend their first night in the garrets. Henrietta made a second and less jubilant tour of the rooms whose luxury had so appalled them, and condemned for removal back to the Louvre several pieces of furniture of wholly worldly appearance. After a few days the nuns descended in answer to her entreaties, and a week later

[1] Clarendon, *Hist.* 13. 44.

Anne of Austria came out from Paris to assist at the first mass celebrated at Chaillot. Interest in the new foundation was heightened by the fact that a body of archers had to guard it by day and night, for fear of a raid threatened by the Comte de Tillières. The Comte, however, went undramatically and unsuccessfully to law, and Henrietta began to experience the peaceful hours for which she had so long hoped.[1]

On an early autumn day Mother Lhulier received the following hastily scribbled note:[2]

To the Reverend Mother, Prioress of the Daughters of the Visitation of St Mary at Chaillot.

MOTHER,

I cannot come to-day to Chaillot as I intended when I left, for I have found more business than I expected, not having been yet to the Palais Royal, on account of the bad news from England, which, nevertheless, I hope is not quite so unfortunate as it is represented. My uneasiness renders me unfit for anything, until I receive the news, which will arrive to-night. Pray to God for the king, my son, and believe me, Mother,

Your very good friend

HENRIETTE-MARIE R.

For some months past, her attendants had noticed that their mistress "whose nature is not to have her mind much wrought upon by any accidents that fall out at a distance", had been "more than ordinarily troubled" by the unpromising rumours from Scotland. The bad news which had now arrived was that of Cromwell's "crowning mercy", the annihilation of her son's army at the battle of Worcester. Charles had set out for England in the same week that had seen the opening ceremony at Chaillot. At Carlisle he had been proclaimed king, but his army had not received the large additions for which he had hoped,

---

[1] Add. MSS. 12186, ff. 264-5, 280. B.M. [2] Everett-Green.

as it passed through Lancashire, and Shrewsbury had shut its gates against him. At Worcester, on September 3rd, his forces, about thirteen thousand in number, had met the army of Cromwell, which was between thirty and forty thousand strong. The king, after bearing himself with conspicuous bravery, had escaped from the field and vanished into space. For nearly six weeks his fate was unknown. "All the world", says Mademoiselle, "went to console the Queen of England, but this only augmented her grief, for she knew not if her son were a prisoner or dead."

CHAPTER VII

THE QUEEN MOTHER

I

HENRIETTA's first news of her missing son came from himself and announced his landing in France. Three days after his arrival at Fécamp on October 16th, he presented himself before his astonished parent at the Louvre. Mademoiselle was an early caller there the next morning. "I thought that my personal inquiries could not be dispensed with." Henrietta, all a-flutter with joy, hastened to warn her niece "that I should find her son very ridiculous, since he had, to save himself in disguise, cut his hair off and assumed an extraordinary garb. At that moment he entered. . . ."

Charles had indeed changed, and in more than appearance. Since his mother had last set eyes on him he had seen the dismembered limbs of Montrose decorating a high place in Aberdeen. He had been crowned King of Scotland at Scone, but in that country he had been harried and humiliated beyond endurance. All his sacrifices seemed to have been made in vain, and he had barely escaped with his life from England after being hunted like a beast. The iron had entered into his soul. An awed lady of his mother's court reports that he reappeared having grown to a majestic stature, manly and powerful in person, but coarse in features and reckless in expression.[1]

Mademoiselle thought him entirely improved. He really had a fine figure. When she realized that he had, as well as attaining a height of six feet three inches, become the master of

[1] Lady Fanshawe.

fluent but inaccurate French, she allowed him to escort her
through the great gallery which connected the Louvre with the
Tuileries, entertaining her *en route* with an account of his recent
adventures. Charles, who was for the flesh-pots now, accordingly made an amusing story of King Charles II hiding in the
oak at Boscobel, and yawning his head off in Scotland, a country
in which, he assured his cousin, there was not a woman to be
had, and people thought it a sin to play upon the violin. His
boredom had been so complete that he regretted his defeat the
less, since it had freed him to return to a civilized realm in-
habited by charming characters, to some of whom he was
deeply attached. The large-nosed spinster striding by his side
had money. Let her feed and divert him. On their next meeting he recurred to the subject of violins. He had heard that his
cousin was the possessor of a very fine string orchestra. He
asked unblushingly to hear it. Mademoiselle, never loath to
display any evidence of her wealth, sent for her musicians.
Presently she found herself giving a dance every day. "All the
young and good-looking people of Paris came. They had no
court to pay to anyone but me, for the queen was not in Paris.
Our assemblies, for they were good enough to be so termed,
began at five or six o'clock in the evening and finished at nine.
The Queen of England often attended them. One evening she
came unexpectedly, bringing her two sons to supper. Although
I kept a much better table than theirs, all food in palaces is the
same, and I was annoyed at not being able to offer them something more exquisite. After supper we played little games. I
resolved to continue these amusements and divide my time
between dancing and playing." The dark, desperate-looking
man, whose unfailing presence at her parties had transformed
her into a successful hostess, had also resolved that she should
do so. But the little games which he played with pretty,
fashionable women at the Tuileries were not the only ones in
which he was engaging himself in Paris. His acquaintance at

this period of his career was catholic, and much resembled that attributed by tradition to Prince Hal. Lucy Walter, poor jade, had not been faithful to him while he was away seeking his crown. He did not blame her but he paid her off. The boon companions with whom, according to Madame de Motteville, he snatched at "whatever pleasures came his way, even those of the most degraded kind", were the young Duke of Buckingham, a man far inferior in ability to his famous father, sly, ill-tempered, and already at three-and-twenty putting on flesh; Harry Bennet, a dry wit, who looked sinister, since he always wore a black plaster across the bridge of a nose broken at the skirmish of Andover; and Thomas Elliott, a man whom the late king had always distrusted.

Hyde, summoned from Antwerp, sent a typical letter to his young master, informing him that his recent distresses had been sent to extend his knowledge of the world, but that his future and that of his kingdom now depended upon his virtue. Henrietta, who had openly declared last year that her son had sacrificed his honour and his conscience, forgot her anger in her delight at having him safe by her side again. She did her best for him. She took him out every week—three times in one week—to peaceful Chaillot. The King of England, "very silent always", dined with his lady mother in the refectory of her favourite convent, waited upon by holy women. In little matters he always obliged her. "Oh, Mr Secretary," exclaimed the exasperated Hyde, "this last act of the King's in making Mr Crofts a gentleman of the bedchamber, so contrary to what he assured me, makes me mad and weary of my life." [1] Charles took his chief adviser to a court masque. When the Queen Mother of France asked who was the fat person seated next to Lord Ormond, her nephew answered loudly and cheerfully, "That is the naughty man who did all the mischieve and set me against my mother".

[1] *Clarendon State Papers*, iii. 59.

The cardinal returned and the civil war began again. Mademoiselle became an Amazon and took the town of Orleans by storm at the head of Frondeur troops. Henrietta congratulated her niece on having imitated the career of the Maid of Orleans so closely. She had begun by driving away the English. The King of England, said his mother, was still passionately in love, but of course, if there was any chance of Mademoiselle marrying her other kingly cousin, he would withdraw his suit. Since the Emperor had chosen as his third wife a Mantuan lady, Mademoiselle had indeed been considering an alliance with the little Louis XIV. He was nearly fourteen, only eleven years and a few months her junior. She had called him her "little husband" when he was a baby, a thing that had annoyed Cardinal Richelieu excessively. Unfortunately for her hopes in this direction, after rescuing Condé's troops in the battle of the Faubourg St Antoine, she ordered the cannon of the Bastille to fire upon her intended husband's forces. Five years' banishment from his court was the little king's comment on this effort to convince him of Mademoiselle's desirability as a bride.

Henrietta had spent a disturbed summer. The roads outside Paris were dangerous for travellers. Frondeurs, disaffected peasantry and footpads haunted them. The Louvre was again surrounded by indignant Parisians, who believed that she and her son supported the cardinal's policy. The Duke of Orleans and the Prince de Condé escorted the Queen Mother and the King of England to the gates of the capital, outside which they were met by a troop of royalist horse. They arrived at St Germain by the light of flambeaux, in heavy rain, on a July midnight, and there remained for three months. Henrietta's attempts to act as a peacemaker between the rebels and Anne of Austria were not kindly received. "My sister," said the Regent, "do you wish to be Queen of France as well as Queen of England?" Henrietta produced one of her best answers: "I am nothing. Do you be something." On the return of the

court to Paris, she was asked to change her lodgings. In future
the King of France would inhabit the Louvre, a more secure
residence than the Palais Royal. Henrietta and her son were
assigned apartments in the discarded Palais Royal.

She had worse vexations. The Fronde, as a civil war, was over.
The whole country, sick of unrest and the rival princes' feuds, was
looking to the throne for order and settled government. England
appeared to have settled down solidly to being a Common-
wealth. Mazarin decided that the time had come for him to
send a minister to London. He could not afford to run the risk
of England supporting his enemies. Over two years ago, Henrietta's hand had shaken so at the very thought of a represent-
ative of her husband's murderers being received in France,
that she had been unable to write a legible letter. Time had
not changed her feelings. Her son James had been fighting for
the last eight months in Marshal Turenne's army. She wrote to
him from Chaillot in an affectionate but dictatorial vein, telling
him that his brother the king would have to leave France. "I
have not yet formed any resolution on your behalf; therefore
you must still act as if you were ignorant of this embassy, and
in case any one speak to you of it, say that you cannot believe
it; do this till we can ascertain what course you must take." In
spite of her use of the word "we", she was obliged to add that
she was ignorant what his brother might have written to him.
"At all events, I wished to inform you of it. When I have cared
for you I shall take care of myself, and I will let you know any
resolution that I may take. I confess to you that since my great
misfortune I have felt nothing equal to this."

Neither of her sons took any immediate action. James continued to serve under the banner of France, and Charles stayed
in Paris, where, within a few months, another of her children
joined her. In February 1653, "Harry Stuart, youngest son of the
late Charles I", had leave "to transport himself beyond the seas".
The death of the Princess Elizabeth had helped to convince

Parliament that royal children were not a useful possession. The young Duke of Gloucester landed in Holland, where he was welcomed enthusiastically by his sister Mary and her great friend and helper, Elizabeth of Bohemia. The two Protestant widows would have liked to keep the boy, but Charles wrote that his mother's natural wish to see her son could not be opposed. He hoped to send Henry back to them as soon as possible. The arrival of another fugitive princeling brought many curious visitors to the Palais Royal. Henrietta, under no illusions as to the reason why her reception rooms were suddenly crowded, wrote to her sister Christine that the French, who always ran after novelty, were all delighted with "this young cavalier". Everybody said that he looked far more Christine's son than hers. "To say this is to praise him enough; I will add no more." Henry, who had been a prisoner ever since he could remember, settled down cheerfully amongst his family. There was no money to be spared, but he must receive the education suitable to his birth. He went daily on foot through the streets of Paris to his riding, fencing and dancing lessons. He was nearly thirteen and growing dark and thin, but his blue eyes were thoroughly English in colour and expression. Like his sister Mary, he reserved the best part of his heart for his fascinating brother Charles. Henrietta was proud of the good impression produced by her strange schoolboy son, but her health was very weak at present. She found her youngest child, a delicate little creature who needed petting and cosseting, a more sympathetic companion. Unless prospects brightened—and they were growing daily darker—her face would be the sole fortune of the Princess Henrietta Anne. Was she going to be a beauty? She must be a beauty. "I am afraid I am a bad judge. . . . My desire that she should be beautiful, makes me, perhaps, believe that she is not."[1] Haggard with anxiety, the black eyes of Henrietta Maria scanned every possibility in the development of Henrietta Anne.

[1] Ferrero.

The poor child was desperately thin. She was growing fast,
and her little back was not perfectly straight. Her skin was
admirable, as white as alabaster, and she had an attractive patch
of brilliant colour in either cheek. Her hair was a lovely shade,
the richest of golden browns, but there was not much of it
and it had lost its curl. Henrietta Maria valued natural curls.
However, Art could always be called in to help Nature here. If
the beauty of her child's person was as great as that of her soul,
reflected the widow sadly, one would have no cause to fear
for the future.

On a chilly February day, a fluttered and muffled-up party
set out from the Palais Royal for the Louvre. The Princess of
England had been invited to take part in a Ballet-Royal, in
which her young cousins, the King of France and the Duke of
Anjou, were also to be performers. It was her first appearance
in public as well as her first experience of the court theatricals
in which her mother had once been so admired an actress. The
subject of the piece presented was classical, of course—the
nuptials of Peleus and Thetis. At last, very unpunctually, as
usual at the Louvre, the curtain rose upon a magnificent
tableau—the future Roi Soleil, seated upon a throne, surrounded
by Muses. Louis XIV, aged fifteen, was Apollo, as he informed
his listeners in a pompous harangue. His power knew no submission except to Love. Out of the group around him stepped a
tiny figure, crowned with roses and myrtle and carrying a lyre
—the Muse of Lovers. Henrietta Anne, aged nine and a half,
accomplished in a clear childish treble twelve lines descriptive
of her high birth, youth and misfortunes. The play flowed on,
but one member of the audience perceived no more than that
everyone present shared her conviction with regard to the
smallest performer. The princess of England might never be a
true beauty, but she was "a little angel". So much grace and
charm must ensure her a life of happiness. She was her mother's
sole comfort. . . .

Henrietta Maria was now forty-five, and for the next four years of her life was to be a very difficult person. The most impressive thing about her during these seasons of her discontent was her list of quarrels.

Tears and protestations had no effect upon her sister-in-law. For reasons of state, said Anne of Austria, regular diplomatic relations with England must be resumed. During the last months of the past year Oliver Cromwell had been installed as Lord Protector. He had concluded an advantageous treaty with Holland. Sweden, Portugal and Denmark were preparing to follow Holland's example. Spain and France were contending for his alliance. "These reasons of state are terrible," said Henrietta, "and I confess I do not understand them. Perhaps it is because they are against me. . . . Nothing since the death of my lord the King, has touched me as nearly as this. . . . It seems like killing his memory."[1] Her eldest son prepared to leave France before he was asked point-blank to do so. He desired his mother to grant a farewell interview to Hyde. If his only parent and his chief minister could not live together in peace, he hoped that they might at least part amicably. Henrietta consented to receive her *bête-noire* "alone in her private gallery". Unfortunately for Charles's hopes, Hyde opened the conversation by asking how he had managed to offend her majesty, and a gust of temper scattered any good resolutions that Henrietta might have had. With "a louder voice and more emotion than usual" she told her son's adviser that she had only consented to receive him at the king's desire, and he had no reason to expect a welcome since he had not visited her for six months, although under the same roof with her. "When her majesty made a pause" her victim defended himself doggedly, beginning by stating that he had never yet been in Bedlam. To have published her majesty's dislike of him by avoidance of her, would have qualified him for entrance into such an institu-

[1] Ferrero.

tion. Bedlam, although he did not divulge this to her, had for some time in his opinion been closely resembled by her household. Henrietta then embarked upon her eternal grievance that her son was encouraged to withhold his confidence from her and disdain her advice. An interview which had begun hotly ended icily, and Hyde went off, and became the innocent cause of a quarrel between her majesty and another of her children. The Princess of Orange, although well aware of her mother's aversion from the Hyde family, proceeded to appoint a member of it one of her maids of honour. Hyde himself begged her to reconsider her philanthropic intention, lest it should annoy the Queen Mother. Mary, however, most undutifully announced that she was mistress in her own house. Anne Hyde, a buxom girl of fifteen to whom she had taken a fancy, arrived in it, and at the Palais Royal the widow's list of heartless oppressors was augmented by the name of her charming elder daughter.

Her relations with her only surviving brother, Gaston, Duke of Orleans, had been embittered ever since he had become a leader of the Fronde. Several reconciliations had taken place between them, but they were never to be true friends again. Her younger son, James, was still fighting gallantly for France. For two days after the battle of Arras, she was uncertain whether he was alive or dead. Reports of his prowess and visits from him gave her pleasure, but the truth was that James and she got on best when they did not meet. He was as determined as Charles and Mary to go his own way, and not half so clever in evading discussion of his intentions. At length the only members of her family with whom Henrietta seemed to be on terms of unalterable affection were her "little puss", in whom nobody could have found any fault, and her sister, the Duchess of Savoy, whom she never saw. Christine's frequent letters, often accompanied by thoughtful gifts of little luxuries such as scent and gloves, were eagerly looked for and exhaustively answered. One present of gloves from Turin arrived just in time for the coronation, and there was a pair amongst them exactly the right size for *"ma petite ici"*. Henrietta Maria with James and Henrietta Anne set off for Rheims to witness the great pageant as private persons. After it, the ladies made on to Bourbon. For three seasons in succession the queen took a course of the famous waters, but their powers seemed to fail with her nowadays. She returned to Paris feeling rather worse than before she had set out. Still she refused to consider herself a hopeless invalid, or indeed hopeless in any sense. On great festival days her carriage was always to be seen outside religious houses. She took her little daughter, on St Ignatius's Day, to visit the Jesuits of the Rue St Antoine. After attending vespers, the queen and princess were shown the treasures of the house, and given an elegant collation composed entirely of fruit. Henrietta Anne was naturally pious. At Chaillot she delighted to wait upon the nuns at table. Father Cyprien, who had been her spiritual instructor since she was two years old, was full of wonder and pleasure at her aptitude and enthusiasm. Lady Dalkeith, now Lady Morton and a widow, always sat in the room during his hours with her pupil. "My dear," said Henrietta Maria to Henrietta Anne, "as you have so much zeal, why do you not convert your *gouvernante?*" The little creature replied that she did try—"as much as I can". "How much was that?" asked her mother. "Madam,"explained Henrietta Anne, "I embrace my *gouvernante,* I hug her, I kiss her, I say to her, 'Madame Morton, be converted! Be a Catholic! You must be a Catholic to be saved. Father Cyprien tells me so very often. You have heard him as well as I. Be a Catholic, *chère dame,* and I will love you dearly.' " Lady Morton, whose plans for a second marriage had been upset by Hyde, became as distraught as nearly everyone else in the Palais Royal. She obtained leave to visit England on account of her financial affairs, and there died. As she lay on her deathbed, a great friend, a Catholic lady, arrived to visit her. "Madam," cried the exasperated *gouvernante,* "talk not to me about religion; urge me not to be a Catholic. I never will be one." Henrietta Anne's education was henceforward carried on by the nuns of Chaillot. Her mother, who could not help her foundation in any other way, hoped by sending her own child as a pupil to attract other parents of exalted birth to follow her example.

Her days at Chaillot were the widowed queen's chief solace now. She went out there increasingly often, and sometimes stayed for weeks together. But even at Chaillot there were disadvantages. Old Mother Lhulier had died, and been succeeded by Mother de la Fayette, a lady only thirty-six years of age. The new prioress, who belonged by birth to the aristocracy of France, and had known the court, was determined that the convent founded by the Queen Mother of England should not, like that founded by the Queen Mother of France, become a fashionable centre of political intrigue. From Chaillot the world could not be too strictly excluded. Henrietta, who had taken great pleasure in entertaining an ingenuous audience with stirring tales of her many adventures, found her habit of joining the nuns every day at their recreation gently discouraged. Realizing that she could not afford to let any action of hers mar her relations with the one community which she found sympathetic, she took precautions to avoid giving annoyance. She refused to see callers who came out from Paris prompted by idle curiosity. No stranger was ever admitted to her private apartments. Visitors who had a genuine reason for seeking her out in her retreat, she received in the common parlour of the convent. When necessity compelled her to summon her physician or her tailor, she interviewed even them through the *grille*. Her religion alone had never failed her. Inevitably, she turned her energies to the work of conversion.

II

Before leaving his brother Henry in her care, the king had extracted from his mother a promise that she would make no attempts upon the young duke's faith. She had been wrong in agreeing to such a condition, for her secret hope in retaining the boy at her side had certainly been to influence him spiritually. Had she admitted this, however, she would unquestionably have lost him for ever, and her belief was that this opportunity had been sent her "to do him good". Three months had now passed, and he showed not the slightest sign of being infected by her example in religion. He strode off, every Sunday, to the Protestant service held in the private chapel of the English Resident in Paris. The necessity of saving the soul of one so dear to her began to obsess the queen's imagination. Overwhelming melancholy alternated by gusts of exaltation and energy were now her portion. She had not, she believed, long to live, but her duty was clear. She began her active campaign by superseding her son's tutor. Mr Lovell, a connection of Lord Leicester, had been a faithful attendant upon the young duke for the past six years. He had instructed the captive children of the late king at Penshurst and at Carisbrooke, and gone personally to London to urge his younger pupil's release after the death of the Princess Elizabeth.

Henrietta wrote to Charles, "Henry has too many acquaintances amongst the idle little boys of Paris, so I am sending him to Pontoise with the Abbé Montagu, where he will have more quiet to mind his book". The Abbot of Pontoise, Walter Montagu, now her Grand Almoner, seemed ideally suited to her purpose. He was a born royalist, the son of an English peer, and a polished author. He had been a man of the world and an adroit secret service agent. He was perfectly acquainted with the tenets of a religion he had himself abandoned, and all the vigour of the convert animated him. Mr Lovell was not crudely dismissed. He accompanied his young pupil out to the picturesque monastic town which had once been important as capital of the French Vexin. The gates of Pontoise opened to admit the English duke and his heretic tutor, and closed behind them. Dr. Cosin had told Mr Lovell that he ought to continue to read Anglican prayers in the duke's bedroom. Mr Lovell looked out at the well-ordered scene beneath him, realized with a sinking heart that he and a lad of fourteen were the only Protestants amongst scores of black-skirted foreigners, and decided that he would not take the risk. Instead he descended to discuss with the ingratiating Montagu the advisability of his taking a trip to Italy. The chief drawback was that he had no funds. When he was recalled to Paris, Mr Lovell went quietly, but before he went he divulged to his pupil the Queen Mother's intentions. She had herself frankly avowed them to him. He had written to the king, but Cologne was far. Abbé Montagu then took charge, confident of an easy victory. But the suave cleric must have strangely forgotten his own youth when he used as arguments in favour of the duke's adoption of Catholicism the poverty of a Protestant prince's prospects in France, and the hopelessness of King Charles's cause. To romantic fourteen, a crust and a roving life with his idolized eldest brother were unquestionably more attractive than a cardinal's hat and "abbeys and benefices . . . to such a value as would maintain him in that splendour as was suitable to his birth". Besides, the typical English schoolboy was swelling with indignation at the "mean and disingenuous action" of his mother in sending him here. He could not attempt to refute the Abbé in religious argument, but he could, and did, declare "that it was shameful to assail him with controversy in his tutor's absence". More than five years had passed since that dark January day when a king, on whom sentence of death had been passed, had taken a child of less than nine on his knee, and warned him solemnly against Rome, but that memory had not faded. Abbé Montagu found unexpected difficulty. A month at Pontoise produced nothing but a violent mutual dislike between royal pupil and new tutor. When Henry asked to be allowed to return to Paris to pay his respects to the Queen Mother and King of France, who had arrived to winter there, his request was granted. All his French relatives were on his mother's side.

His first action on reaching the Palais Royal was to send for Dr. Cosin. He was sure that "the Atlas of the Protestant religion" in Paris, author of many tracts against Popery, could supply him with arguments with which to rout Montagu. Their solemn conference was interrupted by the entry of the Abbé himself, who told his pupil to prepare to accompany him to the Louvre, rated him for having failed to send for the barber, and instructed him as to the exact length to which his hair must be cut.

Young Henry was duly led to court by his mother and his new tutor, where his appearance aroused much friendly interest. There was an awkward moment when Anne of Austria asked her sister-in-law "Was he quite turned yet?" to which Henrietta had to reply, "*Non, pas encore*", but Lovell had advised the duke to behave courteously towards his mother, so Henry controlled himself and behaved as if he had no grievance. Unfortunately finding him charming redoubled Henrietta's anxiety on behalf of his soul. She sent for Lovell, and told him that since she had made up her mind to carry on with the business of the duke's conversion, he had better resign. When that mild person ventured to suggest that the king should be consulted, he was told that such a proceeding would cause unnecessary delay, and in the presence of Montagu he received his *congé*. Henry was luckier in finding his mother unsupported by Montagu, and emerged from his first interview with her decidedly the winner, but discovering him "more obstinate than she had expected from his age", she merely ordered him another dose of Pontoise.

Meanwhile everyone wrote to the king in Cologne. Henry

himself sent a short business-like statement of his intolerable position. Had he remembered to date it, this letter would have been a model. Henrietta wrote that she hoped Charles would not become excited on hearing that she had found it her duty to have his brother enlightened as to her religion. She was not proposing in any way to influence his actions. Jermyn, palpably hating an affair that promised trouble, said practically nothing at great length. Other English Protestant noblemen in Paris, however, assured their monarch, with frenzied eloquence, that until their anxiety for his brother was relieved, they should neither eat nor sleep, and they were prepared to lay down their lives in his defence. Henry, removed again from their midst, was doing his best to defend himself. After lights were out in the abbey of Pontoise two young voices sounded far into the depths of the night. His grace's chamber-boy, a lad called Griffen, recited to him every evening as much as he could remember of a magnificent tract against Popery, specially drawn up for the duke's use by Dr. Cosin, and smuggled into Montagu's kingdom by Lord Hatton. But both boys were aware that should the duke prove intractable he was to be sent to a harsher school. Sir George Radcliffe had, with his own eyes, seen the masons putting the finishing touches to a set of apartments at Clermont, ordered for the youngest son of the Queen of England. In the Jesuits' College, Henry knew he would find a prison faster than Carisbrooke. His only hope was that Charles might act before his mother.

Letters from Charles arrived in Paris on the very day originally fixed for Henry's removal to Clermont. Although obviously written under stress of strong emotion, much acute psychology had been employed in their composition. To his mother the king sent a grave rebuke for having forgotten her promises to a dead husband as well as a son, whom, he could only suppose, she never wished to regain his throne.[1] Three

[1] Clar. MSS. 49. 136, Bodleian Library.

principal noblemen of her household received warmly worded reproaches for neglect of their duty. Montagu, the king failed altogether to notice. He reserved for the soft hide of Jermyn his unkindest cuts. The messenger, sent a few days later to enforce his majesty's commands, was as well chosen. James Butler, Marquis of Ormonde, a great aristocrat, and a great soldier, had always been remarkable for his physical strength, dignified carriage and purity of life. Henrietta displayed less than her usual decision when confronted with this forcible character. She could not, she declared, consider that she had broken any promise given by her to the king, for she had not used violence in her dealings with the duke. The duke would soon be returning to Paris, so it would be quite unnecessary for Lord Ormonde to go out to Pontoise. Promising to consider the whole matter further, she dismissed her son's envoy. A letter to Henry, brought to Pontoise by Sir George Radcliffe, and conveyed secretly to the duke by the invaluable Griffen, was, except perhaps in its opening words, all that the budding martyr would have hoped for.

DEAR BROTHER [read the duke],

I have received yours without a date, in which you tell me that Mr Montague has endeavoured to pervert you from your religion. I do not doubt but you remember very well the commands I left with you, at my going away, concerning that point. I am confident you will observe them; yet letters that come from Paris say that it is the queen's purpose to do all she can to change your religion, in which, if you do hearken to her, or to anybody else in that matter, you must never think to see England or me again; and whatsoever mischief shall fall on me or my affairs from this time, I must lay all upon you, as being the only cause of it. Therefore, consider well what it is to be, not only the cause of ruining a brother who loves you so well, but also of your king and country. Do not let them persuade you, either by force or fair promises; the first, they neither dare nor will use; and for the second, as soon as they have perverted you, they will have their end, and then they will care no more for you.

I am also informed there is a purpose to put you into the Jesuits' College, which I command you, on the same grounds, never to consent unto; and whensoever anybody goes to dispute with you in religion, do not answer them at all. For, though you have reason on your side, yet they, being prepared, will have the advantage of anybody that is not upon the same familiarity with argument as they are. If you do not consider what I say unto you, remember the last words of your dead father, which were to be constant to your religion, and never to be shaken in it; which, if you do not observe, this shall be the last time you will hear from

Dear brother
your most affectionate
CHARLES R.[1]

Ormonde went straight out to Pontoise on the morning after his interview with Henrietta, and carried Henry back to Paris with him. A week passed before the queen nerved herself to a last attack against the powers of evil. Churches were already offering thanksgivings for her child's conversion. After dinner, on a late November day, was the hour chosen by her for her final effort on his behalf. It found both actors in this tragedy in a pitiable condition. The adolescent prince, quick to detect portents of storm, managed, while the room was being cleared after the meal, to despatch the fervent Griffen in hot haste to fetch Lord Ormonde to his aid. When, as he had dreaded, his lady mother signified her intention to speak with him apart, he arose stiff with fright and wrath, to enter with a woman who did not play fair, upon a scene which promised to be terrible.

[1] Clar. MSS. 49. 137.

His worst fears were realized when his mother, having got him alone with her, began to kiss him passionately and insist that only her love for him could make her act with apparent cruelty. Summoning a sweetness which she genuinely felt, but which contrasted painfully with her ghastly look and trembling accents, she told him that she was sure he was as weary as she of his disobedience. The combatants looked upon one another, and each saw that the other was possessed of a devil. The cold blue stare of a young heretic met the glittering black eyes of a honeytongued seductress. Realizing with despair that she was making no headway, Henrietta commanded her son to hear the Abbé's arguments once more, meditate carefully upon them, and send or bring her a full and final answer to her entreaties.

Henry went off to his own room, where the figure of Montagu soon presented itself. After an hour's eloquence, the Abbé asked the duke what answer he might carry to the queen, and received the disconcerting reply: "None". Henry was playing for time till Ormonde should arrive. Montagu retired, baffled, saying that he would come again, but two hours later he had to search the palace for the duke, whom he found in "a lady's chamber on the other side", attended by Ormonde. Without further hesitation, Henry declared that his final answer to the queen his mother was that he meant to continue firm in the religion of the Church of England. "Then", said Montagu, "it is her majesty's command that you see her face no more." He was even empowered to deny the duke a parting blessing from his parent.

One more unhappy scene between Henry and his mother took place, but it was mercifully brief. On the following morning, a Sunday, hearing that she was going to Chaillot, he placed himself in her path as she passed to her coach. Falling on his knees, he asked for her blessing, but Henrietta averted her face. Montagu, when she had swept by, stepped up to ask his victim what her majesty had said which had so discomposed him.

Henry then, for the first time, gave vent to his feelings, and told his persecutor that "It is but reason that what my mother has just said to me I should repeat to you—'Be sure that I see your face no more!' "

He departed defiantly to Church of England service, where he was received with rejoicings, but, on his return to the Palais Royal, found, much to his dismay, that the sheets had been stripped from his bed, his horses were being turned out of their stables, and, by her majesty's commands, no dinner had been prepared for him. When the little Duke of Anjou, sent by Anne of Austria to urge reason upon a hungry cousin, reached the Duke of Gloucester's apartments, he found them bare and tenantless, nor could anyone tell him where their owner had gone. The Protestant Lord Hatton had offered his master's youngest brother food and a bed. Before he had disappeared, however, the schoolboy prince had endeavoured to say farewell to one relation who still loved him. While his mother was at vespers, he asked a servant to take a message to the Princess Henrietta Anne, simply saying that a gentleman wished to see her. The result was disastrous. "*Oh Dieu!* my brother! Oh me! my mother!" screamed the ten-year-old princess. "I am undone for ever; what shall I do?" Henry retreated crest-fallen, but presently Lord Ormonde managed to raise some money by pawning his last jewel, his George of the Garter, and on a December day a happy boy rode out of Paris, bound for Cologne and King Charles.

At the Palais Royal the Princess Henrietta Anne moped. The queen had forbidden her little daughter, under pain of her serious anger, to mention or even think of the Duke of Glouces-ter. With the Duke of York her majesty was at present only communicating by means of the Abbé Montagu. Her second son had committed the dire offence of interceding on behalf of his younger brother. Henrietta scolded her fifth disobedient child. Henrietta Anne howled. Misery flooded the soul of

Henrietta Maria. Gloom reigned supreme at the Palais
Royal.[1]

III

Innocent X had died, having "outlived the understanding
and judgment he had been formerly master of, and lost all the
reputation he had formerly gotten". His successor, Alexander
VII, had wept when discussing the execution of Charles I.
Henrietta wrote to her eldest son, suggesting that the agent
whom she was sending to Rome should ask the new Pope for
funds towards a royalist rising in England. Charles, who "had
in truth very little hope that the new pope would be more
magnanimous than his predecessor", preferred to send his own
messenger. "The Sealed Knot", a band of influential conspirators at work amongst the cavaliers of England, was indeed
assuring him that a revolution in his name was imminent. On
February 14th, 1655, he vanished from Cologne, attended by
Ormonde and a single groom. Six weeks later he reappeared,
having spent the interval disguised as "Mr Jackson", waiting
in Holland for a summons home which had failed to come. As
he had expected, Alexander VII "used the same adage that his
predecessor had done". "He could not with a good conscience
apply the patrimony of the Church to the assistance and support
of heretics." Charles welcomed his sister Mary upon a visit,
and the handsome couple amused themselves by making an
incognito expedition to Frankfurt fair. Henrietta wrote: "I
understand that you have seen the Queen of Sweden, and beg
you to send me word if you find that what people say about her
person and disposition is true. I should be very glad to know it." [2]
The twenty-nine-year-old Queen Christina, who to her subjects' undisguised relief had definitively abdicated her throne,
had departed from her country in male attire, calling herself

[1] Clarendon, *Hist.* 14. 117-20; Carte's *Life of Ormonde*; "Exact Narrative
of the Attempts made upon the Duke of Gloucester", 1655; Evelyn's
Diary, vol. iv.   [2] Lambeth MS. 645. 96.

"Count Dohna", and taken Frankfurt on her road from Flanders to Italy. But whatever impressions of one of the most extraordinary women of his day may have been divulged by Charles II to his mother, they have not been preserved.

France was preparing to sign a treaty of peace with Cromwell. Anne of Austria, a genuinely warm-hearted though very lazy woman, felt sorry for her sister-in-law. Henrietta Maria's tastes were pronounced. It was useless to send her any article for personal adornment. She hung even her bedchamber with black velvet. In the end, Anne decided that her sympathy should be expressed by the gift of a bale of cloth of silver,[1] and an invitation to bring the Princess Henrietta Anne to a private ball at the Louvre. Louis XIV was seventeen now, and theoretically his own master. With the indolence that he had inherited from his mother, he left affairs of state in the hands of the cardinal, but he had begun to realize that he was a handsome young man, and assumed gallant airs. Henrietta, whose dearest wish, ever since she had regained possession of her youngest child, had been to see her Queen of France, built towering hopes on her nephew's improved manners towards her. "He treats me like another person, and has become the most civil being in the world."[2] The entertainment proposed by Anne of Austria was a godsend—a family affair, "only given to show how well the king could dance and divert the Princess of England, who was just growing out of childhood and showing how charming she would become".[3] To have presented her daughter at a court ball, at a date when full dress was elaborate, would have caused Henrietta great difficulty, but an inexpensive imitation of the latest fashion, perfectly suitable to be worn by a young princess at a small party held in her aunt's own apartments, could with care be contrived. Another reason for congratulation was that Minette was a born dancer.

[1] A magnificent bale of cloth of silver, still intact, was found in a wooden chest in Henrietta's country château after her death. *S.P.D.* Fr., 78. 128, P.R.O.   [2] Lambeth MS. 645. 95.   [3] de Motteville.

The great evening arrived, and all promised perfectly. To
mark the informality of the occasion, the hostess had attired
herself in a *négligée* and one of the new *boudoir* caps called
cornettes. The company was extremely select, but there were
enough young people present to form a Grand Quadrille for
the young king, who appeared in tearing spirits. At last the
music struck up for the first dance, the popular old *branle*, and
a brawl indeed it unfortunately proved, for Louis, intent only
on enjoying himself, proceeded to lead out the eldest of Cardinal Mazarin's beautiful nieces. Arising from her chair of state
with a working countenance, Anne of Austria strode after her
son and tore his partner from him. In a furious whisper she
then desired him to invite his principal guest to open the ball
with him. A tiny black-robed figure literally ran after the angry
pair. Her daughter, explained the Queen of England with
pathetic eagerness, would be quite unable to take the floor
to-night. She had hurt her foot. Anne of Austria said stormily
that if the princess could not dance to-night, neither could the
king. "The most civil being in the world" looked daggers at
his poor relations. Finally the shrinking Minette's hand was
forced upon her cousin, who, after the performance of a few
steps with her, sulked for the rest of the evening. At the conclusion of her disastrous attempt at philanthropy, he informed
his mother that "he did not care for little girls".[1]

On a December day Henrietta saw from her windows in the
Palais Royal the illuminations ordered to celebrate a treaty
of peace with England, which insisted upon the exclusion of her
sons from the country of her birth. She seized her pen, and
wrote gallantly to her eldest son that the bonfires had been a
very poor show. Many of the good citizens of Paris had refused
to make them, and indeed some, seeing their neighbours making
them, had hurried to extinguish them.[2]

Mazarin, anxious not to lose the Irish troops in the French

[1] de Motteville.   [2] Lambeth MS. 645. 98.

service, had arranged with the Lord Protector that the Duke of York might take up a command under the Duke of Modena over the French and allied soldiers campaigning in Piedmont, but Charles was refusing to allow his brother to accept such an offer. He had borrowed from his sister Mary enough money to send an embassy to Spain, and in return reluctantly consented that she should accept their mother's standing invitation to visit Paris. Henrietta, hoping that Spain might "go beyond compliments, and come to the sword", wished her son a New Year "happier to you than those which have passed, and such as you could wish it". A mysterious character, "a certain gentleman, a great mathematician", who was an adept at calculating future events, had presented her with a forecast of Charles's career which she forwarded with the warning that "one cannot put too much trust in such things". She prayed God the man might be a true prophet.[1] For herself, she had thought of going to Spain, but since she had been given to understand that she would not be welcome there, she must stay where she was.

Members of the most polite nation in the world, distinctly ashamed of their latest ally, endeavoured to comfort her by speaking disparagingly of England and everything English. She corrected them with dignity. Her son's kingdom was a beautiful place, full of brave, generous and good-natured people. The hardships which she had suffered there had been brought about by the Government falling into the hands of a few desperate fanatics, who by no means represented the bulk of their countrymen.[2]

Everyone except herself and her daughter thought the Princess of Orange's visit to France singularly ill-timed. But Henrietta was nourishing the golden hope that a few weeks of Chaillot might work a wonder with a disconsolate young Protestant widow, and to Mary the word Paris simply spelt magic. For some time past she had been ailing and restless, and her aunt

[1] Lambeth MS. 645. 99. 101.   [2] Reresby.

Elizabeth of Bohemia's unromantic suggestion that she was suffering from nothing but lack of exercise, and would do well to take it in the form of sawing wood into faggots, did not appeal to her. The Jews of Amsterdam were still the possessors of some of the finest jewellery in Europe. Wisely determining to leave the choice of new gowns until she had reached the seat of fashion, Mary proceeded to the congenial business of selecting an array of precious stones calculated to enhance her prestige in the eyes of her mother's host.. To make her purchases she was obliged to anticipate the income of several years, and even, said some disapproving witnesses, pledge estates which she held as guardian for her infant son. Whatever the cost, the result was satisfactory. The arrival of the beautiful Princess of Orange brought so many callers to the Palais Royal that Henrietta pronounced herself "half-dead", and erroneously supposed that her daughter was equally "weary of visits from morning till night". Mary, with her ivory complexion, chestnut curls and dancing hazel eyes, was prepared to be charmed with everything, and charm everybody. She was only twenty-five although she had been a widow for six years. The curious who flocked to admire her had not a single doubt that she had come to set her cap at their king. They wronged her. She had no intention of abandoning her religion in favour of any new husband; the hours of Chaillot, imposed upon her by her mother, had no more effect upon her than water on a duck's back. She had come to Paris to enjoy herself; to show her independence she had brought amongst her attendants the blooming Anne Hyde. She thought that personal acquaintance with so attractive a member of his family must help to overcome her mother's unhappy prejudice against her brother's chief minister. Anne, who had inherited only a little of her sire's brain, and whose other attractions were limited to a pair of languishing blue eyes and a swelling bosom, failed entirely to impress Henrietta, but, quite unknown to the queen, had a complete success with the moody, unemployed Duke of York.

Mary was royally entertained by her French relations. Since Anne of Austria did not consider that widows ought to dance, the Princess of Orange had to remain a spectator at the ball given in her honour by the little Duke of Anjou; but she was not entirely sorry, for she doubted her ability to acquit herself with credit before a fashionable audience. The king opened the ball with her younger sister, "who looked like an angel upon earth . . . and danced so perfectly that a thousand blessings were showered upon her". Anne of Austria also gave a ball for Mary, and the king invited her to a comedy followed by a classical ballet. A banquet offered to her by the Chancellor Séguier surpassed even her expectations of Parisian elegance. The hall in which the court dined was lit by thousands of candles and lined by mirrors, three hundred torches illuminated the gallery leading to the ballroom, and, at the moment that the violins struck up, each cavalier presented his partner with a fragile basket, decked with ribbons and filled with *bon-bons* and rare fruits.[1]

At the close of the season, when the court deserted Paris, Mary showed no inclination to turn home. The great Mademoiselle, who, like the Princess of Orange, had been bored to death for several years, responded eagerly to a suggestion that she should name a date and place for a meeting with her cousin. Mademoiselle, twenty-nine, still a spinster and still an exile from court, chose the beautiful château of Chilly as the scene of her hospitality to Henrietta and Mary, and they presented themselves there on a July morning, attended by "quantities of English and Irish ladies and gentlemen" and a number of Mademoiselle's French friends. Henrietta was led through a succession of splendidly furnished rooms and a gallery, to a bedchamber, where she took a short rest after her drive. Dinner was served in a saloon on the ground floor. On their way upstairs

[1] *Gazette de France*, Feb. 1656.

after the meal, the Princess of Orange attached herself to her hostess and displayed startling friendliness and loquacity. The pretty widow declared that she would have been desolated had she been obliged to quit France without making the acquaintance of someone whom she had loved unseen, from the many descriptions of her brother the King of England. Mademoiselle enquired how the princess liked the French court, and Mary, who did not share her mother's delicacy of feeling with regard to an adopted country, replied that she adored France but had "a horrible aversion" from Holland. When her brother the king was established on his throne she meant to go and live with him in England. Henrietta was conducted to the seat of honour in the circle formed for after-dinner conversation, but her daughter continued to monopolize their hostess. For her visit to her heiress-cousin the Princess of Orange had adorned herself with enormous pendant pearl earrings, a pea-pearl necklace and many diamond bracelets, clasps and rings. Henrietta, very much the French mother, never to be deposed from authority even over married children, drew Mademoiselle's attention to the fact that the princess's dress was perfectly correct for a *visite de cérémonie*. She had insisted that Mary must wear black and a widow's cap to-day. She added in tones of awful warning: "My daughter is not as I. She is magnificent, has jewels and money and loves spending. I tell her that she ought to save. Once I was as she—even more so. Look at me now!" Before leaving, she too mentioned Charles II. "And the poor King of England! You are so unfeeling as not to enquire for him?" Mademoiselle, aware that although an exile she had not ceased to be an heiress, said that she had been waiting for an opportunity. "Alas!" said Henrietta dramatically. "He is so foolish as to love you still!" She offered the optimistic opinion that had her niece accepted Charles's heart and hand, she would not now be exposed to all the caprices of her French kin. She would be her own mistress, and perhaps happily established in England.

"I am persuaded that the poor miserable one will never be happy without you. If only you had married him, he and I would have agreed better than we do. You would have helped him to live on better terms with me." "If he could not live happily with your Majesty," said Mademoiselle unanswerably, "why should he do so with someone else?" [1]

Charles, whose allowance from France was about to be discontinued, had moved his starving court to Bruges. Here, during this month of July, the Guild of Crossbowmen offered him a banquet. A contemporary painting recording the occasion shows a solemn panelled chamber, lighted by many long windows and floored with black-and-white tiles. Scores of grave-faced burghers and servitors, all attired in sober suits with collars and cuffs of spotless linen, are crowded round a table at which, under a silk canopy pendent from the ceiling, is seated the King of England, attended by the Duke of Gloucester and courtiers. Henry, and two of the dogs present, appear keenly sensitive to the atmosphere. Charles alone, with his head cocked slightly aslant, seems to have found some secret source of amusement in the scene.

IV

With September the court returned to Paris and a fresh season of gaieties opened in honour of another royal guest. Christina of Sweden, about whom Henrietta had been so curious, arrived wearing a man's periwig and shoes, a chemise "sticking out all around her petticoat . . . ill-fastened and not over-straight", much powder on a countenance of strong features pitted with smallpox, quantities of pomatum and no gloves on hands which were remarkably dirty. She proceeded to swear, fall into spectacular brown studies, and dance at court balls with astonishing vigour and inelegance.[2] Eighteen

---

[1] de Montpensier.   [2] de Motteville.

months later she presented herself for a second visit, but since on this occasion she superintended the assassination of her major-domo, she received a request to quit France.

The news that her son had developed measles called the Princess of Orange back to hated Holland, after nine months of warmly appreciated French frivolity. The mother whom she had not seen for thirteen years wept at parting from her, but except in love of Charles II the couple had failed to find much in common.

The fifties began to draw towards their close, and Henrietta became conscious of an elderly taste. She had betaken herself "to a private life, studying nothing more than how to live inoffensively", but neither Chaillot nor the Palais Royal exactly suited her needs. A small home of her own, where she could sit in the sun in the garden or by the fireside, surrounded by the pet dogs and some favourite pieces of furniture, and entertaining when she felt like it, a few old friends, was now her ideal. Drives about the suburbs began again, and she found what she was looking for in a village called Colombes. She must not go too far from the capital, for she had a growing daughter to consider. Colombes, although only seven miles north-west of Paris, was perfectly peaceful.[1] It had a sixteenth-century church with a twelfth-century tower, and it lay in a loop of the Seine over which, on fine evenings, the sky reddened behind the forest of St Germain. Unwittingly Henrietta Maria had chosen the scene of her deathbed.

The old château was picturesque and not too large. Anyone clever at such things could soon make it comfortable. Some of the new furniture being made in Paris was fascinating—tortoiseshell and ebony cabinets and mirrors with bronze-gilt inlay. She longed for a few of the pictures which had decorated

[1] The château of Colombes no longer exists. A race-course, numerous villas and boarding-schools now decorate a thriving suburb linked to the capital by tramway.

her English palaces—the portraits of the children by Sir Anthony, so like and so lovely. But she had landed in France with no possessions but hand luggage, and ever since had been too poor to buy anything but necessities. Money was still a terrible consideration. She suggested to Mazarin that since he was now friends with Cromwell he should ask his fine new ally to pay the dowry of the Queen of England. The cardinal, a most avaricious man, actually forwarded the hopeless application. The answer, which he communicated personally to Henrietta, was insulting. Since she had never been crowned queen she was not entitled to any recognition by England. Henrietta said: "This outrage does not reflect upon me, but on the king my nephew, who should not permit a daughter of France to be treated *en concubine*. I was abundantly satisfied with the late King, my lord, and with all England; these affronts are more shameful to France than to me."[1] Anne of Austria added from her own privy purse two hundred livres a month to the pension allotted to Henrietta, as a daughter of France, by the French Government, and Colombes was purchased. Nevertheless '57 was a doleful year for Henrietta. Charles had engaged to collect all his subjects now serving in France and lend them to Spain. In June the Dukes of York and Gloucester both took part in the battle of the Dunes, and in December a rumour reached Paris that the King of England had been seriously wounded in the attempt upon Mardike, where he had exposed himself recklessly. Henrietta wrote:

MONSIEUR, MY SON,

I am very glad that the report . . . is not true. . . . News is always exaggerated, and we easily believe what we fear. It is not, however, altogether unreasonable that I should beg of you to be more careful than you are. Although I do not doubt that God is preserving you for better times, yet you also should not

[1] de Motteville.

tempt Him, and should take care of yourself. My prayers too will not be wanting, if they are worth anything.[1]

During the depths of this particularly severe winter an unexpected convert arrived at Chaillot. On a December morning the Princess Louise of the Palatinate fled from her mother's house and took refuge in a Carmelite convent at Antwerp. Here she was visited by Charles II, the Princess of Orange and the Duke of York, all of whom begged her to reconsider her decision and return to the indignant Elizabeth of Bohemia, who was moving heaven and earth to recover her. Louise answered that she was sorry that she had displeased her mother but "was very well satisfied with her change".[2] Her brother Edward, who had himself abandoned Protestantism some years previously and was now a settled resident in Paris, was making preparations to have her received in France. She met him at Rouen and he took her to Chaillot, where she was given the apartments of the Queen of England.

Everyone expected that the princess would take the veil in the convent founded by her aunt, but the clear-sighted Mother de la Fayette did not encourage her to do so. Louise had no vocation. She had merely realized that she was thirty-six, unlikely to find a husband and sick of penury. She passed on to the Cistercians of Maubuisson, near Pontoise, who eventually made her their abbess. Here she found ample leisure to indulge her taste for painting in oils. She executed an oval "Notre Dame" which she sent to her kind aunt, and Henrietta thought so highly of the convert's effort that she gave it the place of honour over the fireplace in her own bedchamber at Colombes, a room in which it had for companion a "Notre Dame" by Titian. The artist princess thoroughly enjoyed the existence of a wealthy country gentlewoman, never spoke to her nuns except to give orders, and lived to the age of eighty-eight.

[1] Lambeth MS. 645. 105.   [2] Bromley.

Henrietta's relations with Elizabeth of Bohemia, who had never relished being deposed from the position of Arch-Widow of Europe, were naturally not improved by the fact that Louise had gone straight to Chaillot on her arrival in France. In the following year a friendship much dearer to Henrietta was to be threatened.

The court was now much gayer than it had been during the king's minority, and, to her great delight, little Henrietta Anne was invited to three of the many entertainments which took place during this hard winter. Her kind aunt took her to the Chancellor's Assembly, and the cardinal, quite unexpectedly, invited her mother to bring her to a supper party at which the other chief guests were to be the king, the Queen Mother of France, the Duke of Anjou and Mademoiselle, who had at last been allowed to return to Paris. The appearance of the princess of England at grown-up parties was, however, to cause some friction in court circles. A few days after the Chancellor's Assembly, and before his own supper, the cardinal took Mademoiselle apart to ask her if it was true that she had walked out of rooms before the Princess Henrietta Anne the other night. The Duke of Anjou, before she could answer, said: "And if she did, was she not right? Why should people who accept their bread from us take precedence of us? If they are not satisfied with the treatment they get, let them go elsewhere." The story was reported to Henrietta Anne's mother, who wept bitterly. Anne of Austria scolded her son for lack of chivalry, and Mademoiselle explained that she had merely done the honours of the house at the Chancellor's party because she happened to be his nearest relative. She did not wish to miss the cardinal's fête, which promised to be splendid. As it took place on a Sunday evening in Lent, only a bewildering succession of fish dishes was served at it, but there was dancing after the meal, and during the evening the host led the royalties up to a gallery where "everything pretty that comes from China" had been set out. The excited little princess beheld "jewellery, trinkets, crystal chandeliers, mirrors, ornamental tables and cabinets, silver vases, scent, gloves, ribbons and fans, all arranged as in booths at a fair. The only difference was that here every object was expensive." These treasures proved to be prizes for a lottery. No blank tickets were issued, so every guest got a gift. A lucky lieutenant of the king's Guards drew the first prize, a diamond worth four thousand crowns.[1]

On Shrove Monday Anne of Austria gave a masked ball, and the Queen of Sweden, who was making her last appearance in Paris, sent word that unless she could take precedence of the Queen of England, she would not come. Anne of Austria again stood firm. The Queen of England, she said, had no happiness in this world, and this was her one poor opportunity in the year of seeing her daughter dance. Christina could either come in a mask, as a private person, or stay away. Christina came, dressed *en bohémienne*, looking "inconceivably ridiculous", and made such a spectacle of herself on the dancing-floor that people had to look aside to hide their smiles. The Duke of Anjou disguised himself as a fair-haired girl, in which attire his relations considered that he bore a striking resemblance to Mademoiselle. He was nearly eighteen, and had dark-blue eyes and curling black hair. Had his mouth been a little larger, he would have been handsome. His vanity was excessive. The cardinal confided in Mademoiselle that the queen and he wished that, since she appeared to have influence with her cousin, she would use it for his good. "The Queen and I are in despair to see how he cares for nothing but clothes, and dressing himself as a girl. He takes no exercise, and is accustoming himself to a softness most unbecoming to a young man of his age. The Queen and I wish passionately that he would ask to be allowed to join the army."[2]

Louis XIV went off to visit his troops at Mardike, and caught fever there. The rotting corpses of men who had fallen in battle months before, protruded from the dry sands in which they had been unsuccessfully buried, and there was no water to be had in the place. Monsieur stayed close to his mother's skirts at Calais, "like a child". He took her ladies out for walks on the shore, playfully sprinkled their attire with sea water, and was fascinated by the English stuffs and ribbons which he could buy in the town. Even he was relieved when his energetic brother recovered after a dangerous illness.

Louis XIV had fallen in love with the eighteen-year-old Marie Mancini. The cardinal, who had not forgotten that the citizens of Paris had once hung him in effigy at their cross-roads, would not hear of a marriage between his niece and his king, and Marie would consider nothing less than marriage. Obviously a royal bride must be found for the unsettled young man without delay. Anne of Austria had always assured Henrietta Maria that, should her son be unable to mate in Spain, no daughter-in-law would be more welcome to her than the charming Minette. For a long time the Infanta Maria Theresa had been unavailable, since she had been her father's heiress. Now that her stepmother had borne a son, she was still out of the question, for France was at war with Spain. But Minette was not yet fourteen. Looking for a princess who would win the young king's heart and—since the heir-presumptive was inimical to the cardinal—bring France a Dauphin as soon as possible, Mazarin turned his gaze in another direction. The Princess Adelaide, for whom Henrietta had chosen a trousseau seven winters before, had been the youngest of her Savoy nieces, but Duchess Christine had yet an elder daughter unmarried. The truth was that the Duke of Bavaria had considered the Princess Marguerite-Yolande very plain. She was now twenty-three and perfectly healthy. She would get a dowry, and her brother, although not a king, was in possession of his territories. With a chagrin which she must not express, the Queen of England saw her darling passed over in favour of a candidate inferior to her in birth, brains and beauty. The choice of any other woman's child would have been kinder to Henrietta. Her sister Christine, the one member of her family with whom she had never had a shadow of disagreement, went nearly out of her senses with joy at the prospect of so unhoped-for a destiny for her ugly duckling. For several months the friendship of the two surviving daughters of Henri IV hung in the balance. Henrietta, who had again and again discussed by letter going up as far as Chambéry from Bourbon to meet her dear sister, was one of the few prominent people in France during the late summer of 1658 making no preparations to welcome the Duchess of Savoy and the Princess Marguerite at Lyons. She went to Bourbon unusually early this season, and was safely back in Paris before her sister had moved from Turin. Another royalist rising in England had failed. Her two younger sons had narrowly escaped being taken prisoners, when daringly resisting the French attack upon Dunkirk. She wrote to Charles, who was going to see the Princess of Orange at Breda: "I only wish we were in a condition to be able to meet altogether. I assure you that this is my daily prayer. . . . I have been in the greatest possible apprehension for your brothers, and I spend my time ill enough here, seeing all that passes. You may well imagine that I suffer much myself. I hope that *le bon Dieu* will at length put an end to our misfortunes, and will re-establish us, in spite of all the world, and will yet grant me life enough to see for myself that happy day. Believe that these are the ardent wishes of, my son,—your most affectionate mother.[1]

Everyone who felt for the courageous and misfortunate Queen of England hastened to congratulate her on a piece of news which reached Paris about a month before the court left

[1] Lambeth MS. 645. 106.

for Lyons. On September 3rd, 1658, four days after the greatest storm that had vexed England for a hundred years, the spirit of the Lord Protector, Oliver Cromwell, passed from his body. Duchess Christine, who could afford to be generous, wrote at once to hope that this event might make a great difference in the prospects of her sister's family. To her Henrietta proudly replied that certainly there would be changes in England now, "and I have children who will not lose chances". But to the gentle Madame de Motteville she opened her heart: "In truth I thought you would hear with joy of the death of that rascal; yet, whether it be because my heart is so wrapped up in melancholy as to be incapable of receiving any, or that I do not as yet perceive any good advantages likely to accrue to us from it, I will confess to you that I have not myself felt any very great rejoicing, my greatest being to witness that of my friends."

In London the Council had accepted Richard Cromwell as successor to Oliver Cromwell, and the City and Army had followed suit docilely. Charles informed his mother that he had "nothing to propose" at present. "When you command me in anything for your service," answered the indefatigable little woman, "you shall find me as ready as I have ever been. . . . We must wait opportunities to avail ourselves of them. I assure you I will let none slip."[1] Jermyn, whom she had sent to see her son, came back with a tactful intimation that his majesty hoped her majesty would proceed in any way she thought helpful with the greatest caution. Henrietta took the warning in good part, and assured her son that she would "do nothing which could in any possible manner be prejudicial to you. Believe this, I beg you. The court", she added with a trace of bitterness, "is going a grand journey, as you will know; but if there be anything to do, this will not hinder it, for I can always send thither."[2]

But she was to be spared the blow of seeing her child cut

[1] Lambeth MS. 645. 107.   [2] *Ibid.* 108.

out by Christine's child. On the same day that the Princess Marguerite, a stocky, sensible girl, escorted by a highly neurotic mother, arrived in Lyons by one road, Don Antonio Pimental in disguise entered it by another. Louis XIV met his intended bride, and thought her quite agreeable, though rather dark-skinned. Having heard that she was hump-backed, he presented himself while she was making her toilet next morning, and satisfied himself that rumour had lied. Duchess Christine, who like all the daughters of Henri IV had lost her looks prematurely, was pronounced by the court of France to have traces of past beauty and the air of a *grande dame*, but a regrettably sugary manner, and a complexion of extraordinary pallor, easily explained by her devotion to her medicine-chest. Unknown to all of them, the cardinal had already startled and delighted Anne of Austria by the greeting, "Good news, madame. I bring you both peace and the Infanta!" Philip IV, on hearing that his nephew was about to marry a daughter of Savoy, had exclaimed "That cannot and shall not be!" Don Antonio Pimental, sent off post-haste from Madrid, without passports, into a country at war with his own, had arrived just in time to break a match not much fancied by anyone except the bride's mother.

Anne of Austria was overjoyed at the prospect of peace with her brother's country, and the daughter-in-law who had always been her first choice. Her son was not sorry to resume his love affair with the cardinal's niece. Mademoiselle did not mind the king marrying an Infanta. Princess Marguerite had never wanted him. Duchess Christine was reported to have knocked her head against the wall in her first passion of grief, on being informed that her daughter must retire in favour of "the vast grandeur of Spain" and the peace of Europe, but like Henrietta, she could command her emotions in public. Although her eyes were swollen with weeping, she appeared "quite gay" when the cardinal had presented her with a pair of diamond and black enamel earrings and some jewelled scent-bottles, and the king with a document binding himself to marry Marguerite should any accident deprive him of Maria Theresa. On her departure she wept again, but her daughter did not shed a single tear. Henrietta's slighted niece turned home to marry the Duke of Parma and die at the age of thirty. The French court arrived back in Paris late in January 1659. After a pause of just over a year letters between Henrietta and her sister began again in the old friendly vein. The duchess sent a gift of scent and pastilles to Colombes, and Henrietta replied with a portrait of Minette which evoked cries of admiration in Turin.

v

Paris was very quiet during the summer of 1659. The court had set off towards Spain, to bring back peace and the Infanta, and was not to return to the capital for nearly twelve months. Henrietta seemed to have been right when she had prophesied that Cromwell's death would mean changes in England, but that no immediate advantages would accrue to her son. Another royalist rising, planned to take place on August 1st of this year, was betrayed to Parliament by a member of the Sealed Knot. Charles, who had been on the point of embarking for Deal, where he was to have been seized and murdered, decided that he had "scarcely any hopes left but what might arise from the Treaty of the Crowns of France and Spain". Travelling incognito, he reached Fontarabia, where the treaty was being made, late in October. Marshal Turenne, with whom Henrietta had been in touch on her son's behalf, had offered to send over his regiment to assist in a Restoration. The second Stuart king in succession to visit Spain, like his father before him, charmed every influential Spaniard with whom he came in contact, but Mazarin refused to see him and in an interview with Ormonde would commit France to nothing. Henrietta, disappointed but still determined to help, sent Jermyn and the Abbé Montagu down to Toulouse to catch the cardinal on his return journey, "and use instances in her name with him, to furnish her son the king with the succours he wanted for a descent upon England, or at least to connive at those aids of men, arms and ammunition which he might obtain by the affections of the French". Neither her confessor nor her chamberlain was present, therefore, when Charles arrived at Colombes to pay her his first visit since her luckless attempt upon her youngest son's faith. The wandering king reached his mother's picturesque château on a December night, attended by a single groom, and caused immediate merriment by warmly embracing one of her majesty's ladies-in-waiting, whom he mistook for his sister. Six years had passed since he had seen Minette, and he was charmed by the change in her. She was now taller than her mother, of whom she was a more warmly coloured reproduction. The family passed a winter's week of bad weather in the country "with entire satisfaction in each other", and Charles gladdened his mother's heart by discussing his situation without any appearance of reserve. He was in good spirits, and did not despair of being soon upon his throne in England. Henrietta listened to a story which she had heard before. Twelve years before, when his father had written to tell her that the military party was now in the ascendancy in his country, the news had filled her with hope. But her son would be thirty next year; unless the change in his fortunes came soon, it would come too late for her.

At Toulouse, Jermyn and Montagu were finding that they could not prevail with the cardinal "for so much as a connivance". Mazarin refused to be impressed by their assurances of the irreconcilable divisions of their master's enemies and the firm resolution of his friends. He sent word to the queen that her son's visit must be cut short. Henrietta, concealing her despair, told Charles that she thought she could get her sister Christine to advance some money towards his next expedition. These long fireside discussions of hopes and fears, in which she would have taken such eager interest when she had been a little younger, were so amiable, so proper, between a grown son and a wise mother, she must not by any word betray that in her heart hope was almost dead. Charles, after creating his mother's chamberlain Earl of St Albans, left for Brussels in a thaw, promising to write to his little sister and keep his mother advised of every development in his affairs. He arrived back in Spanish territory in the week after Christmas, to find the opinions of his adherents there "not so agreeable to him as those which he had met with on the road".

Yet at this very hour General Monk was beginning his advance on London. The general, "Old Tom" to his troops, was a little apple-cheeked man of fifty, small-eyed, very broad of face and shoulder, and with no air of distinction about him. His father had been a Devonshire gentleman of impoverished estates, and he had been a soldier since he was sixteen. He had served with Sir Richard Grenville against Spain and with Buckingham against France, and for the States-General against Spain, and for Charles I against Fairfax and the Irish and the Scots, and, after the royalist cause seemed hopeless, for Cromwell against the Irish and the Scots. The week of wild weather which had ushered in the death of the Lord Protector had found him at the head of a small but efficient army in Edinburgh. After the fall of Richard Cromwell, he had offered his services to Parliament. General Lambert's attempt to coerce "the Rump" had decided him to march south. Announcing that he was coming to safeguard the Government, he set out from Coldstream at dawn on New Year's Day, 1660. The Border roads were knee-deep in snow, but the weather was exhilarating. As they crossed the Tweed on a dead calm morning of hard frost, the little general's little army could distinguish the very colours of the pebbles in the river's bed. According to his chaplain's account, they never "trod upon plain earth from

Edinburgh to London", but they trod upon clouds, for their progress was an uninterrupted triumph. When Monk reached London he found himself master of England. He declared a free Parliament and got into secret communication with the exiled king. "He is a black Monk, and I cannot see through him", complained that fervent royalist conspirator Lord Mordaunt, fretting at what seemed to him unnecessary delays. But Charles realized that "the most cautious man in the three kingdoms" knew what he was about. The king wrote to his little sister, asking how she was spending her days during this miserable weather. If she was, as he supposed, at Chaillot, a place of which his memories do not appear to have been cheerful, he assumed that she must be "not a little bored".

The Duke of Orleans had died, and Henrietta and her daughter were busy answering letters of condolence. Even the cardinal had written with his own hand to console the queen for the loss of a brother who had been a thoroughly selfish man and very little use to her. Henrietta answered that she was much affected by this evidence of the part the cardinal took in all that concerned her.

Before dawn on the last day of March, Charles left Brussels for Breda. A message from Monk, brought to him by word of mouth the night before, had urged him to leave Spanish territory lest in the event of a Restoration he should be detained by a nation at war with England. In reply he forwarded the famous Declaration of Breda, and letters to the Council of State, the officers of the army, both Houses of Parliament and the authorities of the City of London. Nearly a month later, on old May Day, Charles II was solemnly proclaimed in Westminster Hall. Mazarin, now indeed interested in all that concerned Henrietta Maria, suggested to her that the King of England should negotiate with his subjects from Paris. Thoroughly approving of a scheme which would bring her son to her side, she sent Jermyn to point out its advantages. The newly created earl, nothing loath to approach the fount of honours at so propitious a moment, used his best persuasions, but Charles preferred to accept the invitation of the States-General to move to the Hague. On May 22nd news was brought to the queen at Chaillot that her son intended to embark from Scheveling that day. She wrote to tell him that her prayers would accompany him, but that until she heard of his safe arrival she would know no peace.

"The happy hours" she wished him had already begun, but Charles did not embark on the *Naseby*, now re-christened the *Royal Charles*, until the morning of May 23rd. He entered into his kingdom on May 25th, 1660, by the same port to which his mother had been brought thirty-five years before as a bride, and he wrote next day to Minette from Canterbury: "I was so tormented with business at the Hague that I could not write to you before my departure; but I left orders with my sister to send you a small present from me, which I hope you will soon receive. I arrived yesterday at Dover, where I found Monk, with a great number of the nobility, who almost overwhelmed me with kindness and joy of my return. My head is so dreadfully stunned with the acclamations of the people, and the vast amount of business, that I know not whether I am writing sense or nonsense; therefore pardon me if I say no more than that, I am entirely yours, C."

How low Henrietta's hopes had sunk may be gathered from the fact that, in answer to congratulations, she repeatedly described her son's restoration as "a miracle".

CHAPTER VIII

THE MOTHER OF MADAME

I

ONE of the faithful Progers brought the good news to Colombes, and bonfires were lit in the garden of the château. The king had sent word to his mother that he was being almost torn in pieces by his enthusiastic subjects. He was going to make his triumphal entry into his capital on his thirtieth birthday. Henrietta rose at five o'clock the next morning to write to him that she too was being wellnigh killed with kindness. "You cannot imagine the joy that prevails here." She was setting out "this instant" for a thanksgiving service at Chaillot, after, which she would drive on to the Palais Royal to order bonfires there. "I think I shall have all Paris." [1] Her expectations were not disappointed. The mother of a ruling monarch, a character splendidly free from financial anxiety, closed one of the happiest and most exhausting days in her life by giving largesse to the excited crowd of well-wishers assembled to watch the fireworks being let off outside her palace, and a ball to the large party of old friends who had penetrated to offer congratulations in person.

This exhausting twenty-four hours was a fair example of others to follow. All the Queen of England's days in the immediate future were to be delightfully over-busy. Even at Colombes she found no peace. "Not one poor minute to oneself for the visits and the affairs." [2] A never-ending procession of brave, threadbare cavaliers, who had lost all in the dear late king's service, trooped out to the little village to offer their re-

[1] Lambeth MS. 645. 120.   [2] Ferrero.

spects to the mother and sister of Charles II. They asked nothing. Their only desire was to go to London and kiss the king's hand. But his majesty, they feared, would now be surrounded by new friends and difficult of access. A letter of introduction from the Queen Mother or her royal highness would ensure them the audience which was all that their souls longed for. The rambling family histories of total strangers were listened to by the little royal ladies with tears and smiles, and both set their pens to work. Henrietta Anne sent her brother three notes a day and feared he would think her incorrigible. Henrietta Maria's conscience began to prick her. Recommending a host of old servants to her large-hearted son was at present unavoidable. Those who had been through the storm had a right to expect a place in the sun. But it was not so easy to explain the claim upon the king's time of the family from Jaillais in Maine, or young Sir John Reresby, who listened with such adoration while the princess played the harpsichord to him in her chamber, walked with her in the garden, and sometimes tossed her in the swing that hung between two great trees there. All, however, got their letters. The king was so good-natured, and every one of these poor people had lost a father in the late war. Henrietta Maria dismissed the fear that the little notes, sealed with mourning wafers and addressed in a large scratchy hand, which she was raining upon Whitehall, might become as much dreaded there as they used to be at the Palais Mazarine. Fortunately she had already sent Jermyn to speak to the king about her own finances, and he wrote that his majesty was taking great care in the matter. But the king might not know of the sum settled upon her by his father to provide an allowance for her household in case of her widowhood. She must mention that. . . .

Jermyn was Earl of St Albans now, but she could not remember to call him by his new title. People said that she was married to him in secret. But then people said that the Queen Mother of France was the wife of the cardinal, and that the

Queen of Sweden had superintended the assassination of her
major-domo, and since in the last instance they were right
they were hardly to be blamed for crediting less lurid tales.

Quarter of a century had passed since the scandal-mongers of
England had declared that their beautiful queen looked with
too kindly an eye upon that handsome bachelor, Mr Harry
Jermyn. In appearance, both mistress and man were now cari-
catures of what they had been, but the little shrivelled widow's
"prime servant" was still a gallant bachelor. While other exiled
cavaliers, living *en pension* in Paris by-streets for one pistole a
week, had grown pale and wan, Lord Jermyn, who ate at
the Palais Royal and kept his carriage, had grown decidedly
stout. His strong features, under a fashionably massive periwig,
were highly coloured. He was fifty-six now, "full of soup and
gold", suffered from gout, and was an indulgent uncle to
another Harry Jermyn. *"Le petit Germain"*, who occupied a
post in the Princess of Orange's household, was, said court
gossip, also the secret husband of a widowed mistress, and
Mary, like her mother before her, had refused to dismiss an
agreeable companion in order to quiet slanders. The easy-
mannered Jermyns undoubtedly suited the small vivacious de-
scendants of Henri IV, whom they served faithfully according
to their lights. Young Sir John Reresby, visiting "three cousins
in an English convent in France, one of them an ancient lady,
since abbess of the house", was assured by them that "Lord
Jermyn had the queen greatly in awe of him". She blanched,
they said, when he entered the room. That Henrietta's heart
should miss a beat when she was approached by the man who
had broken the news of her husband's death to her, and who
in virtue of his office was always the person to bring her important tidings, cannot be thought remarkable. Since he had
charge of her finances, Jermyn must have often worn a heavy
countenance; and a sour look on the face of one of the few
people with whom she had never had a quarrel may well have

caused her trepidation. Sir John himself noted that "indeed it was obvious" his lordship had "uncommon interest with her and her concerns; but that he was married to her, and had children by her, as some have reputed", he did not, he says, at the time believe. He adds, however, that "the thing was certainly so". What subsequent proof convinced the young baronet he unfortunately fails to explain, and there are several good reasons for believing that his personal observations on the spot were accurate and his later credulity was a mistake.

Jermyn, although he "had not much religion", lived and died a Protestant. A dispensation from Rome would have been necessary for a marriage between him and the ardently Papist queen, and no such document has ever been traced. After her religion, pride of birth was one of Henrietta's ruling passions. On hearing that the young duke of Buckingham was aspiring to the hand of her widowed daughter, she declared that sooner than see the Princess of Orange so lower her dignity she would tear her in pieces with her own hands. A *mésalliance* actually committed by another of her children at a later date called forth expressions no less strong. The only record of any document connected with her supposed marriage to Jermyn occurs in a footnote appended in 1820 by George Smeeton, the printer and compiler of *Rare and Curious Tracts relating to English History*, to his reprint of *The Life and Death of Henrietta Maria de Bourbon*, first published in 1685. "It is undoubtedly true", announces the antiquarian printer "(though kept out of sight by Clarendon, Hume and other royalist historians who knew it) that Henrietta Maria was married to Jermyn, Earl of St Albans, shortly after the death of Charles, notwithstanding all her pretended grief at the loss of him, and her declaration that she could not live without him." After quoting Reresby as evidence, he adds that "the late Mr Coram, the printseller, purchased of Yardly (a dealer in waste paper and parchment) a deed of settlement of an estate, from Henry Jermyn, Earl of St Albans, to Henrietta Maria as a mar-

riage dower; which besides the signature of the Earl, was sub-
scribed by Cowley the Poet, and other persons as witnesses.
Mr Coram sold the deed to the Rev. Mr Brand for five guineas,
who cut off many of the names on the deed to enrich his collection of autographs; at the sale of this gentleman's effects, they
passed into the hands of the late Mr Bindley." If the document
mutilated by the reverend Philistine was dated soon after the
death of Charles I in 1649 and signed St Albans it was expensive
at five guineas, for Jermyn was not created an earl until 1660.

It is impossible to say to what lengths loneliness may drive a
soul, but until some more impressive evidence than contemporary gossip and a vanished deed can be adduced, Henrietta
must descend to history, as she herself would have wished, as
the wife of the Martyr-King and no other man.

II

Henrietta Anne was now nearly sixteen, exactly the age that
Henrietta Maria had been at the date of her marriage to
Charles I. Charles II sent to Colombes the present of a side-
saddle and horse-trappings of green velvet, richly embroidered
and trimmed with gold and silver lace, and "a little sister who
does not deserve it, but who knows how to be grateful"
scribbled one of her schoolgirl notes to his majesty, expressing
rapturous delight. She was as pretty as her picture, which was
very pretty indeed, but she had been offered in vain to the King
of France and the Duke of Savoy and the Duke of Florence. . . .
Louis XIV, who saw in her nothing but a thin child, "the bones
of the Holy Innocents", had laughingly told the Duke of Anjou
that since nobody else would take her he thought his brother
would have to step into the breach. Already, a month before
the Restoration, rumours of an alliance between "Minette" and
"Monsieur" had reached Duchess Christine in Turin, and she
had written to ask if they were well-founded. Henrietta had

replied guardedly. The same story was current in Paris, but for herself she did not put much faith in such *bruits*. She would keep Christine advised of everything positive. "At last *le Bon Dieu* has looked upon us in His mercy, and has performed, as one must say, a miracle in this Restoration, having changed in an instant the hearts of a people from the fiercest hatred to the greatest possible kindness and submission, marked, moreover, by expressions of unparalleled joy. . . . I don't know yet what I shall do. It is not that the king my son does not press me to return. Even before leaving Holland he ordered his sister to go and find me, to press me to go over with her. . . . I expect she will be here any moment, and I hope, once more before I die, to see my whole family re-united and no longer vagabonds." [1]

She meant to go to England. Everyone expected her to do so, and it would be "regular", always a great consideration with Henrietta. "Where's now the royal mother—where?" sang Mr Abraham Cowley, her poet-secretary, who had nearly put his eyes out deciphering her eternal correspondence during the lean years. But the very thought of London aroused agonizing memories. And now that the great day for which she had been urging everyone to hope for the past sixteen years, had miraculously dawned, she realized with foreboding that she was a born Frenchwoman and settled in her habits. Some day, next spring perhaps, she would return to live dutifully in exile in that beautiful damp England, whose terrible mutton and religion were so much applauded by its new king. She would again occupy her dower-palace of Denmark House, where little Jeffery Hudson had once given her the fright of her life by tumbling out of a window, and Mr Waller, her court poet, the most temperate of men, having been "inhumanly" plied with wine by some frolicsome gallants, had fallen from top to bottom of the water stairs, and, only two years past, the

[1] Ferrero.

body of Oliver Cromwell had lain in state. Meanwhile, it was delightful to sit in the sun at Colombes, answering letters of congratulation, and able at last to send little luxuries to all one's kind friends. The Savoy resident reported that faded *élégante*, her majesty's only sister, to be unusually suffering at present. "I have been ill myself," wrote Henrietta, "but it wasn't very serious. I couldn't help speaking to M. Daguin about your letter, for I think the medicine I use is the best cure in the world for colds, and I wanted to ask him if it wouldn't do you good too. He thinks it would, and even told me I could write and tell you so from him." With pardonable pride she discloses the expensive and novel remedy she is prepared to forward to Turin. "It is Tea, a certain leaf which comes from India. If you would like some I will send it, as I have some of the best in the world. I assure you that there is nothing in my possession which I would not give to restore your health, and be of service to you in any way." [1]

Another consideration, which she must not mention, was detaining her in France. The court had arrived at Fontainebleau after nearly a year's absence. The gayest season for sixteen years was in prospect. Monsieur would be present at every fête. It would be madness at this juncture to remove Henrietta Anne, who spoke little English, and had been bred for a foreign alliance, to her brother's Protestant country. She took her daughter to call upon the new queen. A few days later, Monsieur gave an entertainment at his château of St Cloud, in honour of his mother and the princess of England. He opened his ball with Henrietta Anne. The aesthetic young prince, who was better able than any of his mother's ladies to advise them what colours and materials suited their style of beauty, had for some time shown signs of appreciating his cousin's undeveloped charms.

The two Henriettas, together with Anne of Austria and Mazarin, watched the triumphal entry of Louis XIV and his

[1] Ferrero.

queen to Paris from a balcony in the Rue François Mirron.[1] Before passing into the Rue St Antoine, the procession halted for a moment to salute the tactful relatives who had left all the honours of this day to a young couple. The Duke of Anjou, mounted on a white charger, looked extremely handsome. The king, riding by the side of his bride's coach, was dazzling in cloth of gold and silver. The Infanta Maria Theresa wore black, which was considered a suitable foil to her pink and white complexion, blue eyes and silvery hair. She was low-statured and her teeth were going already. French cookery was to her a delightful revelation, and she was eating enormously in her new country. When asked whether she had ever felt affection for any gentleman at her father's court, "How could I?" she had replied simply. "There were no kings there." She had told Madame de Motteville that ever since she could remember she had been in love with her cousin's portraits, and had looked upon him as her destined husband. She was very pious, very formal, but on her wedding night had startled her new attendants by shrugging out of her clothes without a glance in her mirror, "Quick! quick! the king is waiting."

Everyone in the family group beholding this bridal pageant was thinking of another that would follow it shortly. Within an hour of Henrietta's arrival in the capital, Anne of Austria had paid her a *visite de cérémonie*. The Queen Mother of France had come, empowered by her son, to ask for the hand of the princess of England for his brother. Henrietta's cup of joy now seemed full. Her darling would be "Madame", the third lady in France, mistress of St Cloud, the *"palais des délices"*, of the châteaux of Villers-Cotterets and Montargis, and of *suites* at the Tuileries and Fontainebleau. She would not be leaving the country in which she had been bred, and no religious troubles

---

[1] No. 68, the Hôtel Beauvais, designed by Lepautre in 1665. It has a noble courtyard, an ornate circular vestibule and a heavily carved staircase, the work of a Dutch master.

would vex her married life. She could hardly fail to be happy, safely bestowed at sixteen on a handsome cousin of nineteen, who had always been her playmate. Best of all, Monsieur was, said his mother, violently in love.

No thought of refusing so desirable an offer ever entered Henrietta's head, but she controlled her bliss and answered with suitable formality that too much honour was being done to her daughter, and that she would not fail to let her son know of this proposal. Anne of Austria, with equal care for etiquette, said that her son was proposing to send the Comte de Soissons to London as Ambassador-Extraordinary to treat for the alliance. She then expressed with great elegance her regard for the English royal family, and a thoroughly satisfactory interview ended with the two widows who had been so many trials together, mingling tears of hope and happiness.

Henrietta wrote next day to Charles, telling him of the match she had succeeded in making for his sister, and saying that since there might be some delay before the wooing ambassador set out, she thought he ought to give her permission to announce his satisfaction, meanwhile. The future bride she assured him, was behaving perfectly, displaying exactly the right mixture of pleasure and diffidence, and Monsieur was, equally correctly, mad with impatience.[1] He came two mornings later with his brother and sister-in-law to take Henrietta Anne for a drive, and at one of Cardinal Mazarin's magnificent fêtes arrived, not with the royal family of France, but escorting his future mother-in-law and *fiancée*. For the second time in four months, congratulatory visitors flocked to the Palais Royal, and the unpretentious entertainments given by the Queen of England were universally pronounced much more attractive than those at the Louvre.[2] Anne of Austria and her Spanish daughter-in-law made terrifyingly stiff hostesses, but the two Henriettas took so much pleasure in their own parties, and such

[1] Lambeth MS. 645. 119.   [2] Reresby.

pains to make everyone share their childlike enjoyment, that their flattered guests carried home an indelible impression of royal charm and attention.

The Widow of the Martyr-King seemed indeed now to be entering upon an old age of uninterrupted peace and prosperity. She would settle in her son's kingdom, of course, but as the mother of Madame, she would have an unassailable excuse for frequent and prolonged visits to her native land. She would divide her last years between England and France, an honourable and honoured figure, combining, in the advice which she would give to all her dear children, the wisdom of the serpent with the meekness of the dove.

One of her dear children was being very difficult. She wrote again to the Princess of Orange, telling her that she could not do better, even if the king wanted her in London on her son's affairs, than to take Paris on her journey. Mary could then attend her sister's wedding, after which her mother would perhaps be free to accompany her. They might present themselves at Whitehall together.[1] Mary, owing to a very little naughtiness, had got herself into a hopeless position. The suggestion that her elder daughter and she should hasten to England together, reported by Henrietta to the Duchess of Savoy with such pride on the eve of the Restoration, had not actually come from Charles. It had been Mary's own idea. She had been much taken with the notion of another whiff of Paris fashions and gaiety before settling at her brother's court. Now Charles wrote, telling her on no account to go to France, but come to England directly from her own country. Too late she realized that the arrival of an elderly lady at variance with nearly every prominent official in his administration, and once the most unpopular woman in England, was looked for by the King of England with no impatience. The Queen Mother's detention in France to settle her youngest child's matrimonial

[1] Lambeth MS. 645. 116.

affairs had suited her eldest son excellently. Mary was willing to give up Paris if Charles disapproved, but how to explain her change of plans to Henrietta without giving offence, she could not conceive. Another misunderstanding with "Mam", passing through all the familiar stages of stormy letters, injured silence and finally, touching reconciliation for the sake of the family, was more than she could face. She wrote to Charles, who would understand: "I have let her know your resolution of sending for me directly into England, therefore for God's sake, agree between you, what I have to do . . . and pray do not delay it, for I have a great impatience to be gone from hence".[1] The greatest punishment in this world for her, she added, would be to have to spend the rest of her life in Holland. Charles's decision was prompt, and on September 20th Mary travelled to Brill, attended by the Vice-Admiral of England, who had been sent over with six men-of-war and two frigates, to carry her to her old home. She was feeling unaccountably depressed. A sudden misgiving lest anything should happen to her only child while she was overseas, was haunting her, and the Dowager Princess of Orange, either by design or accident, had failed to arrive in time to see her off. Henrietta's "consent and approbation" to her voyage had been obtained with difficulty. To her son the Queen Mother had written frigidly, "If you had advised me earlier of your wish, it would have been punctually followed".[2] After consigning her strange, clever little son to the care of his kind great-aunt Elizabeth of Bohemia, Mary stepped on board Lord Sandwich's ship and received a piece of news which prostrated her completely during a passage, the trials of which entailed running aground six times on the Kentish coast.

Henry, Duke of Gloucester, who had landed with his brother at Dover on May 25th and tactfully cried "God save General Monk" while everyone else cried "God save the King", had

[1] Thurloe. i. 662.   [2] Lambeth MS. 645. 118.

settled down happily in England, where he had found himself "very acceptable". The story of his early resistance to his Papist mother's attempts on his faith had won him a popularity which had been increased by later reports of his gallant career in arms. Henry of Oatlands had hardened into a tall, thin, blue-eyed young soldier of twenty, "far from insensible to female charms", apparently more inclined to hard work than Charles, and far more affable than James.

Smallpox was rife in London during the early autumn of 1660, so when on September 1st the young Duke of Gloucester's name was added to the long list of distinguished sufferers, it did not arouse any particular interest. On the 12th he was pronounced out of danger. On the 16th he died. Henrietta had prophesied rightly on that unhappy Sunday morning six years past, when she had turned from a kneeling schoolboy with the words that he should see her face no more. On their last meeting on earth she had refused him her blessing, and he had died a heretic. No letter of hers gives any clue as to her feelings on hearing of her bereavement, but one from Henrietta Anne to Charles II, dated nearly a month later, breathes an atmosphere of acute distress. After confessing that she has not hitherto found the resolution to approach the subject of their loss, the little princess decides "I think the best way is to keep silence, so I shall do that".[1] Charles's grief had been violent. Observers reported that never in his life had they seen the king so troubled.

The death of the youngest son of Henrietta Maria in his twenty-first year was to have far-reaching consequences. One ludicrous and immediate result was the culmination of the contest for precedence between Mademoiselle and Henrietta Anne. Mademoiselle, to whose sufferings had lately been added agonies of pique at Monsieur's choice of a bride, had kept away from all entertainments given by her English relations this season. Anne of Austria had scolded her niece, and even gone so far as to tell

---

[1] Lambeth MS. 645. 66.

her that she was behaving like a madwoman. A visit of condolence to the Palais Royal was now unavoidable. Henrietta,
with her unfailing good sense in such matters, ordered her
daughter, on this occasion, to give way to age and absurdity.
In accordance with etiquette, both the royal ladies of England
kept their beds when Mademoiselle presented herself, but the
guest was triumphantly able to announce that her aunt had
admitted her superiority over the future Madame.

Early in October the Louvre, and for that part, Whitehall,
was astonished by the news that the Queen Mother of England
and her daughter were setting out for London instantly. Another
tragedy in her family had spurred Henrietta to swift action.
Her son James, with floods of tears, had confessed to his brother
that he had recently gone through a secret ceremony of marriage. His bride had been a private gentlewoman, the daughter
of his majesty's chancellor, now Lord Clarendon. Anne Hyde
was in the eighth month of a pregnancy for which the heir-
presumptive of England held himself responsible. A little of
Henrietta's emotion may be gathered from the fact that she
poured out the whole story to the Duchess of Savoy. As a rule,
letters to Christine painted a rosy picture of Henrietta's domestic affairs.

"To crown my misfortunes, the Duke of York has married
without my knowledge, or that of the king, his brother, an
English miss who was with child before her marriage. God
grant that it may be by him. A girl who will abandon herself
to a prince will abandon herself to another. I leave for England
to-morrow to try and marry my son the king and unmarry
the other. *Le Bon Dieu* does not wish that I shall enjoy complete tranquillity. But we must thank Him for all things and
reflect that we follow the paths He designs for us. Forgive me
if I stop now. I am so overwhelmed with work that I don't
know which way to turn. I hope to be back by Christmas."[1]

[1] Ferrero.

III

"Mam" was coming, and in one of her worst moods, but the guilty James, who was Lord High Admiral, would have to take the first shock. She was bringing in her train everyone obnoxious—Jermyn, her Jesuits, the Abbé Montagu, the pervert Prince Edward of the Palatine. . . .

Gentle old Father Cyprien de Gamache, suddenly bundled across France in late autumn weather, accepted without reservation his mistress's story that she had to go to England to get a dowry for her daughter and arrange her own finances. Henrietta and her flurried train "took shipping at Calais, in English vessels, in which the highest nobles of the court of England had come to compliment and accompany the Queen on behalf of the King, her son". From Calais she scribbled a last line to Mazarin, assuring him that both her sons were longing to see her. With regard to the Duke of York, she would comport herself as she and the cardinal had agreed. Her first sea passage for sixteen years looked like being her easiest. Father Cyprien did not know if there had ever been seen so dead a calm. The sea was like glass, not a breeze stirred the sails or flags of the large ships sent to carry the Queen Mother home. "In spite of all the efforts of the crews, it took two days to cross from Calais to Dover, though the distance is so short, that, with a fair wind, it may be performed in three hours. The Duke of York, High Admiral, came to receive the Queen, his mother, with the whole Fleet, composed of such a multitude of ships, and ranged in such a manner, that their masts appeared like large trees and resembled a spacious wood. When on board, the guns began to thunder, each ship firing in its turn and order, one after another; they kept up a noise marvellously loud and delightful which lasted for a good half hour." [1]

The miserable James could not do enough for his mother's comfort. At his own expense he had stocked the ship in which

[1] de Gamache.

she travelled with rare and most exquisite viands, well calculated to gratify the palate and satisfy the craving hunger produced by sea air. He charmed Father Cyprien by going personally to order some sturgeon, which he knew that he had on
board, to be cooked for the benefit of the priests who, he had
just learnt, were fasting, since by the Gregorian calendar this
evening was the vigil of All Saints. James had every reason to
be penitent. He was a father by now, or at least he hoped he
was. Harry Jermyn, the younger, Lord Arran and several other
"men of honour" all assured him that his wife's child might as
well have belonged to any one of them. Sir Charles Berkeley
had offered to marry Anne and give her son his name.

Off Dover, the king, Prince Rupert and the Princess of
Orange met the Queen Mother. Henrietta spent her first night
in her son's kingdom in the dark castle which had so affrighted
her suite on her first entry to England, and history repeated
itself, for at supper as soon as the king's chaplain had said grace,
Father Cyprien "in a loud and grave tone" blessed the fare
anew, with great ostentation. He noted with satisfaction that
"the Puritans, the Independents and the Quakers, of whom the
town of Dover is full", were much struck by the liberty he
took at their Protestant king's table. Next morning they were
more astonished "when we said Mass, in a very large apartment,
with all the doors open, in the presence of an innumerable
congregation, most of whom admired the devotion of the
Catholics, others inflamed with rage, from a blind and highly
criminal aversion which they bear to the Romish church".

After such a beginning, it is hardly surprising that the Queen
Mother's arrival in the capital was timed so that she should enter
the city unostentatiously after the dinner hour. Londoners,
however, have a wonderful nose for a show, and before she had
reached Lambeth to cross the river to Whitehall, the Thames was
so crowded by craft that the Secretary to the Navy Board, who had
given a sculler sixpence to take him out in midstream to see the

king's mother pass, could not get near enough for a view. All the riverside stairs were packed with wooden-faced people, cheering solemnly, and the red light of bonfires sprang up into the slightly foggy, unmistakably scented air, as Henrietta Maria landed.

After nineteen years she was back at Whitehall. Inside the palace an impressive group of her son's courtiers had assembled to welcome her. She looked for a familiar face, and recognized that of Charlotte de la Trémoïlle, larger and plainer than ever in widow's weeds. This poor woman, too, had been deprived of the best of husbands by the cruellest of means. She would understand the emotions of such a moment. The massive countess swooped to kiss her old mistress's hand, and Henrietta began to weep.[1] The young courtiers looked on with edification while the two widows, with tears streaming down their faces, yattered in their native tongue the family news of the last quarter of a century. Handsome people with familiar titles but strange faces, and others less well-liking, with familiar faces but strange titles, were duly presented by the king to his mother, and she charmed all by her courtesy.

From the walls of the great stone gallery, where her husband had hung the chief treasures of his famous art collection, many pictures were missing, but her son was doing his best to recover such as could be traced since their dispersal in the great sale of 1649–52.[2] A portrait of Charles I's beloved queen "when she was with child" had been knocked down for five shillings to some stranger then.[3, 4] Since her dower palace of Denmark House was

[1] de Witt.
[2] Mazarin had bought for Louis XIV, furniture and tapestries; the Spanish Ambassador, for his master, several pictures; Christina of Sweden, medals, jewellery and pictures, and the Archduke Leopold, paintings and tapestries. Two Dutch connoisseurs, Eberhard Jabach and Gerard Van Reynst, had bought a large quantity of pictures. Jabach sold to Louis XIV. The States-General bought Van Reynst's collection from his widow, and presented it to Charles II.   [3] Harl. MS. 4898.
[4] Several of the best-known portraits of Henrietta, notably the Vandyke in Dresden and the copy of a Vandyke in the National Portrait Gallery,

hopelessly dilapidated, and her son was a bachelor, the rooms
made ready for her at Whitehall—"the Queen's apartments"
—were the very rooms which only the death of Rubens had
withheld Charles I from beautifying for his consort with
groups of beaming cherubs. They had been splendidly refur-
nished, warmed and lighted for the widow's return, but to the
distress of her ladies, when she found herself alone in them, she
collapsed, weeping and wringing her hands, and announcing
herself "*La reine malheureuse*". "The vicinity to the scene of his
death was breaking her heart. She could not bear to look on
that Westminster Hall where he was arraigned as a criminal,
nor that palace of their former pleasures, the Banqueting House,
before which his blood was shed." She had not been obliged
to pass through the Banqueting House to-night, as she had
arrived at Whitehall by the privy stairs. Outside, joy-bells
were ringing, but Henrietta's comment after her first glimpse
of the court of the Merry Monarch was "Ruins and desolation
are around and about me". The ladies and officers of her household gloomily opined "that her stay would not be long in
England". Other people were hoping the same. Although the
neighbourhood of the palace was loyally illuminated, the City
had only kindled three bonfires in her honour. "Her not coming
through the City" was adduced as "one great reason that no
more joy was made, for many did scarcely know that she was
at Whitehall that night".[1]

Henrietta, however, with one of her lightning changes from
vast despair to composed amiability, was, within two hours of
her arrival, paying a call within the palace. Attended by her
daughter, she visited that evening "in Henry VIII's closet" Mr
Elias Ashmole, Windsor herald.[2] This gentleman, who had been
a close friend of her old Catholic court physician Cademan,

London, represent her at dates when her features were pinched but, according to contemporary taste, the figure of a royal lady was particularly interesting.   [1] Pepys.   [2] Ashmole's Diary.

was now equally celebrated as antiquarian, astrologer and alchemist. In which character the Queen Mother consulted him his reticent diary gives no clue.

Next morning Henrietta was sufficiently recovered to give audience with great graciousness to her son's privy councillors, who waited upon her in a body to offer their congratulations on her return to England. Although they came headed by Hyde, now Lord Chancellor, she received them with a cheerful countenance. She could afford to look with complacence upon the grief-ravaged features of her old enemy. The Duke of York was behaving as she desired, and refusing to go near his wife or new-born child. Henrietta's audience-chamber was thronged the same evening by guests whom she delighted by her quick memory for names and faces, and intelligent enquiries after their families and concerns. All London was longing to see Princess Henrietta, but that exotic little creature kept her room for several days, "wearied with her voyage". Presently a visitor with a special reason for wishing to see her arrived. The Queen Mother told the French Ambassador that he should behold her daughter, "whatever her condition", and the Comte de Soissons, followed by his suite, was led by King Charles into a chamber, where they discovered the future Madame seated at a table playing *ombre* with her sister the Princess of Orange, and her brother the Duke of York. Minette, attired in a mob cap and wrapped in an Indian shawl of a thousand colours, was fully as attractive as rumour had declared, and an inflammable M. Bartet reported to Mazarin, "Monsieur may be told that he never saw her, even in full dress, more beautiful than she was that day. I remember one day when he was leading her through your gallery, I told him that she was as lovely as though she were his little guardian angel, but I had not as much ground for it, even then, as when she was in her *cornette* and Indian shawl at Whitehall."

The Queen Mother went to a banquet offered to her by

General Monk, in the Cockpit at Whitehall, and after supper the king ordered the musicians to play nothing but French music. On her way to dinner every day, she held a little levee, and people had to arrive early in her presence-chamber if they wanted a good place. The Secretary to the Navy Board was pleased when he had managed to install his wife behind the queen's chair, but disappointed at the appearance of the royalties when they arrived. He thought the Queen "a very little, plain old woman, and nothing in her presence in any respect nor garbe, than any other woman". The Princess of Orange he had often seen before. The Princess Henrietta he acknowledged to be very pretty, though much below his expectation. He did not care for her French style of hair-dressing, and considered Mrs Pepys, standing near by, with two or three black patches on, and well dressed, much handsomer than her royal highness.

The weeks sped on towards Christmas, and all appeared to be going well with both Henriettas. They sampled the pleasures of an English watering-place, and during their short stay at Tunbridge Wells the king also visited the fashionable resort. The House of Commons offered its congratulations to the princess, and voted her a present of ten thousand pounds. In a charming letter of thanks, she told the Speaker that although she could not express herself well in English, she had an English heart. Her dowry was to be forty thousand pounds. Many of the Queen Mother's dower lands which had been parted amongst the regicides were pronounced to be so wasted and injured that it was hardly worth while going to the trouble of dispossessing their present owners. In compensation she was offered thirty thousand per annum, to which her son added a pension of another thirty thousand pounds from the Exchequer. Henrietta Anne, who had never before had any money to spend, began to take a great delight in gambling, and the Duke of Buckingham, who had hitherto been an admirer of the Princess of Orange, with whom he had played as a child, shamelessly transferred his marked attentions to her younger sister. A courier from the young Emperor Leopold arrived in London, and the Comte de Soissons heard that Prince Rupert had spoken of making a better match for his niece than that offered in France. In Paris, Monsieur's anxiety kept him awake at nights. Charles II, however, refused to disturb an arrangement on which his mother had set her heart, and to add to his brother's eligibility, Louis XIV created Monsieur Duke of Orleans, a title which had fallen vacant a few months before on the death of the last son of Henri IV.

Mid-December found two members of the English royal family abed at Whitehall. Mary had seldom left the palace during a visit which she had considered spoilt by her brother's outrageous act in presenting her with one of her maids of honour as a sister-in-law. She had ailed ever since she had arrived, and decided sadly that the English air did not suit her. James, who was a contradictory fellow, had soon wearied of his mother's and elder sister's persistently expressed animosity towards a woman with whom he had been passionately in love, but the stories of Sir Charles Berkeley and the rest stuck in his throat. He too began to suffer from feverish symptoms.

Five days before Christmas the court was alarmed by the news that the Princess of Orange had developed smallpox. The Queen Mother hastily sent her younger daughter to St James's,[1] but having no fear of infection on her own account, prepared to visit the patient. A stimulating draught of beer given to the Princess of Orange was reported to have caused the disappearance of her rash, but produced a fainting fit which lasted for several hours. Henrietta's requests to see Mary were discouraged. The princess's physicians feared, not without reason, that the Queen Mother would excite her daughter by making an attempt upon her religion. On the following day the princess was pronounced much better; hopes were even held out that

[1] de Gamache; de Witt; H. M. de B.

her illness was, after all, only measles. Two doctors sent by Henrietta were consulted, and advocated repeated bleeding. Since the Duke of Gloucester's death had been attributed by many to the failure of those in charge of him to bleed him sufficiently, this advice was followed. To the horror of everybody, including her mother, whose grief was increased by the fact that she had not been able to perform the death-bed conversion which she had intended, Mary died on Christmas Eve. The pretty auburn-haired widow, who had pined for another Paris season, had been just nine-and-twenty. Over in Holland, her thin, bright little son "felt her death more acutely than might have been expected from a child of his age".[1] If he suspected that something of grace and frivolity which was never to return had been removed from his life, he was right.

The post-mortem on the Princess of Orange proved to the satisfaction of her physicians that, in addition to her lungs having been affected, she had been suffering from measles, small-pox and putrid fever. Her body was removed by barge to lie in state until December 29th in her mother's dilapidated palace of Denmark House. Her funeral in Westminster Abbey was private, "yet honourable enough", and her brother James arose from his bed to attend it. Mary had been conscious until within a few hours of her death, and had, in her last agonies, "expressed her dislike" of the proceedings to detach her brother from Anne Hyde, an affair to which she had herself "contributed too much".[2] To James's enormous relief, Sir Charles Berkeley now appeared with a complete disclaimer of his former accusations against Anne. Far from having known her too well, "he was very confident of her virtue". He and his friends had concocted their stories "out of pure devotion" to the duke, whom they had imagined to be longing for an excuse to recede from his mésalliance. James at once sent a message to Anne that "he would speedily visit her", bade her "have a care of her son", and

[1] de Witt.   [2] Clarendon, *Life*, i. 392.

rushed to Charles with the good news. Charles, who had been deeply affected by Mary's death, always thought James a fool and always supported the Hydes, wearily prepared to welcome the reconciled Duke and Duchess of York to his court. He knew that one person in it would not easily be persuaded to follow his example. The pusillanimous James left his mother to hear from strangers "that he had made a visit at the place she most abhorred". She retorted by telling him in the presence of strangers that if he brought "that woman" into Whitehall by one door, she would go out of it by another, and never enter it again.[1] Once more the queen and her second son were not on speaking terms. With wrath and scorn Henrietta perceived all who had hitherto applauded her resolution of breaking this marriage, slipping away to congratulate the Hydes. Even Charlotte de la Trémoïlle deserted her old mistress. She wrote to her sister-in-law asking that a waiting woman might do a little shopping for her in Paris. She wanted a French doll, "the most beautiful to be had; that will undress. It is for a little girl whose parents I greatly wish to oblige." The most beautiful doll was designed for a Hyde grandchild.[2]

Anne's story was not as disgraceful as it had at first appeared. She had obtained a promise of marriage from James fully eleven months before the birth of their child, although he had not fulfilled it until almost the last possible moment. Charles had no choice but to accept the lady whom his brother had married with the full rites of the established church of his realm. But Henrietta would listen to nobody. Finally it appeared that if the queen was adamant, so was the king, and since he was master here, her only course was to fulfil her threat of leaving his country.[3] The Queen Mother's return to France, on account of her health, and her daughter's marriage, was announced, and

---

[1] Clarendon, *Life*, i. 394.   [2] de Witt.
[3] Bartet wrote to Mazarin, Dec. 16, 1660, Fr. tr. P.R.O., that when his mother pressed him upon politics the king turned his back and whistled.

again Henrietta's suite found themselves ordered to pack in haste for a winter journey. Then on the very eve of her departure an unexpected thing happened. The Abbé Montagu arrived to tell Lord Clarendon that his mistress "would be good friends with him", and desired to be reconciled to his daughter, who was still living under his roof. Perfectly staggered, Hyde asked bluntly the reason of her majesty's change of face, and was told by the suave Abbé that since she perceived no remedy in the matter of her son's marriage, she was resolved to make the best of it, and only prayed God to bless him and make him happy. A letter from Cardinal Mazarin had convinced her that further opposition would be unwise. His Eminence had told her majesty plainly that she would not receive a good welcome in France if she left her sons in her displeasure, and had warmly extolled the Chancellor's services to the royal family, of which his daughter was now a member. The Chancellor naïvely expressed his surprise at Mazarin's sudden care for the Hyde family, and consented to receive a confirmation of her majesty's pleasure from the Earl of St Albans, a person whom he had always regarded as an enemy.

Yet the "powerful reasons" by which Henrietta's passions had been "totally subdued" ought to have been obvious to an intelligent man. Mazarin's avarice was notorious. He had supported the English royal family at considerable cost and with great unwillingness for sixteen years. With the re-establishment of Henrietta's son on his throne, he had heaved a sigh of relief. His dismay on hearing that she contrived to get on bad terms with everybody in a country which had just consented to supply her with a handsome income, on the understanding that it should be spent within its bounds, and her daughter with a dowry towards a French marriage, had been profound. Henrietta's reaction to his advice was as easily read a character study. Her last supporter had deserted her. The cardinal, who had agreed with her so absolutely just before she had left France, had ranged himself with everyone else in the world to persecute the widow. . . . But this acute man had not abandoned his previous attitude without good reasons, and his letter suggested horrible and undreamt-of possibilities. Nobody in Europe understood better than Henrietta the importance of money. Her child's dowry, her own sixty thousand per annum, had been smilingly promised, to be sure, but they were yet to materialize. Charles would never be vindictive or mean, but James might be both, and the easy-going king's chancellor was now James's father-in-law.

The struggle in the queen's soul was terrific, but its end was inevitable. A good French mother decided that, sooner than submit to the awful indignity of offering a daughter without a *dot*, she would do violence to her feelings. The late king, always so insistent upon a high standard of personal morals in his court, would have died again rather than so sacrifice his principles, but, heaven be praised, he had never known what it was to be left in a palace without a loaf of bread or a faggot. Henrietta Maria enclosed herself for hours together behind locked doors, and when her attendants gained entrance they found their mistress tear-stained and plunged in black gloom. But Gallic logic won, and once Henrietta had made up her mind, she acted, as usual, quickly. The Abbé Montagu, who could persuade almost anyone of almost anything, should be her messenger of peace, and Jermyn, who was so pleasant, should accompany him. The Earl of St Albans, although he had been one of the most shocked by the presumption of the Hydes, accepted his commission with alacrity. He had hated the thought of his queen leaving England on bad terms with her family. He had recently obtained a lucrative appointment to which he was ideally suited—Ambassador-Extraordinary to Paris.

Henrietta was not spared an audience for the scene of her humiliation. The news that she had asked the Duke of York to bring his wife to see her, packed the queen's bedchamber on New Year's Day. Lady Derby, who was a tall woman, got a

good view of the principal actors' movements, but the noise
was so great that she could scarcely distinguish any of their
words. The duchess's actions were very humble. On being led
up to Henrietta by her husband, she fell on both knees. Henrietta bent and kissed her. The little princess hastened to follow
her mother's example. "The Queen immediately directed the
Princess to retire, for she feared that in so great a crowd there
might be some danger from small-pox. But I think", says
Charlotte de la Trémoïlle, "it was for some other reason that
her Majesty led the Duchess from her bed-chamber to the ante-
room, where she made her and the Duke of York sit down." [1]
Next day Henrietta was "kinder to Madame her daughter-in-
law". She seated Anne next to her at dinner. She consented to
be godmother to the baby. Nobody could have guessed from
her serene countenance that she had not liked her son's marriage from the beginning. After the meal, she gave audience to
Clarendon and assured him in magnificently flowery language
of her resolution to be an affectionate mother to his daughter,
"and hereafter to expect all the offices from him, which her
kindness should deserve". Hyde answered with his usual
straightforwardness that he thought her majesty had much to
forgive, and that he should always be obedient to her commands. But before dismissing him, Henrietta again, and unmistakably, drew his attention to the fact that she expected him to
fulfil his share in a bargain. She consulted a paper which she had
been holding in her hand, and "recommended the despatch of
some things to him, which were immediately related to her own
service and interest, and then some persons, who either had
some suits to the king, or some controversies depending in
chancery".[2] She then gladly took coach in St James's Park for
Hampton Court and the Portsmouth Road, attended by Charles
and many of his courtiers. James was not yet well enough
undertake such a journey.

[1] de Witt.   [2] Clarendon, *Life*, i. 402-4.

The citizens of Guildford, "to express their joy to behold both their own king and his royal mother", presented their majesties with a silver basket filled with sweetmeats. Their gift was more appropriate than they knew. Henrietta had failed signally in her proudly avowed intention of unmarrying one son and marrying the other. Charles took no interest in her suggestion that he should promote the most beautiful Mazarin niece to be his queen. Lady Castlemaine, who had the calm features and knee-long tresses of an Early Italian madonna most piquantly combined with the temper of a devil, fulfilled nearly all his domestic needs at present. He saw his mother and sister off at Portsmouth and told Lady Derby that her majesty would be returning soon, to which Charlotte's unspoken comment was "I doubt it". In her majesty's luggage reposed all the superb pearls and diamonds with which the Princess of Orange had decked herself to meet Mademoiselle four summers past. The queen, his grandmother, had thought that this valuable property of the orphan Prince William would be safer with her.[1] Just before the *London* weighed anchor, an unexpected figure joined Henrietta Maria's retinue. The young Duke of Buckingham, having obtained the king's permission to visit France, rushed on board without any luggage. He was madly in love with the Princess Henrietta Anne.

The *London* sailed with a favourable wind, but after twenty-four hours a storm sprang up and the princess began to be sea-sick. Her condition became so alarming that her mother asked Lord Sandwich to give the order for a return to Portsmouth. Running for harbour in heavy seas, the *London* went firmly aground on the Horse-sand. The Duke of Buckingham raged like a madman at the danger to his princess, who continued to suffer, and for some time there seemed a probability that the whole party would be shipwrecked. Eventually, however, they regained Portsmouth, where they disembarked, but

[1] De Witt; Pepys; de Gamache.

as soon as the storm had abated the princess insisted on going aboard again. She still felt very unwell, but Monsieur was writing every day to urge her return to France.

The *London* sailed for the second time, and strong sea-light beating into the cabin where the little princess lay bright-eyed and tossing with fever, revealed on her alabaster skin a nascent eruption. Her frantic mother again asked Lord Sandwich to order their vessel back to Portsmouth. Here all but a few of the queen's attendants went ashore, quiet settled upon the vessel, and Henrietta braced herself to battle against death for the possession of the third of her children within a year to be struck down by a malady hitherto fatal to her family. For several days the princess's life hung in the balance, but Henrietta Anne was to be reserved for a more frightful end than a quiet passing in the cabin of an English man-of-war. Her illness proved to be a severe attack of measles. As soon as she was well enough, she was moved into the town, where she had a relapse. Two doctors sent by her brother longed to bleed her, but Minette, who was accustomed to having her own way, absolutely refused to submit to a treatment which, she hotly declared, had killed her sister. The physicians retired gloomily from so perverse a patient, and Henrietta Anne recovered.[1] The court of France, having no news for fifteen days, sent expresses to know what had befallen Monsieur's *fiancée*, and messengers were sent back with the guarded answer that her royal highness had been ill but was now better. Ships containing her equipage were sailing at once, and she would follow as soon as possible.

Her convalescence was slow, and her mother's suite became extremely bored, detained in January weather in a place whose social possibilities were few. Father Cyprien filled in his time by attending heretic services, struck up a friendship with the local clergyman, and almost, he believed, made a convert. "The Huguenot minister" of Portsmouth town agreed with her

[1] de la Fayette; de Gamache; Pepys.

majesty the Queen Mother's chaplain that much in the religion which he professed was unsatisfactory, "the Catholic was safest". He had, however, a wife and children to support, and no other means of subsistence than his living. Father Cyprien hurried to his zealous mistress with this sad story, and she ordered him to assure his new friend that if he would embrace her faith he should not want for assistance. She would herself grant him an annuity of the same value as his cure. The disappointing man expressed himself deeply flattered by her majesty's interest and kindness, but now discovered that it would be impossible for him to execute his design immediately. He would, if he might, take the liberty of writing about it to her majesty's Grand Almoner and Father Cyprien when they should have returned to Paris. No such letter ever reached Father Cyprien, nor could he afterwards discover from any English travellers the further fate of his Portsmouth acquaintance.

The *London* sailed for France for the third time, and on this occasion had an uneventful passage to Havre-de-Grâce. The Duke of Buckingham had been so troublesome on their voyage that, as soon as they landed, the Queen Mother ordered him to go on to Paris alone. She did not intend to take the direct route, through Rouen, as she had been cautioned that smallpox was rife there. Some members of her train believed that this report was the ruse of a stingy governor and citizens to spare themselves the expense of entertaining royalty, but the Governor of Normandy, who came out in state to meet Henrietta's procession, conducted it to an adjacent château where the hospitality was of the first degree of magnificence. Her majesty's Grand Almoner, who had long desired to have the honour of entertaining her in his abbatial residence at Pontoise, was her next important host. Henrietta and her daughter arrived at the abbey in which Montagu had vainly tried to convert Henry of Oatlands, and were escorted by its owner to view its treasures. While they were admiring his rich pictures, jewellery, porcelain and embellishments, they were surprised by the sound of drums, trumpets and kettledrums. The king, the queen and Monsieur had come out from Paris to see for themselves how Henrietta Anne had stood her journey, and express their joy at their relations' safe arrival. Monsieur could hardly speak for emotion when he saw Henrietta Anne alive and lovelier than ever, offering her cheek for his salute.

They were married eight weeks later in the queen's chapel at the Palais Royal. Since the season was Lent and the bride was still in mourning for a brother and a sister, the ceremony was private. A few days before her wedding, startled by something in her *fiancé's* expression, Henrietta Anne asked her mother to explain to him that she was indifferent to the Duke of Buckingham. Henrietta Maria touched on the subject very lightly, representing the handsome young Englishman's unreciprocated passion for her daughter as a perfect joke in their circle, and Monsieur appeared satisfied.

IV

Over-excitement made the delicate little bride unwell. For several days after her wedding she remained with her mother at the Palais Royal. As soon as she had recovered, her impatient bridegroom arrived to conduct her to the Tuileries. "The thing was just, and according to God", pronounces Father Cyprien, who was a witness of the parting of the two Henriettas, but of course the separation of a mother and daughter who loved one another so perfectly could not be achieved without a scene lacerating to the feelings. Monsieur, who enjoyed assisting at scenes lacerating to the feelings, looked on complacently while his virgin bride and widowed mother-in-law clung to one another, sighing, sobbing and wailing. Most of their attendants also wept; all looked pained. "There was general mourning in the Palais Royal."

The mother of Madame then took herself out of Paris. She settled for the season at peaceful Colombes. Young people were much best left alone during the difficult first months of marriage. She had not forgotten the mischief made between her and her bridegroom by busybodies. In good time she hoped to spend many enjoyable weeks under her son-in-law's roof, but for the moment she would keep away, hoping for the best. She would even cross the terrible sea to England, and reside there, as the world expected. But until she was sure that all was going swimmingly in France, she would keep within call, though out of sight. Her daughter had the best possible foundation for a happy married life, a sound religious education and a pure heart.

She settled down to wait for news from Paris, and her patience was not long tried. The king and queen were at Fontainebleau. They had now been married ten months, and, to her relief, Marie-Thérèse was beginning to believe that she was to have a child. Monsieur's bride was the latest novelty as well as the most important lady in the capital this spring. Although she had lived there nearly all her short life, many people did not know her by sight. Even after her galling penury had been relieved, the Queen Mother of England had kept her daughter close at her side. Paris discovered an angel in its midst, and raised a chorus of ecstasy. "Nothing else was talked of; everyone hastened to sing her praises." Echoes soon penetrated to the suburbs. "All France was at her doors, the men thought of nothing but to pay their court to her, and all the women strove to please her." Madame's complexion of "jasmine and roses", her chestnut hair "dressed in a manner most becoming", her sapphire-blue eyes, "full of the contagious fire on which no man could fixedly gaze without feeling its effects", her rich figure, her majestic air, her perfect teeth (a far from universal asset even amongst beauties) were all rapturously noted. Nor was the princess who had been begotten in an

Oxford College dependent on her physical attractions. "It was a new discovery to find her wit as pleasing as the rest of her." "There was not a soul but what was surprised by her charm, her sweetness and her wit." "Charm", "sweetness", "grace" and "wit" were the words most often repeated in descriptions of Madame. "What the English princess possessed in the highest degree was the gift of pleasing, together with what we call grace. Never had princess been able to make herself so equally beloved of men and women." "Her whole person was adorned with charms. . . . When she was talking to anyone it was impossible not to believe that her only object was to please them." Not all of this was strictly true. Henrietta Anne was over-thin and her little back had never grown quite straight. But if she was not a perfect beauty she was able to make people accept her as one. In this she was luckier than the king's young wife, who, with her regular features, faultless skin and masses of silver-blonde hair, might honestly be called beautiful, but having no animation, failed entirely to please.[1]

The mother of Madame listened with an indulgent smile to the ravings of people who had needed the right jewels, the right *toilettes* to convince them that a princess was wholly admirable. Presently Monsieur took his bride out to St Cloud and on to Fontainebleau, where Madame repeated her triumphs at her brother-in-law's court. The month of May was extremely warm this year. Every day there were hunting expeditions or *fêtes champêtres* in the depths of the forest. Madame made an exquisite Diana, driving in her light chariot to bathe with her nymphs, and returning at sunset on horseback. Every evening there were water parties and concerts. The court embarked in gilded gondolas, under a wide and starry sky, to the sound of string music. Only the young queen was unavoidably absent. She was happily expecting a child in November. Naturally, since Madame was the lady of highest rank present, the king

[1] de Motteville; de la Fayette; de Choisy.

always escorted her. Within a fortnight of her arrival at Fontainebleau he had handed over to her the arrangement of all their entertainments. Madame gave her orders to M. Baptiste, his majesty's "most distinguished buffoon". This character, a Florentine surnamed Lulli, in addition to his genius for stage-management, could compose the most enchanting airs in the world. A noble avenue, terminating in a lawn, was transformed by him into a rural theatre. During rehearsals for Madame's ballets all performers feasted quite informally on the green-sward, sheltered by screens of foliage and flowers. There was much sending of little notes and verses, much wandering off into the gardens and forest. On May 30th (N.S.) Madame paid a flying visit to Colombes, her first since her marriage. Father Cyprien, who was still her confessor, and had attended her at the Tuileries and Fontainebleau, had represented to her that she must not neglect her mother. Madame appeared at the small suburban château like a being from another world, much dressed, in radiant health. Monsieur seemed satisfied with his rôle as husband of a social success. His wife's influence with the King of France was most acceptable to him. But the young couple could only stay three nights. The king could not spare the chief ornament of his court longer. He came as far as the Hermitage in the forest to meet her on her return journey.

June was not quite so good as May, for thunderstorms spoilt some days. Still, on fine nights Lulli's violins throbbed at Fontainebleau until three in the morning, and couples disappeared into the forest for hours together. A court painter depicted the king, Madame, and her maids of honour, in masquing costume. Madame, with a little curled dog sporting at her feet and a crescent in her hair, was the chaste Diana stretching out timid hands towards the half-bared torso of a fine Endymion—his dark young majesty, asleep with a smile on his face. A restraining influence had been removed from the court. During the weeks that had elapsed between the announcement of Madame's engagement and the arrival from Rome of a dispensation for a marriage of first cousins, the cardinal had fallen sick. He had been suffering from gout for years, but this time people said that his illness was serious. On a February day, while the Comte de Brienne waited in a small gallery of the Palais Mazarine, "where there is a tapestry all of wool, representing Scipio, executed from the designs of Giulio Romano", he heard the sound of slippers. He hid behind the tapestry whilst dragging, languishing footsteps approached, and beheld his Eminence "naked in his camlet dressing-gown, furred with squirrel", with his night-cap on his head, muttering despairingly, "I must quit all this!" [1] The cardinal had died fifteen days after removing to the château of Vincennes, on March 9th, 1661 (N.S.), "showing no fear of death, but, to his last breath, an incomprehensible attachment to money". According to Mademoiselle he shared the usual fate of court favourites in being forgotten as soon as he was buried.

Some court ladies presented themselves upon a call at Colombes one afternoon of this thunderous June. Their hostess, delighted to see anyone from a place which she would not approach without a direct invitation, settled herself complacently to listen to further reports of her darling's triumphs. All news from Fontainebleau, as she well knew, would be news of Madame. But there was pathos as well as indulgence in her smiles, for it was slightly pathetic that the King of France, like everybody else, had waited until the princess of England was married to discover that she was the most attractive woman in his realm. The ladies left the mother of Madame not quite so happy as she had been. After sleeping on the matter, she decided to address herself to an old friend of proved discretion. She opened her note to Madame de Motteville in sprightly vein, but she knew that so intelligent a woman would not miss the serious appeal contained in its closing sentences.

[1] Brienne.

"I believe that in your soul you are saying 'That Queen of England has quite forgotten me!' This is not true. M. de Montagu will tell you that I have really had many thoughts of you. By these numbers I must confess to a little laziness, and that I have been to blame for not sending word of my satisfaction in two letters from you. I beg you to continue writing, if you have time, but some ladies who came from Fontainebleau yesterday tell me that you are so much with both queens these days that one cannot get access to you. From the way they spoke, I fear that it is not to be had by letters.

"If you have much noise where you are, I have much silence here, which is more suitable for the remembrance of friends, amongst whom I believe you will be persuaded that you number, and always will.

"You have with you another little edition of myself, who is, I assure you, very much your friend. Continue to be hers. I will say no more." [1]

But "the queen of England, leading a sweet life at Colombes, in a house which she had purchased in search of peace", was to find her policy of non-interference sorely tried. The ladies from Fontainebleau proved to be stormy petrels. Their rumours were soon confirmed by people who had been unwillingly obliged to take an official interest in the frivolities of Madame. The Queen Mother of France had asked the English Ambassador and the Queen of England's Grand Almoner to convey to the mother of Madame her complaints of a daughter-in-law who "took no pains to please her and showed her no consideration". The Earl of St Albans' treatment of an elderly lady whose prestige had been much impaired by the loss of her cardinal had not given satisfaction. He had blandly represented that the day of youth had now come. If her majesty would only be content to let an innocent state of affairs continue, "Madame would serve her with the king, and would endeavour to keep

[1] de Motteville.

them always united". To this the king's mother had hotly replied that when she saw the necessity of being obliged to a third person to do her offices with her own son she would retire to her convent of Val de Grâce, and there end her days in peace. She took her daughter-in-law out to country châteaux and held her there for visits of several days. On Madame's return "everything went on as before". Early in July a summons was sent to the mother of Madame to spend a week at Fontainebleau. She arrived to find universal dissatisfaction with her successful daughter.

The young queen, whose peace of mind was so important just now, had been rendered very unhappy by Madame's selfishness in monopolizing the king's time and attention. The Queen Mother had spoken to Madame and ordered Madame de Motteville to speak to her. Madame had listened with every appearance of friendliness, but immediately reported their interference to the king. Worst of all, Monsieur, who had certainly allowed his bride to enjoy herself "a little beyond the bounds of propriety", was now tortured by jealousy of his brother. The court was beginning to comment on the king's admiration of his sister-in-law and hint that their pleasure in one another's company had "every sign that commonly precedes a grand passion". Even poor old Father Cyprien had his complaint to add. Madame confessed to him and then ran off. She was so taken up with her amusements these days that she never could grant him half an hour in which to warn her against the dangers of courts, the worthlessness of all earthly prizes and the wretchedness and brevity of this miserable life.

The Queen Mother of England stood her ground in defence of a child of whose innocence she was perfectly convinced. Her son-in-law, who was also her godchild, said that he considered her his best friend, and was tactfully comforted by her. When the Queen of England left Fontainebleau the Duke and Duchess of Orleans accompanied her as far as Vaux, the magnificent château of the king's Superintendent of Finances. Within a few weeks affairs seemed to be proceeding more suitably. The king departed on a long overdue expedition into Brittany, where his arrest of his Superintendent of Finances gave his court a new subject for scandal. On his return it was true that he haunted Madame's apartments as much as ever, but the attraction was now said to be one of her maids of honour. Mademoiselle de la Vallière, a gentle, unassuming girl of sixteen, was no adventuress, but the Queen Mother's annoyance was not allayed by the fact that her son had found a mistress in her daughter-in-law's household. Fortunately the matter was kept so quiet that the young queen concluded the whole term of her pregnancy without suspecting it. She was confined at the Louvre on November 1st (N.S.). Her stiff manner had not been evidence of any mental stamina. During her labour, which was long and painful, her cries rent the air, and an unsuitably large audience learnt that "I don't want to have a child. I want to die." The Dauphin, who had been born on All Saints' Day, received the name of Louis Toussaint, and the Queen of England was invited to be his sponsor.

Madame also returned to Paris in November. She arrived in a litter, coughing incessantly. Her features were peaked, and she was thinner than ever. Her doctors ordered her to go to bed and to stay there. She stayed in her room, but every morning, as soon as the curtains of her bed were drawn, she had herself arrayed in a becoming *déshabille* and prepared to receive visitors. Her sick-bed was surrounded by amusing friends from the moment that she woke until nine o'clock at night, when she took the opiates which were her only means of wooing sleep. When she heard that a particularly charming Ballet-Royal had taken place, she had it repeated in her own apartments. At seventeen, and after witnessing her sister-in-law's experience, she was not enchanted by the prospect of becoming a mother. Monsieur's jealousy had now transferred itself to the Comte de Guiche, a handsome young warrior who had been asked to retire from Fontainebleau on account of his too evident admiration of Madame. A greater contrast than Madame's husband and gallant could hardly have been found. Everyone agreed with her mother in believing her pure-hearted, but she had certainly been imprudent. The widow of Charles I found herself completely out of her depth. No maid of honour of hers had ever dared to cast into her lap as she set out on a journey "a volume of papers" which, on being opened, disclosed itself as flaming love-letters from an infatuated commoner. And Madame, since journeys are always so boring, had opened the "volume" and let people know that she had done so. There was another rumour that the same maid had admitted to her mistress's bedchamber a most amusing fortune-teller whom nobody but Madame had recognized as the Count in disguise.

The winter wore out and Madame began to feel better. She moved to the Palais Royal, her mother's residence, and was seen going out in a light carriage to attend religious services. Her confinement took place earlier than had been expected, and found her mother unprepared.[1] On a spring morning, three days after she had received the Spanish Ambassador with suitable dignity, Madame gave birth to a daughter. Monsieur was frankly disappointed. Court gossip said that the pretty young mother, on being told the sex of her child, had told her attendants to throw it into the Seine.

Over in London, "a lady who thinks she knows the news" told Lady Derby that now the Queen Mother would be returning to England. Charlotte doubted it, but her old mistress was indeed beginning to make plans to leave a country where she could find no peace. Before Madame had left her bed, the *Court Gazette* announced that, in acknowledgment of his personal bravery, his majesty had been pleased to appoint the Comte de Guiche, eldest son of the Maréchal de Gramont, commander of the troops ordered to Lorraine. Madame, fatally

[1] de Witt.

soft-hearted, was persuaded to give the unhappy young man a farewell interview. Since she was quite inexperienced in such affairs, it nearly ended in a tragedy. Mademoiselle de Montalais, however, managed to hide the Comte behind a chimney-board before Monsieur came in. . . . Monsieur again carried his woes to his *marraine*, whose own early married life had been most unhappy, and was again soothed. The Queen of England went to see her daughter, "scolded her a little", and told her exactly how much the husband knew, so that she should not rouse fresh jealousy by confessing to unsuspected indiscretions. Two maids of honour, "whose personal conduct left much to be desired", got their *congé*, and a touching scene of reconciliation took place between a young couple who would never become wise and happy parents unless they behaved with more regard for each other's feelings.

Madame made a quick recovery and was soon once more in the saddle and leading every ballet. Her mother prepared to quit France. After all, her son, the king, had always been her favourite child. She bade farewell to Mademoiselle, who was also leaving Paris for the summer, and Mademoiselle accepted with an unmoved countenance her aunt's sugared assurance that had she only married Charles II she would have been the happiest woman in the world. The great heiress was five-and-thirty now, and already people were beginning to distinguish between her and Henrietta Anne's baby daughter, Marie-Louise, by calling the elder princess "*La Vieille Mademoiselle*". In eight years' time she was to fall madly in love with a little gallant whom she would have laughed to scorn in her blooming teens. Charles was well avenged. But he bore her no malice. She had never interested him. Her nose was too big.

Henrietta Maria's furniture and effects were packed to leave the Palais Royal for ever. Her attendants, during the years of despair, had made shocking depredations in this magnificent unhomely home. They had picked off the gilding decorating the famous gallery representing the triumphs of the heroes of France. In order to obtain a few *sols* with which to buy bread, they had destroyed workmanship which had cost enormous sums.[1]

The mother of Madame paid a farewell visit to St Cloud while the last preparations for her journey were being made. Late in July her daughter and son-in-law escorted her towards the coast. At Beauvais they parted with many tears. Monsieur and Madame then took the road back to Paris and their nursery, and the mother of Madame that to Calais.

[1] Reresby.

CHAPTER IX

THE INDIAN SUMMER

I

THE King of England's mother lived in her dower palaces of Greenwich and Denmark House in a style of quiet magnificence. Four-and-twenty gentlemen in black velvet cassocks and gold-embroidered badges waited with their halberds on her majesty when going in her sedan to her chapel, to her meals, or in one of her four coaches-and-six. She had again her Masters of the Buckhounds and the Bows, her Master of the Queen's Games and the Gentlemen of her Music. Twelve liveried barge-men rowed her on the Thames.

She had appointed her household, and no names in her list had attracted surprise. The Earl of St Albans was her Lord Chancellor, the Abbot Montagu her Grand Almoner, the Lord Arundel of Wardour, a great Catholic, her Master of the Horse. Her Secretary, another good Catholic, had first occupied his post a quarter of a century ago. Sir John Winter was past sixty, but still a man of parts. He occupied his leisure hours in making experiments with sea-coal. Her chief Ladies of the Bedchamber were equally unexceptionable—the Dowager Duchess of Richmond, the Duke of Buckingham's sister, and the Countess of Newport.[1] Lady Carlisle was not amongst them. She had died of apoplexy a few months after the Restoration. Young gentlemen urged one another to go and pay their respects to *"Maddam la Mère"*.[2] The king would be pleased; he declared that no

[1] H. M. de B.
[2] She is thus termed in a sonnet, dated 1662, preserved in MS. in a volume once the property of Sir Robert Cotton, Postmaster in Queen Anne's reign.

children ever had so good a mother. She was said to be quite harmless nowadays, interfering in nothing. . . . Young courtiers went, and found themselves much entertained by a small upright figure with a fascinating resemblance to the fairy godmother of children's nursery tales. *"Maddam la Mère"* sat in a favourite "great black velvet chair", backed by "an India screen of six leaves". Her corkscrew curls, which contrasted so strikingly with her tiny parchment-hued face, were, like her rustling gown, her enormous eyes and her waving fan, eternally and defiantly black. Every detail of her antique costume was just right—the finely bound devotional volume in her wasted hand, the single string of large pearls resting on her severe neck-gear. In cold weather she wore over her shoulders "a little mantle of ermines lined with taffetas", and when going abroad, a black velvet surtout furred with sables. She had always had taste. In repose she should be accounted very ugly, for her cheeks were hollow, her nose was broad, and her jaw had fallen in. But in company her features were seldom undisturbed by some emotion. She had seen all the heroes and villains of the past half-century, and would sometimes tell members of the younger generation about them. She said with a sigh, but with a twinkle in her eye, "If I had known the temper of the English some years past, as well as I do now, I had never been obliged to quit this house".

To visit Denmark House became fashionable. The Queen Mother's concerts, where one heard good music well performed, were thronged. On fine summer nights, humble folk passing down the Thames would bid their oarsmen hang upon their sculls while they listened to the sweet strains proceeding from the fine house where the Old Lady lived. Many boats anchored at the foot of her great stone staircase, which had a remarkable echo. If one sang three notes, they were re-

The sonnet proves that even in her old age she had charms. Her "sprightly looke", "sweetness" and "noble grace" are acclaimed by the anonymous poet.

peated many times, and finally sounded in unison.[1] Her restoration of her dower palace would not be completed for several years. She was making some effective additions to Denmark House. All the drawings for a superb new river front, sketched by Inigo Jones at her command in 1638,[2] had been brought forth, and she had ordered a gallery of many full-length windows with a Thames-side view, and an Italian garden with paved walks and avenues all leading to the water's edge. She took a strong interest in her new architects' plans, and even more in their estimates. Her careful majesty, who called for all accounts to be sent in weekly, distributed a good part of her handsome income every quarter amongst the deserving poor. She was particularly sorry for people imprisoned for small debts which they were genuinely unable to pay, and often forwarded the sum necessary to obtain their release. By her orders her priests searched the prisons in and around London for such cases, and also attended every condemned criminal.[3]

Interior decoration still occupied her. Her Great Chamber and Closet, with their well-chosen furniture and pictures and inlaid floors of coloured woods, were considered one of the sights of London. In the summer she liked to make little expeditions to see other people's houses and furniture. Persons with the taste and means for entertaining royalty found the Queen Mother a most agreeable guest. Mr John Evelyn, who had sat so solemnly opposite bold Mrs Barlow in a coach on the road to Fontainebleau thirteen summers past, invited her majesty to honour his poor villa at Deptford with her presence. She came on an August day, attended by her Lord Chancellor and many great ladies and gentlemen, accepted a collation, and was so pleased by Sayes Court that she stayed till very late in the evening. To her flattered host she recounted many observable tales of the sagacity of various dogs she had formerly possessed.[4]

---

[1] Pepys.   [2] Preserved in the library of Worcester College, Oxford.
[3] H. M. de B.   [4] Evelyn.

In the summer she fared well enough in England, but the summer was so short. There were so many mornings when she woke to the creaking sound of heavy rain, or east wind howling in her galleries. On November days, when there was nothing to be seen from the windows of Denmark House but a white blanket, her thoughts turned irresistibly to her small snug château just outside Paris. But its view was, of course, quite dull and quiet compared to that from her London palace. On fine afternoons the clustering, crazy, timber-and-plaster-faced houses on the opposite side of the river, lit by pale winter sunshine, were as pretty and gay as the scenery for a masque. The Thames was always lively, whether clear as a lake, blurred with rain or stirred by wind. Even after dark she could distinguish the large shapes of ships slipping down the dark flood beneath her lighted casements, bound for the Indies and the Levant. Presently they would return, bringing loads of sugar and oranges and tea, and cage-birds all the colours of the rainbow, and best of all, dressing-tables and chests and screens and mirrors of yellow-scarlet and pea-green and shiny black lac, painted with tiny gold people moving under parasols towards temples; and cabinets to be mounted on carved and silvered stands. She had never outgrown the thrill of what her daughter Mary had once described in a childish letter as "A Presant from the East Endy House".

Into the Port of London one day, with a cargo of Eastern rarities, came an extraordinary little piece of goods—a human boy, no size, but perfectly fashioned, with lac black hair and eyes, and a sallow skin smooth as silk. Somebody who remembered her taste for monkeys and pet dogs decided that the Chinese boy, whose disposition was evidently gentle, might do for the Queen Mother. So the Chinese boy found himself brought by water to a noble stone staircase, and into a warm, handsome palace, hung with silks and velvets, where people moved on noiseless feet, and some of the furniture seemed vaguely sympathetic. The old lady (not much larger than himself), to whom everybody bowed down, received him kindly and enquired if he could speak English. He could; in fact, it was so many months since he had heard any other language that he had entirely forgotten how people had talked elsewhere. Henrietta Maria took him under her roof at sight, and delivered him to Father Cyprien with orders to make him a Christian and a Catholic. Father Cyprien got to work, and found that his pupil had no difficulty in believing in the Devil, and a God who had no body, but had created man and the animals and the elements, and the immortality of the spirit and the punishment of the wicked. The mystery of the Trinity puzzled him extremely, but when Father Cyprien had explained that it was a mystery, elevated above Nature, and therefore incomprehensible to natural reason, he acquiesced cheerfully. He listened with emulation to his instructor's stories of virgin saints and martyrs, and soon expressed a desire to be saved from eternal fire. Father Cyprien hurried to tell his mistress of his happy success. With great joy "she not only resolved to attend the ceremony of his christening, but also deemed it no derogation from her royal dignity to perform the office of godmother". As her fellow sponsor she elected the Abbé d'Aubigny, brother of the Duke of Richmond, and the Abbé, when called upon to name the child, bestowed upon her majesty's Chinese lad his own name of Peter. "Thus the young Chinese, so far distant from his country, deprived of his own father and mother, sustained a lucky loss, since he was made, by the grace of baptism, a real heir of Paradise, and had on earth for his spiritual father one of the most illustrious gentlemen of England, and for his mother a mighty Queen who designed to secure to him an honourable subsistence." Peter's christening was attended by a vast concourse of people, many of the Protestants who came being as curious to see her majesty's place of worship as her Chinese godchild.[1]

[1] de Gamache.

Her first thought on her arrival in England had been for her ruined chapel. During her worst days of poverty she had sold all her plate, but before she had left France last year the Duchesse d'Aiguillon had presented her with the gorgeous set of ecclesiastical vessels left to his niece by Cardinal Richelieu. The chapel of Denmark House was now more splendid than it had ever been, and the faithful were flocking to it in such numbers that the queen had been obliged to send into France for additional priests. To the great relief of Father Cyprien, she had summoned seven more Capuchins. Since her Grand Almoner and her Lord Chancellor, "who had great influence over the mind of the Queen", both favoured Oratorians, he had been in terror lest the new-comers should be of that Order. Another cause of satisfaction to the faithful old man was that the spectacle of Peter's christening had brought into the fold a complete English family, and, what was better, the family of a Protestant clergyman.

Henrietta carried on her work of conversion steadily, but at last she showed signs of realizing that, as far as her son's subjects were concerned, her best course was to proceed as unobtrusively as possible. "She desired to live with the least offence imaginable to any sort of man, and therefore was much troubled to hear . . . that her confessor was seen on horseback, brandishing his sword, and to fling his hat by the scaffold where the late king was beheaded, and being asked why he, of all men, should do so, replied that that act was the greatest thing that was ever done to advance the Catholic religion, whose great enemy was that day cut off."[1]

II

Henrietta's was not the only London palace in which Catholic services were now taking place. Protestant England had lately learnt to pray "for our gracious Queen Catherine, and

[1] H. M. de B.

Mary, the Queen Mother". Since it was over three hundred years since a Queen Consort and a Queen Mother had existed simultaneously in the country, much discussion had taken place before this order had been agreed upon.[1] Charles had married at last, and married a Catholic. None of the Protestant princesses proposed had pleased him. "Odd's fish, they are all foggy!" To suit the king, his bride must be a beauty, and for his country's sake, she must be rich. Lord Bristol, sent secretly to Parma to inspect a couple of Italian princesses, had turned tail after a single view of them on their road to church. One was so fat, the other so ugly, he dared not run the risk of recommending either to such a connoisseur as his master. The inventory of the young King of Portugal's only sister sounded ideal to the eldest son of Henrietta Maria: "A Catholic, and would never depart from her religion, but totally without that meddling and activity in her nature, which hath many times made those of that religion troublesome and restless. . . . As sweet a dispositioned princess as was ever born, but bred hugely retired . . . hath hardly been out of the palace ten times in her life. . . . Very beautiful, being somewhat taller than the queen, his majesty's mother. As Portion, half a million sterling in ready money, Tangier upon the African shore, a free Trade in Brazil and the East Indies, and the island of Bombay, with its spacious bay, town and castles. . . ."

Catherine of Braganza had first been offered to him when she was six. A portrait of her, now that she was twenty-four, convinced Charles "that person cannot be unhandsome", and attributing to the malevolence of Spain a rumour "that she could not bear any children", he made the match. Catherine's fate was to be sadder than the rumour promised—she was to prove incapable of bearing a living child.

She arrived in England a few weeks before her mother-in-law, and was married to Charles on a May day at Portsmouth,

[1] de Witt.

wearing a rose-coloured gown trimmed with knots of blue ribbons. She was not a beauty, for her front teeth stuck out, but she was "prettily shaped", and her bridegroom thought her dark eyes "excellent good" and the sweetness of her expression only surpassed by that of her voice. He was determined to be a good husband, and confident that this lady and he would agree very well. Sir John Reresby, less hopefully, saw "nothing visible about her capable to make the king forget his inclination to the Countess of Castlemaine . . . the finest woman of her age", and he was right. Catherine had nearly two months of bliss, while Lady Castlemaine was absent from court giving birth to her eldest son by the king; then the favourite returned to Whitehall and insisted on being appointed a Lady of the Queen's Bedchamber. After a short, bitter struggle, the little bride, who was hopelessly enamoured of the dark, handsome husband who could speak Spanish to her, resigned herself to the second place in his affections. By September Mr Pepys was edified by beholding the king, the queen, Lady Castlemaine, and the king's son by Lucy Walter, all driving away from the Queen Mother's palace in the same coach.

Henrietta professed herself delighted with her unsophisticated Catholic daughter-in-law. At their first meeting she instructed an interpreter to beg the Queen Consort "to lay aside all compliments and ceremony, for she would never have returned to England but for the pleasure of seeing her son's wife, loving her as a daughter and honouring her as a queen". On their second meeting her tact carried her so far as to applaud with enthusiasm a performance by Catherine's Portuguese musicians, generally condemned as execrable. She wrote to Turin that the new queen, who was the best creature in the world, was very beautiful, very sweet, and had plenty of spirit. She saw with joy that the king loved her extremely. Her sister also was having the satisfaction of beholding a favourite son, who had inherited too much of Henri IV, settling down to holy matrimony. The

Duke of Savoy had chosen as his bride one of those little half-sisters whom Mademoiselle went to visit in their Poissy convent school. He had been offered Mademoiselle herself, but "her age alarmed him, for he wanted children". Henrietta was in hopes that her daughter-in-law the queen, for whose happiness the possession of children was essential, was already preparing to present England with an heir. With less enthusiasm she added that she was certain that her daughter-in-law the duchess was again at work. Anne Hyde's marriage was as complete a failure as the most inimical mother-in-law could have wished. James soon began to neglect a woman towards whom he always felt that he had acted with great handsomeness. While the Duke of York gloomily proceeded from mistress to mistress, the duchess bore eight children, of whom only two daughters survived infancy. Even before her father's disgrace and fall, she had become entirely uninfluential, simply a stout lay figure in brightly coloured satin, observable at every public appearance of the complete royal family. Since dinner and the nursery were her only solaces in life, her wit rusted and she grew repellently double-chinned.

Young Mr Crofts, that "most pretty sparke of about fifteen", whom Mr Pepys had seen leaving Denmark House in the king's coach, had come over to England in the train of the Queen Mother. After the death of Lucy Walter, he had been brought up in Paris in the house of a cavalier whose loyalty had extended to bestowing his surname on the king's mis-begot, and representing him as a kinsman. Charles, discovering his son to be a remarkably attractive lad, wished to acknowledge him and give him a title. Catherine objected strongly, gave way to violent emotion, fell ill, and believed herself to have miscarried. Ghoulish courtiers began to discuss whether, in event of the queen's failing to do her duty, the king would appoint his illegitimate son his heir. Some people even said that the boy had been born in wedlock. Mr Pepys dismissed this rumour, together with the one that the Queen Mother was secretly married to my lord St Albans, with the words, "How true, God knows".

Her second Christmas in her son's capital found his mother determined to rejoice. On December 26th Charles announced his intention of dispensing with the execution of the penal laws against all religious dissentients who should live peaceably, Catholics included. Whilst snow began to cover the roofs of London for the first time in three years, a small, stubborn, black-robed figure at Denmark House scratched a jubilant news-letter. The weather was frightful, a plot to surprise Whitehall had been discovered, and her son had not supped with his wife since her illness, but none of this need be admitted. The Queen Mother of England assured her sister in Turin that everything was going well in the best of worlds. Her daughter-in-law the queen, was a saint, entirely *dévote*. "I am most happy in her." Her son, the king, was pressing her to witness some ballets which were going to be performed at Whitehall. She almost thought that, to please him, she would have to break her rule of never appearing at large entertainments. "I believe I shall have to go. This will show you that we have plenty of peace here, should you have heard contrary stories. Some people who have confessed to a design upon the king's person have been hung, which will make other people, who may have shared their sentiments, more wise."

She could hardly attribute her son's action in releasing dozens of good Catholics from prison to any religious motive. James, who was so unhappy, she nourished hopes of influencing, but Charles at present appeared intractable. The fact remained that there would be thanksgiving in countless Catholic homes this season of peace and goodwill. It was one's duty to be gay.

A frost followed the snow, and there was skating in St James's Park, and at Whitehall a gorgeous reception of the Russian ambassadors. Only the Banqueting House would serve for such an occasion. A coach-and-six, attended by two dozen mounted black-velvet-clad halberdiers, passed by torchlight through the snow-hushed streets from Denmark House to Whitehall, and deposited Henrietta Maria at the scene of her husband's execution. She ascended towards noise and radiance, and knew far above her the rosy limbs of Rubens's nine-foot children glowing again in festal light—vast Virtues in whirling sea-blue and blood-red draperies triumphing over mottled umber-fleshed Vices—the birth of Charles I—Peace and Plenty. Harmony and Happiness. . . . But Rubens's ceiling and Inigo Jones's pillars and galleries alone reminded her of old times. Everything else had mercifully changed. Dress was now quite different. So were manners. In her day she had set the fashions. Whitehall now looked to the Louvre for inspiration. But then she had been ahead of her age. Her masques, for instance, had given such offence thirty-odd years ago. Now there were two excellent public theatres in London, where pretty but not virtuous women acted every night to fashionable audiences. London had many novelties—actresses, and champagne, and glass coaches on steel springs, and stage coaches. Embroidery for ladies had come back into favour, and Englishwomen were filling their homes with mirrors and cabinets of white satin, sewn with raised figures with pallid silk faces and curly chenille hair, representing the chaste Susanna bathing, or his gracious majesty out for a walk in a park where hares and hounds were the size of cart-horses. Stump-work, it was called. . . .

The Muscovite ambassadors presented their master's letters and gifts to King Charles II—rich furs, hawks, carpets, cloths of tissue and sea-horses' teeth. The king slipped on a glove wrought with gold, and took one of the hawks on his wrist. Mr Pepys, peering down from the gallery upon the heads of people, noticed that the son of one of the ambassadors was wearing the richest suit of pearl and tissue that ever he had seen. He made out the small figures of the two queens, and the king's son, Mr Crofts, soon to be created Duke of Monmouth, escort-

ing the child Duchess of Buccleuch whom he was to marry. . . .
Next day, when paying a call, he met "a little proud ugly talking lady" who cried up the Queen Mother's court as much as
the gayest nowadays. To be French was to be fashionable, and
the Queen Mother was very French. The cynical guests who
made her palace ring with their laughter lent a willing ear to
the tale that the disconsolate Widow of the Martyr was secretly
married to her gouty, over-blown major-domo. During her
five-months residence in their midst this story had improved.
She was now declared to have borne a child to my lord St
Albans, somewhere, some time, in France.

The English spring brought Madame la Mère nothing but a
persistent cold. Progresses were not for her these days. When
her son's court deserted the capital for a tour into the west, she
went no further than Richmond. Her dower-palace of Sheen,
with its 96-foot-long chapel, its 100-foot-long Great Hall, its
park of 350 acres, and its handsome Elm Walk of 113 trees, had
been sold in the year after her husband's execution, in order
to pay the arrears due to the army. A regicide had given ten
thousand pounds for the antique, rambling, red-brick building,
and had lived in a corner of it, leaving the rest to fall into decay.
Henrietta Maria arrived, to wander like an unquiet spirit
through suites of dark oak-panelled rooms with small leaded
windows, from which, in happier summer days, bright French
eyes had admired the six-year-old Prince of Wales presenting
his mother with a masque, and the Duchesse de Chevreuse
swimming the Thames.

With autumn she rejoined the court in London. Charles's
wife had spent the last weeks of summer at Tunbridge Wells in
hopes of an heir, but all in vain. In October Catherine fell ill
again, and for four days lay between life and death, babbling
of the children she thought she had borne—a son, a daughter,
triplets. . . . When her physician woke her by feeling her pulse,
her first question was, "How do the children?" Memories of her

kind mother-in-law's encouraging anecdotes haunted her. She remembered that the Queen Mother had been shocked when first they had shown her his present majesty, the finest, ugliest baby in the world. In her delirium she fancied that she too had borne a Black Boy. She apologized to her husband for having brought him so ugly a Prince of Wales. Charles, with the tears running down his dark face, assured her, "No. It is a very pretty boy." "Nay", said she in her broken English. "If it be like you, it is a fine boy indeed, and I would be well pleased with it."

Everyone thought that she was to die this time, and perhaps it would be for the best. The king, whose hair was beginning to go grey beneath its great periwig, could then marry his latest flame. "La Belle Stuart", a delicious French-bred tomboy, just sixteen, had been sent to his court by Madame, his sister. She made the king build card-castles, hunt-the-slipper and play blindman's-buff with her. But the unhappy Catherine struggled back to life and hope again, and presently the Queen Mother had leisure to answer the Duchess of Savoy's letters, which had lain unheeded for weeks, a sure sign of great upheavals at Denmark House. Henrietta took up her pen to deny with some indignation that she had ever thought of going to Bourbon this year. She could not imagine how such a tale could have reached her sister. She was thankful to say that she felt in no need of the cure at present. . . . It was irritating, at the very outset of another frightful English winter, to have her attention drawn to the fact that nobody had ever believed that she would endure this climate so long. Her continually ailing sister had been ill again. She concluded her last letter to Turin with the usual kind expressions of concern. She was never to write again, for two days after Christmas Duchess Christine died.

The death of the Duchess of Savoy left a blank in the life of Henrietta Maria. The sisters had not met since they were respectively ten and thirteen, and until they had both become mothers, had not taken much interest in one another. But the arrivals of their children had drawn them together, and founded a friendship which had persisted through storm and shine for thirty-three years. Since the death of Charles I, her correspondence with Savoy had become an increasingly important factor in Henrietta's weekly round. Their often-laid plot for a meeting at Chambéry had long ago deteriorated into a mere polite fiction between the sisters, and on the one occasion when the duchess had visited France, Henrietta had deliberately failed to greet her. But mercifully the tragedy which had then threatened had been averted. With a feeling of desolation the Queen Mother of England realized that she was now the only surviving child of Henry IV, and never again would she have to hurry to catch the Turin mail, or fill pages with mendacious descriptions of her entire satisfaction in wilful children who did not treat her advice with due respect. . . .

Charles confided in her no more than of old. When the sale of Dunkirk had been impending, the French Ambassador had been obliged to ask Lord Clarendon to enquire of the king how much the Queen Mother knew, so that "he might behave himself accordingly". Milord St Albans had been pumping him. Charles, already aware of this, replied blandly that M. d'Estrades "need not take any notice of anything yet".[1] Nevertheless, he did open his heart to one member of his family nowadays. Late at nights, when his subjects imagined him happy with Lady Castlemaine, a weary king wrote long letters to a fair lady in France. Nearly every week he sent Madame, his sister, a bulletin of his news, hopes and fears. All manner of gear filled his sheets—a design for a masquerade at which he thought that his mother's stout major-domo would cut an odd figure, "I believe it were worth seeing my Lord St Albans in such an occasion"— requests for books of devotion for the Queen Consort, for pictures of saints for her to put in her prayer-books—for snuff, for gold sealing-wax, and advice on landscape gardening. . . .

[1] Macray.

England, both in town and country, was "showing an appetite to a war" against the Dutch. Her king was anxious to establish close personal relations with the King of France. His secret hope was to get Louis XIV to exchange his alliance with Holland for one with England. Charles believed that his charming *mondaine* sister, born "an Exeter woman", could and would help him here.

London in June 1664 basked in a heat wave. The king made a hasty finish to a letter before going off to dine with the Queen Mother at Denmark House—was horrified to hear that his sister considered her infant daughter to resemble him, "For I never thought my face was even so much as intended for a beauty". He dined at Denmark House, but St Cloud and the Tuileries got his news.

In October the Queen Mother feasted the whole royal family in celebration of the opening of her new gallery, and the fleet was ordered to sea under the command of Prince Rupert. In November, Parliament voted his majesty two and a half millions for a popular war. It sounded enough, but it was to prove not nearly enough. The year closed stormily, and the famous comet, seen nightly in Paris around Christmas, was only once beheld by the king at Whitehall, "the weather has been so cloudy". His majesty wished his sister an easy confinement. The large Duchess of York had just produced another daughter, after only one hour of labour. Madame's shape was, her brother feared, "not so advantageously made for that convenience as hers is; however, a boy will recompense two grunts more".

Suddenly the weather turned to full winter cold. At White-hall the king's pen slipped in his frozen fingers, and at Denmark House the Queen Mother made her will and decided that she must spend next New Year in France. She had done very well here, much better than anyone had expected. If she waited until the summer to travel, she would have completed three years of permanent residence in England. Her only anxiety was for her chapel. She was afraid that if she left her son's country for an indefinite period, he might be persuaded to close her Catholic place of worship. She approached Charles, and found him most considerate; by no means inclined to detain her in London to the detriment of her health. Her Capuchins arrived in a body to receive her parting commands from her own lips. The little deputation took her quite unprepared, but "as God had endowed her with a shrewd and ready understanding and great fluency of speech", she made a very fine impromptu oration, in which she declared that with the grace of God her journey would not be long, that her chapel would always be open during her absence, and that, although her priests must carry on their work of converting heretics, she wished them to proceed with twice as much caution as if she were present.

In the end, her departure, so long prophesied, took Londoners by surprise. The Plague, which had spoilt her first entry to the capital, hurried her final exit. Mr Pepys, calling in at Denmark House on his way home to dinner on June 29th, 1665, found all there packing up, and was told that the Queen Mother, who was leaving that very day, did not intend to return "till winter come twelve months". A few weeks later, wandering through a picture gallery in the country house of a friend, he had praise but for one portrait—"The Queen Mother, when she was young, by Vandike, a very good picture, and a lovely face. . . ."

Her son the king escorted Madame la Mère to the mouth of the Thames, and the Duke of York saw her to Calais.

III

The mother of Madame spent her summers at Colombes, and her favourite watering-place, and her winters in the Hôtel de la Bazinière,[1] a fine building on the Quai Malaquais, lent to her by Louis XIV.

[1] Built by Mansart for Macé Bertrand, Royal Treasurer. It was much restored in the eighteenth century by the Duchesse de Bouillon, afterwards

She had brought back with her from England a ship-load of furniture, pictures and *bibelots*. At the Hôtel de la Bazinière, where rooms were vast and illuminated by "great lustres of twelve branches", she hung some of the Mortlake tapestry which had once decorated the dower palace of the wife of Charles I— the histories of Vulcan and Venus, of Hero and Leander, and of Polydore. "A great Persian foot-carpet, twenty feet long" ennobled a reception room of her Parisian palace, where the stools and *fauteuils* were "of gold brocade, thick flower'd with crimson velvet", or striped Porte de Paris brocade, also carmine and gold. Her own "great chair, elbow fashion" was "of cloth of gold with a cover of ash-coloured taffeta". The India screen of six leaves, which had shielded her from many an English draught, was re-erected here in company with a towering state bed of black velvet with bunches of ostrich plumes and aigrettes surmounting the corners of its canopy.[1]

She went out to Chaillot for all the great Church festivals, and explained to the good women there that she would have liked to spend the whole year with them, but was afraid that the river mists would affect her weak chest. She intended to die in her own convent, but not yet. All of her children needed her, and none more than her daughter.·

Monsieur now hated his lovely fashionable wife, and suspected her of betraying him with everyone. Even her kindness to her nephew Monmouth, who had been sent over to France to learn good manners, was misinterpreted by a husband whose jealousy was maniacal. Monsieur said that personally his passion for Madame had only lasted a fortnight. This, the courtiers of Louis XIV agreed among themselves, with meaning smiles, was probably true. "The miracle of kindling this prince's heart was reserved for no earthly woman." [2]

During her mother's residence in England, Madame had

became the Hôtel de Chimay, and is now incorporated in the École des Beaux Arts.   [1] *S.P.D. Fr.*, 78. 128, P.R.O.   [2] de la Fayette.

achieved a severe miscarriage, a son destined to live twenty-eight months, and a still-born daughter. A scandalous publication purporting to be a true history of her amours with de Guiche, her brother-in-law and several of his courtiers, had been suppressed after some difficulty. The youngest child of Charles I sat by the side of her mother-in-law's sick-bed and announced that she would not object if her husband took a mistress. "The sensitiveness of wives only hardens the hearts of husbands." [1] Anne of Austria was facing an agonizing end with heroism. She died of cancer six months after Henrietta Maria landed in France. All the news that winter was gloomy. The epidemic which had hastened the Queen Mother's departure from England had developed into the Great Plague of London. Henrietta sent large sums to be distributed amongst families ruined by the loss of the breadwinner, and considered ordering her Capuchins to close her chapel. They pleaded to be allowed to continue holding services, which had never been more necessary or appreciated, and "sooner than one Catholic should die without confession and viaticum" she bade them continue to do their duty. Two of her courageous little band died at their posts.

France was entering into the war on the side of her ally, Holland. The King of England's mother told Louis XIV that "she was sorry he was engaging in an enterprize, wherein she could not go along with him in her prayers". To the Duc de Beaufort she remarked "that she was afraid of him now that he was going to fight the English".[2] The campaign of 1666 went ill for England, and in September two-thirds of London was burnt to the ground. Wild rumours that the Papists had started the Great Fire made the Queen Mother's return to her son's country additionally inadvisable this season, but late in the autumn the portentous figure of my Lord St Albans was seen painfully embarking for his native land. Louis XIV had

[1] de Motteville.   [2] H. M. de B.

empowered his aunt's ancient major-domo to sound Charles II
on the subject of peace. Henrietta Maria suddenly attained a little
political significance. Quiet Colombes was haunted by envoys
and ambassadors, and the kings of England and France exchanged letters sent to the château of Madame's mother, to be
redirected in her handwriting.

Her first eighteen months in her old country were her busiest.
After the peace had been concluded, she retired once more into
obscurity. The disgrace and fall of her old enemy, Hyde, caused
her no satisfaction, rather the contrary. Her daughter's ill-health
and unhappiness occupied her attention to the exclusion of her
own. In the summer of 1667 she was summoned to St Cloud,
where Madame was thought to be dying after a miscarriage. In
the following spring Madame was again so ill that her anxious
brother sent over a physician from England to attend her. Dr.
Fraizer tactfully recommended a prescription of the late Sir
Theodore Mayerne, and Madame made a marvellous recovery.
Her brother refused to decide "whether Mam's masses or Mr.
de Mayerne's pills" had worked the miracle.[1] The Queen Mother,
like many elderly ladies, put little faith in modern doctors, whom
she consistently infuriated by laudatory references to a master of
their craft born in 1573. Sir Theodore, who had seen her through
nine pregnancies, had never let her miscarry. Madame despatched to Whitehall prescriptions which arrived too late.
Catherine of Braganza, whose hopes this time had really been
founded on fact, had already lost her child.

Henrietta Maria, who eighteen years ago had refused to be
comforted by the birth of a grandson, "for myself, I am too old
to see him grow up", had, after all, outlived nearly all her great
contemporaries. Her little household at Colombes included
many withered shanks and trembling hands. Her page of the
backstairs, Richard Lockart, who had "charge of her wardrobe
and beds in all her removals and journeys", was one of the most

[1] Cartwright.

junior of her attendants. He had only a quarter of a century in her service to his credit. Five of her bedchamber women had been with her for forty years. Anthony Goddard, her first footman, was allowed the honourable prefix "old". He had taken up his duties on the dismissal of her French train.[1]

Madame de Motteville, since the death of Anne of Austria, had retired from the court, and occupied apartments at Chaillot. Two widows, hardly distinguishable as far as costume went, from the nuns around them, sat together on fine days on the convent terrace, with its immense view of the course of the Seine through Paris, and beyond that, the blue hills of Meudon and Châtillon. On inclement days they had the same outlook from the windows of a parlour hung with a tapestry of green leaves, where the furniture "much worn" was of gold brocade. The silver-gilt plate on which the Queen Mother's sparing meals were served was also much worn. Some of it was "almost white". It bore an indecipherable coat of arms, which her attendants believed to be Spanish. She had brought none of the splendid stuff from her English palaces to little Chaillot.

The Queen of England and Madame de Motteville discoursed of life and death and long ago. Henrietta Maria confided in the ex-lady-in-waiting her regret that she had not been better instructed in history. All the lessons of statecraft which she knew had been taught to her by the harsh instructor Experience. She detailed many instances in her career in which she now considered that she had acted rashly or misguidedly. Madame de Motteville decided that people who said that this queen had been responsible for her husband's fall were wrong. She was so frank about her mistakes that it was impossible to imagine that she was hiding more serious ones. Silence, said Henrietta Maria with woeful conviction, was golden. "As much out of charity as to avoid making mischief, nothing should ever be repeated. . . ." "Kings should be like confessors, knowing all and

[1] *Cal. S.P.D.*, Sept. 1669.

saying nothing." Both ladies admitted to a terror of death. The queen acknowledged that she did not even care to think about it. "It is better to give one's attention to living well, and hope for God's mercy in the last hour." Madame de Motteville was going to employ the leisure moments of her old age in writing her *Mémoires*. When the ex-lady-in-waiting suggested that her majesty should do her the honour of dictating to her, in this idyllic solitude, the chief events of an amazing career, the widow of Charles I agreed with her usual graciousness. . . .[1]

An event of the winter of 1668-9 disillusioned any who might have believed that her increasing years had affected the spirit of Henrietta Maria. His counsellors had been representing to a king who was "airy and liberal", that he must economize immediately. Charles II's mother had not resided in his country for upwards of three years, and showed no signs of ever returning. She lived a life of complete seclusion. She had even given up buying jewellery. Sixty thousand pounds per annum of English money, therefore, were either going to spread Papistry or being put into a stocking. Lord Arlington, Secretary of State, duly wrote to Lord St Albans that his majesty was most reluctantly compelled to reduce by one-quarter the income received by the Queen Mother from her dower lands in England. Mercifully the winter seas stretched between Whitehall and the Hôtel de la Bazinière. But if anyone had imagined that reducing the income of an elderly French widow was an operation which could be performed painlessly and swiftly, he was much mistaken. Echoes of the mortal screech raised in France were instantly audible in London. A shower of black-sealed notes, commenting in no uncertain language on "this last blow", penetrated to his embarrassed majesty as well as his mouthpiece. Did the king realize that his mother had already reduced her style of living to the exact amount of her revenue? His message had surprised her to a degree very difficult to express, since it

[1] de Motteville.

had never entered into her imagination that he might wish her to retrench yet further. Her majesty felt sure that when his majesty had reflected, he would see that Justice and Right were upon her majesty's side, and that he would not render the remainder of her days, "which will be short", sordid by debts for which he would be responsible, since they had been entered into in confidence of his keeping his word. Her majesty drew his majesty's attention to the fact that since his Restoration she had never greatly importuned him. What touched her heart most was the thought that people would remark on his saving extending to his mother. She could hardly believe that a miserable twenty thousand jacobuses per annum could spell ruin for him. "I hope to have news from you promptly, in order to determine what I am to expect, and what is to become of me." [1]

When Christmas drew his mistress to Chaillot, her majordomo, puffing with relief, wrote to Arlington that he imagined her majesty's devotions would keep her from writing any more upon the subject of her finances for a week.[2] Those who had no stomach for this fight then slipped quietly off the scene, and the unfortunate Arlington was left to deal directly with Henrietta, and suggest some alterations in the proposed arrangement which satisfied her, although they eventually proved entirely ineffective. By Easter she was too unwell to continue the correspondence. Her ailments were nothing new, but her majordomo, who was expected in London, thought her condition sufficiently serious to warrant a warning that he might be obliged to forgo his journey. She recovered, inspired by a new and wonderful hope, and towards the end of April my Lord St Albans set off for Whitehall "by such stages as old men with the gout are wont to make".[3] A second miracle, even more unexpected than the Restoration, was being promised to the Queen Mother. Charles at last seemed to be inclining towards

[1] S.P.D. Fr. Tr., Dec. 9, 1668, P.R.O.
[2] Ibid. Dec. 28.   [3] Ibid. April 17, 1669.

her faith. He was planning, in dead secrecy, a religious and financial alliance with France. Unluckily for his "Grand Design", his sister, his best ambassador to Louis XIV, was childing again. There could be no question of Madame visiting her brother's capital at present. Two persons whose passage between Paris and London could arouse no suspicions, were summoned to open the negotiations. They were Lord Arundel of Wardour, the Queen Mother's Master of the Horse, and Lord St Albans, the Master of her Household. So once more, in the spring of 1669, Henrietta Maria's little château hummed with rumours, of intrigue, and this last intrigue of her lifetime was as thrilling to her as any of which she had ever heard whispers, for the prize actually appeared to be complete freedom for the Catholics of England under a Catholic king. How much Charles confided in her even now is uncertain. Arundel and Madame knew all, but St Albans on his arrival in London had official knowledge of nothing but a projected commercial treaty. The long conferences held between her mistress and Madame, however, had attracted the attention of the Dowager Duchess of Richmond. The chief lady in attendance on the Queen Mother communicated with her brother, the Duke of Buckingham, and Buckingham spoke to St Albans, who believed that there was some business of which he knew nothing. Charles wrote to his sister that how their mother's Chamberlain should have come to know so much, he could not tell. He redoubled his requests for utter secrecy.

Henrietta was to be spared the disappointment of seeing that England would never again tolerate a Catholic king, and that Charles would never declare himself one, but she was also to be denied the joy of knowing that every one of her three surviving children was to die in her faith. Fever and insomnia were undermining her strength. She had begun to alarm her attendants by fainting fits. But it was difficult for anyone to judge how ill she was, for she could not, nowadays, discuss her sufferings. "With the blood of the great Henry she had inherited a courage that was never to be cast down by difficulties, which disguised the sharpness and severity of her pains, and which caused her noble countenance to exhibit an agreeable serenity and a majestic cheerfulness as if she was enjoying perfect health."[1] When she arrived at Chaillot in too weak a condition to walk from her coach to her apartments, she waited with Spartan firmness while a messenger ran to ask if the prioress had any objection to men carrying a chair entering the convent.[2] Father Cyprien often heard her say "that complaints in illness were useless, or if they served for anything it was to show the great weakness and irresolution of the persons who made them. She laughed at those ladies who howl, sob and lament, about a touch of headache or toothache." Only to the sympathetic nuns did she divulge that for twenty years she had not known what it was to pass a day entirely free from trouble of some sort.

Midsummer of this year found her abed, an ominous circumstance, for she usually enjoyed her best health during the warm weather. She rallied, however, for a promised visit to her daughter. Madame must not be disappointed. In London, Catherine of Braganza had again miscarried, and Charles wrote in despair that there had been no accident to explain the matter this time. Madame was expecting her child in the end of August. Everyone who loved her shared her hopes that she might bear an heir. She was approaching her trial in a mood of wild unhappiness. The Chevalier de Lorraine, her husband's favourite, treated her with revolting insolence, and she dared not complain. Last year, when the king had heard, by means of her daughter's governess, that Madame was no longer mistress in her own house, Monsieur had vented his spite by wafting his wife away to Villers-Cotterets, to enjoy no company but that of himself and his chevalier.

The visit of Madame's mother to St Cloud was the usual

[1] de Gamache.   [2] Strickland from inedited MS., Hôtel de Soubise.

success. Monsieur always appeared at his best in her presence. He knew well that, to her, fine manners covered a multitude of sins, and that, like many innocent-minded old ladies, she resolutely shut her eyes to anything she did not wish to see. Before she left, he joined with his wife in insisting that someone so dear to them ought to take better care of herself. The mother of Madame meekly promised to see some more eminent physicians. She would much rather have been allowed to die in peace. When last she had seen Madame de Motteville, she had told that old friend that she was going to establish herself at Chaillot to die, and think no more of doctors or medicines, but only of her soul. Her son-in-law's solicitude touched her. None of her own children had shown great anxiety during her illness this spring. Charles, indeed, had written cheerfully to his sister in March, that since he had heard that Mam, ever unlucky in connection with the sea, had sent him a present by a poor gentleman who had never been seen since his embarkation at Havre, he thought that she ought to pay for the necessary masses for his soul. The children of Henrietta Maria were devoted to her, but they had long since ceased to be harrowed by dark references to their swiftly approaching orphanhood. They considered her not much worse than usual at present, and they were right.

She returned from St Cloud to her own small country château. Her immediate plans were to spend the autumn there and move to Chaillot in time for the feast of All Saints. Her household this summer included a nursery. A stout and unattractive English child, who bumped into things, now stumped about the château of Colombes. The Lady Anne, daughter of the Duke and Duchess of York, was clumsy because she was short-sighted, but also because she was all Hyde. Her parents had sent her over to Paris to receive treatment from a French eye specialist. The Lady Anne of York, who was accustomed to sup unlimited chocolate and whipped cream with her doting mother, was, at four years old, as round as a ball.[1] It was not easy to discover exactly how blind she was, for she was extremely obstinate. Once when walking with her elder sister in Richmond Park, a dispute had arisen as to whether a distant object was a man or a tree. The Lady Mary had been all for its being a man, and so it had proved when they had got closer. But when she had cried "Now, Anne, you must be certain what the object is!" the Lady Anne, averting her countenance had replied, "No, sister, I still think it is a tree".[2]

Madame's child arrived safely on the last day of August (N.S.). "Only a girl", wrote Monsieur. A week later, the Parisian physicians ordered by the Duke and Duchess of Orleans to report on the case of the Queen Mother of England made their appearance at Colombes. There were present that September afternoon grouped around the great state bed containing so small an occupant, enough portentous figures to scare a stronger sufferer—M. Vallot, first physician to Louis XIV, M. Esprit, first physician to Monsieur, M. Ivelin, first physician to Madame, M. Duquesne, resident physician, and Father Cyprien de Gamache. The visitors paid their respects to her majesty, and begged to enquire concerning her complaint. Before Duquesne could open his mouth, the patient took up her parable and explained all her symptoms with such fullness that "she left her physician in ordinary nothing to add except his mode of treatment and the medicines he had been employing". M. Vallot, the most important oracle, was graciously pleased to approve of everything that had been done. After their examination, still acting as leader of the medical chorus, he was blessedly reassuring. By the grace of God, her majesty's complaints, although very painful, were not dangerous. He was, in fact, prepared to add nothing to the admirable treatment already being followed, except something to conquer the persistent insomnia, which was lowering her strength.

[1] Strickland.   [2] Coxe MS. vol. 14, pp. 90-92.

Her majesty's quick ear caught the word "grains", and she interrupted M. Vallot's complacent discourse "to declare positively that she would not take them. She knew from experience that they disagreed with her." Moreover, with great *empressement*, "the famous English physician, M. de Mayerne, had warned her never to take any". His most Christian majesty's first physician, distressingly unmoved by the mention of the great but late Sir Theodore, begged to explain with the greatest respect "that the grains which he was proposing to give were of a particular composition. He would not have been so ill-advised as to prescribe them had he not known for a certainty that they would be conducive to her majesty's health. He begged her majesty to be thoroughly persuaded of this", and much more in the same vein. Henrietta, checked but not convinced, demanded everybody else's opinion on the subject. All present, except M. Ivelin, fully endorsed M. Vallot's decision. Madame's doctor only differed from the rest in declaring "with great moderation and prudence", that he did not know the composition of the grains proposed by M. Vallot. He was, however, sure that anything suggested by so celebrated an expert must be perfectly proper and efficacious.

The visiting doctors returned to Paris, and the invalid arose to follow her usual round. Her habits were very regular. For years past she had begun her days by reading a chapter of the *Imitation of Christ*. Two mornings after the dreaded consultation she had a long interview with her confessor in preparation for receiving the Sacrament next day. When she had made her confession, she told him with great earnestness that she had put all her worldly affairs in order. Her son the king was going to give all her servants two years' wages in advance, in addition to what might be owing to them at the date of her death.

Supper that evening found her restored to gaiety. The small household of withered ladies and stooping gentlemen who sat with her by candlelight at a board served by attendants, some of whom would have been considered past work in any other royal establishment, noted with pleasure that the beloved mistress was eating well and laughing again. Colour deepened in the windows of the château. Outside, trees still heavy with summer foliage were printed black against a clear greenish sky. Not a breeze stirred their shapes. Another long, hot night was beginning. The Queen Mother kept early hours. By ten o'clock she had retired, and all at Colombes sought their beds with easy minds. Nothing unusual was going to happen to-night. Duquesne had decided that, since his patient was already a little overwarm, she had better not take the laudanum. The curtains of her bed were drawn; she sent away everyone, and composed herself to rest. When the lady, who for the past few days had been sleeping in her chamber, arrived to take up her post, the sound of regular breathing from the curtained bed told her that her mistress had fallen immediately into a sweet slumber.

That happy state of affairs lasted for about half an hour. Then Henrietta Maria awoke and began to be restless. In vain she told herself that she had no new reason for disquiet. The visit of the strange doctors, which had been such an ordeal, was successfully overpast. Vallot, the chief of them, that pompous man who had talked her down and shown so little respect for Sir Theodore's opinion, had seen her poor sister-in-law's cancer. Some people said that he had caused the late Queen Mother of France unnecessary suffering. But he had found nothing dire the matter with the Queen Mother of England. He had said that she might live for years. She was glad that she was not to die just yet, for all her children needed her upon earth. Three beloved children, all unhappily married, was enough to keep a good mother awake at nights; and the match made by her was the most disastrous of the lot. Her daughter had succeeded in bearing a living child this time, but not the hoped-for boy.

More trials stretched before her innocent, unwise Minette. She could not see any end to them. The Queen Mother of England perceived herself entering upon one of her bad nights. By day it was possible to be gay and deceive people into believing that one had no worries, but at night it was not possible to deceive oneself. Presently, perhaps, it would be her duty to return to her son's country, to assist in the preservation and promotion of the Catholic religion. She had no great wish to see the fine new capital which he was building. On her last visits she had found enough that was strange and distressing to her in it. The spring-like freshness which had made England so attractive in her spring-time seemed to have quite departed. A glare as lurid as the flames which had consumed two-thirds of a wicked city, lit the London of nowadays. But then, the whole world was much more fleshly minded than it had been in the days of the White King. She had wished so much to sleep well to-night, for she had confessed to-day in hopes of attending early mass to-morrow. She should have done so yesterday, for yesterday had been the festival of the Nativity of the most blessed Virgin, but the doctors had kept her in bed. . . . Her thoughts began to turn to the narcotic ordered by Vallot, for just such an occasion as this. She knew that it had arrived, for Duquesne had considered giving it to her to-night. . . . A gipsy in England had once told her that she should never die except of a grain. . . . Sir Theodore had warned her that she must never take such a thing. But Sir Theodore, as the young experts had hinted, had learned his medicine ages ago. They all said that opium was very good for the heart and nerves. . . .

About eleven o'clock the queen called to the lady sleeping in her chamber, and asked her to tell Duquesne that after all she could not sleep, and would like to take her new medicine. It was brought to her in the white of an egg. Conquering her repugnance, she drank it off resolutely. Her lady resettled her to wait for the good long rest she had now every reason to expect, and breathless quiet fell upon the room again after the little interruption.

But she was not alone in the dark any more, for the curtains of her bed had been left open. On the dim walls she could see the portrait of Madame's daughter and little dead son, holding a lamb in a garland of flowers, and the St Joseph given to her by Cardinal Mazarin, and the oval Notre Dame painted by the Princess Louise, and, over the chimney, James, Duke of York, in black armour. And silhouetted against the radiance of a candle, placed where it should not trouble her eyes, she could see the profile of Duquesne. He had sunk into a chair by the side of her bed, and would remain there faithfully until she was safely asleep. She did not think that he would have long to wait, for already she could tell that the strange doctors had not deceived her. . . . Enormous waves of refreshing sleep were rolling towards her, wetting her with their spray, receding and gathering, only to advance nearer next time. She was sinking over shoes in the sands, and a mariner of England who had slipped across the Channel between two storms last night, was pointing eagerly across the wrinkled waste of waters at a white streak on the horizon, and telling her that those were the cliffs of Dover where his master, her bridegroom, was waiting for her. She had never been on the sea before, but felt only a little afraid, for she was the daughter of the great Henry. Kind people were trying to dissuade her from setting out on such a day. Her ill luck at sea, they said, was proverbial. Her children made a joke of it in their nursery. But she must not hesitate, for she knew that the eyes of the whole spiritual world were upon the lucky princess who had been chosen to bring back the old faith to a lovely country, and the king had written again and again that he was waiting for the guns and money which she was bringing to him for the destruction of his enemies. "Courage, ladies! no queen of England has ever been drowned!" They were all gathering around her, with comically disturbed faces, begging her to rouse herself. Duquesne had moved from his chair, and was feeling her pulse. Somebody was moving a chamber candlestick to and fro close in front of her eyes, but its light no longer vexed her. For this was the worst storm any man had trysted with for many a year. It must last, she knew, for nine days and nights. She could not move from her little bed. She could not move a finger or a toe. Sailors, who had been to the Indies and back, were crying out in their terror of being washed overboard. Only the good Capuchin, who had been a Knight of Malta, had kept his sea-legs. He had brought to her, not without difficulty, the little *curé* of Colombes village, bearing the Blessed Sacrament. That should have been tomorrow. . . .[1]

IV

A coach drawn by sweating horses thundered up to the doors of Colombes in the light of dawn on September 10th, 1669 (N.S.). Old St Albans, fussing amongst his mistress's private papers, was disturbed by the entrance of Monsieur. Her affectionate son-in-law, who had set out instantly from St Germain on hearing of her majesty's illness, learnt with deep emotion that he had arrived too late. She had never rallied after taking the dose which had caused her to sleep too profoundly. She had passed away peacefully between three and four o'clock this morning. When he learnt further that her Chamberlain could not find any trace of a will, he took command of the situation and ordered all her effects to be put under seal. According to the law of France the property of persons who died intestate went to such of their children as were resident in the country. His wife, he fancied, should be the sole inheritress of Henrietta Maria. While the house echoed to the wails of broken-hearted

[1] The two longest and most circumstantial accounts of the death of Henrietta Maria are those contained in Father Cyprien's *Mémoires*, and St Albans' letter of Sept. 10, 1669, to Charles II, *S.P.D.* Fr., 98. 127. P.R.O. But even these two eye-witnesses differ as to the composition of the fatal dose, who administered it, and at what hour.

attendants calling for the blood of Doctor Vallot,[1] my lord
St Albans wrote to Charles II, to Lord Arlington. . . . In his
grief and confusion, he quite forgot to inform the British
Embassy in Paris.

Her majesty's prime servant outlived her by fifteen years.
A mansion in St James's Square and a moated Elizabethan
country seat sheltered his extremely comfortable old age. The
portly figure of the aged earl, being helped from his coach outside a great house where a dinner-party was toward, was still
a familiar sight to Londoners in the eighties of the century. He
grew so blind that he could not tell what was on his plate, or,
after his good meal, what cards he was holding. Still he brought
to his meat and drink "an extraordinary appetite", and afterwards thoroughly enjoyed his gamble, "having one that sits
by him to name the spots on the cards".[2] The earl who planned
St James's Square and built St Albans Market is scarcely remembered,[3] but his surname survives in a London street of whose
amenities he would have been appreciative.

"She was almost always ill", commented Mademoiselle on
her aunt's death. "They gave her some pills to make her sleep,
which were so successful that she never woke again." Other
relations were more affected. The Duchess of Orleans refused
to be comforted by the thought that the little mother, who had
been so much afraid of death, had never even realized that she
was dying. To the day of her own death, little more than nine
months later,[4] the dark-blue eyes of Madame flooded with tears
at any mention of her mother.[5]

[1] Vallot lost much of his reputation, but did not lose his court appointment in consequence of the tragedy of Colombes.   [2] Evelyn.
[3] Destroyed to make room for Waterloo Place and Regent Street.
[4] Henrietta Anne died in agony, after a few hours' illness, in June 1670,
aged twenty-six. She believed herself to have been poisoned, and contemporary opinion pointed to her husband and his favourite as her murderers.
Her death, however, was officially attributed to natural causes, and modern
authorities diagnose her case as one of peritonitis.
[5] de Montpensier.

When an express brought "the unwelcome news" of their loss to the King of England and the Duke of York, "they retired immediately from their intended diversion at New Forest to Hampton Court, where they continued until Whitehall was ready for them".[1] National mourning was ordered. English poetasters produced elegies. Englishmen who had seen her for the first time in the year of her son's restoration, learnt with surprise that the Queen Mother had, after all, been only sixty. She had looked quite seventy, nine years past.

The small, shrunken body of Henrietta Maria, lying in a state bed, remained in the chamber in which she had fallen into her last sleep for a night and a day. It was then embalmed, and lay in state in the hall of her country château, surrounded by tapers and covered by a pall of gold-and-silver brocade lined with ermine, until it was removed to Chaillot, where, in accordance with her wishes, her heart, "laid in a vessel of silver", was presented to the devoted nuns amongst whom she had hoped to spend her last days. Louis XIV took upon himself the whole expenses of the prolonged and magnificent ceremonies, culminating in his aunt's interment by the side of her great father at St Denis.[2]

V

Monsieur did not succeed in his attempt to obtain everything left by Henrietta Maria at Colombes, Chaillot and the Hôtel de la Bazinière. The young Prince of Orange, hearing of his uncle's pretensions, sent word to say that if Monsieur was likely to get a share, he should consider himself justified in advancing a claim. Charles II despatched to Paris a doctor of law, who pleaded that, as a member of his master's household, the late queen could not, by residence in France, have divested

[1] H. M. de B.
[2] During the French Revolution the body of Henrietta Maria shared the fate of those of her royal ancestors in being robbed of its coffin and flung into a common trench behind the Abbey of St Denis.

herself of the English domicile which she had acquired by marriage. Eventually the Duchess of Orleans asked her husband to desist from his efforts on her behalf, the King of England was adjudged his mother's sole heir, and on the last Monday of October 1669 his representatives arrived at Colombes to take an inventory. The doctor of law sent over by Charles II was described by his Parisian hosts as an English gentleman, "*le docteur Jinquin*", but anybody at Oxford University would have known better. Dr. (soon to become Sir Leoline) Jenkins was a Welsh gentleman, and the Master of Jesus College. An unbending Protestant alighted at the Papist Queen Mother's country château with feelings of interest tempered by trepidation. He was curious to behold the entire personal belongings of a lady celebrated for her taste. In a house into which Death has stepped without knocking, much of the owner's secrets must be laid bare. But he foresaw that great tact would be called for during his forthcoming week of hard labour. Already the valuation of her few remaining pieces of jewellery had presented difficulties. The French experts had valued her great cross of diamonds at no more than six thousand pistoles, whereas nine thousand had been paid for it, and Sir Thomas Bond, from Denmark House, bore witness that three thousand had once been offered for its single pendant pearl. . . .

Her late majesty's Grand Almoner and the Master of her Household were awaiting the little party of invasion, which consisted of Dr. Jenkins, two officials from Denmark House and the necessary clerks. Dr. Jenkins' scheme, since he understood that the bulk of her late majesty's effects were to be found here, was to begin at Colombes, go on to La Bazinière and end at Chaillot, taking each residence room by room.[1] He was forthwith invited by their gloomy owner to take my lord St Albans' private apartments first, and his clerks began to scribble notes of twelve dining-room chairs without arms and six with,

[1] Letters of Sir L. Jenkins to Lord Arlington, *S.P.D.* Fr., 78. 128, P.R.O.

all upholstered in Holland brocatelle—colours "greene and Isabelle". . . . In his bedchamber, my lord, bursting forth, announced that the wall hangings had been a present to him from his mistress, "but the king may have them if he pleases".¹

Everyone in this silent house was in a condition of suppressed indignation. "When it is considered how soon Monsieur came amongst them, and how soon the seals were clap't on after the Good Queen's Departure", they were sure that they should be acquitted of responsibility, should aught be missing. Dr. Jenkins was equally, and soothingly, sure that since everything of value possessed by the good queen had been so well known to so many trusted *domestiques* he would find everything in order. Seven trembling, red-eyed ladies in deep mourning introduced themselves as her dressers. Their names were Susan de Mercy, Elizabeth Plansy, Jane l'Espérance, Rebecca Brouncker, Sophia Stuart, Henriette de Vantelet and Henriette Orpe. They had planned to travel to England under the escort of her late majesty's Lieutenant of the Guards, and fling themselves destitute at his majesty's feet, but understood sadly that he did not desire this.

¹ The king's pleasure was to add, in his own handwriting, in the margin of the inventory of everything in these rooms, "To my Ld: St Albans".

Charles behaved very handsomely in his disposal of his mother's effects. He ordered everything at Chaillot "to be left in the monastery". Such of the furniture as was considered by the nuns to be too fine for their use was sold, and produced a sum which built ten new cells and provided for an annual commemorative service in honour of their foundress. The house and lands of Colombes were formally handed over to Madame by the English Ambassador in his master's name, as a free gift for her sole use and benefit. In the margin of the Colombes inventory Charles wrote, "What Madame cares not to have to be distributed amongst the Queen's women"; so every member of Henrietta Maria's household got some memento of the beloved mistress. Charles reserved for himself a selection of such oil-paintings as were "not fix't" into the panelling of the château, and one which was "fix't". He ordered that the picture entitled "Noli me tangere", on which his mother's eyes had rested daily in her little cabinet, should be "Taken away, unknowne to Madame".

They therefore earnestly begged Sir Thomas Bond, from Denmark House, to present their solicitation.

Dr. Jenkins passed into the Guard Chamber of Colombes château, where the hangings were of the brocade made at the Porte de Paris factory—red with a blue ground—and over the mantelpiece, framed into the panelling, stared a portrait of the Duke of York. The Presence Chamber came next, a very fine room with stools, *fauteuils* and hangings all *en suite* in a brocatelle of blue, white and carnation. Two tortoiseshell tables, a tortoiseshell cabinet and a couple of large mirrors completed the furniture of this reception room. The cabinet and both mirrors were "adorned with brass guilt" in the style made fashionable by the talented André Boulle, cabinet-maker to Louis XIV; Vandyck's well-known group of the three eldest children of Charles I had the place of honour here, and the Princess Royal appeared again in a half-length by Honyman. "Great arms of wood to put lights in" occupied the wall space between a Tintoretto of a Venetian senator and five large religious paintings.

The Privy Chamber had Chinese lacquer tables and stands, a clock in a case of Jamaica wood garnished with silver (which, Sir Thomas opined, the king would remember well), a Correggio "Lucrece", and his majesty in buff and armour "fix't over the chimney". All the stools and armchairs here were of black velvet, to match the hangings of a state bed. An enormous representation of the infant Moses "with Pharaoh's daughter and her Women, att large," was, her majesty's attendants assured Dr. Jenkins, "fix't" for eternity. Their mistress had been obliged to leave it here when she had quitted France to take up residence at Denmark House, for its painted frame was plastered into the wall.

The party of inspection had attained the dead queen's bedchamber. Here stood the grey damask bed in which she had fallen into her last sleep. Grey was the predominant colour in the widow's country bedroom, for her stools, *fauteuils*, screens and cushions were all of grey serge, with gold and silver fringe, and a curtain of the same damask as the bed hid the entrance to her cabinet—the little adjacent alcove in which she had said her prayers and written her letters. Here, enclosed in a box containing a stand for its erection, lay the only picture of King Charles the Martyr, at Colombes. The severe Protestant eye of Dr. Jenkins fell upon a large devotional piece entitled "Noli me tangere", a shagreen box, a table of Jamaica wood. . . . Into her majesty's dressing-room had been crammed a collection of family portraits. Except for two flower groups over the doors, every picture on these red and yellow brocaded walls was of a close relation. Her great father and her mother were easily recognizable. The likenesses of a pallid baby, a frank-faced young man and a dark-browed little girl were eagerly explained as her majesty's late son-in-law, her little grandson, Madame's only son—dead, alas!—and Mademoiselle, her granddaughter. Dr. Jenkins' clerks duly entered "the late Prince of Orange", "the Duke of Valois in swaddling clouts" and "Mademoiselle d'Orleans".

Everything in the room furnished for Madame when she had been a maid was bright and pretty—hangings representing the Five Senses, a little bed of crimson damask with gold and silver fringe, two tables of nut-tree, two cabinets inlaid mother-of-pearl, flower-pots of faience. Its sole picture was a Madonna.

The Outer Rooms of the Wardrobe presented a scene of confusion wild enough to daunt the heart of the most methodical, for into them had been cast, on that September morning seven weeks past, everything judged by the officers sent by the King of France to be safer under seal. Floors, tables and beds were heaped with treasures of all kinds and countries. There was a suite of furniture covered with Indian cloth of gold, flowered in red and green, and half of a suite of crimson-rayed satin, and a pile of Persian and Turkey carpets, and her majesty's little blue damask travelling bed, and the trunk containing her dressing-table set, and her red velvet box for pomatum, and her little crystal pocket-glass, and a child's silver spoon, and several tea-pots and a chocolate-pot. . . . The chill October light streamed in upon a ruffled coverlet of white fox-skins and a collar of ermines, and a mantle of cloth of silver lined blue, and another of incarnadine stitched with gold—all relics of her happy days when she wore colours. There was a freshly laundered mountain of body linen—night smocks and day smocks of fine lawn, thirty-four mob caps, twenty-six handkerchiefs, eleven pairs of cotton gloves, several aprons, and a box of Italian fans, and Spanish gloves and pockets, and lace for church furniture.

Dr. Jenkins' clerks noted a nut-cup mounted in silver-gilt, an amber cabinet, an agate cabinet, some pieces of true porcelain, "a greene or willow colour'd sattin carpet, embroidered in gold and silver and Spanish leather (very rich)", and a lemon-coloured bed, a gay bed from Provence, of Avignon rayed taffetas, red and green, with *pommes* and *bouquets* on its canopy.

The jewel-chest of her late majesty, who had been capable of appreciating a fine stone, held nothing very remarkable. The best things in it were her great cross of diamonds and her pendant pearls, punctiliously sent back by Madame, who had long been accustomed to wear them, and some emeralds—a necklace of sixty-nine beads, six drops and a large ring. Everything here, however, must be described, so the clerks made entries of bodkins with heads of sapphires and turquoises, and a set of amethysts —four ear-drops, a bodkin, a brooch and a bracelet, and a little balas ruby, and eight little cabochon rubies, and a cross of sapphires and small diamonds, and a great unset sapphire, and a little cross of gold, from which all the stones except that in the centre had been picked, and a scrap of Indian gold chain and a big box full of cornelians of several sizes but no value. . . .

Her late majesty had been no great reader. One "India trunk" from the passage on the stairs had sufficed as home for her whole library. The Vestibule, almost the end of her story, displayed further evidences of her tastes, for here, in company with the likeness of his majesty when Prince of Wales, in armour, with a pistol in his hand, and five great landscapes in gilt frames, and a Judith holding Holofernes' head, and four great saints, and "the late Duke of Gloucester in sky-coloured coates", hung the head-and-shoulders portrait of a spaniel. . . .

Even the back-stairs at Colombes held elegance, for their hangings were "of Lanskip and Pillars". With "the Little room by the backstayres, called the Trunk Room", which yielded nothing but bundles of hangings and bales of uncut damask and wrought velvet and folding stools, Dr. Jenkins' clerks made an end of their list. They were slightly worried that a previous inventory taken by one Brown contained several pictures which they had been unable to identify, but since they had "many more Madonnas" than Brown, they hopefully "supposed none missing".[1]

VI

The most remarkable service in connection with the death of Henrietta Maria took place at Chaillot. Madame, already the patroness of Corneille and Molière, had invited the foremost religious author in France to aid her in perpetuating the memory of a beloved parent. Jacques Bénigne Bossuet, Bishop-elect of Condom, always painstaking, summoned greatness to meet a great occasion. He interviewed personally everyone likely to be able to give him intelligent information as to the mother of Madame. Madame de Motteville, at his request, supplied him with a *mémoire* recording every important event of the late queen's career as it had been detailed by her own lips. The

[1] "Inventory of all the Goods, Plate and Householde Stuffe belonging to the late Queen, the King's Mother, Colombes, Oct. 31–Nov. 5, 1669," S.P.D. Fr., P.R.O. 78. 128. Brown was probably Richard Browne, who as Under-keeper of Denmark House, took an inventory of the contents of that palace in 1626.

Filles de Sainte Marie tearfully offered anecdotes of a queen who "without pretending to be *dévote* had been remarkably so". By the middle of November, Bossuet, whom Nature had endowed with a voice and language of great strength and flexibility, was ready with a funeral oration destined to link his name for ever with that of Henrietta Maria, and increase the fame of both the preacher and his subject.

The tree-lined Cours de la Reine, up which Henrietta Maria had driven in the summer of 1651 in search of a suitable house for a convent, was on November 16th, 1669 (N.S.), hung with black banners and blocked by the coaches of the French nobility. Within the gates of Chaillot the signs of mourning increased. The walls, floor and even roof of the little chapel were veiled in sable draperies. It was overcrowded to the point of suffocation when the sturdy, white-haired Burgundian preacher, wearing the dress of a simple priest, ascended its pulpit to beg all here to join with him in honouring the memory of the most high, most excellent, most puissant princess, Henriette-Marie, Queen of England, Scotland and Ireland, daughter of the French king Henry the Victorious, wife to King Charles the Martyr, mother of King Charles at present reigning in England, and aunt to his most Christian majesty Louis XIV.

In the centre of the choir, mounted on a bier, covered by a black velvet pall embroidered in gold with her armorial bearings, lay a waxen effigy of the late queen as she had been at the day of her death. The famous preacher's resounding eloquence soon reduced his fashionable audience to tears. As they listened to his heart-rending descriptions of "our great Henrietta's" many narrow escapes from death on land and by sea, in pursuance of her duty as daughter of the Church, as queen, wife and mother, they glanced towards the tiny effigy on the catafalque, and wondered anew that so small a body should have contained so much spirit.

INDEX

Abbeville, 28

Aberdeen, 226

Abingdon, 157

"Abrégé des Révolutions d'Angleterre",
narrative dictated by Henrietta
Maria to Madame de Motteville,
106, 113, 116, 119, 120, 121,
125, 149, 150, 154, 326

Achmet I, Sultan, 3

African negro servants, 72, 83, 88

African shore, 312

Aiguillon, Marie du Pont de Cour-
lay, Duchesse d', 311

"Albani", Alessandro Albini, painter,
93

Alexander I, Emperor of Russia, 151

Alexander VII, Pope, 245

Amboise, 12

Amiens, 28, 29

Amsterdam, 131, 132, 133, 135, 249

Andover, 228

Angers, 14, 161

Angoulême, 7 n., 14

Angoulême, Bishop of, 115, 171

Anjou, Gaston, Duke of, see Orleans,
Gaston, Duke of

Anjou, Philippe, Duke of, see Orleans, Philippe, Duke of

Anne of Austria, Queen of Louis
XIII of France, marriage of, 9,
12; appearance and manners of,
12, 168, 275; neglected by her
husband, 12, 13; favours marriage of Henrietta Maria to
Charles I, 17, 21; relations of
with Buckingham, 28, 43; miscarries, 55; gives birth to Louis
XIV, is widowed and becomes
regent, 148; charity of, to
Henrietta Maria, 158, 159, 163,
168, 172, 193, 206, 216, 222,
246, 247, 254, 256, 257; relations
of with Mazarin, 162, 169, 268;
Troubles of during the Wars of
the Fronde, 191, 193, 195, 213,
229; wishes her son Louis to
marry the Infanta, 258, 259, and
her son Philippe to marry
Henrietta Anne, 274; complains
of Henrietta Anne's conduct,
300, 301, 302; illness and death
of, 323, 333; mentioned, 17, 20,
51, 100, 161, 168, 169, 174, 175,
178, 179, 202, 203, 205, 207,
208, 213, 227, 228, 233, 236,
239, 244, 250, 273, 278, 325

Anne of Denmark, Queen of James
I of England, 38 n., 131

Anne of York, the Lady, afterwards
Anne, Queen of England, 330,
331

Anne, Princess, third daughter of
Charles I and Henrietta Maria,
birth of, 70, 71, 93; death of,
111; mentioned, 101

Antwerp, 80, 82, 118, 131, 134, 228,
255

Arlington, Earl of, see Bennet, Henry

Army Plot, the, 113, 114, 115

Arran, Lord, 281

Arundel, Thomas Howard, 2nd
Earl of, 88

Arundel of Wardour, Henry Arundel, 3rd Baron, 306, 328

Ashburnham, William, 113

Ashby de la Zouche, 149

Ashmole, Elias, 283

Aubigny, Abbé d', 310

Aubigny, Duchesse d', 81

Avignon, 30

347

Aylesbury, 153, 198
Aytoun, Sir Robert, secretary to Henrietta Maria, 74

Banqueting House, Whitehall, 37, 80, 82, 200, 283, 315, 316
Barberini, Francesco, Cardinal, 92, 93, 111
Barberini, Maffeo, Cardinal, see Urban VIII
Barham Downs, 34
Barlow, Mrs, see Walter, Lucy
Barnes, Ambrose, of Newcastle, 145
"Barnino, Monsieur", see Bernini
Bartet, M., French envoy, 284
Bassett, Mistress, lace-woman, 89
Bassompierre, Marshal de, 49, 50, 51, 52, 53, 54, 58, 215, 216, 223
Bastille, 6, 49, 229
Bath, 157, 158, 159, 174
Battles of—
    Arras, 234
    Dunbar, 220
    Ivry, 2, 49
    Naseby, 56 n., 127, 171
    Newbury, 155
    Marston Moor, 170
    Philiphaugh, 172
    The Dunes, 254
    Worcester, 224
Bavaria, Ferdinand, Duke of, 221, 258
Bavaria, Maximilian, Duke of, 221
Bazinière, Hôtel de la, residence of Henrietta Maria, 321, 322, 326, 338, 339
Beaufort, Francois de Vendôme, Duc de, 323
Beaumont, Mademoiselle de, 190
Beauvais, 214, 305
Bedford House, Exeter, 159
Bedford, William Russell I, 5th Earl and 1st Duke of, 154
Bedlam, 87, 233, 234
Bennet, Henry, afterwards 1st Earl of Arlington, 176, 228, 326, 327, 337
Berkeley, Sir Charles, afterwards 1st Earl of Falmouth, 286, 287

Berkeley, Sir John, 186
Bernini, Giovanni Lorenzo, 82, 105
Bertaut, John, Bishop of Séez, 163
Bérulle, Father, afterwards Cardinal, 28
Berwick, 108, 190
Bidassoa, river, 12
"Black Tom Tyrant", see Strafford
Blainville, Marquis de, 49
Blois, 13, 14
Bohemia, Elizabeth, Queen of, see Elizabeth
Bohemia, Frederick, King of, see Palatine, Frederick V, Elector
Bolsover Castle, 84, 146
Bombay, 312
Bond, Sir Thomas, 339, 341
Bordeaux, 12
Borghese Villa, 82
Boscobel, 227
Bosvile, Major, 185, 191
Bossuet, Jacques Bénigne, Bishop of Condom, 344, 345
Boulle, André, cabinet-maker, 341
Boulogne, 16, 27, 29, 30
Bourbon l'Archambault, 162, 164, 166, 213, 235, 259, 318
Boynton Hall, Yorks, 143, 146
Brazil, 312
Breda, 214, 259, 265
Brent, Sir Nathaniel, Warden of Merton College, Oxford, 150
Brest, 161
Bridlington, 126, 141, 143, 145, 171
Brienne, Comte de, 14, 28, 31, 299
Brill, 123, 277
Bristol, Earl of, see Digby, George
Bristol, town, 157, 172
Broom Park, Kent, 85
Brouncker, Rebecca, dresser to Henrietta Maria, 340
Browne, Sir Richard, 210, 222
Bruges, 252
Brussels, 21, 264, 265
Buckingham, George Villiers, 1st Duke of, 16, 18, 19, 20, 21, 27, 28, 35, 36, 39, 42, 43, 44, 45, 46,

49 *n.*, 50, 51, 54, 57, 59, 61, 62, 63, 72 *n.*, 98, 108, 154, 199, 264

Buckingham, George Villiers, 2nd Duke of, 58, 98, 228, 270, 285, 292, 293, 294, 295, 328

Buckingham, Katherine Villiers, Duchess of, 54, 59, 62, 98

Buckingham, Mary Villiers, Countess of, 29, 44, 54, 59, 98

Buisson, Sieur du, 15, 16

Burgos, 12

Burlington Bay, 141

Burton-upon-Trent, 148

Bushell, Mr, inventor, 91

Butler, James, *see* Ormonde

Cademan, Sir Thomas, physician-in-ordinary to Henrietta Maria, 283

Calais, 53, 182, 258, 280, 305, 321

Cambridge, Member of Parliament for, *see* Cromwell, Oliver

Cambridge, University of, 87, 90

Canterbury, Archbishop of, *see* Laud, William

Canterbury, town, 29, 33, 34, 266

Capitol, the, 92

Capuchins in England, 68, 83, 85, 311, 321, 323; *see also* Gamache, Father C. de

Carisbrooke Castle, 187, 189, 218, 219, 221, 237, 240

Carlisle, city of, 190, 224

Carlisle, James Hay, 1st Earl of, 22, 23, 24, 56, 57, 59

Carlisle, Lucy Hay, formerly Percy, Countess of, 59, 97, 98, 99, 121, 190, 306

Carlos, the Infante, son of Philip III of Spain, 21

Carr, Rochester, of Lincolnshire, 86

Castlemaine, Barbara Villiers, afterwards Palmer, Countess of, 38 *n.*, 292, 313, 319

Catherine of Braganza, Queen of Charles II of England, 181, 311,.

312, 313, 314, 315, 317, 318, 319, 324, 329

Catherine, Saint, a picture of, possessed by Henrietta Maria, 94, 185

Cavendish, Lord Charles, 148, 149

Cavendish, William, *see* Newcastle, Duke of

Caversham, 186

Cedrino, oil of, 92

Chaillot, Convent of, 215, 216, 217, 223, 224, 228, 230, 235, 236, 243, 248, 249, 253, 255, 256, 265, 266, 267, 322, 325, 327, 329, 330, 338, 339, 344, 345

Chamberlaine, J., surgeon, 65

Chambéry, 167, 259, 319

Champagne, district, 8

Champagne, wine, 316

Charles-James, eldest son of Charles I and Henrietta Maria, 65, 66

Charles Louis, *see* Palatine, Elector

Charles I, King of England, Prince of Wales, 15, 16; first sees Henrietta Maria, 17; in Spain, 18, 19; negotiations for marriage of with Henrietta Maria, 20 *seq.*; proxy marriage of, 24 *seq.*; marriage of, 34; appearance, manners and education of, 32, 35, 76, 103, 104, 105, 145, 175, 197, 207; coronation of, 42; dismisses his wife's French suite, 45 *seq.*; complains of her to Buckingham, 44, and Bassompierre, 50; goes to war against France, 53 *seq.*; makes peace with France and Spain, 66; his relations with his wife improve, 54, 61, 63; weeps on hearing of Buckingham's murder, 63; becomes devoted to his wife, 64, 66, 67, 68; births of the children of, 66, 69, 70, 71; "The White King", 64; clothing and possessions of, 76, 201; penuriousness of, 35, 79; his love of the fine arts, 79, 92, 93; visits Scotland, 86, 107, 110, 117, 118, 120; high moral tone of his court, 88; sacrifices Strafford, 116; his fatal ductility, 128, 130, 212; raises the royal standard at Nottingham, 136; "The Man of Sin", 138; at Oxford, 144, 150 *seq.*; says farewell to Henrietta Maria for the last time, 157; defeated at Naseby, 173; delivers himself to the Scottish army, 177; instructs his children to obey their mother, 181, 198; a prisoner, 181, 185, 186, 187, 191, 192; is tried and condemned to death, 197; last hours of, 198 *seq.*; execution of, 200, 201; mentioned, 228, 230, 233, 237, 238, 240, 245, 254, 264, 269, 270, 271, 276, 282, 283, 290, 296, 313, 316, 317, 319, 322, 323, 325, 326, 334, 335, 341, 342, 345

Charles II, King of England, conception and birth of, 67, 69, 76; christening of, 69; early wit and ugliness of, 70, 73, 102; his mother's favourite child, 72, 208, 213, 304; is slow to learn her language, 73, 180, 184, 208, 227; portraits and descriptions of, 73, 80, 179, 226, 341, 344; manners and education of, 102, 206, 207; a suit of armour for, 164; his mother wishes him to marry "La Grande Mademoiselle", 173, 180, 181, 183, 207, 209, 210, 229, 251; arrives in France, 178 *seq.*; wishes to serve against Spain, 186, 187; sails for England, 190; returns to Holland, 191; affection of for his youngest sister, 183, 263, 265, 271; King of England, 203, 204; does not desire his mother's advice, 205, 211, 212, 213, 214,

234, 319; offers marriage to "La Grande Mademoiselle", 207 *seq.*; his opinions of a husband's duty, 210; sails for Jersey, 213; experiences in Scotland, 214, 220; returns to France, 226; leaves France, 233; disapproves of his mother's attempt to convert the Duke of Gloucester, 237 *seq.*; attempts to regain his throne, 245, 248, 259, 262; visits Spain, 262, and Colombes, 263; forwards the Declaration of Breda, 265, and sails for England, 266, 267; welcomes his mother to his kingdom, 281 *seq.*; marries, 312, 313; recognizes his illegitimate son, James, 314, 316; corresponds with his sister, 319, 324; reduces his mother's pension, 326; hears of her death, 338; generous disposal of her effects, 340; mentioned, 38 *n.*, 95, 101, 108, 110, 119, 120, 126, 127 *n.*, 136, 137, 150, 151, 157 *n.*, 173, 174, 177, 189, 198, 217, 218, 219, 222, 229, 230, 234, 246, 247, 249, 251, 252, 253, 255, 268, 272, 273, 275, 276, 277, 278, 279, 285, 288, 289, 290, 291, 292, 293, 304, 306, 317, 318, 339, 340, 345

Charlotte de la Trémoïlle, afterwards Stanley, Countess of Derby, *see* Trémoïlle

Chateauneuf, Marquis de, 67

Cheapside, 51, 89

Chelmsford, 101

Chester, 145, 157

Chevreuse, Claude de Lorraine, Duke of, 20, 26, 27, 31, 39, 109

Chevreuse, Marie de Rohan-Montbazon, Duchess of, 20, 34, 40, 59, 96, 97, 99, 108, 109, 163, 165, 317

Chilly, château of, 250

China, rarities from, 11, 89, 256, 257, 309, 341
Chinese boy, see Peter
Chipping-Norton, 91
Cholmely, Sir Hugh, 145
Christ Church, Oxford, 90, 91, 151
Christina, Queen of Sweden, 245, 246, 252, 253, 257, 269, 282 n.
Christine, Duchess of Savoy, sister of Henrietta Maria, 10, 15, 21, 55, 66, 67, 76, 100, 102, 118, 127, 167, 206, 211, 215, 231, 234, 258, 259, 260, 261, 262, 264, 271, 272, 273, 276, 279, 313, 315, 318, 319
Ciphers, used by Henrietta Maria, Charles I, Charles II, 122, 125, 126, 127, 167, 170, 186, 187
Civil War in England, outbreak of, the first, 136; the second, 191
Clarendon, Edward Hyde, 1st Earl of, see Hyde, Edward
Clermont, 240
Cleveland, Duchess of, see Castlemaine, Countess of
Cleveland, Thomas Wentworth, 1st Earl of, 62
Coldstream, 264
Cologne, 131, 134, 238, 239, 244, 245
Colombes, château and village of, 253, 254, 262, 263, 267, 271, 273, 296, 298, 299, 300, 321, 324, 330, 331, 333, 336, 338, 339, 341, 342, 344
Compiegne, château of, 28, 208, 209
Concini, Concino, Marshal d'Ancre, 11, 13, 14
Concini, Leonora, 11, 13
Condé, Charlotte de Montmorency, Princess of, 4, 8
Condé, Henry de Bourbon II, Prince of, 4, 10, 11, 16
Condé, Louis de Bourbon II, Prince of, 213, 229

Conn, George, Canon, first papal nuncio to the count of Henrietta Maria, 93, 94, 95, 96, 185
Consières, château of, 14
Conti, Armand de Bourbon, Prince of, 213
Conway, Edward, 1st Viscount, 21, 29
Corpus Christi College, Oxford, gardens of, 151
Corneille, Pierre, author, 344
"Correggio", Antonio Allegri, painter, 93, 341
Cosin, John, afterwards Bishop of Durham, 222, 238, 239, 240
Covenant, the Solemn League and, 181, 185, 214
Coventry, 144
Cowley, Abraham, poet, Secretary to Henrietta Maria, 170, 176, 271, 272
Crofts, James, see Monmouth
Crofts, Lord, 228, 314
Cromwell, Oliver, 38 n., 56 n.; consults a doctor, 64; sits in the Short Parliament as a member for Cambridge, 109; raises troops of horse, 144; general, 156; is present at meeting of Charles I with his children, 186; signs the death warrant of Charles I, 198; in Ireland, 213; wins the battle of Worcester, 224, 225; Lord Protector, 223, 248; makes a treaty of peace with France, 246; refuses to pay Henrietta Maria's dowry, 254; dies, 260; body of lies in state, 273; mentioned, 187, 262, 264
Cromwell, Richard, 260, 264
Croxall, 149
Cyprien, Father, see Gamache

Dalkeith, Elizabeth Villiers, afterwards Douglas, Countess of, afterwards Countess of Morton, 165, 174, 181, 182, 203, 235, 236

Darnley, Henry Stuart, Lord, 70

Dartmouth, 174

D'Avenant, Sir William, Poet Laureate, 109, 113, 157

Davy, the Lady Eleanor, prophetess, is consulted by Henrietta Maria, 56, 57; prophesies the birth and death of Henrietta's first child, 57, the deaths of Buckingham, 61, Laud and Strafford, 68 n., and the birth of Charles II, 68; is sent to prison, 68 n.

Deal, 262

Delft, city of, 133

Delft ware, 79

Delos, 80

Denbigh, Susan Villiers, afterwards Fielding, Countess of, 126, 139

Denham, Sir John, poet, 186

Denmark, Christian IV, King of, 131, 140

Denmark House, dower-palace of Henrietta Maria, 38, 47, 52, 53, 73, 87, 95, 99, 104, 272, 282, 287, 306, 307, 308, 309, 314, 315, 316, 318, 320, 321, 339, 341

Derby, Charlotte de la Trémoïlle, afterwards Stanley, Countess of, see Trémoïlle

Derby, James Stanley, 7th Earl of, see Strange

Derby, William Stanley, 6th Earl of, 58

Dieppe, 161

Digby, George, 2nd Earl of Bristol, 113, 134, 188, 312

Digby, Sir Kenelm, 79, 81, 183

Diver, a Dutch, in the service of Charles I, 54

Dohna, Count, see Christina, Queen of Sweden

Dover, Castle and town of, 29, 30, 31, 48, 122, 137, 182, 266, 280, 281, 335

Dover, Mayor of, 29

Drury Lane, 84

Dugdale, Sir William, 145

Dunkirk, 319

Duquesne, M., resident physician at Henrietta Maria's château of Colombes, 331, 333, 334, 335, 336

Durham, Bishop of, see Cosin, John

Durham, city of, 138

Easenwood, Gabriel, coachman to Henrietta Maria, 83

Edgehill, 150

Edinburgh, 118, 265

Eleanor of Mantua, wife of Ferdinand III, Emperor, 229

Elizabeth, Princess, second daughter of Charles I and Henrietta Maria, birth of, 70, 71, 89, 102; appearance of, 70, 197; early piety of, 95; nicknamed "Temperance", 198; proposal for marriage of, 103; delicate health of, 112; scholarship of, 127 n., 218; a prisoner, 181, 186; her last interview with her father, 197; illness and death of, 217, 218, 219, 220, 221; mentioned, 101, 114, 230, 237

Elizabeth, Queen of Bohemia, 22, 42, 66, 81, 88, 89, 90, 123, 124, 136, 139, 222, 231, 249, 255, 277

Elizabeth, Queen of England, 4 n., 13, 36, 77, 80

Elizabeth, Queen of Spain, sister of Henrietta Maria, 10, 12, 15, 19, 55, 66, 168

Elliott, Thomas, 176, 228

Enstone, 91

Epernon, Jean de Nogaret, Duke of, 2, 6, 14

Espérance, Jane l', dresser to Henrietta Maria, 340

Esprit, M., first physician to Philippe, Duke of Orleans, 331

Essex, Robert Devereux, 3rd Earl of, 136, 149, 155, 159, 167

Estrades, Godefrai, Comte d', French Ambassador, 319
Evelyn, John, 210, 308
Exeter, 71 *n.*, 158, 159, 160, 165, 174, 181, 186, 218, 320

Fairfax, Ferdinando, Baron, 147, 264
Falmouth, 160, 165, 171
Fanshawe, Anne, Lady, 152, 226
Fayette, Louise de la, Mother Superior of Chaillot, 215, 236, 255
Fécamp, 226
Felton, John, 61, 62
Ferdinand III, Emperor, 19, 180, 184, 207, 209, 210, 229
Ferine, Jean-Baptiste, perfumer to Henrietta Maria, 77
Fiano, Duchess of, 92
Fire of London, the Great, 323, 334
Fitzroy, James, *see* Monmouth, Duke of
Fletchers of the Hague, merchant-bankers, 135
Florence, Duke of, *see* Tuscany
Flushing, 123
Fontaine, Louise de la, 215
Fontainebleau, Palace and forest of, 11, 178, 179, 180, 273, 274, 296, 297, 298, 300, 301, 303, 308
Fontarabia, 262
Ford, Sir Edward, 186
Fraizer, Dr Alexander, 324
Francis, St, of Sales, 214, 215
Frankfurt-on-Main, 245, 246
Fronde, Wars of the, 189, 191, 195, 213, 228, 229, 230, 234
Fryer, Colonel, Sir Thomas, 62

Gainsborough, siege of, 149
Galigai, Leonora, *see* Concini, Leonora
Gamache, Father Cyprien de, 83, 85, 93, 164, 182, 196, 202, 204, 205, 235, 280, 281, 293, 294, 295, 298, 301, 310, 311, 329, 331
Garter, Order of the, 82, 201

Geddes, Jenny, 107
"Generalissima", name given by Henrietta Maria to herself, 143, 149, 157, 160
Gentile, Charles, chief embroiderer to Henrietta Maria, 76 ,
Gerard, Charles, afterwards 1st Earl of Macclesfield, 149
Gloucester, siege of, 155
Goddard, Anthony, footman to Henrietta Maria, 325
Gondomar, Diego Sarmiento de Acuña, Count of, 18
Goring, George, 1st Baron, afterwards Earl of Norwich, 27, 113
Goring, George, 2nd Baron, 113, 114, 115, 120, 136
Gouda, 133
Graham, James, *see* Montrose
Grenville, Sir Richard, 264
Greenwich, Palace of, 38, 65, 69, 71 *n.*, 110, 306
Griffen, attendant upon Henry, Duke of Gloucester, 240, 241, 242
Grignan, M. de, French Ambassador, 193, 194
Guernsey, 115
Guiche, Armand de Grammont, Comte de, 302, 303, 304, 323
Guienne, 11
Guildford, 292
Guildhall, the, 120
Guise, Claude, Duke of, 26
Guzman, Gaspar de, Count of Olivarez, Duke of St Lucar, *see* Olivarez

Hacker, Colonel Francis, 200
Hague, The, 100, 123, 125, 129, 131, 133, 134, 135, 136, 137, 170, 211, 220, 266
Hall, Mistress Judith, 149
Hamilton, James, 3rd Marquis and 1st Duke of, has his infant son painted by Vandyck, 81: at York, 146 *n.*; tries to prejudice Henrietta Maria against Mon-

trose, 147; is taken prisoner, 191

Hamilton, Mary, nun, 215

Hammond, Colonel Robert, 187

Hampden, John, 121

Hampton Court, 38, 41, 50, 91, 95, 120, 122, 186, 187, 291, 338

Harborough, 177

Harcourt, Henri, Comte d', French ambassador, 155, 159

Harvey, William, discoverer of the circulation of the blood, 156

Harwich, 100

Haselrig, Sir Arthur, 121

Hatton, Christopher, 1st Baron, 240, 244

Havre-de-Grace, 294, 330

Hay, James, *see* Carlisle, Earl of

Hay, Lucy, *see* Carlisle, Countess of

Helvoetsluis, 123

Henrietta Anne, Duchess of Orleans, fifth daughter of Charles I and Henrietta Maria, birth of, 71, 159; baptism of, 165; escapes to France, 181, 182; reared in the Catholic faith, 182, 235; descriptions of, 182, 183, 231, 232, 234, 263, 275, 296, 297; nicknamed "Minette", 183; early poverty of, 192, 193, 246; education of, 235; her mother's ambitions for, 212, 246; love of her brothers, 212, 246; scorned by Louis XIV, 247, 258, 259; projects of marriage for, 271, 273, 274, 275, 276; in England, 284 *seq.;* 290, 291; contracts measles, 292, 293; arrives safely in France, 294, 295; unhappy marriage of, to Philippe, Duke of Orleans, 296, 301 *seq.,* 322 *seq.;* births of her children, 303, 323, 331; correspondence with Charles II, 319, 320, 324, 328, 330; devotion to her mother, 337, 344; death of, 337 *n.;* mentioned, 195, 203, 253, 256, 257, 268, 278, 279, 297, 298, 299, 300, 318, 336, 339, 342, 343

Henrietta Maria, Queen of Charles I of England, birth of, 2; first appearances at court ceremonies of, 8, 10, 11, 13, 14; education of, 8, 73, 74, 75, 76; negotiations for marriage of, 16, 19 *seq.;* betrothal and proxy marriage of, 24, 25, 26, 27; marriage of, in England to Charles I, 34; appearance and accomplishments of, 17, 21, 22, 29, 30, 33, 34, 103, 104; sails for England, 29, 30; ill luck at sea of, 30, 123, 124, 139, 140, 330, 335; first meeting with Charles I, 31, 32, 33; taste in dress of, 30, 43, 35, 74, 77, 114; unhappy early married life of, 35, 36, 39, 40, 43, 44, 49, 50; unpopularity in England of, 40, 41, 42; nicknamed "the Popish brat", 138; insolence of the Duke of Buckingham to, 43, 44; her French suite banished, 45 *seq.;* refuses to share her husband's coronation, 24; her supposed pilgrimage to Tyburn and penances, 52; her relations with her husband improve, 54, 61, 63, 64; wishes to become a mother, 57, 60; consults a soothsayer, 57; her friendship with Lady Carlisle, 59; becomes pregnant, 64; birth and death of her first child, 65, 66; her courage in adversity, 66, 140; becomes pregnant again, 67; gives birth to Charles II, 69; and subsequently to seven more children, 70, 71; her happiness, 72; her chapels, 25, 39, 68, 95, 112, 148, 311, 321, and devotion to the Roman Catholic faith, 9, 25, 40, 321; her dower palaces, 38, 306, 317; a bad linguist, 30,

52; her love of dogs, 72, 83, 141, 142, 151, 308, 344, music, 74, 307, flowers, 58, 82, 83, jewellery, 77, 102, 131, furniture and interior decoration, 77, 246, 253, 308, 309, and theatricals, 77, 87, 109, 232, 316; her letters and handwriting, 76, 118, 125 *seq.*, 143 *seq.*, 151, 174; portraits of, 23, 80, 81, 282; aversion from Scotland, 86, 107; chastity of, 93, 94; goodness to her servants, 104, 332; visits Oxford, 90, 91; her good-fortune wanes, 103; first political intrigues, 106 *seq.*; slanders against her private character, 110, 148; her indiscretion, 121; sails for Holland, 122, 123; pawns and sells crown jewels, 125 *seq.*; purchases armaments, 134 *seq.*; dictates to her husband, 128 *seq.*; sails for England, 138; is bombarded on landing, 141, 142; at York, 146 *seq.*; her relations with Montrose, 147, 148, 188, 214; impeached by Parliament, 148; travels south, 148, 149, 150; with Charles at Oxford, 150 *seq.*; becomes pregnant, 156; parts from her husband for the last time, 157; her death reported, 158; gives birth to the Princess Henrietta-Anne at Exeter, 159; flies to France, 161; her ill-health and loss of beauty, 162 *seq.*; is established at the Louvre and St Germain, 168, 172; her relations with Jermyn, 116, 169, 268, 269, 270, 271, 315, 317; hears of her husband's defeat at Naseby, 172; discontent in her court, 173, 180, 213; urges Charles I to Scottish alliance, 174, 176; wishes Charles II to marry "La Grande Mademoiselle", 181 *seq.*; 251; recovers

possession of her youngest daughter, 182; her children call her "Mam", 183; her husband a prisoner, 181, 185, 186, 187; her poverty, 190, 191, 246, 247, 254; offers to share her husband's captivity, 193; receives the news of his death, 196, and his farewell letter, 203; assumes perpetual mourning, 204, 205; relations with Charles II, 205, 209, 211 *seq.*, 234; founds the convent of Chaillot, 215, 216, 217, 223, 236; receives news of the deaths of her daughter Elizabeth, 217, 219, and her son-in-law, 220; and of the defeat of Charles II at Worcester, 224, 225; removes to the Palais Royal, 230; her ill-health and quarrels, 233 *seq.*; attempts conversion of the Duke of Gloucester, 237 *seq.*; ambitions for her daughter Henrietta Anne, 246, 258, 259, 274, 275; visited by her daughter Mary, 248 *seq.*; buys château of Colombes, 253, 254; her opinion of England, 240, 254; Cromwell refuses to pay her dowry, 254; her lack of vindictiveness, 260; hears of her son Charles's Restoration, 265 *seq.*; death of her son Henry, 278, and marriage of her son James, 278; sails for England, 280; at Whitehall, 282 *seq.*; accepts Anne Hyde as daughter-in-law, 289 *seq.*; nurses her daughter Henrietta Anne, 293, 294, and parts with her on her marriage, 295; anxiety for her, 299 *seq.*; appearance of, in later life, 285, 307; her household in England, 306 *seq.*; last days in France, 324 *seq.*; her pension reduced, 326, 327; her failing health, 327 *seq.*, and death, 336;

furniture and effects of, 322, 325, 340 seq.; funeral of, and memorial services for, 338, 344, 345

Henry VIII of England, 37, 69, 283

Henry IV of France, 1 seq.; murdered, 5-6, 30, 49; resemblance to his daughter Henrietta, 8; aversion from matrimonial alliances with Spain, 9; mentioned, 49, 55, 70, 99, 115, 142, 161, 189, 192, 204, 214, 259, 261, 269, 313, 319, 329, 335, 338, 342, 345

Henry, "of Oatlands", Duke of Gloucester, 71, 110, 127 n., 181, 186, 197, 198, 218, 230, 231, 237, 238-44, 252, 254, 259, 263, 277, 278, 287, 294, 344

Henry, Prince of Wales, 15, 60, 70, 199

Herbert of Cherbury, Edward, 1st Baron, 17

Herbert, Sir Thomas, 198

Herbert, William, see Pembroke, 3rd Earl of

Héroard, Jean, physician to Louis XIII, 10

Hertford, William Seymour I, 2nd Earl of, 119

"Hipparc" (Hyde Park), 52, 151

Holland, Henry Rich, 1st Earl of, 20, 21, 22, 23, 31, 45, 97, 98, 154, 155, 190, 191

Holland, States-General of, 89, 133, 136, 139, 189, 264, 266, 282 n.

Holles, Denzil, 121

Holmby House, Northamptonshire, 94, 185, 186

Holy Island, 137

Hopton, Sir Arthur, diplomatist, 81

Hounslerdike, 123

House of Commons, see Parliaments of Charles I

House of Lords, 115, 121, 193, 194

Hudson, Jeffery, favourite dwarf of Henrietta Maria, 68, 72 n., 125, 160, 166, 272

Hull, 122, 130, 132, 137, 148

Humber, river, 135

Hume, David, historian, 270

Huntingdon, 64

Hurst Castle, 192

Hyde, Anne, afterwards Duchess of York, 234, 249, 279, 286, 287, 288, 289, 290, 291, 314, 320, 330

Hyde, Edward, 1st Earl of Clarendon, 175, 212, 222, 228, 233, 234, 235, 270, 279, 284, 289, 290, 291, 319, 324

Imitation of Christ, the, read daily by Henrietta Maria, 332

Indian: canoe, 80; cloth of gold, 342; gold chain, 343; natives, 88; tea, 273; trade, 312; trunk, 343; screen, 322; wares, 309

Infantas, see Maria Anna, Infanta of Spain; Maria Theresa, Infanta of Spain; and Catherine of Braganza, Infanta of Portugal

Innocent X, Pope, 170, 183, 245

Ireland, 108, 109, 120, 183, 186, 205, 213

Ireton, Lt.-General Henry, 186

Isabella, daughter of Philip II of Spain and wife of the Archduke Albert of Austria, 21

"Isabelle", cipher name for either Lady Roxburgh or Lady Denbigh, 126

"Isabelle", colour, 217 and n., 340

Isle of Wight, 187, 218

Ivelin, M., first physician to Henrietta-Anne, Duchess of Orleans, 331, 332

Ivry, see Battles

Jackson, Mr, see Charles II

James, Duke of York, birth of, 70, 71; appearance and character of, 70, 206, 207, 211; escapes from England, 189, 206; his brother's heir-presumptive, 203; military career of, 230, 234, 248, 254, 259; relations with his mother, 211, 221, 222, 234, 244; love-affair and marriage with Anne Hyde, 249, 250, 279, 280, 281, 284, 286, 287, 288, 290, 291, 314; mentioned, 101, 120, 127 *n.*, 132, 136, 150, 151, 186, 198, 210, 213, 214, 222, 227, 235, 255, 278, 315, 321, 331, 335, 338, 341

James I, of England, 15, 16, 18, 20, 22, 23, 24, 25, 35, 38, 59, 60, 66, 84, 88, 151, 181, 199

Jansens, Cornelius, painter, 144

Jenkins, Sir Leoline, Master of Jesus College, Oxford, 338, 339, 340, 341, 342, 343, 344

Jermyn, Henry, 1st Baron Dover, "Le petit Germain", 269, 281

Jermyn, Henry, 1st Earl of St Albans, early career of, 97, 98, 99; appearance and manners of, 97, 169, 269; sent to France, 108; negotiates between conspirators in Army Plot, 113 *seq.*; flies to France, 108; said to be Henrietta Maria's lover, 116; joins her in Holland, 126, 134, 136; accompanies her to England, 141, 149; created a baron, 154; accompanies her to France, 160, 161; where he acts as her Chamberlain, 169, 170, 195; breaks the news of the execution of Charles I to her, 201; sent by her upon diplomatic missions, 260, 263, 265, 268, 323, 324, 328; created Earl of St Albans, 264; said to be the husband of Henrietta Maria, 269, 270, 271, 289, 290, 315, 317; old age of, 337; mentioned, 127, 155, 157, 159, 160, 166, 167, 171, 172, 188, 205, 207, 208, 209, 213, 240, 241, 280, 300, 308, 311, 319

Jermyn, Sir Thomas, 99

Jersey, 115, 161, 180, 213

Jerusalem, the Temple of, 80

Jesus College, Oxford, 339

Jones, Inigo, 37, 38 *n.*, 39, 41, 80, 82, 109, 308, 316

Jonson, Ben, 74

Joyce, Cornet, 186

Joyeuse, François, Cardinal de, 10

Juxon, William, Bishop of London, afterwards Archbishop of Canterbury, 82, 91, 198, 199, 200, 201

Katharine, Princess, fourth daughter of Charles I and Henrietta Maria, birth of, 70, 107; death of, 71, 107

Kensington, Henry Rich, Baron, *see* Holland, Henry Rich, Earl of

Kettel, Dr Ralph, President of Trinity College, Oxford, 152

Kew Palace, 85

Kineton, vale of, 150

King's Norton, 149

"La Grande Mademoiselle", *see* Montpensier

Lambert, Lt.-General John, 264

Lambeth, 281

Lambeth Palace Library, 127 *n.*

Lambeth ware, 79

Lapland, a conjuring drum from, 80

Lathom House, 58, 188

Laud, William, Archbishop of Canterbury, 56 *n.*, 64 *n.*, 66, 68, 87, 90, 96, 107, 108, 110, 111, 148, 153, 199

Laval, Comte de, 188

Lavardin, Marshal de, 5

"La Vieille Mademoiselle", *see* Montpensier

Legg, Robin, 149, 176

Leicester, Dorothy Percy, afterwards Sidney, Countess of, 218

Leicester, Robert Sidney, 2nd Earl of, 218, 237

Leicester, town, 144

Lennox, Katharine Stuart, Duchess of, 34
Leopold I, Emperor 19, 286
Lesley, Sir Alexander, 149
Le Sueur, Hubert, 77, 82, 91
Lhulier, Mother, 215, 216, 236
Liesse, shrine of Our Lady of, 141
Lincoln, 148
Lincoln's Inn, 87
Lister, Sir Matthew, Royal Physician, 158
Lithuania, Dukedom of, 88
Loches, 14
Lockhart, Richard, page to Henrietta Maria, 324
Longueville, Henri d'Orléans, Duke of, 213
Longueville, Hôtel de, 1
Lord Mayor of London, the, 69, 120
Lord Mayor's Show, 51
Lorraine, Charles, Duke of, 170, 171, 221
Lorraine, Philippe, Chevalier of, 329
Louis XIII of France, accession, 7; character, 9; early education, 9, 10, 11; and marriage of, 12; rebels against his mother's tyranny 13, 14; refuses offer of Don Carlos as bridegroom for Henrietta Maria, 21; illness of, 27, 28; objects to the dismissal of Henrietta Maria's French attendants, 47, 49; is represented in a masque, 51; goes to war against England, 53; death of, 148; mentioned, 92, 99, 108, 137, 138, 215
Louis XIV, King of France, birth of, 100; appearance of, 168, 246; coronation of, 235; scorns his cousin, Henrietta-Anne, 247, 271; serious illness of, 257, 258; falls in love with Marie de Mancini, 258; schemes for his marriage, 258, 261, 262; admires his sister-in-law, 298, 299, 301; falls in love with Louise de la

Vallière, 302; pays for funeral of Henrietta Maria, 338; mentioned, 172, 175, 178, 179, 180, 184, 208, 213, 229, 230, 232, 238, 249, 250, 254, 256, 273, 274, 282 n., 286, 295, 296, 320, 321, 322, 323, 328, 329, 331, 332, 341, 342, 345
Louis Toussaint, Dauphin of France, son of Louis XIV, 302
Louvre, Palace of the, 1, 4, 5, 6, 13, 16, 20, 24, 27, 53, 167, 168, 172, 176, 188, 189, 192, 193, 194, 195, 204, 205, 217, 224, 226, 227, 229, 230, 232, 246, 275, 279, 302, 316
Lovell, Mr, tutor to Henry, Duke of Gloucester, 237, 238, 239
"Lucinda", see Carlisle, Lucy Hay, Countess of
Ludgate Hill, 87
Lulli, Baptiste, 298
Lucas, Sir Thomas, 152
Luxembourg, Palace of the, 12, 27
Luynes, Charles, Marquis d'Albret, Duke of, 13, 14, 15, 20
Lyons, 259, 260, 261

Maas, river, 135
Macedo, Souza de, Portuguese agent, 175
"Madame", title of (1) Henrietta Maria as only unmarried princess of France, 14; (2) Henrietta Anne, 274 seq.
"Mademoiselle", see Montpensier, Anne Marie Louise d'Orléans, Duchess of, and Orléans, Marie Louise d'
Madrid, 18, 96, 213, 222, 261
Magdalen College, Oxford, 152
Magdeleine of St Joseph, Mère, gives Henrietta Maria religious instruction, 10, 25
"Mam", name given to Henrietta Maria by her children; see Henrietta Maria

"Mamie St George", *see* St George, Jeanne, Madame de

Mancini, Laure, de, afterwards Duchesse de Mercœur, 247

Mancini, Marie de, afterwards Constabless Colonna, 258, 261

"Man of Sin", *see* Charles I

Mantua, Carlo Gonzaga 1st, 2nd Duke of, 79

Mardike, siege of, 254, 257

Marguerite de Valois, 2, 10

Maria Anna, Infanta of Spain, afterwards first wife of Ferdinand III, Emperor, 17, 19, 20, 24, 30, 39, 180, 207

Maria, of Tyrol, second wife of Ferdinand III, Emperor, 207, 209

Maria Theresa, Infanta of Spain, afterwards Queen of Louis XIV of France, 258, 261, 262, 274, 275, 295, 296, 297, 301, 302

Marie de Medicis, Queen of Henry IV of France, coronation of, 2; gives birth to Henrietta Maria, 2; widowed, 6-7; Regent, 8, 9, 13; appearance of, 9, 75, 102; arranges marriages for her children, 12, 15, 20 *seq.*; is banished to Blois, 13; escapes from, 14; is again banished, 16; returns to court, 16; says farewell to Henrietta Maria, 28; a good linguist, 30; instructions from, 31, 33, 44, 49, 54, 168; receives a gift of beagles from Henrietta Maria, 41; decreases in influence, 43; is represented in a masque, 51; a possessive parent, 8, 9, 73; is disappointed at her lack of grandchildren, 55; sends a midwife to Henrietta Maria, 65, 68; education of her children, 10, 11, 30, 76; visits England, 99 *seq.*; encourages her daughter in political intrigue, 103, 118; attends the wedding of her grand-daughter, 114; leaves England, 117, 118; last illness of, 131, and death of at Cologne, 134, 135; mentioned, 190, 192, 342

Marriage treaty of Charles I and Henrietta Maria, secret clauses in, 24, 42

Marston Moor, *see* Battles

Marten, Colonel Henry, 198

Martine, Saint, 92

"Martyr-King", the, *see* Charles I of England

Mary, Princess of Orange, eldest daughter of Charles I and Henrietta Maria, birth of, 70, 71, 76, 89; portraits of, 80, 341; appearance of, 70, 122, 220, 249; possesses a rosary, 94, and goes to Mass, 99; is betrothed, 112, and married, 114, to William, Prince of Orange; leaves for Holland, 122; in Holland, 123 *seq.*; parts from her mother, 139; miscarries, 189; is widowed, 220; gives birth to a posthumous son, 220; shows hospitality to her brothers, 231, 259; quarrels with her mother, 234; loves her brothers, 231, 245; visits France, 248 *seq.*; is said to be married to "Le petit Germain", 269; in England, 277, 281, 284, 285, last illness and death of, 286, 287, 288; mentioned, 101, 110, 117, 118, 120, 123, 124, 134, 206, 211, 222, 219, 222, 255, 266, 270, 272, 292, 309

Mary of York, the Lady, afterwards Mary II, Queen of England, 331

Mary, Queen, official name of Henrietta Maria as Queen Consort, 39, 41, 312

Masques, court, 17, 53, 80, 84, 109, 228, 232, 317

Massacre of St Bartholomew, 2, 6

Matthew, Sir Tobie, 29

Maubuisson, abbey of, 255

Mayerne, Sir Theodore Turquet de, first physician to Henrietta Maria, 60, 61, 64, 66, 96, 111, 118, 119, 158, 160, 217, 218, 324, 332, 333, 334

Mazarin, Jules, Cardinal, 92, 138, 151, 161, 162, 163, 166, 168, 169, 172, 174, 179, 187, 189, 191, 192, 193, 213, 221, 222, 228, 229, 230, 246, 254, 256, 257, 258, 259, 261, 262, 263, 265, 273, 275, 280, 282 n., 285, 289, 290, 292, 299, 335

Medicis, Catherine de, 216

Medicis, Marie de, see Marie de Medicis

Meldrum, Sir John, 149

Mende, Daniel du Plessis, Bishop of, 45, 47, 51

Mercy, Susan de, dresser to Henrietta Maria, 340

Merton College, Oxford, 150, 151, 155, 156

Michiel, Giovanni, Venetian Ambassador, 125

Middle Temple, 89

Mildmay, Captain, 187

Militia Bill, the, 132

Milton, John, 15 n.

"Minette", see Henrietta Anne

Mitte, favourite dog of Henrietta Maria, 141, 142, 160

Modena, Francesco d' Este I, Duke of, 248

Mogridge, Yeoman of the Leash to Henrietta Maria, 83

Molière, Jean Baptiste Poquelin de, 344

Monk, General George, afterwards 1st Duke of Albemarle, 264, 265, 266, 277, 285

Monmouth and Buccleuch, Anne Scott, Duchess of, 317

Monmouth and Buccleuch, James Scott, also known as Fitzroy

and Crofts, Duke of, 210, 313, 316, 317, 322

"Monsieur", see Orleans, Gaston Jean Baptiste, Duke of; Henry, Duke of; Philippe, Duke of

Montagu, Walter, abbot of Pontoise, 74, 112, 138, 155, 156, 188, 222, 237, 238, 239, 240, 241, 243, 244, 263, 280, 289, 290, 294, 300, 306, 311, 339

Montalais, Mademoiselle Françoise de, 303, 304

Montbazon, Duke of, 16

Montglat, Madame de, "Mammanga", 10

Montpensier, Anne Marie Louise d'Orléans, Duchesse de, "La Grande Mademoiselle", birth of, 54; appearance of, 167, 184, 227; her first meeting with Henrietta Maria, 167; her arrogance, 167, 173, 256, 278, 279; her matrimonial projects, 173, 180, 207, 210, 229, 314; her descriptions of Charles II, 179, 184, 227, of Henrietta Maria as widow, 205, 206, and of James, Duke of York, 207; her military activities, 229; and subsequent banishment, 229; entertains the Princess of Orange, 250 seq.; is consulted by Mazarin, 257; "la Vieille Mademoiselle", 304; mentioned or quoted, 127 n., 187, 211, 221, 225, 262, 292, 299, 314, 337

Montreuil, Jean de, 115

Montreuil, town, 29

Montrose, James Graham, 5th Earl and 1st Marquis of, 146, 147, 151, 156, 172, 175, 188, 213, 214, 226

Moorgate, 120

Mordaunt, John, Baron, 265

Mortlake, tapestries manufactured at, 80, 322

Morton, Countess of, see Dalkeith, Countess of

Motteville, Françoise Langlois, Madame de, 163, 165, 169, 178, 179, 190, 192, 195, 202, 203, 215, 228, 260, 275, 299, 325, 326, 330, 344

Moulton, Yorks, 146

Muscovy, Ambassadors from, 11, 87, 315, 316; money from, 214

Mytens, Daniel, painter, 80

Napier, Lilias, 188

Naseby, see Battles

Nene, river, 54

Nevers, 163, 166

Newark, 148, 149, 167

Newbury, see Battles

Newcastle-on-Tyne, 137, 140, 141, 145, 181, 185

Newcastle, William Cavendish, 1st Duke of, 73, 138, 146, 147, 153, 154, 155, 156, 170

Newcastle, Margaret Lucas, afterwards Cavendish, Duchess of, 152, 153

New Forest, the, 41, 338

Newmarket, 87, 131, 133, 142

New Place, Stratford-on-Avon, 149, 150

Newport, I.O.W., 218

Newport, Anne Boteler, Countess of, 306

Nicholas, Sir Edward, 180

Nonesuch, palace of, 38, 48, 61

Northampton, 144

North Sea, 125, 135, 141, 146

Northumberland, Algernon Percy, 10th Earl of, 97, 107, 115, 154, 197, 218

Notre Dame, 26, 27, 28, 113, 168

Oatlands, palace and park of, 38, 67, 71, 84, 110, 118, 119, 120, 181, 182

O'Hartegan, 170, 171

Olivarez, Gaspar de Guzman, Count of, 18

Orange, Amelia of Solms, Princess of, 124, 133, 139, 220, 277

Orange, Frederick Henry, Prince of, 103, 112, 114, 117, 122, 123, 124, 131, 132, 133, 134, 136, 139, 170, 183, 189

Orange, Louise, Princess of, 181

Orange, Mary, Princess of, see Mary

Orange, William II, Prince of, 103, 112, 114, 117, 123, 133, 139, 183, 205, 214, 220, 221

Orange, William III, Prince of, afterwards King William III of England, 211, 220, 221, 249, 253, 277, 287, 292, 338

Orleans, Anne Marie, Duchess of, see Montpensier

Orleans, city of, 12, 163, 229

Orleans, Gaston Jean Baptiste, Duke of, 3, 10, 24, 27, 28, 55, 99, 166, 167, 174, 186, 213, 229, 234, 265

Orleans, Henrietta Anne, Duchess of, see Henrietta Anne

Orleans, Henry, Duke of, 9, 10

Orleans, Maid of, 229

Orleans, Philippe, Duke of, character of, 168, 256, 257, 258, 330; the marriage of, to Henrietta Anne, arranged, 271, 273, 274, 275, 284, 286; the marriage of, takes place, 295; and proves unhappy, 301 seq.; jealousy of, 301, 304, 322, 329; claims Henrietta-Maria's effects, 336, 338, 339, 340; mentioned, 232, 244, 278, 293, 331

Orleans, Philippe Charles, Duke of Valois, 323, 335, 342

Orleans, Marie-Louise d', afterwards queen of Charles II of Spain, 304, 320, 335, 342

Ormonde, James Butler, 1st Duke of, 228, 241, 242, 244, 245, 262

Orpe, Mlle., attendant upon Henrietta Maria, 188, 340

Oseney, mill at, makes gunpowder, 153

"Ox", the, see Pym, John

Oxford, city and University of, 40, 63, 64, 90, 91, 144, 150, 151, 152, 153, 154, 155, 156, 157, 174, 176, 177, 339

Palais, Royal the, 175, 184, 224, 230, 231, 232, 235, 239, 244, 247, 249, 253, 267, 269, 275, 279, 295, 303, 304
Palatinate, Edward, Prince of the, 255, 280
Palatinate, Louise, Princess of the, 123, 255, 256, 335
Palatinate, Maurice, Prince of the, 136, 156
Palatinate, Rupert, Prince of the, 89, 90, 123, 135, 136, 137, 144, 149, 153, 154, 170, 172, 184, 188, 286, 320
Palatine, Charles Louis, Elector, 89, 90, 114, 132, 156
Palatine, Frederick V, Elector, King of Bohemia, 18, 69
Palladio, Andrea, 37
Panzani, Gregorio, Canon, 92, 105
Paris, Jean de Gondi, Archbishop of, 25, 26, 216
Parliamentary Commissioners, 78, 185
Parliament, "Rump", the, 264
Parliaments of Charles I—
  I, 29, 40, 42, 84
  II, 42, 45
  III, 58, 66
  IV, "The Short", 108, 109
  V, "The Long", 111 seq., 129, 155, 185, 186, 194
Parma, Ranuccio Farnese II, Duke of, 262
Parkinson, John, botanist, 83
Parr, Thomas, "Old Parr", 88
Pembroke, Philip Herbert II, 4th Earl of, 84, 87
Pendennis Castle, 160
Penshurst, 218, 231
Pepys, Samuel, 281, 285, 313, 314, 321

Percy, Algernon, see Northumberland, Earl of
Percy, Dorothy, see Leicester, Countess of
Percy, Henry, 97, 113, 115, 126
Percy, Lucy, see Carlisle, Countess of
Peronne, Madame, sage-femme, 65, 66, 68, 100, 158
Persia, Ambassador from, 87; carpets from, 322, 342
"Peter", Chinese godchild of Henrietta Maria, 309, 310
Petition of Right, the, 58
Philip, Father Robert, confessor to Henrietta Maria, 48, 67, 93, 94, 115, 116, 159, 187, 222
Philiphaugh, see Battles
Philip III, King of Spain, 9, 178
Philip IV, King of Spain, 12, 18, 20, 173, 207, 258, 261
Piedmont, Christine, Princess of, see Christine
Piedmont, Victor Amadeus, Prince of, see Savoy
Pimental, Don Antonio, Spanish envoy, 261
Plague, in England, 34, 40, 87, 321, 323
Plansy, Elizabeth, dresser to Henrietta Maria, 340
Plessis, Armand du, Cardinal de Richelieu, see Richelieu
Plymouth, 57, 160
Poissy, 210, 314
Poitiers, 12
Poitou, 11
Poland, Maria Louisa of Mantua, Queen of, 175
Poland, Ladislas VII, King of, 90
Poland, money from, 214
Pollard, Sir Hugh, 113
Pontefract, 148
Pontoise, Abbey of, 237, 238, 239, 240, 241, 242, 255, 294
Pontoise, Abbot of, see Montagu, Walter

"Popish Brat of France", *see* Henrietta Maria

Portland, Frances, Countess of, 81; *see also* Weston, Richard, 1st Earl of Portland

Portland stone, 37

Port Meadow, Oxford, 152

Portsmouth, 54, 61, 62, 114, 115, 116, 120, 136, 214, 291, 292, 293, 312

Portugal, Alphonso VI, King of, 312

Preston, 191

Prettyman, William, 176

Prince of Wales, *see* Charles I, Charles II and Henry, Prince of Wales

Prinne, William, 87

Progers, family, messengers between Henrietta Maria and Charles I and II, 176, 267

Prynne, William, *see* Prinne, William

Puritans, 108, 121, 145, 153, 281

Pym, John, 115, 121, 126

Quakers, 281

"Queen of Hearts", *see* Elizabeth, Queen of Bohemia

"Queen's Rebellion", *see* Ireland

"Queen's Room," Merton College, Oxford, 150, 151

Raconski, Johannes Albertus, Lithuanian Ambassador, 88

Radcliffe, Sir George, 240, 241

Raphael, *see* Sanzio

Ravaillac, François, 5, 6, 7

Raynham Hall, Norfolk, 85

Recusancy laws in England, 23, 24, 25, 29, 42, 49, 108, 315

Rembrandt van Rijn, *see* Van Rijn

Reresby, Sir John, 268, 269, 270, 313

Retz, Jean de Gondi, Cardinal de, 192

Rheims, Abbey of, 8, 235

Rhenen, 222

Richard, Lewis, Master of the King's Musick, 109

Richelieu, Armand du Plessis, Cardinal de, 14, 16, 21, 23, 24, 27, 43, 45, 49, 96, 99, 105, 107, 116, 134, 138, 163, 166, 189, 215, 229, 311

Richmond and Lennox, Frances Stuart, Dowager Duchess of, 69

Richmond and Lennox, Frances Theresa Stuart, Duchess of, *see* Stuart

Richmond, Mary Villiers, afterwards Herbert and Stuart, Duchess of, 81, 139, 306, 328

Richmond-on-Thames, *see* Sheen, palace of Richmond Park, 331

Rochefoucauld, Cardinal de la, 10, 25

Rochelle, 53, 54, 61, 63

Rochester, town, 156

"Roi Soleil, le", *see* Louis XIV

Romano, "Juilio" Giulio Pippi, painter, 93, 299

Rosetti, Count, second papal nuncio to the court of Henrietta Maria, 96, 109, 112

Rotterdam, 123, 135

Rouen, 255, 294

"Roundheads", the, 138

Roxburgh, Jane Drummond, afterwards Ker, Countess of, 126, 139

Royal Slave, The, play, 91

Royston, palace of, 84

Royston, Richard, bookseller to Charles I, 145

Rubens, Sir Peter Paul, painter, 9, 12, 60, 80, 178, 283, 316

Rupert, Prince, *see* Palatinate

Sabran, M. de, French envoy, 159

St Albans, Henry Jermyn, Earl of, *see* Jermyn, Henry

St Alban's Market, 337

St Cloud, Palace of, 11, 273, 274, 297, 305, 320, 324, 329, 330

St Denis, Abbey of, 2, 7, 8, 338

St George, Hardouin de Clermont, Seigneur de, 10

St George, Jeanne, Madame de, "Mamie", 10, 33, 34, 45, 46, 47, 48, 70, 75

St Germain, Palace of, 11, 172, 178, 182, 189, 193, 195, 202, 207, 210, 213, 229, 253

St James's, Palace, park and gardens, 37, 38, 39, 48, 52, 68, 69, 70, 71 n., 79, 82, 84, 101, 102, 104, 110, 117, 123, 197, 199, 206, 286, 291, 315

St James's Square, 337

St John's College, Oxford, 78, 90, 91

Sandwich, Edward Montagu, 1st Earl of, 277, 292, 293

Sanzio, Raffaello, painter, 80

Sarto, "Andrew of", painter, 93

Savoy, Adelaide Henrietta, Princess of, 222, 258

Savoy, Charles Emmanuel I, Duke of, 3

Savoy, Charles Emmanuel II, Duke of, 127 n., 258, 271, 313, 314

Savoy, Christine, Duchess of, see Christine

Savoy, Marguerite Yolande, Princess of, 258, 259, 261, 262

Sayes Court, Deptford, 308

Scarborough, 137, 145, 148

Scheveningen, 139, 140, 266

Scone Palace, 226

Scotland, troubles in, 66, 107, 110; peace with, 108; invading army from, 156; Montrose raises loyalists in, 156; Campaigns of Montrose in, 172, 188, 214; Charles II in, 214, 226, 227

Scott, Anne and James, see Monmouth

"Sealed Knot, The", 245, 262

Séguier, Pierre, Chancellor of France, 150, 256

Ségur, Canon, 13

Serre, Sieur de la, 101, 102

Shakespeare, William, 37, 74, 149, 150

Sheen, Palace of, 38, 40, 119, 317

"Shipside", see Cheapside

Shrewsbury, 225

Sidney, Algernon, 211

Sidney, Dorothy, see Leicester, Countess of

Sidney, Robert, Colonel, 211

Sidney, Robert, see Leicester, Earl of

Smallpox, contracted by—
Elizabeth, sister of Henrietta Maria, 12
Lady Carlisle, 39
Charles I, 86
Charles II, 191; and causes the deaths of William, Prince of Orange, 220
Henry, Duke of Gloucester, 279
Mary, Princess of Orange, 286, 287

Smallpox, Henrietta Maria's fearlessness of infection from, 59, 86, 286

Smeeton, George, 270

Smith, John and Tom, aliases of Charles, Prince of Wales, and George, Duke of Buckingham, 16, 17

Soissons, Eugéne Maurice of Savoy, Comte de, 275, 284, 286

Soissons, Louis de Bourbon, Comte de, 15, 20, 21, 26

Somerset, Edward Seymour, Duke of, 38

Somerset House, 79; see also Denmark House

Somme, river, 28

Spa, 118

Spalding, John, historian, 142

Stamford Bridge, 146

Stamford Hill, 120

States-General of Holland, see Holland

"Steenie", see Buckingham, George Villiers, 1st Duke of

Strafford, Thomas Wentworth, 3rd Earl of, 58, 67 n., 108, 109, 111, 112, 113, 114, 115, 116, 117, 121, 134, 197

Strand, The, 84

Strange, James Stanley, Lord, afterwards 7th Earl of Derby, 58, 81, 188

Stratford-on-Avon, 37, 149

Strickland, Walter, Parliamentary agent at the Hague, 136, 143

Strickland, Sir William, 143

Strode, William, 121

Stuart, Frances Theresa, afterwards Duchess of Richmond and Lennox, 318

Stuart, Sophia, dresser to Henrietta Maria, 340

Suckling, Sir John, poet, 113, 115

Sully, Maximilien de Béthune, Duke of, 2, 3, 6, 7

Swakeleys, Middlesex, 85

Syon House, 197

"Tabula Crytographica", see Ciphers

Tamworth, 148

Tangier, 312

Tea, 79, 273

Tennis, 10, 86, 98

Thame, 153

Thames, river, 35, 37, 40, 41, 88, 103 n., 191, 281, 282, 308, 309, 317, 321

Theobalds, Palace of, 38, 64

Thomlinson, Colonel Matthew, 199, 200

Thouars, Charlotte de la Trémoïlle, Duchesse de, 48, 50, 58

Thynne, Lady Isabella, 152

Tillières, Comte de, 223, 224

Tillières, Comtesse de, 46

Tillières, Leveneur de, Comte de, 16, 31, 34, 43, 49, 54

"Tintoretto", Jacopo Robusti, painter, 89, 341

Titchfield, 41

"Titian", Tiziano Vecellio, painter, 89, 255

Toulouse, 263

Touraine, 11

Tours, 163

Tower of London, the, 41, 42, 111, 113, 114, 115, 116, 156

Trémoïlle, Charlotte de la, afterwards Stanley, Lady Strange, Countess of Derby, 58, 77, 81, 188, 282, 288, 290, 291, 292, 303; see also Thouars

Trinity College, Oxford, 151, 152

Tuileries, Palace and gardens of the, 4, 11, 195, 227, 274, 295, 298, 320

Tunbridge Wells, 67, 285, 317

Turenne, Henri de La Tour d'Auvergne, Vicomte de, 213, 230, 262

Turin, 15, 65, 67, 77, 100, 221, 234, 259, 271, 313, 315, 318, 319

Turkey, carpets from, 79, 342; galleons from, 72 n.; 80; embroideries from, 217

Turquet, Theodore, de Mayerne, see Mayerne

Tuscany, Ferdinand de Medicis II, Duke of, 271

Tweed, river, 264

Tyburn, 52, 62 n.

Typhus, outbreak of, amongst the garrison at Oxford, 156, 157

Urban VIII, Pope, 3, 24, 25, 29, 92, 99, 100, 110, 112

Utrecht, 133

Vale of the White Horse, 157

Vallière, Louise de la Baume le Blanc, Duchesse de la, 302

Vallot, Antoine, first physician to Louis XIV, 331, 332, 333, 334, 337

Valois, Duke of, see Orleans

Van Dijck, Antoon, see Vandyck, Sir Anthony

Vandyck, Sir Anthony, 78 n., 80, 81, 82, 90, 101, 102, 105,254, 282 n., 321, 341

Van Rijn, Rembrandt, painter, 129

Vantelet, de, Madame, dresser to

Henrietta Maria, 48, 65 & n., 340

Van Tromp, Admiral Cornelis, 214

Van Tromp, Admiral Martin Harpertzoon, 112, 139, 142

Vaux-le-Vicomte, Château of, 301

Vendôme, César, Duke of, 70, 202

Vendôme, Francoise of Lorraine, Duchess of, 202

Verneuil, Catherine d'Entragues, Marquise de, 4 n., 6

"Veronese", Paolo (Paolo Caliari), painter, 93

Villers-Cotterets, 274, 329

Villiers, Barbara, see Castlemaine

Villiers, Eleanor, 98, 99

Villiers, Elizabeth, see Dalkeith

Villiers, George, see Buckingham, 1st Duke of

Villiers, George, see Buckingham, 2nd Duke of

Villiers, Katharine, see Buckingham, Duchess of

Villiers, Mary, see Buckingham, Countess of

Villiers, Mary, see Richmond, Duchess of

Villiers, Susan, see Denbigh, Countess of

Vincennes, Château of, 299

Vinci, Leonardo da, artist, 93

Vitry, M. de, 1

Voorne, Island of, 123

Wales, Princes of, see Charles I, Charles II and Henry, Prince of

Waller, Edmund, poet, 74, 272

Walsall, 149

Walter, Lucy, "Mrs Barlow", 191, 210, 211, 228, 308, 313, 314

Warrington, 191

War-ships—
The Lion, 137
The London, 292, 293, 294
The Naseby, 266
The Neptune, 53

The Princess-Royal, 139, 141
The Royal Charles, 266
The Triumph, 54

Webster of Amsterdam, merchant-banker, 135

Welbeck Abbey, 84, 146

Wellingborough Spa, 55, 56 n., 60, 61

Wentworth, Thomas, 3rd Earl of Strafford, see Strafford

Westminster Abbey, 42, 66, 115, 287

Westminster Hall, 109, 121, 134, 197, 265, 283

Weston, Richard, 1st Earl of Portland, 85, 98

"Whitecoats", regiment raised by 1st Duke of Newcastle, 146

Whitehall, 37, 40, 41, 46, 51, 53, 59, 71 n., 84, 101, 104, 106, 109, 110, 114, 115, 116, 120, 122, 199, 215, 268, 279, 281, 282, 283, 284, 285, 286, 288, 313, 315, 316, 320, 326; see also Banqueting House

"White King", the, see Charles I

Wigan, 191

Wilmot, Henry, 1st Earl of Rochester, 113, 188, 210

Wilton, 41, 84

Winchester, 87

Windsor, 38, 122, 192

Winter, Sir John, Secretary to Henrietta Maria, 306

Wintour, Sir John, Physician to Henrietta Maria, 157, 160

Woodstock, 91

Worcester, battle of, see Battles

Yeoman of the Guard, 47

Yeoman of the Leash, 83

York, city of, 110, 130, 131, 132, 138, 143, 144, 146, 147, 148

York, Duchess of, see Hyde, Anne

York, Duke of, see James

York House, 49 n., 51

York, Ladies Anne and Mary of, see Anne and Mary